Communist
Strategies
in Asia

Communist
Strategies
in Asia

A COMPARATIVE ANALYSIS
OF GOVERNMENTS AND PARTIES

Edited by

A. DOAK BARNETT

GREENWOOD PRESS, PUBLISHERS
WESTPORT, CONNECTICUT

Library of Congress Cataloging in Publication Data

Barnett, A   Doak, ed.
    Communist strategies in Asia.

    "Originally presented, in briefer form, as
papers for a symposium on 'Communism in Asia' held
during the 1962 annual meeting of the Association
for Asian Studies."
    Reprint of the ed. published by Praeger, New
York, which was issued as no. 132 of Praeger publications in Russian history and world communism.
    Includes bibliographical references.
    1. Communism--Asia--Congresses. 2. Asia--
Politics and government--Congresses. 3. Communist parties--Congresses. I. Title.
[HX383.5.B37 1976]   335.43'095   75-32454
ISBN 0-8371-8547-5

© 1963 by Frederick A. Praeger, Inc.

Originally published in 1963 by Frederick A. Praeger,
Publishers, New York

Reprinted with the permission of Praeger Publishers, Inc.

Reprinted in 1976 by Greenwood Press,
a division of Williamhouse-Regency Inc.

Library of Congress Catalog Card Number 75-32454

ISBN 0-8371-8547-5

Printed in the United States of America

Preface

The individual chapters that make up this volume were originally presented, in briefer form, as papers for a symposium on "Communism in Asia" held during the 1962 Annual Meeting of the Association for Asian Studies. Subsequently, the authors revised and greatly expanded them, incorporating considerable new, up-to-date material on the rapidly changing situations affecting Communism in Asia.

Both the authors and the editor have benefited from extremely helpful advice provided by a number of sources. We are pleased to acknowledge especially the suggestions and criticisms made by Zbigniew K. Brzezinski, Allen S. Whiting, and Howard L. Boorman, both at the above-mentioned Association for Asian Studies symposium, and in further discussions and correspondence.

A. D. B.

Contents

vii

Communist
Strategies
in Asia

Introduction

by A. DOAK BARNETT

A process of profound ferment and change has been under way in the Communist world for several years. The fundamental causes of this ferment are numerous: Communist China's rise to power as a second major ideological and political center within the Communist world movement; Stalin's death and the subsequent destruction of the myth of Stalinist infallibility and monolithic Communist unity; the steady growth of "polycentrism" (or at least decentralization) within both the Communist bloc and the Communist world movement as a whole; and the emergence of intense conflict between Moscow and Peking.

These and other recent developments have set in motion new forces that already have had a great impact on Communist regimes and parties everywhere and will doubtless have a continuing impact in the years immediately ahead. Even though the long-range consequences of these developments cannot be foreseen clearly, many of their immediate effects are clearly evident—and important. Gradually, authority within the Communist world has become increasingly diffused. A significant process of differentiation between Communist regimes and parties has been steadily taking place. And complex new interrelationships have begun to develop among the varied members of the Communist bloc and Communist world movement. Clearly, there are still forces working for unity in the Communist world, but now there are also important centrifugal forces working for increased variation and differentiation.

It is hardly necessary here to stress the importance of understanding this process of change. Increased knowledge of it is essential for accurate assessment, not only of the nature of the challenge that Communism presents to the non-Communist world, but also of the range of possible policy responses that can be adopted to meet that challenge successfully.

Therefore, it is imperative today, perhaps more than ever before,

3

to analyze the differences as well as the similarities among various Communist regimes and parties. It is necessary to study local applications and adaptations of the so-called "universals" of Marxism-Leninism, to discover the complex interrelationships developing among the various states and movements that make up the Communist world, and to assess the impact that the Sino-Soviet dispute has had upon them. There is great need, in short, for systematic study of what might be called "comparative Communism."

This volume represents an attempt to analyze these questions as they relate to Communism in Asia. The need for comparative studies of Asian Communist regimes and parties and of their relationships to the rest of the bloc and the world Communist movement is especially great. For a variety of reasons, research on Asian Communism has lagged behind the study of Soviet and European Communism. Most specialists of Asian affairs have lacked the necessary skills—including knowledge of Marxist-Leninist doctrine and of Communist practice in non-Asian areas—to examine Asian Communist movements in the context of both world Communist trends and indigenous revolutionary situations. Most specialists on Soviet and European Communism have lacked the necessary skills —including knowledge of Asian societies and languages—to assess Asian varieties of Communism.

The contributors to this volume have been drawn from the few specialists in the United States who do possess sufficient knowledge of both Communism in Asia and the world Communist movement to approach such a study. Before writing the papers constituting this volume, they agreed that, to the extent practicable, they would deal with similar questions and issues in order to provide as much basis for comparability as possible.

One of the fundamental questions to which all of the contributors have addressed themselves is what the impact upon Asian Communist movements has been of the Sino-Soviet conflict and the emergence of two major Communist "models"—Soviet and Chinese. These models differ significantly in their detailed prescriptions for strategy and tactics, even though they still concur on many ideological fundamentals. Two of the contributors analyze some of the distinctive characteristics of these models; the others examine their impact upon six Asian Communist parties—three that are struggling for power and three that already control established Communist regimes.

The problem of defining what constitutes a distinctive "model" is not a simple one. What is meant when one speaks of Soviet and

Chinese Communist models and their impact on various Asian Communist movements? Does the term mean simply the influence of major Soviet and Chinese theoretical and ideological formulas? Or the "examples" of specific policies, programs, and methods of operating used by the Soviets and the Chinese in applying Marxism-Leninism in their own countries at various times? Or Soviet and Chinese "influence" in an even broader sense, exerted politically and economically as well as ideologically?

The contributors to this volume have attempted to analyze all these questions. They have examined, in short, not only the impact on particular Asian parties of the Soviet and Chinese ideological models, but also other forms of Russian and Chinese influence, including the examples provided by past Soviet and Chinese policies and experiences, and other political and economic "influences" emanating from Moscow and Peking—influences that have become increasingly competitive in recent years as a consequence of the Sino-Soviet dispute. They have also studied the indigenous factors shaping the growth of national Communist movements, and the chapters dealing with the Communist movements in particular countries provide in some detail an analysis of the ways in which national movements have attempted to translate Marxist-Leninist theory into concrete policies adapted to local problems and situations.

Almost all Communist parties struggling for power are confronted by a number of crucial questions, most of them concerning strategy and tactics, that demand answers. What is the nature of the local society and what are the special features of the "class struggle" presumed to be operating in it? Who should be defined as the main targets—the primary enemies—of the revolution at any particular period of time? Who, at any particular stage, are potential allies whom the Communists should try to bring into a united front under their control, and what kind of united front should it be? What "stages" must the revolutionary process go through, and what should be the minimum program—the immediate goals—at each stage? What forms of revolutionary struggle are considered to be both necessary and feasible? Armed struggle? Parliamentary and other forms of "peaceful" struggle? Underground political struggle? Or a mixture of several forms?

For Communist parties that have won the struggle for power and have embarked on the long, hard "road to socialism," there are different sorts of questions to answer. What should be the forms of political organization and state power? What does the local situa-

tion demand in regard to developmental stages and processes of
political, economic, and social change that must be carried out at
each stage? How fast can and should the processes of change be?
How, and when, should socialization, collectivization, and industrialization be pursued? What policies should be adopted toward
key "nonproletarian" groups in the population—the national bourgeoisie, petty bourgeoisie, rich peasants, intellectuals, minorities?

There are significant differences between the ways in which the
Russians and the Chinese have attempted to answer such questions.
How are various Asian Communist parties and regimes now attempting to answer them? To what extent are their answers determined mainly by local factors—by their own assessments of the
nature of local society and its revolutionary potential, by the immediate problems to be solved, and by their own organizational
history and special attitudes and aspirations? To what extent are
their answers significantly affected by Soviet or Chinese influence—
by the ideological models they provide, by the examples inherent
in their past experiences, or by direct advice or pressures?

And what, specifically, has been the impact to date of the Sino-
Soviet conflict on individual Asian Communist parties and regimes?
What is the long-range impact likely to be? Are they likely to
"choose sides" and to strengthen their alignment with, and emulation of, either Russia or China? (Do alignment and emulation
necessarily go together?) Are they likely to be ambivalent and confused and to experience internal factionalism and splits over what
course they should follow? Are they likely to attempt to play the
difficult game of maintaining as close relations as possible with both
Moscow and Peking, avoiding clear alignment with, or subordination to, either? Or are they likely, in a situation where there are
now two competing centers of authority and influence, to turn
more inward, to exercise increased independence and autonomy,
and to show greater tendencies toward local innovation, initiative,
and originality?

These are some of the questions examined by the contributors to
this volume. Their studies of individual Communist parties treat
only a few of the many existing in Asia, but the ones described are
important. They include the regimes in all three small Communist
states in Asia (North Korea, North Viet-Nam and Outer Mongolia), as well as the parties struggling for power in the three largest
and most important non-Communist Asian countries (India,
Japan, and Indonesia). The authors would readily agree that their
studies do not provide final and definitive answers to many of the

questions explored, but they do throw important new light on Communist movements in Asia and on the ways in which Asian Communism has been affected by the changes that have been taking place in recent years in Sino-Soviet relations and in the Communist world as a whole.

The over-all picture that emerges from these studies is one of ferment, of changing relationships, and of increased differentiation in the Communist movements in Asia as well as elsewhere. But the impact of these changes, and the local responses to them, have not by any means been uniform. In Outer Mongolia, the Russians, reacting to Peking's efforts to reassert Chinese influence, have stepped up their own activities in the area, and apparently the Mongols have felt compelled to "choose sides"; in any case, they have definitely strengthened ties with Moscow and have aligned themselves more closely with the Soviet Union than other Asian Communist parties have to date. In India, serious factional struggles have ruptured the local Communist Party—struggles in which competing groups have split both in their views toward Moscow and Peking and on issues regarding domestic strategy. In most of the other countries treated, the local Communist movements have shown varying degrees of ambivalence and vacillation, and their attitudes toward Moscow and Peking—viewed both as ideological models and as power centers—have been far from unambiguous or free from contradictions. Clearly, there have been strong pressures to choose sides and line up with either Moscow or Peking, but many parties have resisted doing so in any clear-cut way. In some respects, Chinese influence seems to have grown slowly but steadily. Nevertheless most Asian Communist parties still seem to be trying to maintain relations with both Moscow and Peking without being excessively dependent upon, or subordinate to, either.

In this situation, it is still not clear what the long run effects of Sino-Soviet competition will be. Despite the pressures to align with either the Soviet Union or Communist China, some important Asian Communist parties appear, for the moment at least, to be relying less on outside guidance and to be showing greater initiative in determining their own policies. They appear, in short, to be asserting a higher degree of independence and autonomy than shown in the past. Some others, however, appear to be greatly influenced by mounting pressures to align clearly with one of the major centers of world Communism.

Whichever one of these tendencies wins out in the long run, growing "polycentrism" is already resulting, in Asia as elsewhere, in increased differentiation of viewpoints and policies, substantial diffusion of lines of authority and influence, and decreased unity and coordination in the Communist world. This is a development of great importance. Whatever its final result may be, it deserves serious and continuing study.

ONE

THE "MODELS"

1. Some Comparisons Between the Russian and Chinese Models

by DONALD S. ZAGORIA

In 1919, looking forward to future Communist revolutions in Asia and other underdeveloped regions, Lenin wrote that Asian Communists would have to adapt themselves to "peculiar conditions which do not exist in the European countries" and to find "specific forms" for waging the revolutionary struggle.[1]

The Chinese Communist revolution was to confirm Lenin's prophecy. Both in its tactics for gaining power and in its subsequent policies for "building socialism," the Chinese Communist Party has displayed a number of "peculiarities" in relation to Soviet norms. At the same time, there has been much in Chinese Communist strategy and tactics, both for gaining power and for "building socialism," that is clearly patterned on Soviet experience. It is the relationship between China's general conformity to the Soviet model for building "socialism" and her particular departures from it that will be explored here.

To what extent the Soviet model must be followed in other Communist countries has been the subject of much discussion in the Communist world since the appearance after World War II of eleven new Communist states. Since the death of Stalin, and particularly since the Polish and Hungarian events of 1956, the Russians have continually tried to define the limits of permissible diversity in the methods for "building socialism."[2] While acknowledging since Stalin's death that all bloc countries must find a way to socialism in accordance with their own peculiar historical and national circumstances, the Russians have never ceased to emphasize the overriding importance and universal validity of certain elements in Soviet experience. In 1957, indeed, they codified these elements as "basic laws" of socialist construction.

The Russian attitude toward the limits of permissible diversity has changed substantially with the passage of time. Under Stalin, these limits were extremely narrow; immediately after his death, a "New Course" was introduced in the U.S.S.R. and most countries of the bloc. The New Course involved large cuts in heavy industrial investment, concessions to the peasantry, greater religious tolerance, wage increases, and other popular measures. In the "people's democracies," for the first time, the peculiar domestic problems of each country were taken into consideration. The scope of the New Course varied significantly from country to country: Whereas in Hungary the reforms were substantial, in Poland they were minor.

While the Russians, after Stalin's death, were increasingly ready to adopt a more flexible and even permissive attitude toward diversity, they were concerned lest the resulting relaxation in the domestic political climate of the Communist states lead to political or ideological disunity. Their worries crystallized during 1956 and 1957, when they had to face the growth of a bloc-wide revisionism whose sponsors argued that the Soviet model was largely irrelevant for other Communist states and pleaded for national autonomy, and even genuine independence, throughout the Communist bloc. The Russians, reacting to this unprecedented challenge, began to warn with growing frequency that the policy of allowing different roads to socialism could not be used as a pretext for encouraging disunity within the bloc. Haunted by the prospect that national autonomy would degenerate into Titoism, they began to attack the "claptrap about 'national Communism.' "[3]

At the Moscow Conference of 81 Communist Parties in November, 1957, one of the principal subjects at issue was the extent of permissible divergence from the Soviet model. From the speeches made to the conference and from the resolution subsequently adopted, it became clear that a compromise had been reached between the advocates of diversity and the champions of conformity. The resolution stated that there were certain "basic laws" of socialist construction confirmed by Soviet experience, but that there was also a "great variety of historic national peculiarities . . . which must by all means be taken into account." For the first time, these "basic laws" of socialist construction were enumerated.

> These laws are: guidance of the working masses by the working class, the core of which is the Marxist-Leninist Party, in effecting a proletarian revolution in one form or another and establishing one form or other of the dictatorship of the proletariat; the alliance of the working class and the bulk of the peasantry and other sections of the

working people; the abolition of capitalist ownership and the establishment of public ownership of the basic means of production; gradual socialist reconstruction of agriculture; planned development of the national economy aimed at building socialism and Communism, at raising the standard of living of the working people; the carrying out of socialist revolution in the sphere of ideology and culture and the creation of a large intelligentsia devoted to the working class, the working people and the cause of socialism; the abolition of national oppression and the establishment of equality and fraternal friendship between the peoples; defense of the achievements of socialism against attacks by internal enemies; solidarity of the working class of the country in question with the working class of other countries, that is proletarian internationalism.[4]

The distinguishing characteristic of these "laws" is their high order of generality within a common ideological frame of reference. So long as the process of socialist construction is led by a Communist Party and includes nationalization of industry, collectivization of agriculture, and loyalty to the Soviet Union, it would seem that the attitude toward diversity reflected in this document is quite permissive. Indeed, it seems likely that the "laws" of socialist construction have been deliberately phrased in general terms so as to give the Communists sufficient doctrinal flexibility both to accommodate diversity within the bloc and to welcome new revolutionary regimes into the fold. Moscow, for example, has specifically recognized that the revolutions in Asia, South America, Africa, and the Middle East, in view of the vast diversity of social conditions to be found in those areas, will give rise to "new forms of working people's political power."[5]

In short, Khrushchev seems prepared to tolerate departures from Soviet practices, and he may be willing to tolerate even larger margins of experimentation in revolutions yet to come, so long as the resulting diversity does not threaten Soviet hegemony in the Communist world. The primary Soviet consideration must be the maintenance of Russia's dominating position in that world. It is in this very area of power politics that China has become a special problem for the Soviet Union.

Because China is the largest Communist power in Asia and consciously seeks to apply its own revolutionary model to other Asian Communist states, the Russians are faced with a thorny question: Can they grant the Chinese model's applicability to other underdeveloped Asian countries without conceding at the same time a measure of their leadership in the bloc? If it is true that China's revolutionary experience is more applicable than Russia's to North Viet-Nam, North Korea, Outer Mongolia, and other Asian countries, does it not follow that the Chinese should guide the Communist parties in these countries? This, of course, is a question for Communists to answer. For the Western specialist, the problem is to estimate how far the Chinese have, in fact, been influenced by the Soviet model and to identify the ways in which they have departed from it. We must try to ascertain, particularly, whether the Chinese model is, by reasonably objective criteria, more suitable than the Russian for Asian countries.

While we have a good idea from the published record of how the Russians and Chinese view the problem, an objective assessment is greatly complicated by the fact that the study of Chinese Communism in the West lags considerably behind the study of Russian Communism. On some aspects of Chinese Communism, even the simplest groundwork studies remain to be written. Until they are written, it is doubtful that we shall be in a position to make satisfactory comparisons of the Soviet and Chinese political, social, and economic systems, methods of control, ideologies, Party organizations, approaches to collectivization and industrialization, and so on. Even if such comparisons were now possible, there would still be the problem of determining what elements in the Chinese model are peculiar to China and what elements represent responses to problems that China shares in common with other underdeveloped Asian states seeking to build Communism.

With so many gaps in research waiting to be filled, it is virtually impossible to present systematically the differences in Russian and Chinese development strategies. Instead, an attempt will be made here to suggest a number of factors that distinguish the Russian revolution from the Chinese one and that may account for some of the differences between the Russian and Chinese roads to socialism. This, in turn, should put us in a position to inquire how far one or another of these factors is present elsewhere in Asia.

THE COMMUNIST APPROACH TO THE PROBLEM

It is necessary to begin with a discussion of what the Russians and Chinese themselves say about the relevance of their own revolutionary models to other Asian states. Does China claim, and does Moscow grant, that the Chinese model is more relevant than the Soviet one for Asia?

One can trace in Chinese Communist pronouncements after 1940 a rather persistent theme—that Mao has transplanted Marxism-Leninism to "the East" (in Communist jargon, not only Asia but all underdeveloped areas) and that the Chinese Communist revolution is the classical model for all subsequent revolutions in these countries. These claims have been resisted, diluted, or distorted by the Russians, in some periods more than in others.

The dialogue between Moscow and Peking on this question was particularly intense in two periods: the first from late 1949, when the Chinese Communists took power, until the fall of 1951; the second from 1958 to the present. In both periods, the Chinese and Russians wished to pursue divergent strategies in the so-called "colonial and semi-colonial" areas. The Chinese wanted to place greater emphasis than the Russians on armed liberation struggles. But an underlying political issue in both periods was whether or not the Russians would concede a Chinese Communist sphere of influence in Asia and in some other parts of the underdeveloped world.

The Chinese Communists want a sphere of influence in Asia because most of their short- and middle-run objectives relate to that continent. They have come to realize that the priorities they assign to these objectives are not always the same as those assigned by the Russians. The Soviet Union faces a problem, which Zbigniew Brzezinski aptly calls "domesticism," over the tendency of this or that Communist Party to emphasize domestic objectives and interests at the expense of the broader international goals set by Moscow, and to view the interests and priorities of the international movement largely in terms of national or sectional problems.

In both periods (1949 to 1951 and 1958 to the present), the Chinese Communists wanted the Russians to take greater risks in support of Chinese objectives in Asia than the Russians were prepared to take. The Russians were not willing to take these risks for a variety of reasons. There was the danger of local war with the West. Perhaps more important, they had larger fish to fry in the advanced capitalist countries of Western Europe. For example, they were unwilling to give much support either to the Viet-Minh or to the Algerian rebels because they calculated that weaning France away from the Western alliance was, for them, a much bigger prize than a Communist-dominated Algeria or Viet-Nam. The Russians have evidently decided that the encouragement of neutralism and pacifism in Western Europe through the "peace movement" is a more important goal than stirring up colonial wars, and this assignment of priorities has been bitterly resented by the Chinese. The problem is that in framing world-wide Communist strategy, the Russians, unlike their Chinese allies, have had to look at the world as a whole, particularly at Europe and the United States. The Chinese Communists, looking at the world from Peking, have often acted, not unreasonably, as if their own goals and interests in Asia were just as important as Soviet world-wide goals. When Soviet and Chinese aims do not actually conflict, they are not viewed in Moscow and Peking with the same sense of urgency.

The phenomenon of "domesticism" can be observed not only in divergencies over global strategy and the priorities to be assigned to this or that objective, but also in the adaptation of general Marxist-Leninist principles to the complex and manifold tasks of "building socialism." In 1956, Gomulka, faced with problems peculiar to Poland, and not because he was a "disloyal" or "national" Communist, adopted a "right-wing" agrarian policy. Thus he came into conflict with Moscow, which perceived in this policy an infection that might threaten the cooperative system elsewhere in Eastern Europe and ultimately in the U.S.S.R. itself.

In 1958, because Mao was faced with critical difficulties in food production, dwindling food reserves, a rapidly growing population, and mounting disaffection among the peasantry and rural cadres—and not because he was "irrational"—he abandoned the Soviet cooperative model and invented the "left-wing" commune, which had its root in the decision to mobilize labor power on a scale unprecedented in human history. This decision led to conflict with Moscow primarily because the Chinese infused it with an ideological content. They suggested that the communes represented a blueprint of the Communist future for which Moscow was still groping. They also strongly implied that the communes and the "Great Leap" represented a solution by Mao of the problems of building socialism and Communism in all underdeveloped countries. Thus the Chinese presented the communes, not as a specifically Chinese reaction to peculiarly Chinese problems, but rather as an original discovery by Mao of the keys to the "earthly paradise"—keys that could be used by all backward Eastern countries. This was in itself testimony to the Chinese aspiration for a sphere of influence in the underdeveloped areas.

The Maoist attempt to distinguish the Chinese revolution, as a model for all backward areas of the East, from the Russian Revolution, which was the model only for the more advanced capitalist countries, can be traced back at least as far as 1940, when Mao's *On New Democracy* was published. There Mao distinguished the "new democratic republic," which he said would be established in China, from both the bourgeois "dictatorships" in the old European-

American democratic states *and* the dictatorship of the proletariat in the U.S.S.R. The "new democratic republic," he wrote, "is the transitional form of state to be adopted by revolutions in colonial and semicolonial countries." "To be sure," Mao continued, "revolutions in different colonial and semicolonial countries necessarily have certain different characteristics, but these constitute only minor differences within a general framework of uniformity."[6]

In the spring of 1946, in an interview of extraordinary importance, Liu Shao-ch'i told Anna Louise Strong that Mao had discovered an Asian form of Marxism, that Marx and Lenin were Europeans and therefore, by implication, not very interested in or capable of solving Asian problems, that Mao was the first to have succeeded in adapting Marxism to China, and that Mao's revolutionary theories charted a path to power not only for the Chinese people, "but for the billion folk who live in the colonial countries of Southeast Asia."[7]

No sooner had the Chinese Communists conquered the mainland than they began to claim that their own path to power, "the road of Mao Tse-tung," was in general the one to be taken by other colonial countries. Liu Shao-ch'i told the trade union conference of Asian and Australasian countries in November, 1949:

> The road taken by the Chinese people in defeating imperialism and in founding the Chinese People's Republic is the road that should be taken by the peoples of many colonial and semicolonial countries in their fight for national independence and people's democracy. . . . This is the essential road on which the Chinese people marched to achieve victory in their country. This road is the road of Mao Tse-tung. It can also be the basic road for liberation of peoples of other colonial and semicolonial countries, where similar conditions exist.[8]

In 1951, Lu Ting-i and Ch'en Po-ta, two of the most prominent Chinese Communist ideological writers, amplified these claims. Lu, in a well-known speech, said flatly: "The classic type of revolution in imperialist countries is the October Revolution. The classic type of revolution in colonial and semicolonial countries is the Chinese revolution."[9] Ch'en saluted Mao's writings as "the development of Marxism-Leninism in the East."[10]

In this period (1949–51), the Russians resisted Chinese claims that the Chinese revolution provided the classical model for colonial and semicolonial countries. They attributed the success of the Chinese revolution to the fact that it was "relying on the extremely rich experience of the CPSU" and particularly to the working out by Marx, Lenin, and especially Stalin of a program on the national-colonial question that provided "the only correct road leading to liberation from imperialism and feudalism."[11] Stalin's works, it was asserted, contained a "finished theory of national-colonial revolutions in general, and the Chinese revolution in particular."[12] Finally, in November, 1951, the well-known Soviet orientalist Ye. Zhukov told a conference of the Oriental Institute of the Academy of Sciences of the U.S.S.R. that "it would be risky to regard the Chinese revolution as some kind of 'stereotype' for people's democratic revolutions in other countries of Asia."[13]

In 1952, Moscow and Peking evidently reached some sort of compromise on this basic question of whether Peking's model was applicable to other Eastern countries. Throughout 1952, the Chinese desisted from extended public discussions of the problem. Then, on September 27, 1952, there appeared in the Chinese journal *Shih-chieh Chih-shih* an article on the subject by none other than Ye. Zhukov. This article, "China's Revolutionary Victory and Its Influence Over the Liberation Movement of the Various Peoples of Asia," was evidently designed to announce the terms of the compromise between Moscow and Peking. It was unusual for an article on this subject to be written by a Russian for a Chinese journal at the "request of the Chinese editors." It could not have been accidental that the Russian selected was the very same man who, a year earlier, had warned against applying the Chinese model in other countries of Asia. While making it quite clear that the Soviet Union occupied the leading role in the Asian revolutionary movement and that the liberation struggle in Asia "followed the road pointed out by the great proletarian leaders, Lenin and Stalin," Zhukov now made some concessions to the Chinese position. He said the Chinese had provided an "example" that could "stimulate" and "inspire" other Asian peoples in their search for independence. More important, for the first time a Soviet spokesman recognized how "especially significant" was the "rich revolutionary practice of the Chinese Communist Party" for carrying out a revolution of national liberation.

How far, if at all, this "compromise" affected political realities it is difficult to say. In any event, beginning in 1952, the extravagant claims for "Mao's thought" and the Chinese example ceased to be made by the Chinese Communist Party (CCP) in such a blatant way as in 1949–51. This was probably because there began in 1952 a shift in Chinese Asian strategy from a "hard" to a "soft" line, a shift that anticipated the "Bandung spirit" and the *rapprochement* with India. As China's attention turned from promoting armed revolution to a more flexible approach to its Asian neighbors, there was naturally less emphasis on the Chinese revolutionary model. Having failed to promote widespread revolution in Asia, the Chinese began to employ the more traditional diplomatic, economic, and political instrumentalities in an attempt to win friends and influence in Asia. They offered themselves as leaders, not of an Asian Communist revolutionary movement, but rather of an Asian anti-imperialist and nationalist movement. This reduced tensions with the Russians for several reasons. First, the new political strategy reduced the risks that a war with the West might be forced on Russia by a reckless partner in pursuit of revolutionary aims that seemed far less urgent to Moscow than to Peking. Second, it meant an abatement of the Chinese challenge to Soviet hegemony over the Asian revolutionary movement. The Chinese probably retained hopes of dominating the Communist movement of Asia, but the need to do so was reduced once the decision was made to change to a "soft" tactical line. The main problem now became one of manipulating Asian governments rather than Asian Communists.

The rivalry between Moscow and Peking over leadership in Asia broke out once again in 1958, and the same conflict of interests produced it. By late 1957, the Chinese wanted to abandon their "soft" strategy, which had resulted in fewer gains than they had expected, and to promote "armed struggle" in the colonial and semicolonial areas under the shield of the new Soviet nuclear-missile deterrent. To pursue a forward strategy by exploiting Soviet military-technical advances, however, required Soviet acquiescence, if not active cooperation. Yet the Russians refused to abandon the "soft" line toward the nationalist leaders which they had adopted in 1955. They were in no mood to risk nuclear war on China's account.

If the Chinese were going to adopt a more militant strategy without Soviet backing, they must inevitably encroach once again on the Soviet prerogative of leadership over the Communist movement in Asia and other underdeveloped areas, however much the strategy suffered from lack of Soviet cooperation. The full extent of the increased Chinese activity in the Communist and nationalist movements of the underdeveloped areas since 1958 has yet to be revealed. Yet there is good reason to believe that the Chinese have with considerable success been seeking in recent years to build up pro-Chinese factions in the Communist parties of these areas and to convince local Communists there that the Russians are betraying their interests by seeking an arrangement with the West.

The cult of Mao has assumed unprecedented proportions, and there have been a number of articles whose purpose is to demonstrate that the Chinese model both for taking power and for building socialism is more suitable for underdeveloped countries than the Russian experience. The references to "building socialism" and "socialist construction" represent a new element that was not present in the Chinese claims of 1949–51. The communes provided a unique opportunity to make such claims. No sooner had the Chinese taken the decision to establish them than Ch'en Po-ta suggested that they formed part of the blueprint for Communism in all underdeveloped countries.[14]

The Russians, of course, did not accept such claims, because they immediately perceived in them a Chinese attempt to overturn the "compromise" that had been reached in 1952 and to force the Russians into recognizing Chinese leadership of the revolutionary movement in all underdeveloped countries. At their Twenty-first and Twenty-second Party Congresses, the Russians declared that they were showing the path to Communism for both Europe and Asia and that anyone who wanted to know what Communism was had better study the Soviet Party program and documents.

It is difficult not to conclude even from this brief chronicle that one essential question in the Sino-Soviet ideological tug of war is the question of whose authority is to be recognized as final in the African, Asian, and Latin American Communist movements.

Having looked at the Russian and Chinese controversy concerning the relevance of their models for other Asian states, as viewed by the Russians and Chinese themselves, we may now try to assess from our own point of view the differences in the two models and the relevance of these differences for other countries in Asia.

THE ECONOMIC DIFFERENCES[15]

The first point to be noted in any comparison of the Soviet and Chinese "roads to socialism" is that the Russia of 1917 was underdeveloped only by the standards of the advanced European countries. China of 1949 was underdeveloped by any standards. A few simple figures bear this out. It has been estimated that if the rate of increase in per capita consumption achieved by China in the First Five-Year Plan (1953–57) continued, it would take twenty years to reach the level achieved by the Russians in 1928, when the Russians' own First Five-Year Plan began. In other words, so far as consumption is concerned, it would take China twenty-five years to reach the point where Russia stood even before she embarked on industrialization. To take another simple comparison, the per capita Soviet steel output in 1928 was twelve times that of China in 1952.

The special difficulty of the Chinese task is also reflected in the contrast between population-land ratios in the two leading Communist countries, perhaps the most critical of all the differences between them. The average annual rate of population increase in Russia since 1928 has been about 0.6 per cent; in the past decade, China's population has expanded by about 2 per cent a year, starting from a much higher base. To put this contrast more starkly, the total population increase in the Soviet Union from 1913 to 1960, roughly 50 million, will be added to China's population in the next three or four years. Particularly in rural areas, China is critically overpopulated. In the Soviet Union, the farm population, has, in fact, declined since the Communists took power in 1917, while in China it has grown by more than 60 million since 1949.

The arable land available to feed this rapidly growing Chinese population in 1956 amounted to only 0.2 hectares per inhabitant. As Oleg Hoeffding has pointed out, even if in ten years China succeeds in adding her planned maximum of 33 million hectares of arable land to her present 112 million, she will possess only two-thirds of the present arable acreage of the U.S.S.R., and her population will be nearly four times as large. It is simply not possible for China to bring her virgin lands under cultivation on a sufficiently large scale to meet her needs. Hence the Chinese have labored to develop novel methods of deep plowing and close planting in order to raise agricultural yields.

Another critical difference is the low level of Chinese mechanization compared to Russia's. Most of the work in the Chinese countryside is still done by human labor power. This has a number of implications. First of all, it means that the state has less control over the farm produce than it would have if agriculture were mechanized. Second, it means that the will to work plays a much larger role in China's agriculture than in Russia's.

China stands apart from Russia, too, in her critical shortage of trained manpower, a fact that has contributed to the periodic Chinese "blooming and contending" campaigns, which have been designed to encouraged the Chinese technical intelligentsia to participate in socialist construction.

Even before the communes and the Great Leap Forward of 1958, the Chinese sought to meet their special problems by devising policies with an emphasis peculiar to themselves. In China's First Five-Year Plan, although agriculture was neglected in comparison with industry, the Chinese Communists gave more attention to raising agricultural production than Russia had ever done. Not until 1953 did the Soviet Union give first priority to increasing agricultural production. In her agricultural policies, moreover, China from the start emphasized irrigation, water conservation, and traditional "labor-intensive" methods, while the Soviet Communists in their early days emphasized mechanization.

In the early stages of Chinese Communist rule, the very fact that China was so backward facilitated tasks that had proved much more difficult in Russia of the 1920's. This was particularly true of collectivization. In China, there was no appreciable lowering of the peasantry's already low living standards during the collectivization drive as there was in Russia. Moreover, the lower productivity of the Chinese peasantry meant a lowering of their ability to resist state control as compared with their Russian counterparts. Finally, Soviet collectivization was accompanied by mechanization, which meant large changes in the countryside. The revolution in the Chinese village was not nearly so profound in technical terms as it was in the U.S.S.R. Because it was generally not mechanized, the Chinese collective was a more frail organization. While it is difficult to break up a mechanized kolkhoz into individual peasant holdings, it is not so difficult to do so with a nonmechanized kolkhoz. While the requirement of mechanization made the Russian task initially more difficult, it also made their collectives more stable than those of the Chinese.

Prior to 1958, although the step-by-step collectivization process in China had been much smoother than collectivization in the U.S.S.R., the difference between the Russian and Chinese models was largely one of degree. With the inauguration of the Leap Forward and the communes, it became a difference in kind. The differences between the Soviet approach to economic development and that of the Chinese since 1958 are well known. The important point for our present purposes is that, by 1957, it was becoming apparent to the Chinese Communist leadership that the problems of "building socialism" in an underdeveloped Asian country, with little machinery, modern technology, or trained manpower, a rapidly growing population, a relatively stable area of arable land, and an impoverished agricultural sector, were quite different from the problems that had faced the Soviet Union at any time in its history.

Throughout the period of the Leap Forward and the communes, the Chinese Communists repeatedly emphasized the "special conditions" in their country that made it necessary to find a new and distinctive path to socialist construction. These conditions, specified by Mao and others and explicitly distinguished from conditions in the U.S.S.R., were: a large population coupled with a relatively small amount of arable land, a predominantly agrarian economy, and a low level of mechanization. These critical differences between Russian and Chinese factor endowments had been largely ignored in China's First Five-Year Plan, which was closely modeled on earlier Soviet plans.

Peking concluded in 1957 that the key to China's agricultural problem was to mobilize the underemployed rural labor force on an unprecedented scale. The lack of modern equipment and machinery would be made up by putting vast labor gangs to work where their work would be most effective—in irrigation, fertilizer accumulation, and the building of dams and reservoirs. This massive mobilization of labor, moreover, would have to be achieved with almost no material incentives, since it was the essence of the scheme that, to maximize the rate of capital accumulation, slogans and ideological incentives would be substituted for tangible rewards. Similarly, the program was designed to accelerate agricultural production with the least possible diversion of investment from industry. Since it was imperative to establish machinery through which the Party could control the new rural labor armies, the communes were introduced.

The industrial component of the program required more rapid industrialization with a minimum expenditure of capital. This was to be accomplished through the construction in rural areas of thousands of small-scale industrial installations. Of these, the backyard blast furnaces received the most publicity in the West, but the promotion of small-scale industry also embraced machine shops, fertilizer production, power generation, coal extraction, and the more traditional textile and food-processing industries. This solution, it has been suggested, bore much greater similarity to Japanese than to Soviet precedents. However, where the Japanese confined their small-scale industry to such things as baskets, pottery, and consumer goods, the Chinese extended theirs into metallurgy and other fields where large-scale production generally produces economies.

If successful, the small-plants campaign could conceivably have considerable influence on the planners of other underdeveloped countries. The principal advantage of such plants is that they require little capital. Because they are widely distributed to match the local availability of labor, they also allow savings in transportation. Furthermore, they require little technological skill or imported machinery and thus reduce dependence on foreign suppliers.

Initially, the Chinese claimed that small plants could be designed for almost every branch of light and heavy industry. So much was expected of them that China's industrial plan for 1958 was revised sharply upward. Nevertheless, as is well known, the backyard iron and steel campaign was a failure because the product was defective in quality. Yet Chinese planners seem to have learned from their failures, and small plants are still being encouraged on a more modest and rational basis.

It remains to be seen whether the Chinese Communists, having launched a radical experiment that has in many respects failed, will in the future hew closer to the Soviet line or whether they will cast about for new, original solutions to their acute problems. The evidence of recent years suggests that Soviet experience, particularly as it relates to the organization of the countryside, is seriously deficient when superimposed on an underdeveloped, overpopulated Asian country. But it is by no means clear that the Chinese Communists have yet evolved a system better suited for such countries.

BENEFITING FROM PAST SOVIET MISTAKES

A second factor that helps to explain some of the differences in method between Chinese and Soviet approaches to building socialism is that Mao could benefit both by Stalin's mistakes and from those made by the Chinese Communists themselves during their Kiangsi Soviet and Yenan days. This was particularly true in agriculture, where Mao's initial approach (until 1955–56) was a much more gradual and well-prepared one than Stalin's. With their own and Russian experience behind them, the Chinese consciously set out to avoid ultra-left mistakes in agrarian policy. Thus, unlike the Russians, they did not immediately nationalize all land after the revolution. Although the landlord class was treated harshly, the well-to-do and upper-middle-class peasants were treated much more generously during the land reform than their Russian counterparts during the period immediately after the Revolution. One might even say that the Chinese Communist approach to social classes in the countryside immediately after the revolution was closer to that of the right-wing Social Revolutionaries in the U.S.S.R. than to that of the Bolsheviks. The Bolsheviks wished to begin immediately by supporting the poor peasant against the kulak and by encouraging class warfare in the countryside. The right-wing Social Revolutionaries (SR's) wanted to conduct the struggle exclusively against the landlords. They believed, for example, that land held by individual peasants, no matter how wealthy, was untouchable and that only confiscated landlords' estates should be redistributed. This was essentially the tactical line followed by the Chinese Communists, whose initial purpose was to destroy the power of the rural landlord class while seeking to unite the vast bulk of the peasantry behind them. Thus, according to the 1950 agrarian-reform law, land owned by rich peasants and cultivated by them or by hired labor was not to be touched. The idea was to neutralize the rich peasant initially, not to liquidate him.

The difference between the SR's and the Chinese Communists was, of course, that for the SR's land reform was an end; for the Chinese Communists it was a means to an end. But it was the skill with which the Chinese Communists played their cards that led some Western observers to conclude that they were merely agrarian reformers.

During the early stages of collectivization, Mao again benefited from Soviet mistakes and made much greater use than Stalin did of lower and intermediate types of cooperatives. He began with seasonal mutual-aid teams, which were then made permanent. The next step was gradually to lead the peasants into low-level, then high-level, agricultural producers' cooperatives. When the peasants first entered the cooperatives, the Chinese, in sharp contrast to the Russians, paid a dividend to peasants who had contributed land to them. The farmer retained title to his land and received a share of the cooperative's annual joint product in proportion to his previous private holdings. Indeed, for a number of years the Chinese Communists emphasized that their mutual-aid and cooperative organizations were built on the foundation of private ownership; they denied any similarity between these organizations and the Soviet collective farms; and they made it absolutely clear that there was to be no infringement of private property after the peasant pooled his land in the cooperative. Members withdrawing from a mutual-aid team or cooperative were legally entitled to withdraw their investments in capital and reserve funds. Moreover, a member of a cooperative was not, at this stage, bound to pool any other means of production besides land. If he did so voluntarily, he was entitled to full compensation.

In industry, too, the Chinese were intent upon avoiding Soviet mistakes, and their transition from a private to a socialist economy was made gradually. Joint state-private enterprises were used to bring industry and trade under state control, and frequently the former bourgeois manager was retained on a salary.

Many other examples of how the Chinese profited from Soviet mistakes or experience could be cited. The Chinese were able, for example, to take over the Soviet concept of central planning immediately after the revolution without having to go through an initial utopian phase such as that in which the Russians considered abolishing money as a medium of exchange. The many Soviet advisers in China during the First Five-Year Plan undoubtedly helped the Chinese to avoid some of the planning mistakes previously made by the Russians themselves.

A final important economic factor concerns foreign aid. Soviet material assistance played a crucial role in Chinese industrialization. Chinese imports from the U.S.S.R., particularly machinery and equipment, formed a bigger portion of the total Chinese Communist investment over the past decade than Soviet imports from the West at a comparable stage of development. "Building socialism" in backward Asian countries may require more outside aid than was available to the Russians in early stages of their development.

THE DIFFERENT ROADS TO POWER

Besides differences of economic situation and the cautionary effect of past Soviet mistakes, there is a third factor that plays an even more profound part in distinguishing the Chinese revolutionary model from the Russian one. The Chinese Communists spent close to three decades together in battle and faced great dangers and tremendous obstacles in the course of a protracted civil war. Most of the Russian revolutionary leaders lived in exile; they had neither fought together nor shared the same hardships. They spent much of their time in hurling abuse and polemics at one another. The second generation of Soviet leaders who now rule are not even welded together by the struggle against the old regime, since most of them joined the Party after it had taken power.

The long and bitter Chinese Communist struggle for power undoubtedly explains a great deal of the distinctiveness of the Chinese revolutionary model. For one thing, it helps to explain why Chinese Communist organizational control is so much more effective than the Russian. As H. F. Schurmann has pointed out,[16] the territorial fragmentation of Communist power, particularly during the Yenan period, necessitated control at the local level and self-discipline because centralized army discipline could not effectively govern the actions of thousands of guerrilla groups. It was in this period that the Chinese Communists achieved their extraordinary organizational perfection. The long struggle for power is undoubtedly also an important factor in explaining the peculiar Chinese emphasis on remolding individuals through "thought reform" and "rectification," processes that have no real analogues in Soviet Communism. Because the Chinese Communists were outnumbered by such great odds for so long, their very survival hinged on their ability to recruit allies from all classes and groups and to convert their enemies into friends. Perhaps for the same reason, Mao has placed great emphasis in his ideological pronouncements on the "people" as a whole. He seems to see himself not only as a Communist leader but also as a leader of the entire nation.

The "populist" component of Chinese policy finds expression particularly in the Chinese attitude toward minorities and various social groups. Mao has always stressed the "united front," not only as essential for taking power but also as a means of consolidating power. The Chinese Communist Central Committee, unlike the Russian, has a special united-front department under Li Wei-han, whose work is primarily concerned with integrating minorities and various social groups into the Communist system. As late as 1959, fourteen out of forty-nine ministries of the central government were headed by members of non-Communist parties.

Another reason for the relatively tolerant Chinese attitude toward the bourgeoisie, of course, is that the skills of the latter are much more important to the Chinese Communists than the skills of the Russian bourgeoisie were to the Bolsheviks. The great need to win the allegiance of the scientific, medical, and technical intelligentsia is reflected in many of the regime's policies, and this need will doubtless be present in most other Asian countries.

THE TIMING OF THE CIVIL WAR

A fourth source of the differences between the Chinese and Russian models is the fact that in Russia the civil war took place after the Communist seizure of power, while in China it occurred before. This had several ramifications. First, it meant that in Russia, unlike China, the period of "war Communism" came while the Communists were in power. This period of enforced rationing and scarcity could not but damage the relationship between the Russian Communists and the peasants. In China, on the other hand, the period of "war Communism," coming as it did during the war against Japan, affected only the Party, not the relationship of the Party with the peasantry. Second, it meant that the Chinese Communists, unlike the Russians, could begin immediately their step-by-step transition to socialism without having first to go through a long period of recovery. In China, there was no need for a policy akin to the New Economic Policy in Russia, when for a while peasant proprietors became entrenched in the countryside. Hence the task of collectivization was easier in China than it had been in Russia.

DIFFERING STAGES OF DEVELOPMENT

A fifth factor that must be mentioned in comparing the Russian and Chinese models is the present difference between Russia and China with regard to socio-economic development. First of all, however, let us compare China of the Great Leap with Russia of the early 1930's. There are some suggestive similarities. Both countries were striving desperately to accumulate capital; both sought to hasten the growth of capital by restricting peasant consumption and inculcating revolutionary zeal; both, in attempting to surmount incredible difficulties, were obsessed with speed of development even at the cost of imbalance. Here are the words of Liu Shao-ch'i in 1959:

> In high-speed development, it is more likely that certain imbalances will occur. We should not, however, give way to "fear of the wolf in front and of the tiger behind," vainly hoping for a haven of peace by adopting the method of reducing speed unjustifiably to achieve a balance.[17]

A year earlier, he said:

> The speed of construction has been the most important question confronting us since the victory of the socialist revolution. The aim of our revolution is to expand the social productive forces as quickly as possible. . . . Karl Marx prophesied that the proletarian revolution would usher us into a great epoch when "20 years are concentrated in a day." If in past revolutionary struggles we experienced such great times, then is not our present socialist construction another great time again?[18]

In Khrushchev's Russia, such a view is condemned as "left-wing adventurism." But on the eve of the big collectivization push, the prominent Soviet economist S. G. Strumulin wrote: "Our task is not to study economics, but to change it. We are bound by no laws. There are no fortresses which Bolsheviks cannot storm. The question of tempo is subject to decision by human beings."[19]

When he sounded the call for forced collectivization in 1927, Stalin, like the Chinese Communists of 1958, presented that solution as the only alternative to suicide. The following passage from Leonard Schapiro's description of the early 1930's in the Soviet Union sounds somewhat familiar to the student of China in 1958–60:

> As the years wore on, to an ever mounting crescendo of self-congratulation from the Party leaders, exaggerated claims of success, faked statistics and exhortation to yet greater efforts, the more sober realities of the situation produced a corresponding depression. In the place of the promised plenty, there was food shortage.[20]

One should not push too far these parallels between the Russian outlook during the First Five-Year Plan and the Chinese outlook in the period of the Great Leap. There is obviously a need for systematic comparisons of the two countries in these two periods, and until they are undertaken parallels must be drawn with caution. Yet it seems that a common characteristic of both periods was the fact that the leaders had come to a serious impasse in their drive toward rapid industrialization. In the Russia of the late 1920's, there was the well-known grain problem caused by the refusal of the peasantry to deliver surplus produce to the state. In the China of the "leap," there was also a grain problem, though for different reasons—bad harvests and an expanding population on a limited amount of arable land. In both cases, an extremely weak agricultural sector threatened to retard the industrialization process. In both cases, the reaction of the regime was to look for extreme organizational solutions and to deck these out in fancy ideological trimmings.

In 1958, the Chinese displayed remarkable ideological agility. They substituted the concept of "uninterrupted revolution" for that of revolution by stages and contended in effect that a new stage in socio-economic development toward Communism need not await the prior development of productive forces. The Russians, with good reason, accused them of jumping over necessary stages in the advance toward Communism, of trying to introduce new advanced "production relations" (social institutions) without the requisite technology and industrial base, which the Chinese could not hope to have for many years to come. The Chinese countered with the criticism, equally reasonable from a Marxist point of view, that the Russians were not "developing" the Communist system, but were bringing it to a standstill. In 1960, Lu Ting-i, a prominent Chinese theoretician, without specifically mentioning Moscow, berated "the kind of theory" which holds that:

> . . . there is no need to develop the socialist system, but only to consolidate it, and even if it is to be developed, [in order] to go forward to Communism, [that] still there is no need to undergo a struggle and to pass through a qualitative leap; and thus [that] the process of the uninterrupted revolution of human society goes up to this point and no further.[21]

It is difficult to avoid the impression that the models for social construction currently offered by Russia and China differ fundamentally because of the hard fact that China is compelled to advance to the self-sustaining stage of economic growth at breakneck speed or risk stagnation and defeat of the revolution, whereas Russia has long since reached the stage of self-sustaining growth.

Why, it may be asked, did neither the Chinese nor the Russians, in their early post-revolutionary stages, set aside longer periods to put through their development plans and thus avoid the strains and problems faced by the Russians in the 1930's and by the Chinese since 1958. In each case, the Five-Year Plan developed a momentum of its own. Development in a priority sector implied development in other sectors. More tractors meant more steel and more coal, and so on. The greatest pressure for breakneck economic development, however, sprang from the fact that both Russia of the 1930's and China of 1958 took it almost as an article of faith that a showdown with the imperialists was inevitable. Russia today, by virtue of its weapons developments, can afford to be somewhat more confident that war is not "fatalistically inevitable" than China, whose defense (as well as revolutionary ambition) depends on a Soviet deterrent that is not available to them to exploit as they would like.

CONCLUSIONS

To sum up, the Russians and Chinese themselves have rather persistently disagreed on whether or not the Chinese model for revolution and socialist construction is more relevant than the Russian for underdeveloped areas. This disagreement seems to be intimately bound up with a struggle for power and spheres of influence in Asia and other underdeveloped areas, a struggle that has become intense in recent years. The Soviet economic model has proved to have important weaknesses when applied in China, an underdeveloped Asian country with little machinery, modern technology, or trained manpower, a rapidly growing population, and a relatively stable and inadequate area of arable land. But it is by no means obvious that the Chinese Communists have as yet discovered a more suitable model for themselves, let alone for other Asian countries.

Of the factors that account for the divergence of the Russian and Chinese roads to socialism, the most important seem to be the great difference in population-resource ratios; the fact that the Chinese have learned from Soviet mistakes and have benefited from Soviet help; the Chinese Communist experience of twenty or more years of regional power; the considerable differences between the paths to power of the Soviet and Chinese Communist parties; the fact that in Russia the civil war took place after and in China before the seizure of power; and, finally, the differing stages of socio-economic development in which Russia and China now find themselves.

Other Asian countries that have unfavorable population-resource ratios and are extremely underdeveloped will doubtless find, as the Chinese did, that Soviet experience cannot in itself offer solutions to their numerous and peculiar economic problems. They will be able, however, to take advantage of Soviet and Chinese mistakes and successes.

In the Communist world of tomorrow, diversity and polycentrism are likely to increase as a result of the Sino-Soviet conflict and the consequent gradual erosion of Soviet authority in some areas. Already the Sino-Soviet conflict has had a considerable impact on the smaller Communist parties throughout Asia, particularly those in power. Of these three, only Outer Mongolia joined in Khrushchev's attack on Albania at the Twenty-second Party Congress, in the fall of 1961. The refusal of the vast majority of the Asian parties out of power and the two key parties in power, the North Vietnamese and North Koreans, to echo Khrushchev's action is an indication of the considerable limits of Soviet authority in the Asian Communist movement.

But it would be too great an oversimplification to assume from these developments that the smaller Asian parties in or out of power will become Chinese satellites. The North Koreans, for reasons of their own, have been staunch supporters of the Chinese in their dispute with Moscow since 1960, while the North Vietnamese sought for a number of years to mediate the dispute and only recently have moved closer to the Chinese on some issues. Nevertheless, both the North Koreans and the North Vietnamese continue to take economic aid from both the Russians and the Chinese. So long as there is no open and formal split, they will probably continue to maneuver between Peking and Moscow, extracting support from both. In this manner, they will be able to gain even greater independence from Russia and China in both foreign and domestic policies. There are already a number of indications that the North Vietnamese Party has a high degree of independence from both Russia and China in its operations in Laos, for example. At home, both the North Vietnamese and the North Koreans can be expected eventually to develop their own peculiar brands of "socialist construction" which, in all likelihood, will be modeled in part on both Russian and Chinese experience but with a large dose of local variation. Khrushchev himself recently gave the green light to "national roads to socialism" when he told the East German Party Congress, in January, 1963, that it was possible for Communist parties to diverge even on important ideological questions and that the real question now was only "who owns the means of production and who controls state power." Khrushchev was, in effect, saying that a Communist Party's road to socialism and Communism is its own business.

Thus, the Sino-Soviet conflict has shattered the single-centered international system created by Stalin and has opened the door to pluralism in the Communist world. Communism is no longer homogeneous and monolithic. The common ideology is increasingly being stretched to fit diverse national conditions and circumstances. This is perhaps the most significant and lasting consequence of the historic struggle within the Communist world.

NOTES

1. "Address to Second All-Russian Congress of Communist Organizations of the Peoples of the East," Nov. 22, 1919.

2. Zbigniew K. Brzezinski, *The Soviet Bloc* (Cambridge, Mass.: Harvard University Press, 1960; New York: Frederick A. Praeger, 1961 [rev. paperback ed.]), *passim*.

3. *Pravda*, July 15, 1956.

4. G. F. Hudson, Richard Lowenthal, and Roderick MacFarquhar (eds.), *The Sino-Soviet Dispute* (New York: Frederick A. Praeger, 1960), p. 51.

5. *Fundamentals of Marxism-Leninism* (Moscow: Foreign Languages Publishing House, 1959), p. 660.

6. Mao Tse-tung, *Selected Works* (New York: International Publishers, 1954), III, 119.

7. Anna Louise Strong, "The Thought of Mao Tse-tung," *Amerasia*, XI, No. 6 (June, 1947), 161.

8. *Wen-hui Pao* (Shanghai), November 25, 1949; cited in Arthur Cohen,

Phillip Bridgham, and Herb Jaffe, "Chinese and Soviet Views on Mao as a Marxist Theorist and on the Significance of the Chinese Revolution for the Asian Revolutionary Movement," an excellent unpublished monograph on the differences between Chinese and Soviet views between 1949 and 1951. (Notes 9 through 13 below are given as cited there.)

9. "The World Significance of the Chinese Revolution," *Hsueh-hsi*, July 1, 1951, pp. 26–27.

10. "Mao Tse-tung's Theory of the Chinese Revolution Is the Combination of Marxism-Leninism with the Chinese Revolution," *Hsueh-hsi*, July 1, 1951, p. 20.

11. Ye. Kovalev, "Historic Victory of the Chinese People," *Bol'shevik*, No. 19 (October, 1949), pp. 42–54.

12. A. N. Kheyfets, "Problems of the Chinese Revolution in the Works of J. V. Stalin," *Voprosy Filosofii*, No. 3 (1950, published in January, 1951), pp. 53–74.

13. "On the Character and Peculiarities of People's Democracy in Countries of the East," *Izvestia Akademii Nauk SSSR, Seriya Istorii i Filosofii*, IX, No. 1 (1952), 80–87.

14. *Hung Ch'i (Red Flag)*, No. 4 (July 16, 1958).

15. In the discussion that follows, the author has drawn on Oleg Hoeffding, "Soviet State Planning and Forced Industrialization as a Model for Asia" (The RAND Corporation, August 4, 1958); Ygael Gluckstein, *Mao's China* (Boston: Beacon Press, 1957); Alexander Eckstein, "A Study in Economic Strategy," *Survey*, October, 1961; Shao-er Ong (under the direction of Theodore H. E. Chen), "Agrarian Reform in Communist China," February 15, 1952; the unpublished and published work of William Hollister; W. W. Rostow, *The Prospects for Communist China* (Cambridge, Mass.: Massachusetts Institute of Technology, 1954); Otto Schiller, "A Comparison of the Agrarian System in the Soviet Union and China" (paper delivered to Third International Conference of Sovietologists, September 18–25, 1960); and the very perceptive and pioneering article of Robert Vincent Daniels, "The Chinese Revolution in Russian Perspective," *World Politics*, January, 1961, pp. 210–30.

16. H. F. Schurmann, "Organization and Response in Communist China," *The Annals*, January, 1959, pp. 51–61.

17. New China News Agency release, October 1, 1959.

18. *Report to the Second Session of the Eighth Party Congress*, May 5, 1958; reprinted in Robert R. Bowie and John K. Fairbank (eds.), *Communist China 1955–59* (Cambridge, Mass.: Harvard University Press, 1962), pp. 424–29.

19. Quoted in Leonard Schapiro, *The Communist Party of the Soviet Union* (New York: Random House, 1960), p. 364.

20. *Ibid.*, p. 387.

21. Lu Ting-i, "Unite Under Lenin's Revolutionary Banner," *Long Live Leninism* (Peking: Foreign Languages Press, 1960), pp. 94–95.

2. Two Revolutionary Models: Russian and Chinese

by ROBERT C. NORTH

RUSSIAN AND CHINESE COMMUNIST VIEWS

The great struggles of the mid-twentieth century, like the crucial conflicts man has fought in earlier eras, have emerged, to a large degree, from differences over how people should combine, or organize, and how resources should be allocated and exchanged. However, because of man's recent and spectacular achievements in a third sphere, the reordering of his environment, the current struggle over how to combine and how to allocate resources has raised peculiarly favorable opportunities, as well as gross dangers unknown in previous periods of history.

Modern technology has provided people in the so-called "underdeveloped" regions with a variety of new possibilities for substantially altering their environment and rendering it less hostile. The example set by the technologically "advanced" countries and the transmission of this "image of possible advancement" have thus become political phenomena of extreme relevance. At the same time, however, the development of nuclear weapons has raised unprecedented possibilities for destructiveness.

It is entirely possible for a people who have achieved sophisticated techniques for improving their environment to transmit—in one fashion or another—their organization, skills, and surplus energies to underdeveloped areas. This transmission of knowledge affords great opportunities for reshaping such areas, but it also gives rise to conflicts over who shall do this transmitting and what organizational forms—both political and economic—shall be put into practice.

Marxist-Leninist theory and practice have played a powerful role in altering political and economic forms and in hastening the transmission of technology from developed to underdeveloped

34

areas. Classical Marxism argued that inequities in the allocation of resources within a given capitalist country would lead to the over-throw and destruction of the bourgeois political structure and the substitution of a new system that would provide a different kind of allocation. Lenin, through his theory of imperialism, placed initial emphasis elsewhere: Revolution was more likely to be generated in the underdeveloped countries than in those where technology was highly developed. Marxism-Leninism thus became a system for communicating new political, economic, and technological goals to colonial and "semicolonial" areas and also for introducing new means—in all three categories—for transforming underdeveloped environments.

Viewed broadly, Marxism-Leninism provides a body of theory, a strategy, and a manual of tactics for breaking up traditional economic and political structures, pulverizing them, so to speak, and reintegrating them into a new kind of system. Today, however, there are two major Marxist-Leninist models of world conflict and integration—two somewhat distinct programs for combining human efforts in order to alter and control the environment—the Chinese Communist and the Soviet Russian. It is important that we understand both their similarities and their differences.

DIFFERING WORLD VIEWS

A subtle and often elusive source of conflict resides in the fact that men have differing views of the world and of the role of human beings in it. This is a difficulty of long standing. Depending upon their experiences and cultural conditioning, men have always maintained a diversity of philosophies, religions, world views, and ideologies. It seems clear, however, that certain relatively recent developments have aggravated the difficulties of moderating those collisions between organized groups of people that have persistently characterized human history.

We may visualize man as having no contact with his environment or with his fellow man except through two filter lenses—the lens of his senses and the lens of his experience, upbringing, and cultural conditioning. And just as an individual who suffers color blindness sees his environment somewhat differently from the way a person with normal vision views it, so we may suppose that a man who has been conditioned by one set of experiences will perceive his surroundings somewhat differently from his fellow man from a different milieu.

Virtually any organizational effort in human history is characterized by an attempt on the part of the group to standardize at least a part of the lens used by each of its members. This is an essential purpose of all rule books, catechisms, educational systems, and codes of law. Groups and societies differ, however, in their views of how much and what particular parts of each lens should be synchronized with all other lenses in the system.

A troublesome factor in the world conflict today is that one of the major contending organizational systems, the Communist, is founded upon the premise that one lens—and only one lens—provides a "correct" view of the world and of man's role in it. This system acknowledges that not all human beings wear this prescription, but anticipates that in due course all men will inevitably be so equipped and that when this comes about, there will be an absolute minimum of essential difference from one set of glasses to the next. Yet it is becoming increasingly evident that even Communist lenses are often differently shaped and offer somewhat different views.

THE MARXIST-LENINIST WORLD VIEW

The essential aspects of the Marxist-Leninist world view are well known and do not require extensive recitation. We need only to remind ourselves of a few crucial features: The world view is put forward as absolutely comprehensive, embracing the laws governing the whole physical universe as well as man and all his works. The fundamental laws it identifies are inescapable, irreversible, unalterable, and governed by materialistic processes which—in the current stage of history—manifest themselves through class conflict. Man's behavior and the processes of his cognition are wholly subject to these materialistically engendered laws. Nothing is inherently unknowable. Virtually all men—since they are unavoidably subject to these processes—will, in due course, achieve "true" cognition, will therefore increasingly perceive the universe and their fellow men in the same way, and will, in the long run, react the same way to the same stimuli. All interactions within this total context are inherently conflictual, but beyond a certain point—as men are conditioned more and more in the same way—these contradictions will become less and less antagonistic and more and more reciprocally corrective.

Human beings all over the world, in short, will tend to accept the same world view, the same long- and medium-range goals and—increasingly—will tend to select the same immediate means for achieving these goals.

MAJOR ANTAGONISMS OR CLEAVAGE POINTS

Marx saw the major struggle emerging from the conflict between capital and labor in the advanced industrial societies. His view was focused largely on Great Britain, Western Europe, and the United States. Lenin made crucial alterations in this concept, and, as a consequence, Communism came to be more and more concerned with the underdeveloped countries, which he referred to as the "colonies and semicolonies."

Having accumulated vast surpluses of capital in the industrial nations, the bourgeoisie, according to Lenin, had found it necessary to seek new fields of investment. These they had found in the colonies and semicolonies of the economically underdeveloped areas of the globe. Taking advantage of cheap labor in these regions, the capitalists of the industrial nations could buy raw materials at low cost, process them, and sell the products back to the populace at great advantage. With these profits, the bourgeoisie could "bribe" their own proletariats through higher wages and thus stave off the revolution in their own countries. So it was that capitalism had thrown its net over the surface of the globe.

Marxist-Leninist theory identifies three major antagonisms or hostile contradictions in the world: (1) the antagonisms among competing imperialist powers; (2) the antagonism between the imperialist powers and the colonies and other "exploited" nations; and (3) the antagonism, within a given country, between the capitalist "exploiter" and the proletariat and other classes suffering exploitation.

By holding his chisel at the correct cleavage point, a skilled stonecutter can split a boulder into its natural parts. Analogously, we find the Soviet Russian and the Communist Chinese chisels somewhat differently placed—though the discrepancies are largely of emphasis. In fact, both the Russians and the Chinese recognize the same antagonisms. The problem emerges in practical terms: How much time and energy and how many resources shall be allocated to exploiting the various conflicts? Today, in some respects, the Chinese may be closer to Lenin than the Russians.

Generally, Lenin saw world Communism emerging from the chaotic wake of imperialist wars and from wars of national liberation in the colonies and semicolonies. In these latter areas, however, the circumstances were complicated further.

Necessarily, as Lenin saw it, the bourgeois imperialists would ally themselves with local elements seeking to preserve the *status quo*, but unavoidably and in spite of themselves they would also sow the first seeds of revolution by introducing new technologies and educating the populace to new possibilities. In the colonies, indeed, the imperialist bourgeoisie—by recruiting and training native armies —were creating the armed forces that would eventually be used against them.

This bourgeois exploitation of colonial and semicolonial markets, Lenin believed, was changing the class structure of colonial areas in a crucial fashion and releasing a new revolutionary potential.

Nineteenth-century Marxism would have assumed it to be necessary for these colonies and semicolonies to work their way—or "struggle" their way—dialectically through stage after stage into full capitalism, thence to the dictatorship of the proletariat, and finally to pure Communism. But with the establishment of the Soviet Union as an ideological inspiration, an organizational base, and an arsenal of the proletariat, Leninism saw the possibility for a foreshortening or telescoping process. With support from the Soviet Union and from the Communist parties of the Western nations, the emerging proletariats in the colonies and semicolonies could speed the struggle and bypass full capitalist development.

At the heart of the Leninist program for revolution in the colonies and semicolonies was the concept of a temporary collaboration between the Communists and the local nationalist revolutionaries.

TACTICAL ALLIANCE

As early as 1920, Lenin asserted that during initial stages of the struggle in a colonial or semicolonial country, the national bourgeoisie would "march with the revolution" in a four-bloc alliance (national bourgeoisie, petty bourgeoisie, peasantry, and proletariat) against the counterrevolutionary, reactionary classes (imperialists, feudal militarists, and compradors). The Lenin theses, somewhat modified by the ideas of the Indian revolutionist M. N. Roy, became the theoretical foundation for Communist-led revolutions in Asia and in the colonies and semicolonies elsewhere.[1]

The task of the proletariat, under revolutionary circumstances, is to collaborate with the other three classes in the revolutionary bloc —but also to maintain "hegemony" over them. In later stages of a given struggle, as the more revolutionary classes in the bloc—particularly the peasantry and the proletariat—begin to "raise new demands," such as land reform, the national bourgeoisie will desert the revolution and "go over to the imperialists," leaving a three-class bloc (petty bourgeoisie, peasantry, and proletariat) in place of the earlier four-class alliance. It is the responsibility of the proletariat to see that this three-class bloc is strong enough to withstand the defection of the national bourgeoisie and level new attacks against the imperialist bloc (now augmented by the defected bourgeoisie).

The Communist leadership must recognize, of course, which sections of the bourgeoisie—at a given revolutionary phase—are the appropriate target for the "main blow" and which should be conciliated or neutralized.

It is assumed that during subsequent revolutionary stages at least a section of the petty bourgeoisie will "go over to the imperialists," and in due course the rich peasants will also "betray the revolution" before the demands of the proletariat and the poor peasants for the confiscation of rich peasant holdings.

The peasantry, as Lenin saw it, was an extremely complex class displaying some components that were essentially capitalist and others that were proletarian. Insofar as a rich peasant owned land, stock, and implements, depended on hired labor, and sold his own grain in the market, he was fundamentally capitalist. To the degree that a poor peasant hired himself out for labor on another man's land he was essentially proletarian. A middle peasant, owning a small but insufficient plot of land and finding it necessary to hire himself out a part of the time, or to hire out his sons, partook of both classes. In a revolutionary struggle, the proletariat should support or attack the rich peasant according to the dialectical circumstance. The middle peasant could be counted upon as an ally. The poor peasant would march with the proletarian forces.[2]

The task of the Soviet Union and of the Communist parties of the imperialist states, theoretically, was to support the proletarian movements in the colonies and semicolonies and guide them in their struggles. A major difficulty with this analysis and, indeed, with the whole concept of class struggle, lay in the fact that Communist theoreticians seldom defined with any clarity the precise criteria for recognizing a class or for delineating its boundaries. The problem was especially troublesome in Asia where economic groupings did not necessarily fit the class stereotypes familiar to Europeans. Increasingly, in fact, a group and its leadership tended to be assigned to a given class not only on the basis of its economic characteristics but also according to its attitude toward the Communists.

EARLY ATTEMPTS AT APPLICATION

In 1926 and early 1927, the Soviet Russians looked upon Chiang K'ai-shek as a national bourgeois leader "marching with the revolution" who could be counted upon as an ally for some time to come. Even earlier, the Stalinists had proposed a Communist coalition with Chiang, on the assumption that the Communists could gradually take over by subversion.

As it turned out, however, Chiang "went over to the imperialists" sooner than Stalin or his agents in China expected, and the Communists were caught off balance. Those who suffered most from this miscalculation were members of the Chinese Communist Party, who were not only driven underground or into the mountains by Chiang K'ai-shek, but were also held responsible by Stalin for what amounted to his own mistake.

During the early 1920's Comintern theoreticians tried to apply this fundamental analysis of class conflict not only to China but also to India, Japan, Indonesia, and other regions of Asia. The historical record suggests that each country presented its own peculiar problems.

In 1924, M. N. Roy told the Fifth Congress of the Communist International that national capitalism was growing rapidly in India. The national bourgeoisie, in fact, had already been won over to support the British Empire, and it would be a mistake for the Communists to rely upon them. Other Comintern theoreticians were similarly cautious. "The anti-imperialist bloc must be organized much more carefully in India than in China," G. N. Voitinsky wrote in 1925, "because the upper Indian bourgeoisie has already become a conservative class, a class that fears revolution within the country much more than it fears national oppression by imperialists."[3] Because of the Congress Party and its strength and also because of other factors such as the organizational weaknesses in their own movement, the Indian Communists found it difficult to make much headway.

Japan was different because the country was itself an imperialist power. In 1922, a draft platform had stated that because of the semifeudal nature of the Japanese state, the Japanese Government was opposed not only by the workers but also by other strata of Japanese society: the peasants, the petty bourgeoisie, and the so-called liberal bourgeoisie. Consequently, the Japanese Communists were to support the bourgeois-democratic revolution temporarily—on the assumption that the triumph of the bourgeois revolution would serve as a prelude to the proletarian revolution.[4] Five years later, the Comintern altered its viewpoint by noting that "the hope that the bourgeoisie can in any way be utilized as a revolutionary factor, even during the first stages of the bourgeois-democratic revolution, must be abandoned now."[5] Analogies with China would not stand. "China was and is an object of imperialist policy, whereas the Japanese bourgeoisie is itself a first-rate imperialist power." The driving forces in the Japanese revolution were, above all, the proletariat and the peasantry, with the proletariat providing indispensable leadership.

After the failure of two Communist-inspired uprisings against Dutch authorities in Java in November, 1926, and Sumatra in January, 1927, the Communist International recognized special circumstances in Indonesia. "The national revolutionary movement in Indonesia differs above all from similar movements in the colonies in that, owing on the one hand, to the lack of a native bourgeoisie, and, on the other hand, to the existence of concentrated proletarian masses in the big factories of the imperialists, this movement followed a different path, and the working class succeeded comparatively easily in playing an active role in this movement."[6] The uprisings had failed because the Indonesian Communist leadership had betrayed "the lack of an earnest political and organizatory preparation of this movement as a whole."[7]

THE NEW DEMOCRACY

After gaining control of the Chinese Communist movement in the mid-1930's, Mao Tse-tung accepted Lenin's perception of the class structure and primary class antagonisms in China and other underdeveloped countries, but he refused to put much trust in national bourgeois leaders. Rather than rely on national bourgeois troops and governmental structure as Stalin had done, Mao went into the countryside and organized his own Red Army and his own governmental institutions, thus assuring "proletarian hegemony."

The special characteristic of the Chinese revolution, according to Mao Tse-tung and his colleagues, was a struggle of the "armed people opposing armed counterrevolution."

Essentially, Mao distrusted a tactical alliance with the national bourgeoisie until his "revolution from below" had achieved control over the whole "four-class alliance" of national bourgeoisie, petty bourgeoisie, peasantry, and proletariat. This Party hegemony took the form of the New Democracy, a governmental instrument for imposing sovereignty over all the classes and guiding the revolution through its phases by exercise of the power inherent in the Communist movement. Under the New Democracy, there was assurance that the national bourgeoisie could not do serious damage when it "went over to the imperialists." The whole revolution was under tight Maoist supervision.

Thus the New Democracy was essentially an instrument for imposing the power of the Communist Party and for carrying out a tightly controlled revolution. At each stage, the regime mobilized as broad a coalition base of tactical class alliances as was feasible under the program at hand. Once the class enemy of that particular revolutionary phase had been disposed of and Communist power consolidated, the least "revolutionary" class of the coalition—or the most reactionary class—was assumed to have "gone over" to the imperialists and was treated accordingly. Thus the imperialists, feudal elements (landlords), and bureaucratic capitalists (compradors included) were eliminated first, and then the national bourgeoisie—having "betrayed the revolution"—were put under attack, and after them, at appropriate stages, the petty bourgeoisie and the rich peasants.

The assumption was, of course, that as the class struggle progressed—as the strength of the counterrevolutionary forces abated and the power of the worker-peasant alliance increased—the governmental class composition and structure would alter, appropriately reflecting the dialectic changes taking place in the society as a whole.

The New Democracy, then, represented a transitional stage telescoping economic, political, and social "struggles" and hastening progress into Communist-style socialism.

It is against this theoretical background that the Chinese Communists have placed major emphasis upon the need for armed struggles and especially for "wars of national liberation" by the oppressed peoples against the imperialists, with tight Party control over tactical alliances with the bourgeoisie.

Stalin was reluctant to acknowledge the advantages of Mao's model. Even after World War II, he is reported to have urged the Chinese Communists to pursue "revolution from above" by forming a new coalition with Chiang K'ai-shek and boring from within rather than relying on the Chinese Red Army. Mao agreed—and then proceeded in his own way, using the Chinese Red Army to sweep Chiang and his Nationalist forces off the mainland of China.[8] This was essentially a Maoist—as against a Stalinist—victory.

Thus Soviet Russia has, over the years, tended to favor "revolution from above," whereas Communist China has been inclined toward "revolution from below." It should be reiterated, of course, that the discrepancy between the Russian inclination and the Chinese tendency is one of emphasis, and the respective policies are not, in all cases, mutually exclusive. We can postulate, however, that Peking and Moscow must encounter difficulties in coordinating programs.

CHALLENGE OF THE NUCLEAR EPOCH

ROADS TO POWER

As early as 1946, Liu Shao-ch'i—who succeeded Mao Tse-tung in 1959 as Chairman of the Chinese People's Republic—told Anna Louise Strong that Mao had changed Marxism from a European to an Asiatic form. "The basic principles of Marxism are undoubtedly adaptable to all countries," Liu asserted, "but to apply their general truth to concrete revolutionary practices in China is a difficult task. Mao Tse-tung is Chinese; he analyzes Chinese problems and guides the Chinese people in their struggle to victory. He uses Marxist-Leninist principles to explain Chinese history and the practical problems of China. He is the first that has succeeded in doing so."[9]

Mao had thus created a Chinese or Asiatic form of Marxism, Liu declared.

China is a semifeudal, semicolonial country in which vast numbers of people live at the edge of starvation, tilling small bits of soil. Its economy is agricultural, backward, and dispersed. In attempting the transition to a more industrialized economy, China faces the competition and pressures—economic, political, and military—of advanced industrial lands. This is the basic situation that affects both the relations of social classes and the methods of struggle toward any such goal or national independence and a better, freer life for the Chinese. There are similar conditions in other lands of Southeast Asia. The courses chosen by China will influence them all.[10]

In 1949, after the Chinese Communists had seized power on the mainland, Liu Shao-ch'i suggested again that the "path taken by the Chinese people" was in many circumstances the path that should be taken by people of other "colonial and dependent countries in their struggle for national independence and people's democracy."[11]

Over the succeeding dozen years, the problem of how Communists should achieve power—both in the underdeveloped countries and also in the advanced industrial states—became an important issue in the Sino-Soviet controversy. Generally, the Chinese Communists have tended to see local revolutionary conditions within a given country as crucial, while the Russians assert that the "essence, content, and nature of the decisive tasks of the present epoch" are overriding. The Russians, moreover, have been emphasizing "peaceful" approaches.

The possibility of "peaceful" roads to power is not a wholly new concept in Marxist-Leninist theory. "In the remote future," Stalin declared in a lecture delivered at Sverdlov University in April, 1924, "if the proletariat is victorious in the most important capitalist countries, and if the present capitalist encirclement is replaced by Socialist encirclement, a 'peaceful' path of development is quite possible for certain capitalist countries, whose capitalists, in view of the 'unfavorable' international situation, will consider it expedient 'voluntarily' to make substantial concessions to the proletariat."[12] But Khrushchev is clearly pushing the concept further than either Lenin or Stalin had done.

For the most part, in the aftermath of World War I, Marxism-Leninism had perceived the imperialist powers caught irrevocably in further herculean struggles against each other and predisposed toward aggression against the Soviet Union and other Communist states. It was out of the chaos of these turbulent conflicts that world Communism would eventually emerge.

Since then, however, the world situation had undergone radical changes, Khrushchev told the Twentieth Congress of the CPSU (Communist Party of the Soviet Union) in February, 1956. The forces of "socialism and democracy" had grown immeasurably throughout the world, whereas capitalism had become much weaker: Socialist encirclement of capitalism was beginning to replace the former capitalist encirclement of socialism. The "decisive advantages" of socialism over capitalism were becoming increasingly evident, moreover; increasingly, the workers, peasants, and intellectuals "of all countries" were finding that socialism had a great power of attraction. "The ideas of socialism," he said, "are indeed coming to dominate the minds of all working mankind."[13]

SOVIET VIEWS ON THE NEW EPOCH

The main distinguishing feature of the epoch, according to Khrushchev, was "the fact that the socialist world system is becoming the decisive factor in the development of human society."[14] This means that socialism is increasingly in a position to determine the character, methods, and trends of international relations—to encourage conditions of "peaceful coexistence." With this growth in the might of the socialist system, moreover, there emerge increasingly favorable conditions for socialist revolutions. "The transition to socialism in countries with developed parliamentary traditions may be effected by utilizing parliament, and in other countries by utilizing institutions conforming to their national traditions."[15]

There were other basic characteristics of the new epoch. Particularly, in the view of Khrushchev, the development of nuclear weaponry had made large-scale war unfeasible.[16] Only "madmen and maniacs" could call for another world war.[17] At the same time, Marxism-Leninism had become a "living reality" and "a mighty material force," Khrushchev asserted subsequently. In all the world there was no longer any power capable of barring the road to socialism. The day was not far off when Marxism-Leninism would dominate the minds of the majority of the population of the globe.[18]

Under these circumstances, Khrushchev declared, large-scale war was not "fatalistically inevitable." There might be "local wars," such as "the aggression of Britain, France, and Israel against Egypt," but even the possibilities for starting wars of this kind were diminishing.[19] There would also be "wars of liberation" in countries dominated by the "imperialists"—though here, also, various new alternatives were becoming available.

"In order to be loyal to Marxism-Leninism today," Otto Kuusinen of the CPSU Presidium asserted in April, 1960, on the anniversary of Lenin's birth, "it is not sufficient to repeat the old truth that imperialism is aggressive. The task is to make full use of the new factors operating for peace in order to save humanity from the catastrophe of another war."[20]

The prevention of war had become "the question of questions."[21] Khrushchev developed the course of his reasoning even further: Across the face of the earth, from certain of the highly developed capitalist states to certain of the so-called underdeveloped countries, the minimizing and even the avoidance of violent conflict was becoming increasingly feasible. In the countries where capitalism was still strong and had a huge military and police apparatus at its disposal, the reactionaries, of course, would inevitably offer serious resistance. There the transition to socialism would be attended by a sharp revolutionary struggle.[22]

"At the same time," Khrushchev declared, "the present situation offers the working class in a number of capitalist countries a real opportunity to unite the overwhelming majority of the people under its leadership and to secure the transfer of the basic means of production into the hands of the people." The right-wing bourgeois parties and their governments were "suffering bankruptcy" with increasing frequency. In these circumstances, the working class, by rallying around itself the working peasantry, the intelligentsia, and "all patriotic forces," and resolutely repulsing the opportunist elements who were "incapable of giving up the policy of compromise with the capitalists and landlords," would be in a position to "defeat the reactionary forces opposed to the interests of the people," to capture a stable majority in parliament, and to transform parliament from an organ of bourgeois democracy into a genuine "instrument of the people's will." In such an event, according to Khrushchev, "this institution, traditional in many highly developed capitalist countries, may become an organ of genuine democracy—democracy for the working people."[23]

Khrushchev made clear that he did not refer to a survival of bourgeois parliamentarianism. On the contrary, by using parliamentary means, the proletariat would smash the military-bureaucratic machine and set up "a new, proletarian people's state in parliamentary form."[24]

It was probable, Khrushchev asserted, that more forms of transition to socialism would appear. In 1917, bourgeois counterrevolution and foreign intervention had "prevented a peaceful transformation." Since then, however, the historical situation had undergone radical changes. Throughout the world the forces of socialism had grown immeasurably, and capitalism had grown much weaker.[25]

The Russians began to see possibilities for a transitional "democracy of a new type" in certain highly developed capitalist countries. This new variety of "democracy" would be neutral; it would demand the elimination of war; it would press for the nationalization of monopolies. In such circumstances, the transition to socialism could be greatly facilitated.[26]

The December 6, 1960, Moscow Declaration of the Conference of Representatives of 81 Communist Parties, moreover, put forward the concept of "national democracy"—a transitional form of government between bourgeois nationalism and "socialism" and without the proletarian hegemony of Mao's New Democracy. It was envisioned that a national democracy would "fight against imperialism" and the "penetration of imperialist capital," and reject Western in favor of Soviet aid, undertake agrarian reform, and allow Communists a prominent, though not a leading, role in policy-making. Such "national democracies" would represent a transitional stage prior to Communist achievement of power.[27]

SOVIET CONCEPTS OF "REVOLUTION FROM ABOVE"

With regard to the underdeveloped countries, Moscow continued to emphasize "revolution from above"—by support for "national bourgeois" leaders (even without proletarian hegemony) and also through technical assistance to newly emerging nations.

"The working class is the most consistent enemy of imperialism," *Pravda* admitted in an article on the bourgeoisie of the new nations. "Nevertheless, Lenin considered it natural that *at the beginning* of any national movement the bourgeoisie plays the role of its hegemonic force (leader) and urged that in the struggle for the self-determination of nations support be given to the most revolutionary elements of the bourgeois-democratic national-liberation movements."[28]

Pravda complained that "doctrinaires" and "leftists" were permitting themselves to criticize forms of the national liberation movement that did not fit into the usual patterns. In many of the Asian countries, and especially in Africa, the populations were preponderantly peasant. Under these circumstances, "the central task in freeing themselves from the yoke of imperialism" would remain —for a comparatively long time—that of "struggle not against capital but against survivals of the Middle Ages." In these regions, the workers, peasants, and intelligentsia would undoubtedly cooperate with "that part of the national bourgeoisie that is interested in independent political and economic development of its country and is ready to defend its independence against any encroachments by the imperialist powers."[29]

Referring to the emerging nations, Khrushchev told the Twenty-first Congress of the CPSU in February, 1959:

> Many public figures in these countries say they want to build social-ism. True, it is hard for them to utter the word "Communism," and it is not always clear what they mean by socialism. There is no doubt, however, that these figures are benevolently oriented toward the socialist countries, do not regard them as antagonists, do not consider that the socialist countries oppose their desire to build a new life without imperialists and without colonial oppression. For this reason the socialist countries have established good, friendly relations with these states and are developing normal economic ties with them.[30]

The Russians justify economic and technical assistance to countries like India, Indonesia, and the emerging countries of Africa in similar terms.

Close alliance and fraternal friendship, "mutual assistance and cooperation in building socialism and communism"—these had been considered the foundation of Soviet foreign policy. But in the new epoch "we have a broader understanding of the international duty of our socialist country," Kuusinen declared on Lenin's anniversary, and "we understand it as rendering assistance to those liberated peoples, too, who are not included in the world system of socialism."[31]

CHINESE COMMUNIST RESERVATIONS ABOUT "PEACEFUL COEXISTENCE"

The Chinese Communists have tended toward a more traditional analysis. Mao Tse-tung wrote in 1957:

> The First World War was followed by the birth of the Soviet Union with a population of 200 million. The Second World War was followed by the emergence of the socialist camp with a combined population of 900 million. If the imperialists should insist on launching a third world war, it is certain that several hundred million more will turn to socialism; then there will not be much room left in the world for the imperialists, while it is quite likely that the whole structure of imperialism will utterly collapse.[32]

Mao Tse-tung and his colleagues made it clear that they were "against war and in favor of peace." Nor did they discount entirely the possibilities for avoiding war and even—in special circumstances—achieving socialist power without violence. But Lenin's theory of imperialism was not obsolete, and "none of the new techniques like atomic energy, rocketry, and so on" had changed the basic characteristics of imperialism and its epoch nor the principles of proletarian revolution pointed out by Lenin. "The capitalist-imperialist system absolutely will not crumble of itself," Peking declared on the anniversary of Lenin's birth. "It will be overthrown by the proletarian revolution within the imperialist country concerned, and the national revolution in the colonies and semicolonies."[33] Imperialism, according to Peking, would never reconcile itself to its own destruction.

It would be in the best interests of the people, Peking declared, if the proletariat could attain power and carry out the transition to socialism by peaceful means. It would be wrong not to make use of such a possibility when it occurred. Whenever an opportunity for "peaceful development of the revolution" presented itself, Communists must seize it, as Lenin had done, so as to realize the aim of the socialist revolution. "However, this sort of opportunity is always, in Lenin's words, an extraordinarily rare opportunity in the history of revolutions."[34]

The strong implication of Chinese Communist reasoning was that local conditions were still overriding considerations, even in the new epoch. Crucial decisions depended upon local circumstances and could not necessarily be reached in Moscow.

The proletariat must never allow itself to assume that the bourgeoisie will accept peaceful transformation, Peking declared. On the contrary, the working class must keep in mind the assurance of Mao Tse-tung that "the most abundant strength in war" lies in the masses and that "a people's army organized by awakened and united masses of people" will be invincible "throughout the world."[35] By following these precepts the Chinese Communists had triumphed over Chiang K'ai-shek following World War II—despite dire warnings from certain "right opportunists"—and in Korea against the United States with its superior weapons and equipment.

"At a time when Chiang K'ai-shek with the backing of U.S. imperialism expanded his army to well over 4 million men," Peking declared, "that is to say at the time when the counterrevolutionary state machine of China's big landlords and big bourgeoisie reached its peak, Comrade Mao Tse-tung penetratingly pointed out that the Chiang K'ai-shek reactionaries were nothing but paper tigers and that the Chinese people should prepare themselves."

What was the outcome? "Things turned out exactly as Comrade Mao Tse-tung predicted," according to Peking. "The massive counterrevolutionary army under Chiang K'ai-shek, hammered and battered by the People's Liberation Army, rapidly fell to pieces in just over three years."[36]

Weaponry—even nuclear weaponry—was not the crucial factor, any more than the alleged desire of the bourgeoisie to avoid war was a crucial factor. Rather, the proletariat must rely closely "on the masses of its own class and on the semiproletariat in the rural areas, namely, the broad masses of poor peasants," and establish a worker-peasant alliance led by the proletariat. "Only then is it possible, on the basis of this alliance, to unite with all the social forces that can be united with and so establish a united front of the working people with all the nonworking people that can be united with in accordance with specific conditions in the different periods."[37]

Whether the transition would be carried out through armed uprising or by peaceful means was a question to be decided locally. "It is an internal affair of each country," Peking declared, "one to be determined only by the relation of classes in that country in a given period, a matter to be decided only by the Communists of that country themselves."[38]

CHINESE EMPHASIS ON THE HEGEMONY OF THE PROLETARIAT

The Chinese Communists have considered theoretically falla- cious the Soviet tendency to link peaceful coexistence—internation- ally—with the essentially local problem of how the proletariat should achieve power in a particular state. From the Peking view- point, these are two separate and distinct issues. Modern revisionists

> . . . hold that peaceful coexistence of countries with different so- cial systems means that capitalism can peacefully grow into social- ism, that the proletariat in countries ruled by the bourgeoisie can renounce class struggle and enter into "peaceful cooperation" with the bourgeoisie and the imperialists, and that the proletariat and all the exploited should forget about the fact that they are living in a class society, and so on. All these views are diametrically opposed to Marxism-Leninism.[39]

The struggle for peace and the struggle for socialism are two dif- ferent kinds of struggles, according to Peking, and it was a mistake not to make a distinction between them.

Peking also accused the revisionists of confusing seizure of power with the possibility of a peaceful transformation to socialism *under the hegemony of the proletariat*. For the proletariat and the masses to seize political power, smash the old state machine, and set up a new machine was one thing, Peking declared. It was quite another thing, having taken political power, having established hegemony, to proceed to the socialist transformation. "It is a misconception to confuse these two things—the seizing of political power by the pro- letariat and the carrying out by the proletariat of socialist trans- formation by peaceful means after it seizes political power." The basic question in any revolution, according to Peking, is the ques- tion of who holds state power.[40]

On the basis of their own historical experience, the Chinese Communists distrusted the national bourgeoisie and saw little pos- sibility of effective collaboration until the proletarian forces had "established their hegemony." The bourgeoisie, according to Pe- king, "cannot," "dare not," and "will not" lead a "true peasants' revolution."[41] Yet the "democratic revolution" is essentially "a peasants' revolution" from the Chinese Communist viewpoint.

Speaking at a meeting held in commemoration of the fiftieth anniversary of the 1911 revolution, Vice Chairman Tung Pi-wu argued that this revolution had been a failure because of its leadership by the national bourgeoisie. He said:

> As everyone knows, in the epoch of imperialism there is no country in which the national and democratic revolution can achieve complete victory under the leadership of the bourgeoisie; neither the plan for a bourgeois republic nor that for any other form of bourgeois state can enable these countries to embark on the road of completely independent development. In the present epoch, only under the leadership of the proletariat, and by obtaining the help of the socialist countries, will it be possible for any country to win complete victory in its national and democratic revolution and, after the success of the revolution, to advance along the path of independent development.[42]

Later, in the 1920's, according to Liu Shao-ch'i, the "right opportunists" had pursued a policy of capitulation toward the bourgeoisie and had regarded the democratic revolution mainly as the concern of the bourgeoisie. "They did not rely on the worker-peasant alliance, but mainly on the united front with the bourgeoisie, and only united with them without waging the necessary struggles. In doing so they gave up the hegemony of the proletariat and, at the time of the betrayal of the revolution by the bourgeoisie, made the revolution suffer defeats and made the cause of the proletariat and the masses of the people suffer serious setbacks."[43]

The firm grasping of hegemony by the proletariat through the Communist Party, Liu Shao-ch'i declared, is the key to victory in "democratic revolution and the successful switch-over from the democratic revolution to the socialist revolution."

The specific historical conditions underlying the revolution are usually not identical in various countries, the Chinese Communists insisted. In Russia, the Bolshevik Revolution started with "the armed uprising of the Russian working class in the capital" and was characterized by the taking over first of the cities and then of the countryside. By contrast, the Chinese revolutionary war, which began in the autumn of 1927—"namely, the revolutionary war under the independent leadership of the Chinese Communist Party"— had succeeded first in a number of rural areas on the basis of the agrarian revolution, followed by victory later in the cities. "In other words, its course was characterized by growth from setting up small revolutionary bases in the rural areas to large revolutionary bases;

from the establishment of a few revolutionary bases to the establishment of many and from encirclement of the cities by the rural
areas to the ultimate taking over of the cities."[44] "This course of
development of the Chinese revolution," Peking emphasized
pointedly, "was propounded by Comrade Mao Tse-tung . . ."

In thinly veiled rhetoric, Peking was pointing out that whereas
the Chinese revolution had emerged victorious under "independent
Chinese Communist leadership," it had failed miserably in periods
of close Russian supervision.

The Balance of Unity and Conflict

SOURCES OF SOVIET AND CHINESE COMMUNIST BEHAVIOR

Orthodox Marxism-Leninism identifies the physical environment as the prime mover of human behavior, but emphasis is placed
overwhelmingly upon changes in the modes of production and exchange, upon the "contradiction" between the way goods are produced and the way they are distributed.

Standing outside the Communist framework, we can conceptual-
ize Marxism-Leninism equally well as a highly complex system for
the manipulation of man's perceptions—and, through his perceptions, his behavior.

Here we postulate that it is not strictly the environment that
shapes the way man acts, *but his perception of it,* the way his lenses
are shaped. If the individual human being (or the group) *perceives*
the environment as eminently satisfactory—if the *status quo,* or the
"is," seems good enough to serve as the "ought to be"—he will not
expend much energy in efforts to change it. If, on the other extreme, the perceived difference between "what is" and "what ought
to be" is too great, the individual (or the group) will assess his own
energies or capabilities too low, relative to the task at hand, and
will be discouraged from ambitious attempts toward change. But
if the difference between the "is" and the "ought to be" is sufficient
to cause enough—but not too much—tension, then the individual
(or the group) will work persistently in an effort to close the gap.

These premises allow us to argue that human conflict emerges
not only from "contradictions" between the way goods are produced and the way they are distributed, but also from a host of
other circumstances under which man's perceptions are unsatisfac-
tory or at odds.

From a non-Communist viewpoint, it seems evident that the
perceived "is" and the perceived "ought to be" can take abstract as

well as concrete and material shape. Some men (and some nations) hunger as much for recognition or status as for economic well-being, and this kind of gap can be as potent as any other. Undoubtedly the Chinese are motivated in part by a determination to restore the power, prestige, and perhaps the uttermost boundaries of the ancient Chinese Empire at the peak of its ascendancy. Undoubtedly, also, they are in part driven by recollections of how, during the nineteenth and early twentieth centuries, the European powers and later Japan reduced China to virtually a tributary status. Here we have powerful dynamics for Mao Tse-tung and his colleagues to harness and direct.

In many instances, of course, the revolutionary leader will harness basic tensions arising from inadequacies in the environment and seek to focus upon and aggravate them by animation, that is, by directing attention toward enemies—the "inside enemy" (bad landlord, running dog, kulak, wrecker, traitor) and the "outside enemy" (aggressor, imperialist, invader)—who are dedicated to evil obstructions of progress. By playing upon these symbols, he can frequently achieve cohesive efforts, which otherwise might be discouraged by the obstacles of a stubborn and inanimate environment.

In Communist China the difference between the "is" and the "ought to be" is undoubtedly great, and in view of the imbalance between the exploding population and the rate of production, it is difficult to foresee how the gap can be significantly narrowed. For the Soviet Union, on the other hand, the prospects are different. During early decades after 1917, the gap was undoubtedly severe, but increasingly since World War II, the Russians have been making rapid strides, and one might expect their gap to be somewhat narrower than that of the Chinese and their tensions somewhat lower. In view of the wide open spaces of the U.S.S.R. and the relatively smaller population, we might postulate that, over the long run, the Soviet "is" might increasingly tend to approach the "ought to be."

Khrushchev, moreover, has committed the Soviet Union to a program of intense economic and technological development over the next twenty years. The goal is to overtake and even surpass the United States as a consumer society. These purposes require careful maneuvering on the part of Khrushchev: He must avoid large-scale war, but instigate sufficient external tension to justify domestic controls and to maintain internal submission and cohesion; he must support a large security budget, but build at the same time a consumer society. It must be clear to the Chinese that Khrushchev does not propose to—and indeed cannot—take Communist China along on this rising curve of development.

For China, with its excruciating internal problems, the maintenance of discipline is crucial. Both the internal enemy and the external enemy must be maintained at peak threat. Mao and his colleagues cannot afford the luxury of a "de-Stalinization" program or of moves toward a *détente* with the West.

An intense content analysis of three recent periods in Sino-Soviet relations reveals, in fact, that there is a significant difference not only in Soviet and Chinese means and middle-range ends, but also in their emotional levels.

The time periods selected for analysis were January and May, 1960, and April, 1961. Generally, Communist China emerged several points higher than the Soviet Union—on a nine-point scale— in terms of frustration, hostility, and a desire to change the *status quo* radically.[45]

SPECIFIC SINO-SOVIET DIVERGENCIES

Other important differences emerged from this analysis. The Chinese Communist leadership was more inclined to see the United States as the chief enemy, whereas the Soviet Union frequently placed major emphasis upon West Germany as the primary threat. In Asia, the Peking regime saw the United States threatening aggression through its bases in Japan, through support of Taiwan, through the Seventh Fleet, and through its influence in South Viet-Nam and Laos. The Soviet Union, although cognizant of United States' interests in these spheres, remained less deeply disturbed than the Chinese.

Peking persistently saw the United States as both a "real tiger" and a "paper tiger." The United States was perceived as undeniably strong, but Mao and his colleagues remained convinced that time is on the side of Communism in Asia and throughout the world. The United States was seen as weak in places like Laos and South Viet-Nam, where the society is weak—not only in a military sense, but economically, politically, and psychologically. Moscow also tended to see Communism victorious in the long run, but there was less contempt for the United States in Soviet statements—and not infrequently a touch of admiration for American skill and productivity.

The Chinese Communists were more inclined than the Russians to emphasize what they saw as the "occupied" or "semi-occupied" status of Japan. Increasingly, however, the Peking regime became concerned with Japan as "an accomplice" in the United States "aggression" in Laos. Peking took pains to link United States "imperialism" with the World War II imperialism of Japan and raised repeated warnings about a renaissance of Japanese militarism. The Chinese Communists also revealed a fear of Japanese competition for Asian markets.

The Soviet Union was more inclined to stress "good-neighborly relations" with Japan. Peking made a sharper distinction between the "bad" Japanese Government and the "good" Japanese people.

Chinese perceptions of the "enemy" appeared sharp and deeply institutionalized, whereas Khrushchev—relatively—was more concerned with international law and diplomacy, customs and usage, and the role of the Soviet Union as a great power among other great powers. Considerable areas of the *status quo* appeared desirable to the Soviet leader, whereas Peking perceived "things as they are" as essentially evil and subject to radical change.

Soviet Russian and Chinese Communist behavior, then, has been separately shaped by their distinct national interests; by the differences in their fundamental perceptions, that is, by the cultural and experiential "color" of their lenses; and also by the relative widths of the gaps they perceive between the *status quo* and the environment as it "ought to be."

SINO-SOVIET DEBATE

In recent years, Sino-Soviet divergencies have led to open debate. Although both sides have put forward tentative, conciliatory overtures, the public debate has nevertheless become increasingly vitriolic. According to Peking, "certain comrades of a fraternal Party" were pinning their hopes for world peace not on struggle, but on the "wisdom of the heads of major powers."[46] Referring back to the Camp David talks in September, 1959, Peking charged these "comrades of a fraternal Party" of proclaiming "incessantly" that war could be abolished "even while the imperialist system and the system of exploitation of man by man" continued to exist in a large part of the world.[47] The Chinese were openly critical of what they perceived as a "soft" Soviet policy in the Cuban crisis of April, 1961, and October, 1962. These same "comrades of a fraternal Party," according to Peking, had not only given "political support to the anti-China policy of the Nehru government," but had also been "supplying that government with war matériel." Instead of condemning such "wrong actions," these comrades had acclaimed them as a "sensible policy."[48]

It was "a fact of particular gravity," moreover, that "late in June, 1960, someone went so far as to wave his baton and launch an all-out and converging surprise attack on the Chinese Communist Party at the meeting of the fraternal Parties in Bucharest." Then, after this meeting, "some comrades who had attacked the Chinese Communist Party lost no time in taking a series of grave political steps to apply economic and political pressure, even to the extent of perfidiously and unilaterally tearing up agreements and contracts they had concluded with a fraternal country, in disregard of international practice." These agreements and contracts, according to Peking, were to be counted "not in twos and threes or in scores, but in hundreds." These "malicious acts" extended ideological differences into the sphere of state relations and were "out and out violations of proletarian internationalism."[49]

In a *Jen-min Jih-pao* editorial of March, 1963, Peking even charged that the Soviet Union, by criticizing China, was reopening old and dangerous territorial disputes between them. The Chinese Communists listed nine treaties that Peking considered "unequal" and not permanent. Three of these instruments—the Treaty of Aigun (1858), the Treaty of Peking (1860), and the Treaty of Ili (1881)—had ceded Chinese territory to Czarist Russia.[50]

The Soviet Union defended its policy on the grounds that peaceful coexistence—"as the most expedient form of class struggle"[51]—represented a minimal prerequisite for Communist survival and eventual victory in the world. How could the Communist countries benefit by a world-wide thermonuclear catastrophe? Khrushchev asked this question at a gathering in East Berlin of delegations from seventy national Communist parties on January 16, 1963. Only people who consciously closed their eyes to the truth could think so. Marxist-Leninists could not conceive of "the creation of a Communist civilization on the ruins of the world cultural centers, upon an earth deserted and poisoned by nuclear fallout."[52]

Again and again during the 1950's and early 1960's, according to the Russians, Soviet policy had prevented the outbreak of war or the explosion of small wars into major wars. The Cuban crisis of October, 1962, was a particularly crucial instance in which Soviet decisions had prevented world conflict and, indeed, a nuclear holocaust.

The Chinese were in tragic error, Moscow declared, when they dismissed the United States as a "paper tiger" or underestimated the destructive capacity of nuclear weapons. At present, Khrushchev told the gathering of delegates in East Berlin, ". . . the

United States has roughly 40,000 nuclear bombs and warheads. Everyone knows that the Soviet Union has more than enough of this stuff. [Khrushchev himself boasted of a 100-megaton bomb.] What would happen if all that nuclear armament were dropped on human heads? As the result of the first blow alone, 700–800 million people would have perished. All the big cities would be wiped out . . . [not only in] the United States and the Soviet Union but also in France, Britain, Germany, Italy, China, Japan, and many other countries."[53]

When the Chinese Communist delegation chief tried to answer the various charges leveled against his Party, delegates from the Soviet Union and from many other Communist parties shouted, whistled, stamped, jeered, and reviled him from the Congress floor.

The Russians charged their critics with provoking a possible "split in the international Communist movement."[54]

IMPLICATIONS FOR THE FUTURE

Against this background, it will not be surprising if Communist China tries increasingly to assert its self-perceived role as the chief model and inspiration for revolutionary struggle not only in Asia but also in Africa and Latin America and even in the world at large. But the international Communist movement is not structured to accommodate major centers of Party and national power in competition with each other. The system will be subject to excruciating strains, and centrifugal forces will work to pull it asunder. At the same time, we may expect powerful forces of common interest—threats from outside the bloc, for example, and the drive for expanding Communist influence and for achieving a world order—to operate toward holding the system together.

The concept of an out-and-out split is probably too dichotomous: Nations enjoy possibilities for—and normally range over—a wide spectrum of intermediate relationships between close alliance and utter withdrawal or large-scale violence. What we may expect is a frequently shifting, only partially stable equilibrium in which national interests are balanced against common interests and in which conflictual interactions compete with behavior that is reciprocally supportive.

Under these circumstances, it is likely that the Communist world will become increasingly pluralistic as events unfold.

NOTES

1. *Vtoroi Kongress Kominterna, iiul–avgust, 1920 g* (*Second Congress of the Comintern, July–August, 1920*) (Moscow: Partiinoe izd-vo, 1934), pp. 491–99.

2. V. I. Lenin, *Selected Works* (New York: International Publishers), III (1935–38), 145–46; also *Sochineniia* (Moscow: Gos. izd-vo), XXIV (1926–32), 314.

3. Voitinsky, "Kolonialnyi vopros na rassherennom plenume I.K.K.I.," *Kommunisticheskii Internatsional*, XLI, No. 4 (April, 1925), 64–66. An English translation appears in Xenia Joukoff Eudin and Robert C. North, *Soviet Russia and the East, 1920–1927* (Stanford, Calif.: Stanford University Press, 1957), pp. 342–43.

4. For an English translation of this document, see Eudin and North, *op. cit.*, pp. 330–33.

5. Theses of the Executive Committee of the Communist International (ECCI) on Japan, July 15, 1927, *Nihon mondai ni kansuru hōshin-sho, ketsugi-shū*, pp. 12–36. Translated by Kay K. Kaneda and Hidemi Fumino in Eudin and North, *op. cit.*, pp. 338–39.

6. The ECCI on the tasks of the Communists in Indonesia, *International Press Correspondence*, (English ed.; Vienna), VII, No. 69 (December 8, 1927), 1562.

7. *Ibid.*, p. 1563.

8. Vladimir Dedijer, *Tito* (New York: Simon and Schuster, 1953), p. 322.

9. Anna Louise Strong, "The Thought of Mao Tse-tung," *Amerasia*, XI, No. 6 (June, 1947), 161–74.

10. *Ibid.*

11. New China News Agency (hereafter cited as NCNA) release, November 23, 1949.

12. Joseph Stalin, *Problems of Leninism* (Moscow: Foreign Languages Publishing House, 1947), p. 45.

13. N. S. Khrushchev, *Report of the Central Committee, 20th Congress*, (Soviet News Booklet No. 4; London: Soviet Embassy, 1956), p. 30.

14. Khrushchev, "For New Victories for the World Communist Movement" (Results of the meeting of representatives of the Communist and Workers Parties), *World Marxist Review*, IV, No. 1 (January, 1961), 5.

15. *Ibid.*

16. Khrushchev, "On Peaceful Coexistence," *Foreign Affairs*, XXXVIII, No. 1 (October, 1959), 1.

17. "Nikita Khrushchev's Speech at the Third Congress of the Rumanian Workers Party," *Soviet News* (London: Soviet Embassy), No. 4292 (June 22, 1960), p. 240.

18. Khrushchev, "For New Victories for the World Communist Movement," p. 3.

19. *Ibid.*, p. 13.

20. Otto Kuusinen, "Lenin Anniversary Meeting at Moscow Sports Palace," *Soviet News*, No. 4255 (April 25, 1960), p. 64.

21. Khrushchev, "For New Victories for the World Communist Movement," pp. 11–12.

22. Khrushchev, *Report of the Central Committee, 20th Congress*, p. 31; also "For New Victories for the World Communist Movement," p. 22.

23. Khrushchev, *Report of the Central Committee, 20th Congress,* p. 30.
24. Khrushchev, "For New Victories for the World Communist Movement," p. 22.
25. Khrushchev, *Report of the Central Committee, 20th Congress,* p. 30.
26. *Fundamentals of Marxism-Leninism* (Moscow: Foreign Languages Publishing House, 1959) pp. 591 ff.
27. Quoted in *The New York Times,* December 7, 1960, p. 15.
28. "*Pravda* on Supporting the 'Bourgeoisie' in New Nations," *Current Digest of the Soviet Press,* XII, No. 34 (September 21, 1960), 18.
29. *Ibid.*
30. Leo Gruliow (ed.), "The Documentary Record of the Extraordinary 21st Communist Party Congress," *Current Soviet Policies,* III (New York: Columbia University Press, 1960), p. 201.
31. Kuusinen, *op. cit.,* p. 63.
32. Mao Tse-tung, *On the Correct Handling of Contradictions Among the People* (Peking: Foreign Languages Press, 1957), p. 64.
33. "Long Live Leninism," *Hung Ch'i (Red Flag),* No. 8 (April 19, 1960), as translated in *Peking Review,* No. 17 (April 26, 1960), p. 13.
34. *Ibid.,* p. 18.
35. *Ibid.,* p. 12.
36. "A Basic Summary of the Victorious Experience of the Chinese People's Revolution," *Hung Ch'i,* No. 20–21 (November 1, 1960), as translated and released by NCNA on December 22, 1960.
37. *Ibid.*
38. *Ibid.*
39. "Long Live Leninism," p. 22.
40. *Ibid.*
41. Wang Chia-hsiang, "The International Significance of the Chinese People's Victory," in *Ten Glorious Years* (Peking: Foreign Languages Press, 1960), p. 275.
42. NCNA release, Peking, October 9, 1961.
43. Liu Shao-ch'i, "The Victory of Marxism-Leninism in China," *Peking Review,* No. 39 (October 1, 1959), p. 7.
44. "A Basic Summary of the Victorious Experience of the Chinese People's Revolution," pp. 1–14.
45. For each of these months, all available foreign-policy statements from the leaderships of the two countries were collected. Analysts then isolated and recorded separately each statement of intended policy or preference and each statement of a past decision. Strict rules were laid down to determine what statements were to be accepted and how the analysts were to know where one such statement ended and another began. Tests were administered from time to time to ensure that all analysts were observing these rules and recording the same categories of statement.

Essentially, each one of these policy statements—or *policy conditions*—represented a link in a means-end chain: a Soviet Russian *perception* of a Soviet Russian means-end link; or a Soviet Russian *perception* of a Chinese means-end link; or a Soviet Russian *perception* of a link in some third power's means-end chain; or a Chinese Communist *perception* of a Chinese Communist means-end link; and so on. Each perception was recorded as the perceiver stated it.

Once these statements had been obtained, they were scaled according to whether they revealed more or less hostility, more or less frustration, more or less specificity, more or less desire to change the *status quo,* and so forth. The statements were sufficiently masked so that the scalers did not know which were Chinese assertions and which were Russian. All statements were scaled by at least two judges, and by three or four if there was more than a small difference between their judgments.

When the scaling had been completed, each policy statement was punched on an IBM card with notches to indicate the scale values, the country making the statement, the country or countries about which the statement was made, and the country or countries toward whom the policy was directed. The cards were then placed in an electronic computer, which calculated percentages, averages, and pertinent correlations within a matter of minutes. The results were carefully charted and graphed.

Findings obtained in this way were then analyzed by specialists in Soviet and Chinese Communist affairs and interpreted in terms of what the various policy statements had explicitly asserted and against the background of what was already known about Sino-Soviet relations. The statements were also checked for inconsistencies, contradictions, *non sequiturs,* and other flaws that might reveal propaganda patterns, bluffs, or ambivalences on the part of the policy-makers.

46. Editorial, *Jen-min Jih-pao (People's Daily),* February 27, 1963, as translated in the *Peking Review,* No. 9 (March 1, 1963), p. 9.

47. *Ibid.*

48. *Ibid.,* p. 13.

49. *Ibid.,* p. 11.

50. Editorial, *Jen-min Jih-pao,* March 8, 1963, as translated in the *Peking Review,* No. 10–11 (March 15, 1963), p. 61.

51. Editorial, "Cementing the Unity of the Communist Movement Is Our Internationalist Duty," *World Marxist Review,* VI, No. 2 (February, 1963), 5.

52. "Report of Comrade N. S. Khrushchev to the VI Congress of the Socialist Unity Party of Germany," *Pravda,* January 17, 1963, p. 3.

53. *Ibid.*

54. "Cementing the Unity of the Communist Movement . . . ," p. 4.

TWO

STRUGGLES FOR POWER: COMMUNIST PARTIES IN OPPOSITION

3. Independence or Subordination: The Japanese Communist Party Between Moscow and Peking

by PAUL F. LANGER

Although the Japanese Communist Party (JCP) is one of the oldest Communist organizations in Asia, its troubled history and its slow pace on the road to power have prevented it from occupying a seat of honor among the world's Communist parties. Some of the Japanese Communists' failures can be explained by certain unfavorable factors inherent in the local and international environment; others must be attributed to a combination of weaknesses peculiar to Communism in Japan.

The Japanese Communist Party has rarely enjoyed conditions in which it might have evolved a consistent strategy and gained a feeling for the realities of the Japanese situation. Before World War II, government restrictions forced it to operate furtively, and police action disrupted the continuity of its leadership. In the postwar period, the Party has been racked by internal disputes and by policy changes originating outside Japan. Its leaders have never been able to make up their minds whether their principal role is to work toward seizure of power irrespective of the requirements of the Communist bloc's larger objectives or to aid the Party's sponsors abroad at the expense of political advancement at home. As a result, the Japanese Communist Party, vacillating between "rightist" and "leftist," "hard" and "soft" strategies, remained for much of the postwar period without a formal policy guide. Only after years of debate did the Japanese Communist leaders finally succeed, in July, 1961, in coming to an agreement on a strategic formula for Japan—and only after the international Communist congress held in Moscow in 1960 had resolved the JCP's major doubts.

63

The Party suffers not only from uncertainty about objectives and strategy, but also from a distinct deficiency in leadership. One looks in vain in the Japanese Communist hierarchy for a man of the stature of Mao Tse-tung, Ho Chi Minh, or D. N. Aidit. It is true that the JCP has as its Chairman Nozaka Sanzo, once a member of the Comintern Presidium, who spent the 1930's in Moscow and later moved to Yenan to work with Mao. But the seventy-one-year-old Nozaka, essentially a sober research analyst rather than a dynamic political leader, lacks the aura of prestige that such qualifications would normally confer. This applies not only in Tokyo and within his own Party, but apparently also in Moscow and Peking. Nor have Miyamoto Kenji, the Secretary-General, or Shiga Yoshio and Hakamada Satomi,[1] both veteran Party leaders, succeeded in creating a reputation corresponding to their high positions and long Party records. Certain adverse experiences and conditions have contributed to the lack of strong and creative leadership within Japanese Communist ranks. Much of the prewar experience of the Japanese Communists was limited to small-scale underground operations that often led to prison or to exile. Again, in the postwar period, during the years of Communist militancy in the early 1950's, the Japanese Communist leaders preferred to desert the battlefield and flee abroad or hide out within the country. Just as Japanese Communist historical experience, therefore, has tended to isolate the leaders from the realities of Japanese life and politics, so it has also made for an unusually heavy dependence on outside assistance and advice. Because both phenomena have played such a decisive role in influencing JCP strategy, it may be useful to examine them a little more closely.

Like that of many other Communist parties, the leadership of the Japanese Communists is primarily drawn from the urban intellectual or semi-intellectual sectors of society. The Communist movement in Japan has never succeeded in taking root in the countryside. There have been no able and forceful Communist peasant leaders. Nor, on the whole, have Japanese trade unions provided the Communist Party with men of real ability. Before the war, this was largely due to the immature state of the Japanese labor movement and to the severities of police restrictions. Today, successful Socialist competition for control of the labor movement, as well as the entrenched position of the intellectuals in the Communist hierarchy, impedes the rise of labor leaders in the JCP.

The Japanese intellectual is probably more "intellectualized" than his counterpart in any other country of Asia, and perhaps more than any in Europe. He has felt, and still feels, a high degree of "separateness" from other groups in his society, rather like the Russian intelligentsia of the nineteenth century; and like them, too, he has a high sense of mission. The Japanese intellectual has an exceeding fondness for theoretically "perfect," "neat," and "ideal" solutions. He tends to see the world in terms of black and white—and the present social order in Japan seems to him largely black. He enthusiastically endorses the need for radical change as a prerequisite for creating an ideal world. He is a natural dogmatist, a born theorist, and a master of criticism (frequently sterile). These characteristics, of course, are bound to leave their mark on a Communist Party dominated by intellectuals.

The direction of the Japanese Communist Party has almost always been in the hands of intellectuals of the purest water. The historical experience of the Japanese Communist movement, as we have seen, condemned its leaders to remain largely within the realm of intellectualization and intensified their natural tendency toward barren scholastic quarreling, intellectual inbreeding, and mental and political isolation. Never confronted with the challenging political opportunities enjoyed by Communists in India and Indonesia, the Communist strategists of Japan have been inclined to force reality into the Procrustean bed of Marxist dogma and have adopted foreign Communist prescriptions wholesale, ill-suited as they were to the Japanese scene.

In trying to reconcile the compulsion of events with the demands of Marxist theory, the Japanese Communist leaders lack the rich practical experience as well as the flexibility of a Mao Tse-tung; they often appear to lack even the desire to detach themselves from their traditional theoretical position. But as they reluctantly learn from past failures, as younger men move up in the Communist hierarchy, as the Sino-Soviet conflict compels them to review their strategy and to make independent choices, the Japanese Communists are beginning to free themselves very gradually from the shackles of their negative past.

Numerically and financially feeble, deprived of strong and continuing leadership, yet confronted with an overwhelmingly powerful and repressive state apparatus, the prewar Japanese Communists were compelled to draw their strength from abroad. Their basic strategy guides, therefore, have until recently been written in Moscow, sometimes with little Japanese participation. Personnel, funds, and propaganda literature have been funneled into Japan time and again from Moscow, Shanghai, or Los Angeles.[2] For years, the Japanese Communist movement could survive only because of frequent blood transfusions from abroad. Reliance on such aid, therefore, has become almost second nature and today constitutes a serious obstacle to the evolution of a Japanese Communist strategy suited to conditions in Japan.

Another obstacle to the growth of Communism has been the relationship between Communism and nationalism in Japan, strikingly different as it is from that existing in other parts of Asia and reminiscent rather of conditions prevailing in the West. Disguising itself as a "national liberation movement," Asian Communism has generally directed its fire against "Western imperialism," with considerable success, as the Communist-directed or infiltrated fronts have shown. In China, Viet-Nam, and Indonesia, the local Communist parties have effectively combined the Communist and the nationalist leitmotivs. The Japanese Communists were in a very different position. Until World War II, they suffered under and fought against a chauvinistic, imperialist government of native rather than Western origin. The tendency of the Japanese Communists was to view their task as a struggle against the political domination of the indigenous capitalist. In an independent Japan, there could be no "national bourgeoisie" bent on "national liberation." Hence there was little or no basis for the creation of a "united national front."

After the war, when "American imperialism" replaced "Japanese imperialism" as the main obstacle to a Communist seizure of power, conditions both within the Party and without proved most unfavorable to a substitution of the new enemy for the old. The current Communist appeal to the Japanese people to rally under the banner of a "struggle against American imperialism" is occurring at a time when nationalism is not much in vogue in Japan and when the benefits of "American imperialism" are fairly obvious to the Japanese people (despite their awareness of the implied risks of alignment with the U.S.). Moreover, in the light of its past history, the JCP appears to the average Japanese as an unlikely convert to, and spokesman for, nationalist sentiments. Whatever remains of Japanese nationalism tends to follow the prewar pattern: The nationalists not only reject an alliance with Communism but see their principal objective in fighting Communist doctrine, its supporters in Japan, and its powerful patrons abroad.

In contrast to other Communist movements in Asia, therefore, the Japanese movement has failed in its attempt to effect a fusion of Communism and nationalism. As a result, one of the most potent weapons now being used against the U.S. by Communists elsewhere in Asia is blunt and ineffective in Japan.

COMMUNIST OPPORTUNITIES AND DILEMMAS

In October, 1945, the surviving leaders of the Japanese Communist movement were released from prison at the instruction of the Supreme Allied Commander (SCAP). A few months later, Japanese Communism's ambassador abroad, Nozaka Sanzo, returning in triumph from Mao Tse-tung's headquarters in Yenan, joined his comrades in Tokyo.[3] As the Japanese Communist Party reconstituted itself, enjoying for the first time the status of a legal organization, it faced a radically changed and seemingly most favorable situation.

Since 1945, the Japanese Communists, like the members of any other political group in Japan, have been free to agitate for their objectives, to organize for political activity, to run candidates in local and national elections, and to publicize their views. Perhaps of equal importance in creating a favorable context for expanding Communist influence has been the rapid transformation of Japanese society: the freedom to organize labor unions and to call strikes; the temporary eclipse of the prewar leaders of political, economic, and cultural life; and the chaos and instability created by the aftermath of the war and by the postwar reforms.

The fiction of an "*Allied* occupation of Japan" that included the Communists' patron, the Soviet Union, as a partner and ally of the U.S., persisted for some time after Japan's surrender and gave the Japanese Communist Party another advantage, but one that gradually disappeared as the world moved into the Cold War; it vanished altogether with the outbreak of hostilities in Korea. Only the Communists could collectively lay claim to having opposed Japan's militarist policies, and from there it was only one step to a Communist attempt to monopolize the attractive labels "progressive" and "democratic."

Yet the very circumstances that facilitated the spread of Communism have also given rise to new problems for the JCP. In the early postwar period, the Allied authorities, having created conditions that incidentally stimulated the growth of the Communist movement, had the foresight to set limits to this growth by curbing Communist labor offensives and mass movements, by encouraging the Japanese Government to impose a number of measures restricting radicalism, and, last but not least, by carrying out a whole range of social, economic, political, and legal reforms.

By 1952, when the bulwark of SCAP military and administrative control was removed and Japan regained full independence, the pendulum had swung back in the direction of political conservatism, the economic situation had improved, and the Korean War had aroused apprehensions among the Japanese people about the nature of Communism and the intentions of the Communist bloc. After its initial, although relatively modest, electoral successes, the JCP made no further headway. Since 1949, when it polled nearly 10 per cent of the total vote, the Party's attraction for the Japanese voter has sharply decreased, and it now fluctuates between a mere 2 and 4 per cent.[4]

The conspicuous failure of the Japanese Communists to create a solid base of popular support for an eventual seizure of power, despite circumstances that appeared to favor Communist growth, is due not only to Japan's recovery of a fair degree of internal balance and prosperity. Other factors have played a contributing role: the Party's inability to transform and expand its organization rapidly enough to profit from the temporarily disturbed political, social, and economic equilibrium; the JCP's inability to develop and apply without loss of time a strategy appropriate to the situation (much time was lost in debates over the "correct strategy" in conditions of "semi-independence"); the prewar "foreign flavor" of the JCP and the popular image of the Party as a conspiratorial organization out of place in a democratic Japan, an image that was waning after 1945, but was revived in 1950 by the JCP's sudden adoption of a militant strategy at the behest of the Cominform.

But the most fundamental obstacle to Communist growth in Japan since the war has been the character of the Japanese Socialist Party. The political scene in postwar Japan is characterized by bipolarization. This is partly the result of an electoral system that does not favor small parties, but more basically it reflects an electorate that prefers sharply contrasting solutions and approaches and thus reveals the deep ideological cleavages that continue to characterize modern Japan. The popular protest vote against a permanently entrenched conservative government, and against certain defects inherent in the social and economic structure of Japan, tends to go to the opposition Socialists, who on almost every issue hold radically different views from those of the conservatives. The Socialists, on the whole, are as fervent believers in orthodox Marxist dogma as the Communists. They advocate many of the same ideas and policies, but are not burdened with the Communists' conspiratorial past or with their reputation for maintaining foreign ties.

While the ideological affinity between Socialists and Communists presents obvious opportunities for a Socialist *apertura a sinistra*, a cautious instinct seems to prevent the Japanese Socialists from making common cause with the Communists except in short-term crises such as that arising in 1960 from the mass protest against the U.S.-Japanese security pact. Socialist caution springs from a complex combination of factors and considerations, doubtless including: (1) the relatively small size of the JCP, which makes an alliance unprofitable for the Socialists; (2) the comparatively large number of Socialists who are suspicious of the Communists or even strongly anti-Communist, raising the specter of a further deepening of the schism within Socialist ranks should an alliance with the Communists ever be concluded (as was evidenced when a Socialist-Communist *rapprochement* in 1959 exacerbated antagonisms within the Socialist Party and gave birth to a splinter group, the anti-Communist Democratic Socialist Party); and (3) the clumsiness and haste with which the Japanese Communists generally pursue their objectives whenever they succeed in building up or taking over a front organization, as witnessed in the history of the Japanese anti-nuclear movement. In the late 1950's and early 1960's, Gensuikyo (the Council Against A- and H-Bombs) became so heavily infiltrated by Communist elements and began to pursue such an outspokenly radical, militant, biased, and anti-Western line that the Socialists, in 1961 and again in 1962, felt compelled to attempt to recapture the movement and to oust the Communists. By 1963, the Socialist-Communist conflict had led to chaos within the organization, to the resignation of its Lenin Prize–winning Chairman, Yasui Kaoru, and to the virtual paralysis of the organization's activities. Another recent example is the anti–security pact movement of 1960, when many Socialists let themselves be goaded into extreme actions only to be sobered up when they faced public criticism and their own guilty consciences a few months later.

Indeed, a serious dilemma for the Japanese Communists arises from this cardinal fact of Japanese politics: The Socialist Party is *sufficiently far to the left* to draw the antigovernment protest vote and to steal much of the Communists' thunder, yet *not radical enough* to wish to enter an organizational alliance with the Communists. So far, therefore, the Japanese Communists have been unable to devise a strategy that would lure the Socialists into a permanent "anti-imperialist united front." Not surprisingly, therefore, the Communist-Socialist relationship has gone through predictable cycles of mutual attraction and repulsion.

Being good Marxist-Leninists and extreme dogmatists, fond of ideologically "correct" solutions, the Japanese Communists have wrangled among themselves for years over where Japan, given her advanced economic development, should be placed in the Marxist taxonomy of Asian states awaiting revolution. The question obviously has important political implications. These discussions reach back to the days when the Comintern set up study committees in Moscow and wrote "action theses" analyzing the situation in Japan. It is obvious to the Japanese Communist that, whatever feudal remnants may still exist, postwar Japan is an advanced capitalist country and *ipso facto* "imperialist." But this raises for the Marxist strategist a host of embarrassing questions: Where, then, are the symptoms of Japanese imperialism? What about the role of American imperialism in Japan? Which should be the main target of the revolutionary struggle, American imperialism or Japanese imperialism? Should the revolution in Japan be a one-stage socialist revolution, as the advanced state of Japan's economic development might suggest? Are the political conditions ripe for such a revolution? And if not, why not? These questions must be answered before deciding the "correct revolutionary strategy in Japan" and "the main point of attack," and we shall return to them shortly. Meanwhile, they may help us to understand a basic Communist dilemma: The level of Japan's economic development and her political independence would suggest a one-stage revolution aimed primarily against Japanese "monopoly capitalism," whereas the requirements of world-wide Communist strategy point toward a two-stage revolution that would permit the alignment in the first stage of a broad array of forces against the external enemy, the United States, and her position in Japan.

The long-standing debate among Japanese Marxists on the question of revolution by stages and the identity of the main enemy is all the more significant because a major difference between Communists and Socialists concerns precisely the problem of where the revolutionary thrust should be oriented. The Socialists assign a pre-eminent place to the domestic enemy, Japanese capitalism in general and "monopoly capital" in particular, while since 1950 the Communists have emphasized the primacy of the "American enemy."

At times the Japanese Communists, in their desire to serve the cause of Communist-bloc strategy while remaining faithful to Marxist dogma, have gone so far as to describe Japan as a "semi-colonial dependency" of the U.S. and have directed their fire wholly against the U.S. position. At other times, mostly before 1950, the Party has tended to minimize the American role and to emphasize the "imperialist" and "advanced" nature of Japan's economic development.

STRATEGY AND TACTICS

Communist strategy in postwar Japan has gone through a number of stages.[5] These have included: (1) the "soft-line" period of Nozaka's so-called "lovable Communist Party," an era that lasted from Japan's surrender to early 1950 and was characterized by the JCP's heavy emphasis on the exigencies of the local situation, often at the expense of attention to the Communist cause abroad; (2) the period of perhaps misinterpreted Cominform directions, a period that coincided with the Korean War, when the JCP's "hard-line" operations were directed from underground and from abroad and the Party equipped itself with "Molotov cocktails" and launched rather amateurish armed assaults against the existing order in Japan; (3) the epoch of confusion, soul-searching, faction-alism, ideological debates, and mutual recriminations; and (4) a transitional stage in the mid-1950's when a new strategic formula was gradually being evolved. This new formula was officially sanctioned by the Japanese Communist Party's Eighth Congress, held in Tokyo in July, 1961.

As early as 1958, at the Seventh Party Congress, there had been attempts to codify this emerging strategy, but sharp ideological clashes forced postponement of the final decision. For three years, the Japanese Communists anxiously looked toward Moscow and Peking for ideological and strategic advice, but at the same time they continued their inconclusive discussions. These centered around three interrelated issues: the main target of the struggle for power, the stages of that struggle, and the instruments to be used in the struggle. Some authoritative answers to these questions were supplied from Moscow when eighty-one Communist parties, including the JCP, met there in November, 1960, to draw up the Moscow Statement, a universally valid blueprint for Communist action. It was only then that the Japanese Communist majority leaders decided to read the vociferous opposition faction out of the JCP in order to be able to adopt "unanimously" a new Party thesis.

This new program answers the requirements of Communist-bloc strategy while meeting to some extent the demands of the local situation.[6] The "enemy" is defined as having two heads: American monopoly capitalism and Japanese monopoly capital. But the latter, being described as clearly subordinate to the former, is assigned a strategically less important role. In other words, the JCP has accepted the prescriptions of the Moscow Conference of the Communist and Workers' Parties, which read:

> In some non-European developed capitalist countries which are under the political, economic, and military domination of U.S. imperialism, the working class and the people direct the main blow against U.S. imperialist domination, and also against monopoly capital and other domestic reactionary forces that betray the interests of the nation. In the course of this struggle all the democratic, patriotic forces of the nation come together in a united front fighting for the victory of a revolution aimed at achieving genuine national independence and democracy, which create conditions for passing on to the tasks of socialist revolution.[7]

That this passage was meant to apply to Japan (and possibly to a very few other non-European, but not Asian, countries) is clear.[8] European Communist literature tends to place Japan in the same class as Western Europe insofar as the stage of its economic development is concerned. Japan is considered an "advanced capitalist" country.[9] On the other hand, the Moscow Statement indicates, and the JCP's new program confirms, that in Communist eyes Japan's relationship to the U.S. sets it apart from Western Europe. Soviet, Chinese, and Japanese Communist literature of recent years suggests that Japan is not merely "dependent" on the U.S., as some European nations are, but is a "*semi-occupied* dependent country" because Japanese monopoly capital is much more dependent on its U.S. counterpart than is the case in Western Europe. Taking into account also Japan's military dependence on the U.S., they view Japan as being essentially an occupied country requiring first a "new national democratic revolution."[10]

This latter point, in turn, suggests the answer to the problem of the road to power. The Moscow Statement, in a passage obviously applying to Japan—and interpreted as such by the JCP—recommends:

> In the countries where the imperialists have established war bases, it is necessary to step up the struggle for their abolition, which is an important factor for fortifying national independence, defending sovereignty, and preventing war. The struggle of the peoples against the militarization of their countries should be combined with the struggle against the capitalist monopolies connected with the U.S. imperialists. Today as never before, it is important to fight persever-

ingly in all countries to make the peace movement thrive and extend to towns and villages, factories and offices.[11]

The JCP's strategy, therefore, calls for a "united national democratic front" (*minzoku minshu toitsu sensen*) that will rally all whose interests are in conflict with those of the "American occupiers." This front is to be quite an inclusive one. Scrutinizing the class structure of Japan, the JCP finds it to be made up of 44 per cent workers, 38 per cent peasants, and 16 per cent "urban middle sections," leaving about 2 per cent for the remainder, namely, the "capitalists." Closer examination reveals to the Communists that most of the Japanese capitalists are actually medium and small employers and, therefore, material for the "united national democratic front." This front's principal aim being the removal of U.S. influence from Japan, it must emphasize broad issues that can capture the emotions of the Japanese people while striking at the base of U.S. power. From this reasoning emerges the principal Party slogan: "Struggle for peace, independence, and democracy." Yet, even the Moscow Statement and the JCP program leave an important question unresolved. In directing the JCP to strike the main blow against "U.S. imperialist domination," it is not clear whether this blow is to be primarily a blow for "peaceful coexistence and general disarmament" or for "national liberation." This uncertainty in turn gives rise to a whole set of questions relating to the present differences between Moscow and Peking.

The past year has witnessed the full application of the new strategy. The Japanese Communist Party has recovered some of the strength lost during the years of violence and confusion. It polls more than a million votes even if, because of the Japanese electoral system, it sends only a handful of representatives to the Japanese Diet. Today the JCP may have as many as 90,000 or 100,000 members—twice as many as the much more popular Socialist Party can command.[12] These members still come almost entirely from urban areas, with workers (42 per cent) and intellectuals constituting the majority. Efforts to create Communist Party organizations in the countryside are running into difficulties as a result of the farmer's deep-rooted conservatism, the success of the American-sponsored land reform, and a rising level of prosperity.

The Party's main task, the creation of a *permanent* broad national front, directed primarily against the U.S., has not been fulfilled, but neither has it been a complete failure. As the mass movement against President Eisenhower's visit and against the U.S.-Japanese security pact demonstrated in 1960 and, as subsequent smaller mass actions in 1961, 1962, and 1963 have shown, the Communists in Japan are not operating in complete isolation. The elements that go to make up mass movements in which the Communists can participate continue to exist. On the other hand, these elements can be held together only by very general demands such as "peace" or "democracy." Only sharp domestic crises originating in tactical mistakes on the part of the government or in situations threatening Japanese involvement in war can galvanize the Left into unity. A united front,[13] even when achieved, tends to be unstable and temporary and to lack the official Socialist endorsement that would give it organizational strength and political impact. Moreover, as the Communist experience with front organizations has demonstrated time and again, separate action for a common end leads to some degree of cooperation, then to Communist seizure of leadership and extremist action, and finally, to a withdrawal of most of the non-Communists. The consequence is either a breakup of the front organization, leaving the Communists in command of a rump group and isolated from the Socialist Left, or a successful curbing of Communist influence within the over-all organization. Despite determined and often skillful Communist efforts, the Socialists and the unorganized forces of the Japanese Left remain today, as in the past, immune to permanent incorporation in a Communist-dominated front.

On the other hand, the Japanese Communists have succeeded in keeping alive the issues of nuclear weapons, of the stationing of U.S. forces and equipment in Japan and (especially) Okinawa, and of Japan's foreign-policy orientation—the American alliance versus a neutralist alignment. Neither the Japanese Government and people nor the U.S. has been allowed to develop an atmosphere where cool reasoning and debate could prevail. As long as the above issues remain the focal points of a heated debate, the Japanese Government's freedom of action will be severely circumscribed, and the Communist bloc will benefit from the resulting paralysis.

THE JCP AND THE COMMUNIST WORLD

The past and present close ties of the JCP with Moscow and Peking are a matter of record. So is the Party leadership's responsiveness to advice emanating from the Communist power centers.

Probably the most dramatic illustration of foreign Communist influence over Communist policy in Japan occurred in January, 1950. Nozaka's "soft" strategy stressing a gradualist approach and peaceful path to revolution had garnered 3 million votes for the JCP in 1949, as compared with 1 million in 1947. Suddenly, on January 6, 1950, an editorial in the Soviet-controlled Cominform journal accused Nozaka of following a line that "had nothing whatever in common with Marxism-Leninism," labeled his policy "anti-patriotic" and "anti-Japanese," and attacked his strategy as serving only "the imperialist occupiers in Japan and the enemies of independence." Soon Moscow added official Soviet support to the Cominform's criticism of Nozaka, and, on January 17, Peking's *Jen-min Jih-pao* (*People's Daily*), the official Chinese Communist newspaper, echoed Moscow's voice. Nozaka and the JCP apologized. The Japanese Communists, belatedly following other Asian parties, adopted a militant anti-American line. Soviet pressure for a *Gleichschaltung* of world-wide Communist strategy in the direction of militancy and armed action (the Korean War) had succeeded in Japan, but as a result the Japanese Communist Party lost much of its popular appeal, which it is only now beginning to recover.

The Japanese Communists' consistent refusal to back Japanese territorial claims against the U.S.S.R. and the Party's hearty approval of Soviet nuclear testing in 1961 and 1962 may have cost the Communists much sympathy at home, but these attitudes demonstrated again that the JCP is continuing to subordinate its objectives to those of Moscow.

As long as international Communist policy was interpreted exclusively by the Kremlin, Communist strategists in Japan followed Moscow's guidance without much hesitation. When Communism conquered China, the JCP felt, if anything, heartened, ideologically and strategically, since the Communist world at first continued to speak on all but minor issues with a single voice. But gradually, in the late 1950's, it must have become clear to the Japanese Communist leaders that different emphases, even different approaches and strategies, were being developed in the two power centers.

One might expect, therefore, that the Japanese Communists, as early as 1957, were faced with the immediate need to decide whether Moscow or Peking should from hereon be their ideological Mecca. Four factors may explain why this was not the case.

First, there is no convincing evidence of a distinct "Moscow faction" or of a "Peking faction" within the Japanese Communist hierarchy. (This is not meant to suggest, however, that certain Japanese Communist leaders do not incline toward one or the other Communist power center or that Moscow and Peking factions could not crystallize in the future as a result of the continuation or sharpen-

ing of the Sino-Soviet conflict.[14]) Second, since 1956, the Soviet and
the Chinese Communist governments may have followed somewhat divergent policies toward Japan, but these have been by no
means incompatible and in some respects may actually have been
complementary.[15] Third, both Communist powers agree that the
Japanese Communists should concentrate their attack on the American position in Japan rather than on indigenous barriers to a seizure
of power. Fourth, until recently no tactical opportunities had presented themselves that would require the JCP to make a choice
between the policies of Peking and Moscow, and in both Communist China and the Soviet Union there appears to have existed
agreement on the limits of the revolutionary potential in Japan. As
late as 1961, Peking appears to have refrained from lending support
to a JCP faction that claimed to derive its inspiration from Mao
Tse-tung and, in true "national liberation" style, urged the launching of guerrilla warfare in Okinawa and Japan.

But the differences between the two Communist world powers
could not indefinitely develop without eventually causing repercus-
sions in the JCP. In the first place, Moscow-Peking friction over the
meaning, significance, and strategic role of the "national liberation
struggles," "coexistence," and "the nature of imperialism and its
relationship to war" gave rise to confusion in Japanese Communist
thinking. The confusion was doubtless also related to the protracted
Japanese inner-Party debate over the new Party program that was
to replace the outdated thesis of 1951. While the Moscow Statement of 1960, a compromise between Moscow and Peking, seemed
to ease the ideological dilemma of the JCP, subsequent events in
the Communist world made it evident that the Moscow-Peking
gap had not really been bridged and that the basic issues remained
unresolved. Slowly, it also became clear that the Japanese Communists' hope for a reconciliation of the two powers' world views had
been premature.

No doubt the ideological issues at stake and their strategic implications were of less immediacy in Japan than in most other countries of Asia. The Japanese Communists were certainly more remote
from seizing political power than, for example, the Indonesian
Communists, and the domestic situation in Japan was distinguished
by stability and a solidly conservative government. But the question
of Sino-Soviet rivalry over authority within the international Communist movement already confronted Japan. Perhaps the problem
was more baffling for the Japanese Communists than for other
Asian Communists, since they had always been particularly depend-

ent on foreign advice, were accustomed to emphasize theoretically perfect and universally "correct" solutions, and, consequently, needed the re-establishment of a center of international ideological authority more than most.

This issue of authority over the world movement was clearly posed at the Twenty-second Congress of the CPSU, in October, 1961, when Khrushchev launched into an open and virulent attack against the "Albanian deviationists" and by implication criticized Communist China. As he demanded that other Communist parties repudiate the Albanian foe from the rostrum, the JCP was, for the first time, compelled to take a public stand. Until then it had been allowed to face the questions at issue within the inner-Party circles or in off-the-record international Communist gatherings.

Today, therefore, the Japanese Communists, like other Asian Communists, have to admit, even if only implicitly, that Moscow and Peking are exercising antagonistic pulls.

To evaluate the effect of this reluctant realization upon the Japanese Communist Party and its policy, we must first examine a number of factors that affect the attraction for the JCP of the two great rivals for Communist authority. An important consideration that immediately comes to mind is the relevance of the models offered to Japan by the Soviet Union and China. "Model" is interpreted here broadly as including the sum of conditions and experiences the Russian and Chinese Communists have confronted prior to their seizure of power, as well as the road to the seizure of power itself.

In prewar days, one could perhaps pretend, as most Japanese Communists did, to see instructive parallels between Czarist Russia and Imperial Japan. References to "Japan's coming 1905 revolution" and the like may then not have sounded too incongruous. But the rapid modernization of Japan during the past three decades, especially the fundamental changes brought about since Japan's defeat in World War II, and the important cultural, historical, and institutional differences between Russia and Japan, made Lenin's road to seizure of power largely irrelevant for the Japanese Communists except in the most general terms of political strategy. Nor does the Communist pattern of revolution in Eastern Europe have much relevance for present-day Japan, which is threatened but not dominated by Soviet military power.

At first glance, Mao's Communist model would seem more apposite. China and Japan are located in the same part of the world and are linked by common cultural and historical experiences. The

Chinese Communist seizure of power occurred in the recent past when the world had already entered the atomic age and was experiencing the confrontation of two contending world systems. But upon closer examination, one cannot but conclude that the environment in which the Japanese Communists must operate today, the obstacles they face, and the capabilities at their disposal are so drastically different from those which Mao Tse-tung encountered and skillfully handled that the Maoist pattern can at best supply only fragments of an effective Communist strategy for Japan.

Without going into detail, let us set side by side in schematic form some (though by no means all) of the more important contrasts between Chinese and Japanese conditions as they affect the question of seizure of power:

China	*Japan*
Underdeveloped large country.	Developed small country.
Social structure and role of foreign capital permits creation of broad national front, including "national bourgeoisie."	Social structure and role of foreign capital does not favor creation of Communist-directed national front.
Extreme social and political instability; civil war; value system in flux.	Relatively high degree of stability and public order.
Corrupt and ineffective state apparatus lacking popular support.	Efficient and centralized state apparatus enjoying comparatively broad base of popular support.
Absence of non-Communist alternative to national government.	Socialist alternative to conservative government.
Peasant base and guerrilla warfare leading to Communist seizure of power.	Capture of cities prerequisite for seizure of power; guerrilla warfare an unlikely road to power.
Absence of strong foreign military forces committed to a fight against Communist seizure of power; Soviet Union in position to aid sympathizers.	Presence of powerful U.S. bases and armed forces committed to a defense against Communist seizure of power; Soviet Union in no position to give much assistance to its allies in Japan.

It would seem, then, that neither the Soviet nor the Chinese Communist road to power has much relevance for Japan. On the other hand, the Japanese Communists need not on that account forgo such ideological guidance and material assistance as the big powers choose to give them. There is also the question of Soviet and Chinese Communist experience in other countries and of the degree to which the latter might be offered as models for revolutionary development in Japan. Here again, however, the Japanese Communists are not likely to find much inspiration or guidance. Neither the North Korean Communist seizure of power nor that in North Viet-Nam could be duplicated in Japan. Where Communist parties in Asia have been comparatively successful, as in Indonesia or perhaps in India, conditions differ substantially from those in Japan. Paradoxical as it may sound, the situation faced by Western European Communists is perhaps closer to that in Japan. This is especially true of Italy, where the Communists operate in a similar context of rapid modernization, where they can count, as in Japan, on some degree of cooperation from the Socialist Left, and where they must dislodge a seemingly permanent conservative government. Significantly, Italian Communist behavior does not follow the Soviet model; it is a new development in the Communist world. As such, it is having a profound effect in Japan—as evidenced by the central role of the Italian concept of "structural reform" in the discussions of Japan's political Left.

There is also the question of the relative importance of the material assistance that is reaching the Japanese Party in various, mostly devious, ways from both Peking and Moscow. During the past few years, contacts between Japan and the two Communist powers have developed substantially. Although Japan maintains no diplomatic relations with Communist China, travelers go back and forth, virtually unhampered, between Tokyo and Peking. The same is true of Japan's relations with the Soviet Union, where, despite the absence of a peace treaty, economic, cultural, and political contacts have increased from year to year. The presence of an official Soviet mission in Tokyo may tend to encourage the JCP to lean toward Moscow, but this practical consideration is balanced by others, such as a greater Japanese affinity for China and the feeling on the part of the Japanese Communists that through closer relations with Peking they can participate in the developing struggle for Asia, in which Japan as a whole has a traditional stake.

As important as the material incentives that Peking and Moscow can provide for the Japanese Communists are the natural orientation of the Party, its fundamental character, and the way its leaders feel about their Communist neighbors. The Japanese Communist

Party, of course, has long-standing and substantial ties with the
Soviet Union. Many of its leaders have visited that country. Others
have been trained at the Communist University of the Toilers of
the East (KUTV) in Moscow or have worked in various capacities
with the Comintern. On the other hand, we should not forget that
much of this experience was in the Stalin era, that some Japanese
Communists disappeared in the purges, that others were exposed
to ruthless Stalinist pressures, and that almost all of them saw a
Russia that must have seemed materially and intellectually backward compared to Japan.

In many respects the Japanese Communists—from their top leaders, Nozaka and Miyamoto, down to the ordinary Party member—
must feel much closer to their comrades in Peking. This is not only
a matter of the latent hostility of the Japanese toward Russia and
the attraction and admiration that they feel toward China, although these feelings are by no means negligible in their political
implications. There is also the question of the personal experience
of the Japanese Communists in non-Communist and Communist
China. In prewar times, Shanghai was a refuge from the Japanese
police and from direct Soviet control. Later, Mao Tse-tung's Yenan
became the first, if somewhat remote, Communist stronghold on
Asian soil. Nozaka, escaping to Yenan in 1943 from the pressures
of life in the shadow of the Kremlin, found an extraordinarily backward country where people lived in caves, but where there was a
feeling of optimism, of purpose, of a bright future. When Nozaka
organized his antiwar league to encourage defections from the Japanese Army, he had the full support of Mao Tse-tung and of the
Chinese Communist elite. In the early 1940's, the Japanese Communists in Yenan were no longer, as they had been in Moscow, mere
translators, researchers, or "yes men," but were active fighters for a
common cause whom the Chinese honored and frequently con-
sulted.[16] As the JCP moved underground on the eve of the Korean
War, the late Secretary-General, Tokuda Kyuichi, and most of the
Party leaders transferred their headquarters from Tokyo to Peking,
where, once more, they seem to have lived in a congenial atmosphere. It may be symbolic that the Japanese Communist movement's first internationally important figure, Katayama Sen, lies
buried in the walls of the Kremlin, but that his successor, Tokuda
Kyuichi, rests in Peking.

However strongly attracted they may be to Communist China,
however, the Japanese Communists can hardly overlook the effect
that an adoption of the Peking-preferred strategy of militancy and

"national liberation" would have in Japan. Even if it is true that Communist China seems to press more strongly than does the U.S.S.R. for a change in the Far Eastern *status quo*, the means it employs would tend to render more difficult the JCP's struggle for power. In contrast, Moscow's policy of utilizing Soviet power to press relentlessly, but within well-defined risk limits, for a removal of American influence from Japan, its attempts to play on the fear of nuclear war and to stress peaceful coexistence and disarmament rather than the inevitability of military conflict, would seem more realistic and effective a strategy in a war-weary Japan.

Since 1959, the dichotomy in Japanese Communist thinking caused by the conflicting pulls exerted by Moscow and Peking has been accentuated by increased Soviet and Chinese efforts to ensure the JCP's allegiance. In recent years, Communist leaders from Japan have become familiar figures in Moscow and Peking. Japanese Communist missions have been invited to tour Communist China and the U.S.S.R. and have been treated there with evident signs of esteem.[17] Khrushchev and Mikoyan are as ready to grant them interviews as Mao Tse-tung, Chou En-lai, and Liu Shao-ch'i. Japanese Communist newspapermen move among the Chinese Communist and Soviet dignitaries.[18] Joint Japanese-Chinese declarations are issued and given much publicity.

Not only has the official record of the JCP's Eighth Congress been published in the Soviet Union, but even the writings of individual JCP leaders (including Nozaka, Miyamoto, and Shiga) and of Japanese Communist novelists are now being introduced to the Soviet and Chinese reading public. Soviet and Chinese newspapers carry articles by Japanese Communist leaders. Meanwhile, Japanese-language editions of Soviet periodicals are being exported in increasing numbers to Japan. Peking, in its turn, prints a monthly specially tailored to the Japanese Communist reader, to acquaint him with developments on the Chinese mainland. Another indication of the JCP's enhanced international importance could be seen in the summer of 1961 when the Communist parties of both the Soviet Union and China decided to send to the Eighth JCP Congress delegations drawn from the highest level of Party officialdom.[19]

The language of the Soviet and Chinese Communist press has reflected this new situation. Where once the editors limited themselves to brief notices or impersonal reports on Communist policy in Japan, they now refer to the JCP and its leaders in the warmest tone. The Japanese Communist Party is now "heroic," "brave," and "glorious" and a "model of internationalism"; its policy is praised as "correct," and its leaders are said to have "intimate and friendly talks" with their counterparts overseas.

Much flattery—or belated recognition—was bestowed on JCP Chairman Nozaka Sanzo as he celebrated his seventieth birthday in March, 1962. Back in 1950, Moscow and Peking had severely reprimanded him for his "anti-Marxist" policies, but now Mao Tse-tung himself sent fraternal greetings that called Nozaka a "long-tested and staunch fighter" and "a close friend of the Chinese people and the Communist Party of China" and praised him for "holding aloft the banner of Marxism-Leninism, the banner of internationalism and patriotism" and for carrying out a "titanic task and sustained fight." The Chinese Party's Central Committee elaborated on this theme in another message that spoke of Nozaka as "a fine son of the Japanese working class" who had made "important contributions to the defense of peace in the Far East and the world" and had "waged a selfless struggle against the common enemy." The message concluded with the assurance that "the Chinese people are proud to have a friend like you." As if this were not enough, *Jen-min Jih-pao* carried reminiscences (by his Chinese deputy director of the Yenan school, Li Ch'u-li) about Nozaka's life in wartime Yenan, while Teng Hsiao-p'ing, Secretary-General of the Chinese Communist Party, published an article about him entitled "Outstanding Fighter of the Japanese People."[20]

Meanwhile *Pravda's* front page conveyed to Nozaka the birthday greetings of the CPSU Central Committee, while *Izvestia*, the official newspaper of the Soviet Government, carried a similar message under the title "Staunch Fighter." Where Mao Tse-tung had emphasized Nozaka's fight against "U.S. imperialism," *Izvestia* stressed the Japanese Communist leader's "struggle for peace."[21]

To a striking degree, Moscow and Peking have stepped up their press and radio coverage of the JCP. They show far more interest than previously in the Communist movement in Japan. But it is clearly China that is the more eager to make an ally of Japan and the more concerned about details of the Communist struggle there. This difference in the importance assigned to the JCP by Moscow and by Peking is, of course, partly the result of geographical propinquity and related factors, but it also appears to reflect the fact that Peking is on the offensive in Asia and is exerting itself mightily to incorporate the JCP into its sphere of influence.

THE FUTURE: INDEPENDENCE OR SUBORDINATION?

The emergence of Peking as a second major Communist power center has fundamentally altered the situation in Asia that existed in Stalin's time. Peking has proved strong and determined enough to challenge Moscow over world strategy, but it cannot hope in the foreseeable future to become the one and only source of Communist authority. Meanwhile, Khrushchev's greater tolerance of "different paths to socialism" and his waning control over the Communist Parties outside the bloc tend to foster within the Asian Communist movement the development of ideological diversity and the adoption of a whole range of differing strategies that are attuned to local traditions and requirements. Each Asian Communist Party is beginning to develop, so to speak, a personality of its own. In the process, it finds that it is now permissible, within certain limits, to disagree on some points with Moscow or Peking.

A particular Party may have serious doubts about specific Soviet policies, yet acknowledge Moscow's leadership for reasons of power politics, traditional outlook, and so on. It may implicitly criticize aspects of Moscow's foreign or domestic policies, and it may even lean toward Peking's views on the same issues, without losing the Kremlin's ostensible good will. It may actually proclaim policies that seem at variance with the line laid down by Moscow and still be considered by the Kremlin a pillar of strength in its contest with Peking. A Communist Party in a country outside the bloc may now enjoy the privilege of refraining, at least temporarily, from declaring itself on an issue about which Moscow and Peking are in dispute— for example, in 1961, when Khrushchev demanded a general condemnation of the Albanian leaders for their "Stalinist deviation," many of the "fraternal parties" of Asia abstained from voting.

Even in the relatively permissive atmosphere of today, however, no Communist Party can forever avoid committing itself on such key issues as coexistence and the likelihood of war. When a Party decides to come down on one side or the other and to adapt its strategies to the ideological norms of either China or Russia, it may be said in a sense to have joined one of the two "camps" or to have entered one of the two spheres of influence. But as long as there is no evidence of firm and consistent subordination either to Moscow or Peking, as long as Communist parties outside the bloc retain substantial freedom of action, as long as Sino-Soviet differences remain susceptible of adjustment, and while these differences have only a limited significance for the domestic strategies of some parties, it will be safer for us to think in terms of "affinities"—developing, intermittent, or consistent—rather than of Peking or Moscow spheres of influence. In examining the Japanese Communists' position on the Moscow-Peking spectrum, the term "developing affinity" seems to describe best their present relationship to the Chinese Communists.

It is only recently that events—such as ideological strife among the Japanese Communists, Khrushchev's insistence that each Party make known its stand on the Albanian issue, and the intensified efforts of Peking to press its views on other Communist parties—have compelled even the fence-straddling Japanese Communists to depart from their stated position on the Sino-Soviet conflict, which was simply that the conflict did not exist. Up to that point, the JCP had pretended that friction between Moscow and Peking had no significance for international Communist policy or for Japan.

Under the surface and in inner-Party discussions, the effect of the Sino-Soviet conflict must surely have been felt for some time also in Japan. Two recent developments shed some light on this question and suggest the direction the Communist Party of Japan appears to be taking as a result of the relentless pressures from abroad—and increasingly also from its own members—to define its position in the international Communist movement. The first development relates to the "Kasuga deviationist revolt"; the second concerns the Albanian issue.

As stated earlier, when the Japanese Communist Party held its Seventh Congress in 1958, it was unable to agree on a new program. For three more years, the internal debates continued,[22] until in July, 1961, at the Eighth Party Congress, a program was unanimously adopted. This fell into line with the prescriptions laid down in the Moscow Statement of December, 1960. The new program had the full support of Moscow and Peking, which sent congratulatory messages and presented the program to the Soviet and Chinese reading public. The document was adopted, however, over the fierce opposition of a faction in which the Moscow-educated Communist veteran Kasuga Shojiro[23] and the theorist Sato Noboru were the leading figures. On the eve of the Party Congress, realizing that their cause was lost, Kasuga and some of his followers resigned from the Party to pursue an independent course and to set up their own organization.

Kasuga denied the supreme importance of "American imperialism" as the principal obstacle to socialism in Japan. He viewed Japan as an essentially independent nation, no different from any of the countries of Western Europe, and asserted that the Communists' fight must be directed against the capitalist enemy at home and against incipient fascist trends. He further argued that Japan, like Western Europe, had already had its "democratic revolution" and that the next step would be a socialist revolution. Such a revolution, he stated, could be accomplished, in the main, peacefully, by continuous pressure for domestic reforms that would shift the balance of domestic power toward the left. In arguing thus, Kasuga was following the "structural reform" theories advanced by the Italian Communist leader Togliatti and also by many Japanese Socialists, among whom Togliatti's theories have recently found much response.[24] Kasuga further asserted that U.S. "imperialism" could be ousted from Japan without a revolution, simply by canceling the U.S.-Japanese alliance. He implicitly and sometimes openly criticized the two Communist great powers; withheld support for the Soviet decision to resume nuclear testing; described Soviet socialism as "undemocratic"; and quoted frequently from the writings of the Yugoslav Communists.

These theories placed Kasuga, ideologically speaking, close to the Yugoslav Communists, and in the camp of the "revisionists."[25] At the same time, Kasuga's views are so like those of the Japanese Socialist Party that, by implication, they seem to deny the need for separate Communist and Socialist organizations. Obviously, these views are unacceptable not only to Peking but also to Moscow, so that they could hardly be the cause of a split in the JCP along the lines of the Moscow-Peking conflict.

The importance of this inner-Party conflict in Tokyo lies, however, not only in the substance of the issues at stake but in the way the Japanese Communist leaders chose to deal with the "deviationists." Ever since Kasuga's defection, Japanese Communist Party organs have poured forth a veritable torrent of articles, comments, and statements about the deviationists, attacked the personalities and records of their leaders, and denounced their views as "treacherous anti-Party actions."[26]

In concentrating its fire against the "structural reform" theories of Sato Noboru and Togliatti, the JCP does not go so far as to deny the validity of the doctrine in relation to Italian problems. It simply characterizes these views as exceedingly harmful if applied to Japan. The tone of the indictment, however, strongly implies the JCP's disapproval of Togliatti's doctrine as such. Togliatti, of course, is the exponent of ideological positions akin to those of the Yugoslavs and diametrically opposed to those of the Chinese Communists.

The deviationists are said to accept uncritically the "mistaken and harmful views of the Yugoslavs" and the vitriolic criticism of Peking by Yugoslav leader Kardelj.

Another theme in the JCP's criticism of Kasuga and his group is his "underestimate of the role of U.S. imperialism" and his alleged "disinclination to fight it." Furthermore, the rebels are again and again attacked for "the irresponsible, mechanistic way in which they transfer foreign parties' theories" to the Japanese environment, in spite of the "special character of the Japanese revolution," which must be "clarified both in theory and in action." Kasuga has even been accused of attempting to make JCP regulations conform, "in a formalistic fashion," to the new Soviet Party regulations.[27]

The present JCP leadership has been compelled to lash out against "revisionism" mainly because the principal challenge to their authority comes from the revisionist right, as embodied in Kasuga's faction of pro-Togliatti reformists. Acceptance of Kasuga's theories would have drawn the condemnation of Moscow, and even more of Peking. Worse still, had Kasuga's strategy proved successful by creating a united front of the Left, it could only have done so at the expense of the Communist Party's existence as a separate entity.

Even if they recognized the powerful domestic pressures that induced the JCP to act as it did, the Chinese Communist leaders must have congratulated themselves on the violent language used by the Japanese leaders to make their points, the emphasis they placed on the rejection of Western European models, and the passionate way in which they defended Peking against Kasuga's charge of belligerency.

The above evidence would seem to suggest that between 1958 and 1961 the Japanese Communist Party was beginning to lean toward Peking. But we should not draw rash conclusions from a single though admittedly important episode, for it would have been difficult, in any case, for the Japanese Communist leaders to fight the challenge from the extreme right wing of their Party without taking positions that generally have been identified with those of Peking.

If the JCP's reaction to the "Kasuga deviation" is susceptible to varying interpretations, Japanese Communist behavior in the well-known Albanian affair added more distinct indicators regarding the JCP's position in the international Communist movement. When Khrushchev, at the Twenty-second Congress of the CPSU, anathematized Albanian Communist leader Enver Hoxha as a die-hard Stalinist and an enemy of peace, each Communist Party represented at the Congress was under strong Soviet pressure to join in the condemnation. It will be recalled that Chou En-lai confirmed the existence of a Peking-Tirana axis by leaving the Moscow conference abruptly and returning to Peking, and that certain parties, especially those of Asia, by refraining from comment on the Albanian incident, implicitly disavowed if not Khrushchev's world strategy at least his handling of the matter. Nozaka Sanzo, representing the Japanese Party, was one of those who withheld support from Khrushchev on this historic occasion.[28] Needless to say, this was a turning point for the Japanese Communist Party, which never before had openly hesitated to follow Moscow's lead.

While Nozaka's silence could still be interpreted in a variety of ways, its significance for JCP policy became clearer during the following weeks. On November 22, 1961, the official Party newspaper, *Akahata (Red Flag)*, carried the text of Nozaka's report on the Soviet Party Congress. A very brief passage admitted the existence of an "Albanian question" and conceded that differences of opinion could arise among Communists of various countries. The report insisted, however, that these could be settled through application of the principles enunciated in the Moscow Declaration of 1957 and the Moscow Statement of 1960 and that in this way Communist international unity could be further strengthened. Nozaka had already made this point at the Moscow Congress, in reply to Khrushchev's attacks on Albania. It is significant that Nozaka in his report described the two documents as "programs" for Communist parties throughout the world. Evidently, he disagreed with the way Khrushchev had been handling the Albanian affair, and, just as evidently, he felt that the problem should have been settled through quiet consultation among those concerned and not on the speaker's rostrum at the Soviet Party Congress. On the other hand, the JCP Chairman refrained from commenting on the substantive issues posed by the Albanian case.

During the following weeks, discussion of the Albanian affair apparently continued on the highest level in the JCP. In a long report on one of its meetings, the Japanese Central Committee briefly referred to "the appearance of difficult problems within the Socialist camp like the matter of Soviet-Albanian relations."[29] On December 29, an *Akahata* editorial repeatedly appealed for unity in the international Communist movement and then proceeded to announce that the Party had decided to publish pertinent materials on the Albanian question to permit Party members and Communist sympathizers to study the issue. The very next day, *Akahata* carried the full text of the Indonesian Party's December 15 resolution on the subject, which was generally unsympathetic to Khrushchev and called for resistance to Yugoslav revisionist influence. The Albanian side of the story followed shortly thereafter in a Party publication meant for a more restricted public.[30] As exemplified by Chinese and Japanese Party cooperation in publishing a Japanese-language edition of Mao Tse-tung's *Selected Works*,[31] relations between the JCP and the CCP were if anything closer after the Albanian affair than before. The JCP also continued to maintain contacts with the Albanian Communist Party, although this must have irritated the Soviet leaders. On the occasion of Nozaka's birthday, for example, Enver Hoxha sent him a warm message which was cordially acknowledged by the Japanese Communist leader.[32]

The JCP's behavior in this instance, as in that of the Kasuga "revisionist deviation," might easily be interpreted as proof of the Party's all-out support for Peking's policies. However, the Japanese Communist Party's reaction to the Sino-Soviet conflict—and to the opportunities created by it—appears to be more complex, as evidenced by JCP policies during 1962 and early 1963. It is true that the JCP has at last cut the umbilical cord that linked it to the Soviet Union since the Party's birth shortly after World War I. But this Moscow tie has not been replaced—at least not as yet—by a similar tie to Peking. Meanwhile, the JCP gives evidence of a modest degree of independent thinking.

That the JCP was beginning to view critically Soviet behavior was already suggested by Nozaka's unwillingness in 1961 to lend his support to Khrushchev's open attack against Albania. During 1962 and 1963, the Party went further. It admonished Khrushchev and his supporters repeatedly—but without mentioning Khrushchev by name—stating that "for one fraternal party to criticize unilaterally and openly another fraternal party is not the proper way to settle a disputed question."[33] The JCP also indicated its disagreement with Soviet policy on the Sino-Indian border war by attacking those who placed some blame for it on Peking. Furthermore, the Party failed to endorse Khrushchev's Cuba policy. It gave passionate support to Castro's refusal to submit to international inspection, expressed doubts that President Kennedy had ever pledged not to use force against Cuba,[34] and then topped it off by proclaiming in an editorial devoted to the Cuban and Sino-Indian conflicts that "peace pledges by the imperialists have absolutely no value."[35] The implicit disapproval of Soviet policy was further indicated by the fact that Castro's ability to survive was credited to his

stalwart determination to resist U.S. threats rather than to any Soviet protection and assistance.

In the eyes of the JCP, Peking can now claim near-equal status
with Moscow in the leadership of the international Communist
camp. This conclusion emerges not only from the general tone of
JCP statements, but from the specific and no doubt carefully
worked out wording of recent Party documents. Thus, the most
important JCP policy statement on the Sino-Soviet dispute, the
resolution of the Fifth Central Committee Plenum of February 15,
1963, after pointing to the fact that China represents a quarter of
mankind and two-thirds of the population of the Communist bloc,
asserts that the emergence of the Chinese People's Republic has
completely changed the situation in Asia, Africa, and Latin America and that the international Communist movement is inconceiv-
able without either Moscow or Peking. Repeatedly, the CPSU and
the CCP (in this order) are referred to as forming together the
"nucleus" of international Communism.[36]

It would be wrong, however, to assume therefore that the JCP is
hostile to Moscow or firmly in the Chinese camp. The Japanese
Communists to this day continue to be well represented in the col-
umns of the *World Marxist Review,* from which Peking and its all-
out supporters have withdrawn.[37] Nor is the JCP following Peking's
lead in its discussion of the Sino-Soviet dispute. Thus, *Akahata*
published the important Soviet policy statement of January 7, 1963
(printed in *Pravda* of that date), two days later, while Peking hesitated to make it public until February 21. Neither does Moscow's
comment on the Japanese Communists or their treatment at official
functions in the Soviet sphere of influence suggest that the JCP is
now considered in Moscow to be committed to a Peking-Tirana
line. In this respect, it is interesting to compare the JCP with the
North Korean and Indonesian Communists. North Korean and to
a lesser extent Indonesian comments on Soviet and especially Yugoslav policies use much harsher language than that found in the
Japanese Communist press. A Japanese representative was allowed
therefore to address the Congress of the German Socialist Unity
Party in January, 1963, and to plead for a "correct" solution of the
Sino-Soviet conflict, whereas the North Korean delegate was si-
lenced by the hosts. In the carefully planned proceedings of Communist congresses, the gradations of applause have, ever since
Stalin's time, been good indicators of official sanction. In the thoroughly pro-Soviet atmosphere of the Berlin congress, the appearance of the pro-Peking North Korean delegate rated only "ap-

plause," the Vietnamese and Indonesians—less committed to support of Peking—were received with "strong applause," but the Japanese delegate—representing a party that remains on good terms
with both major Communist power centers—received an ovation
that was described in the congress proceedings as "strong, prolonged
applause." Clearly, in early 1963, the JCP continued to be courted
by both Moscow and Peking, and it pursued an independent path
even though it leaned generally toward Peking.

The Japanese Communist leadership has repeatedly stated that
it sees little benefit to itself or to the Communist movement at
large in arguing who is right and who is wrong in the Sino-Soviet
dispute. There may be a good deal of wishful thinking in such an
attitude, but it is clear that the JCP views its role as that of a mediator between Moscow and Peking—one sufficiently independent to
reach its own conclusions after careful and dispassionate study. It
has sought to prepare the ground for a Moscow-Peking accommodation while cautiously acquainting its members with the issues at
stake.

In its role as mediator, the JCP has called for inter-Party consultations and the eventual convening of an international Communist
conference. It has tried to avoid giving offense to either Peking or
Moscow—for example, by omitting from its recent official statements any direct references to Yugoslavia or Albania. It has sought
to minimize the seriousness of the conflict by calling it "temporary," "minor," or "natural" and by magnifying in its press whatever
remains of Sino-Soviet cooperation. (An *Akahata* headline of February 15, 1963 read: "Rallies in Moscow and Peking Commemorat-
ing the [Anniversary] of the Alliance—Unshakable Solidarity.")
The JCP has gone out of its way not to get directly involved in the
name-calling between Moscow and Peking. At the same time, it has
begun to spread before its members a somewhat sanitized collection
of documents expressing the views of the Soviet, Chinese, Indonesian, Korean, Italian (Togliatti), German, and other parties. This
presentation of opposing views in the official Party daily, *Akahata*,
and the documentary periodical *Sekai Seiji Shiryo* (*Materials on
World Politics*) may not always have been perfectly fair to both
sides, but then the balancing act has been a difficult one, and there
is as yet no clear JCP consensus as to the merits of particular features of Soviet and Chinese strategies.

Although the JCP refrains from openly taking sides between
Moscow and Peking, its own domestic and foreign-policy positions
are clearly closer to those of Peking. It is therefore not surprising

that the official Peking daily *Jen-min Jih-pao* reprints Japanese Communist policy statements more frequently than *Pravda,* and that the *Peking Review* of February 1, 1963, could state with conviction that the JCP has "consistently followed a correct line." The JCP in 1963 gives vociferous support to the "national liberation struggle" in all its manifestations, and tends to de-emphasize the Soviet slogans "complete disarmament" and "peaceful coexistence." It minimizes more than the Soviets (although less than Peking) the significance of nuclear weapons. On the domestic scene, the Party has not gone so far as to return to its earlier strategy of armed action, but it has intensified its anti-American policy even at the risk of alienating the Socialist Left—as evidenced in its insistence on a hard line in the anti-nuclear movement, which resulted in a split in the Socialist-Communist front after the Eighth Congress of the Council Against A and H Bombs, held in August, 1962. The Party has also clearly stated that it considers Communist dogmatism (i.e., the Chinese and Albanian view) a minor danger, and that the real enemy to the Communist movement in Japan is "revisionism"— being careful at the same time to direct its fierce attack ostensibly only against the local brand of revisionism and only through publication of Indonesian, Chinese, and Korean documents criticizing the Yugoslav Communists.[38]

Meanwhile, the Japanese Communists are strengthening their ties with other Asian parties, especially with the successful and independent-minded Indonesian Communist Party (PKI).[39] In this context, it is significant that Japanese Communist writings increasingly stress the need for "a creative application of Marxism-Leninism."[40] It may well be that the JCP now sees its future role as part of a group of Asian Communist parties that will remain on friendly terms with both Moscow and, especially, Peking, without automatically accepting instructions and ideological guidance from either of the two Communist power centers.

The Japanese Communist Party may be assuming a more independent position in the conviction that it can serve its own interests *and* the cause of international Communism better this way than by leaning to either side. In this, the Party may merely mirror a general Japanese trend of thought—or wishful thinking—which sees Japan's destiny as a bridge between contending powers. This tendency to avoid involvement in the Moscow-Peking struggle reflects itself in many ways and reaches into the all-important realm of Party indoctrination. When the JCP recently published its recommended reading list,[41] it included—as might be expected—the works of Marx, Engels, and Lenin. There were also the writings of the more important Japanese Communist leaders, past and present. But one looks in vain for the works of the controversial trio—Stalin, Khrushchev, and Mao Tse-tung. Have they been sacrificed because the Japanese Communists are returning to the original sources and expect to build their own theoretical edifice on Marx, Engels, and Lenin? Or have they been sacrificed because the Party leaders are as yet uncertain of the outcome of the Moscow-Peking struggle and of its meaning for the future of Communism in Asia and in Japan?

Only time can tell whether the Japanese Communists will emerge from the present period of transition and searching as a truly independent entity, both ideologically and organizationally, or whether they will return to their past tradition of subservience to foreign influence. One cannot help but recall that the present Chairman of the Japanese Communist Party, Nozaka Sanzo, attempted, back in 1950, to develop his own strategy for Japan, that he was attacked by Moscow and Peking for doing so, and that he meekly surrendered. On the other hand, more than a decade has gone by since then, Stalin is dead, and what was once a monolithic Communist bloc is today a realm of contending power centers. Even the notoriously submissive Japanese Communists must sooner or later reflect the profound changes that have taken place in the international relations of the Communist world.

NOTES

1. Miyamoto, a well-educated intellectual and a Marxist literary critic of some prominence, joined the JCP while in his twenties. He became an important figure in the illegal Communist Party, was arrested in 1933, and thereafter remained in prison until the end of the war. In the postwar period, he opposed at times the dominant Tokuda-Nozaka faction, but today Miyamoto represents the Party's mainstream and is considered its "strong man." His recent illness, however, has placed his Party career in doubt. Shiga, another intellectual with outstanding educational qualifications, was also active in the prewar Communist movement and is Miyamoto's senior in terms of Party affiliation. He was arrested in 1928 and remained in prison until Japan's surrender. In the postwar era, Shiga has at times worked with Miyamoto against the predominant faction. Today he is one of the Party's few Diet members and, with Nozaka, one of the Party elders. Hakamada has also been active in the Communist movement since prewar times, as have all important figures in the JCP. He is a graduate of the KUTV (Communist University of the Toilers of the East)—a predecessor of Lumumba University—in Moscow. Like all the other prominent JCP figures, Hakamada has spent many years in Japanese prisons. All three men are members of the JCP Presidium, which in 1963 had eleven members (including two candidate-members).

2. There is an interesting mimeographed Japanese Government document

(*Kominterun shin-hoshin no waga kuni ni okeru han-ei jokyo*, issued by the Peace Preservation Bureau, Police Division, Japanese Home Ministry) in the collections of the Hoover Institution in Stanford, California, which reports on Communist liaison work between the U.S. and Japan during the mid-1930's. A similar printed collection of propaganda materials smuggled into Japan from the U.S. is in the Library of Congress. For an over-all view of the JCP's foreign relations in prewar years, see Rodger Swearingen and Paul Langer, *Red Flag in Japan* (Cambridge, Mass.: Harvard University Press, 1952), chaps. vi and vii.

3. In Yenan with the Chinese Communists, Nozaka carried on antiwar propaganda among Japanese defectors and tried in various ways to undermine the discipline of the Japanese forces fighting in China. He established a school in Yenan for the indoctrination of future Japanese "progressive" cadres. While in Yenan, Nozaka worked closely with the Chinese Communist leaders. His appearance at the Chinese Communist Party Congress as a speaker suggests that his role in China was a fairly important one. He has recorded some of his memories of Yenan in an autobiography, *Bomei juroku-nen* (*Sixteen Years in Exile*). Travelers recently returned from Yenan (officially Fushih) report that a sign commemorates Nozaka's old residence there.

4. The postwar electoral record of the JCP is shown below. The figures, which refer to elections for the House of Representatives, indicate that the number of seats held by the JCP is far smaller than its proportionate share of the electorate.

Year	Votes for JCP (in millions)	Percentage of total vote	No. of seats won by JCP (out of total of 464–67)
1946	2.14	3.8%	5
1947	1.00	3.7%	4
1949	2.98	9.7%	35
1952	0.90	2.6%	0
1953	0.66	1.9%	1
1955	0.73	2.0%	2
1958	1.01	2.6%	1
1960	1.16	2.9%	3

The most recent elections (July, 1962) involved only the House of Councilors and are not directly comparable to those for the House of Representatives. However, they confirm that the JCP is making a slow comeback at the polls, although it is still far from equaling its 1949 peak. This trend was also evident in the local elections of April, 1963.

5. For an excellent discussion of the meandering course of Japanese Communist strategic thinking in the early postwar years, see Toshio G. Tsukahira, *The Postwar Evolution of Communist Strategy in Japan* (Cambridge, Mass.: Massachusetts Institute of Technology, 1954). For an account of the history of the Japanese Communist movement in the 1950's, see Paul F. Langer, "Communism in Independent Japan," in Hugh Borton (ed.), *Japan Between East and West* (New York: Harper and Brothers, 1957).

6. It is characteristic of the change that has taken place in international Communist thinking that Nozaka, writing in the February, 1962, issue of *World Marxist Review*, the official international Communist organ, could say of the new Party program that it "creatively applies the fundamentals of Marxism-Leninism to the conditions of Japan," while back in 1950 he had been

assailed by the Cominform for attempting "the naturalization of Marxism-Leninism in Japanese conditions."

7. For the official English text of the Moscow Statement, see *World Marxist Review*, III, No. 12 (December, 1960).

8. Hakamada, who led the Japanese delegation to the conference, states that it was clearly understood that this passage applied to Japan and Canada. This was also confirmed by the Canadian Communist Party.

9. Raymond Guyot, for instance, writing in the official French Communist monthly, *Cahiers du Communisme*, March, 1961, mentions Japan as being in the same class as France and other European countries.

10. One could render "national revolution" also as "people's revolution," since the term used by the JCP—*jimmin*—is identical with the term used in "People's China" (*Jimmin Chugoku*). Much of the modern Japanese Communist terminology has been colored by Mao's style. How far this has actually affected Japanese Communist ideological orientation is, however, another matter. Other important points of this new JCP program are:

1) The united front will establish a government on the foundations of a fight against both imperialism and monopoly capital; depending on circumstances, a government constituted essentially of a labor-farmer dictatorship is not ruled out.

2) Peaceful as well as nonpeaceful revolutions are considered possible, the choice depending on the attitude of the "enemy."

3) The democratic revolution will "pave the way to the transition to socialist reconstruction and, rapidly and consistently, grow into a revolution which will abolish capitalism."

4) On the controversial issue of the inevitability of war, the Party program declares that the nature of imperialism has not changed and that the danger of war continues to be with us, but that the forces of peace are today superior to those of war and that if they continue to exercise the necessary vigilance and fight in unity, war can be prevented. No distinction is made between general and local war.

11. *World Marxist Review, loc. cit.*

12. These figures, cited by Party sources as well as others, constitute a very substantial increase over 1959—probably at least a doubling of Party membership. Communist Party membership among Japanese Government and public corporation employees is particularly large (in 1962, about 17,000). The JCP daily, *Akahata* (*Red Flag*), had a circulation of about 150,000 in 1963 (against 53,000 in the spring of 1960 and 104,000 in mid-1961) with the Sunday edition selling about 300,000 copies. According to an official JCP statement of November 15, 1962, this figure represents a tenfold circulation increase within three years. The JCP monthly *Zen'ei* (*Vanguard*), devoted to Communist theory, and the several other JCP publications are considerably less popular.

13. The JCP generally applies the "united front from below" formula, but continues to press vigorously for a full-scale front on all levels. On the national level, it is often only partially or temporarily successful, but on the local level it has had more success. In Kyoto, in April, 1962, for instance, it was permitted to join a united front set up to assure re-election of a progressive candidate as governor of the area. The opponent, a conservative backed by the government party, was defeated. A year later, the Party was backing the gubernatorial candidate of the Socialist Party for the Tokyo area who, however, was defeated by his conservative opponent. In the summer of 1963, the JCP was seeking to

draw the Socialists into a common front opposing the deployment of U.S. jet fighters (F-105D's) to Japan and the planned visit of U.S. nuclear-propelled submarines.

14. Some official Japanese sources express the conviction that a pro-Peking faction had indeed emerged by 1963 and is now in control of the JCP.

15. For a discussion of this point, see Paul F. Langer, "Moscow, Peking, and Tokyo" in Kurt L. London (ed.), *Unity and Contradiction: Major Aspects of Sino-Soviet Relations* (New York: Frederick A. Praeger, 1962).

16. In September, 1959, Nozaka revisited China to attend the tenth-anniversary celebrations of the Chinese People's Republic as official representative of the JCP. According to a Peking broadcast, the Japanese Communist leader, addressing the Chinese and international Communist audience, recalled the memory of those days in Yenan in these terms:

> Over ten years ago, I personally shared the joys and sorrows with Chairman Mao Tse-tung and other Chinese Communist leaders in Yenan during their war against Japanese imperialist aggression in China. A thousand emotions are welling in my mind now as I look back upon China at that time. The marvelous construction of People's China and the glorious celebration of the tenth anniversary of the People's Republic of China appear miraculous to me, when I think of the life in the caves in Yenan.

(Incidentally, the Chinese honored Nozaka and the JCP on this occasion by allowing him to be the first speaker from among the many delegates representing Communist parties of non-Communist countries.) It is interesting that Nozaka, who served even longer with the Comintern in Moscow than in China, mentioned this fact, but did not add such wistful observations when reminiscing about life near the Kremlin.

17. Among the many official Communist Party missions to the U.S.S.R. and China, the following were probably the most important: January, 1959—delegation to the Twenty-first Party Congress in Moscow, with Miyamoto as chairman; February–March, 1959—again Miyamoto, this time in Peking, meeting with Mao; September–October, 1959—Nozaka, Hakamada, and several other JCP leaders attend the tenth anniversary of the C.P.R. and meet with Mao; November–December, 1960—Hakamada leads delegation to Moscow Conference of 81 Communist Parties; June, 1961—Shiga and other JCP leaders have interviews with Mao, Liu Shao-ch'i, Chu Te, and Chou En-lai, and two of the Japanese Communists make a side trip to Ulan Bator to attend the Fourteenth Congress of the Mongolian People's Revolutionary Party; September, 1961—JCP Diet-member delegation, headed by Shiga, visits Moscow at the invitation of the Supreme Soviet; October, 1961—Miyamoto and another Central Committee member attend the Fourth Congress of the North Korean Communists before proceeding to join Nozaka and other JCP leaders in Moscow for attendance at the Soviet Twenty-second Party Congress; November–December, 1962—Hakamada and another Central Committee member go to Moscow and Eastern Europe and return via Peking, where they join up with another group of JCP leaders and meet Mao, Liu Shao-ch'i, and Teng Hsiao-p'ing before traveling back to Tokyo in January, 1963. It should be added that most JCP leaders visiting the U.S.S.R. have had an opportunity to meet with Soviet leaders of the Presidium level (including Khrushchev) and that, whether going to China or to the U.S.S.R., they often have stayed for several weeks' discussions and inspection. Generally, when visiting Moscow, the JCP

leaders have stopped over in Peking (and sometimes also in Pyongyang) or gone there before returning to Japan. As the above, no doubt incomplete, list of JCP missions shows, all top leaders of the Japanese Communist Party have had a chance to get acquainted with the views of both the Chinese Communist and the Soviet leadership.

18. An *Akahata* delegation toured China during November and December, 1961, for example, and was received by Mao and Chou En-lai. A few months later, in May, 1962, the Soviet Union balanced the situation by hosting another *Akahata* delegation on the occasion of the fiftieth anniversary of *Pravda*. They were received by Mao and Chou's counterparts, Khrushchev and Mikoyan.

19. Actually, the Chinese Politburo and Soviet Presidium members did not visit Japan because the Japanese Government refused to issue entry visas to prominent foreign Communists. Mikoyan, during the same year, was allowed to visit Japan, however, since he came as a government and not as a Party official.

20. *Jen-min Jih-pao*, March 30, 1962.

21. See *Pravda*, March 30, 1962, and *Izvestia*, March 29 and 30, 1962. The same issue of *Pravda* carried a five-column article by Nozaka.

22. The inner-Party debate apparently continued to rage right up to the eve of the Party Congress. The following incident illustrates the situation: In June, 1961, *Gekkan Gakushu* (*Monthly Learning*), a JCP publication, carried a number of ideological definitions of such key terms as "monopoly capitalism" and "imperialism." On June 29, 1961, *Akahata* in a short notice announced that the definitions were in error and would soon be corrected; meanwhile, they should be considered invalid. On July 14, the "correct definitions" were published by *Akahata*. A study of the differences between the two versions shows two views which, within the limits of a common Marxist framework, clearly represent different interpretations of the Japanese situation. Thus the "incorrect" version contains no reference to the important role ("correct" version) of "American imperialism" and declares the time ripe for a transition to socialism. But what is especially interesting about this incident is its timing. Only two days before the notice of correction appeared in *Akahata*, Shiga had returned from lengthy discussions in Peking. Had he also brought back the conviction that the "strike America first" formula had to be pushed through even at the risk of a Party schism?

23. Kasuga held the post of Chairman of the Party Control Commission before he resigned on the eve of the Eighth Party Congress. He had been an organizer in the radical labor movement of the early 1920's prior to being selected by the Japanese Communists to study in the U.S.S.R. He attended the KUTV (Communist University of the Toilers of the East) in Moscow, graduating under the name Kawamura in 1926. Arrested after his return to Japan, he spent, except for a very brief interlude, the entire prewar and wartime period in prison.

24. Increased Japanese interest in Togliatti and his theories is also reflected in the decision of a major Communist publishing firm, in 1962, to issue a Japanese-language edition of the Italian Party's history.

25. It is rather ironical that in June, 1950, Kasuga criticized the JCP leadership and especially Nozaka for its "right opportunism," its "parliamentarianism," and its emphasis on a peaceful road to revolution, pointing out that the Cominform had correctly called the JCP's attention to the dangers of creating

a hotbed for Titoism. See *Nihon Kyosanto 50-nenmondai shiryo-shu* (A Collection of Documents on the So-Called 1950 Problem of the JCP) (Tokyo: Shin Nihon Shuppansha, 1957), I, 132–39.

26. For the JCP side of the story, see especially the many pertinent articles that appeared in *Zen'ei* during 1961, 1962 and 1963; the numerous articles, editorials, and Party resolutions published during the same period in *Akahata*; *Nihon Kyosanto Ketsugi Kettei-shu* (Collection of Resolutions and Decisions of the Japanese Communist Party) (Tokyo: Central Committee of the JCP, 1961 and 1963), VII and VIII; and Hakamada's article in the Tokyo monthly *Bungei Shunju* (*Literary Chronicles*) of October, 1961. For the other side of the controversy in its early phase, see Kasuga's article in *Bungei Shunju* of September, 1961, and several articles by Sato Noboru, especially those in the Tokyo monthlies *Sekai* (*World*) of February, 1961, and January, 1962, and *Chuo Koron* (*Central Review*) of August, 1961.

27. This is one of the accusations Nozaka leveled against Kasuga in a report ("Upon Returning from the Soviet Union") that appeared in *Akahata* of November 22, 1961. Nozaka's reaction was to reject Kasuga's "formalistic" attempts at imitating the Soviet Union (Kasuga liked the relatively liberal position reflected in the Soviet Party regulations) as "impossible" since "in the first place, objective conditions are entirely different."

28. Nozaka only obliquely referred to the Albanian issue by calling attention to the Moscow Declaration of 1957 and the Moscow Statement of 1960 and their provisions for the settlement of intra-Party conflicts. He softened his implied criticism of Khrushchev by reaffirming the everlasting friendship linking the Japanese and Soviet peoples. It is perhaps significant of the JCP's relationship to Moscow that in recent years it has signed joint statements with the Chinese, Indonesian, and other Communist parties in Asia, but not, it seems, with the CPSU.

29. *Akahata*, December 23, 1961.

30. Enver Hoxha's views appeared in a January, 1962, special Albania issue (No. 140) of the Tokyo publication *Sekai Seiji Shiryo* (*Materials on World Politics*), published three times a month by the JCP to acquaint Communists in Japan with important foreign Communist documentation. The same issue contained pertinent Soviet documents, as well as materials from a variety of Communist parties, including those of Indonesia, Australia, France, Italy, Poland, Bulgaria, Czechoslovakia, and Rumania.

31. According to *Jimmin Chugoku* (*People's China*), a periodical edited in Peking for the Japanese reader, the translation and editing of Mao's work was a major enterprise undertaken jointly by the Japanese and Chinese Communist parties. When one pieces together the available information, the following picture emerges. The basic translation was made in Tokyo and sent to Peking for review. The corrected translation was then returned to Japan for further study and improvement, then again returned to Peking for further study. Finally, an official Japanese Communist delegation of Central Committee level went to Peking to discuss with its Chinese counterparts the finer points of the draft. The result was taken back to Tokyo for publication. (A comparison of the Chinese, English, and Japanese versions of the fourth volume of Mao's work indicates that the only textual differences are found in the explanatory notes, which were prepared separately for each edition and tailored to the needs of the respective readers. Examination of these notes suggests that apart from certain omissions and additions, no doubt owing to the different nature of

the languages and the different degree of familiarity with terminology and place names, a number of notes in the Chinese and English editions appear to have been revised to minimize any anti-Japanese implications in the original wording.) The significance of the fourth volume in Chinese eyes is suggested by a discussion of the work in the Chinese Communist periodical *Shih-chieh Chih-shih* (*World Knowledge*) of November 20, 1960, which states: "*The Selected Works of Mao Tse-tung*, Volume IV, reflects and summarizes that Marxism-Leninism that has guided the great revolution of the Chinese people to national victory. . . . The entire volume is a summary of the experiences of the victory of the Chinese people's revolution against imperialism and against American imperialism in particular." An article in the June, 1962, issue of *Zen'ei* in turn takes up the same theme and, alluding to Mao's well-known formula "Despise the enemy strategically, but respect him tactically," suggests that this formula, like the entire volume, is full of important lessons for the Japanese Communist Party in its struggle for seizure of power.

32. *Akahata*, March 31, 1962, carried Hoxha's congratulatory message.

33. See *Akahata*, January 11, 1963. Similar remarks are found in all major JCP utterances regarding the Sino-Soviet conflict and also in the authoritative resolution of the Fifth Central Committee Plenum of February 15, 1963.

34. *Ibid.*, December 15, 1962.

35. *Ibid.*, November 24, 1962.

36. *Ibid.*, February 19, 1963.

37. On the other hand, the JCP decided toward the end of 1962 to "censor" the Prague edition of the *World Marxist Review*. It has since been printing a Japanese-language version, which is no longer a complete translation of the original but omits articles that are considered to be "controversial" (i.e., that might give offense to Peking). Such articles are often published later on in the Party's *Sekai Seiji Shiryo*, a periodical that is read only by the Party elite or by the scholarly inclined.

38. The only conspicuous exception was an article by Ide Jun'ichiro, which appeared in *Akahata*, November 8, 1962. The author, a member of the editorial committee of another JCP publication, vigorously attacked "Tito and his ilk." It is interesting that the official Peking daily, *Jen-min Jih-pao*, reprinted the article in its issue of May 9, 1963 (half a year later!), apparently to remind the vacillating JCP of its antirevisionist duties.

39. Within the Asian region, the JCP appears to be developing particularly close ties with the Indonesian Communist Party (PKI). This is, among other indications, evident from the increasingly frequent publication of PKI resolutions and related materials in the Japanese Communist press and from the coming and going of Communists between the two countries. Secretary-General Aidit, for example, came to Japan in September, 1961, and visited JCP headquarters. (This, incidentally, was also the month in which the JCP published and recommended for study the record of the PKI Sixth Congress.) In April, 1962, Presidium-member Kurahara Korehito addressed the PKI Congress and remained in Indonesia for a full month. Before returning to Japan, he signed, on May 23, 1962, a joint statement with Aidit which Japanese Communist literature shortly thereafter called "a powerful weapon." On May 31, 1963, Chairman Aidit gave a dinner in Djakarta for JCP Presidium member Kikunami Katsumi, who had arrived for the celebration of the forty-third anniversary of the PKI. In the JCP message read on that occasion, there was much emphasis on the PKI's struggle for the unity of the Communist movement,

and the closing words were: "Long live the monolithic unity of the international Communist movement." Three principal reasons probably account for the growing JCP affinity for the PKI: (1) respect for the PKI's performance in building within a few years the non-Communist world's largest and most influential Communist Party ("Our Party learned from the experiences of the PKI," *Akahata* proclaimed); (2) sympathy with the PKI's announced and pronounced efforts to adapt Communism to local conditions; and (3) misgivings about Khrushchev's handling of the Albanian issue and both Parties' desire to re-establish Soviet-Chinese unity. These points are confirmed by the tenor of the previously mentioned joint statement of the two parties. It should also be noted that the JCP was of some help to the PKI in maintaining pressure on the Japanese Government to support Indonesia's claims to West Irian. There exists also an important parallelism between the political use, at home, that JCP can make of claims to American-occupied Okinawa and the political use the PKI made of the West Irian issue. These tactics tend to weaken the position of the Western enemy and create embarrassment for its ally Japan.

Otherwise, only the Korean Party appears to have especially close ties with the JCP. This is evidenced by the frequent visits of JCP leaders to Pyongyang; the recent publication of Kim Il-sung's works in Japanese and under JCP sponsorship; and the publication in *Akahata* of important North Korean policy statements such as the *Nodong Sinmun* editorial of January 30, 1963, on the international Communist movement. The reasons are partly historical, Korea having long been part of the Japanese Empire, so that in prewar times there was considerable cooperation between the two movements. Moreover, the presence in Japan of half a million largely underprivileged Koreans is helpful to the JCP. So is North Korea, as a bridge for illegal contacts with the continent. And both parties have a vested interest in creating trouble for the United States. The Indian Communist Party, on the other hand, seems as yet remote when viewed from JCP headquarters in Tokyo. The political contexts are radically different. In India, it is a matter of displacing a government (and a ruling party) that is neutralist, progressive, and to a degree socialist. It is also a country that has a popular leader, borders on China, and is involved in conflict with its Chinese neighbor. None of this applies to Japan, where the government is solidly conservative, where the Socialists make up the opposition, and where the Communists must first succeed in breaking the hold of the Socialists over the antigovernment elements or somehow infiltrate the competitor. The gradual broadening of the JCP's horizon beyond Moscow and Peking extends also to contacts with the European Communist parties. Quasi-permanent JCP representatives or observers are stationed in Europe, and European Communist materials are studied for ideological and tactical guidance. This is evidenced in the increased geographic spread of translations published by the JCP. In July, 1961, for example, a volume on *Prospects for Revolution in Japan and the International Communist Movement*, issued by the JCP, contained, in addition to Moscow and Peking documents, East German and Czechoslovakian theses which were recommended to the reader for their significance with regard to the problem of revolutionary stages.

40. Indicative of the trend is an article in the July, 1962, issue of *Zen'ei*. The article, prompted by the publication of official statements by Secretary-General Miyamoto Kenji, places heavy emphasis on the "creative aspect" of Japanese Communist strategy—for instance, calling the new Japanese Com-

munist formula for revolution "a new proposition, rare in the history of Marxism-Leninism."

41. This list, published in *Akahata*, May 7, 1962, was compiled in connection with the decision of the 1961 Party Congress to establish a Central Party School for ideological training. The school was opened in February, 1962, and continues in operation. *Akahata* reports that local Party schools are also in the process of being established. The importance of the reading list is underlined by the fact that the Party republished it several months later in *Akahata* to impress upon its members its significance.

4. The Communist Party of India: Sino-Soviet Battleground

by HARRY GELMAN

The repeated efforts of the Soviet and Chinese Communist parties to pressure other parties in the world Communist movement into committing themselves in the struggle against the fraternal antagonist have fostered evident dissension, recrimination, and factional struggle in the ranks of many Communist parties, but nowhere more than in the Communist Party of India (CPI). As a result of numerous factors—geography, the importance of India, and the Indian Party's own history—the CPI was destined to become a sort of borderline region in the Communist internecine conflict, an arena where the opposing influences of the CPSU and the CCP have clashed more openly and on more equal terms than in almost any other Communist Party of comparable importance.

The Indian Party has occupied a borderline position in another sense as well. Especially since the CPSU's Twenty-second Congress, the response of the world's Communist parties to the Soviet call for support against its adversaries has shown a striking geographic pattern: some form of public backing for Moscow—through denunciations of Tirana and, in many cases, of Peking as well—has been forthcoming from nearly all the Communist parties of Europe, the Western Hemisphere, North Africa, and the Middle East, while nearly all the Far Eastern parties have refused to render such support, their reactions ranging from polite criticisms of Khrushchev's attack on Hoxha to explicit endorsement of Chinese policy positions.[1] Between the broadly pro-CPSU Middle Eastern parties and the Far Eastern Communist parties generally sympathetic to the CCP lies India, where the Party—long under Soviet tutelage—now has a large and vociferous anti-CPSU and pro-Chinese minority which until very recently controlled several of the provincial Party organizations and was also well represented in the Party center.

This minority cannot be purged without a major split in the Party; such a schism has now become a serious possibility.

FACTORS IN THE DECAY OF CPI DISCIPLINE

The present situation in the CPI has come about as a result of forces that have been at work within the Party for over a decade, some of them independent of the Sino-Soviet conflict. They include the growth of unprecedented factionalism and lack of discipline, with a corollary weakening of the authority of the Party center at the hands of defiant provincial Party committees; the emergence of incompatible views among the rival factions on the line to be taken toward Nehru's "national bourgeois" government; the declining authority of the CPSU and the growing prestige of the CCP in the eyes of many Indian Communists; and finally, the steady polarization of the Party into leftist and rightist factions divided along pro-Chinese and pro-Soviet lines.

This process received its initial impetus during the internal CPI battles, between 1947 and 1951, over the methods of struggle the Party should follow, the immediate goals it should pursue, and the classes it should admit into its alliance. At that time, the left-faction leader, B. T. Ranadive, took control of the CPI as General Secretary and, in conformity with what he thought was CPSU policy, led the Party in the application of violent insurrectionary tactics against the Nehru government. Modeling his efforts on the Russian Revolution, Ranadive gave primary emphasis to the struggle in the cities rather than in the countryside; and he called for a one-stage revolution to overthrow both the imperialist enemy and all sections of the Indian bourgeoisie simultaneously and bring about immediate Communist Party rule in India. Ranadive's tactics failed dismally and were disastrous for the Party. When opposition to him rose throughout the CPI, he attempted to suppress it ruthlessly, increasing the chaos within the organization.

The leaders of the Andhra provincial Party committee then came forward and attacked Ranadive's line; citing a relatively successful peasant revolt that had been going on for some time in the Telengana district of south India, they called for the Party to abandon insurrection in the cities and to rely instead upon armed struggle in the countryside. They also demanded that the CPI ally itself for this purpose with antifeudal sections of the well-to-do peasantry, as well as with anti-imperialist sections of the urban bourgeoisie (the "national bourgeoisie"). Thus they wished the Party to aim at a two-stage revolution in which efforts would be aimed first at ousting from power what were regarded to be the agents of imperialism and feudalism, and only later at securing firm Communist control of the Indian Government. The Andhra leaders explicitly stated that the Chinese Revolution, rather than the Russian Revolution, was their model, and they fervently hailed Mao Tse-tung as their inspiration and guide.[2]

Ranadive responded with public attacks not only upon the Andhra leadership, but also upon Mao; he attempted to portray Mao's advocacy of an alliance with the national bourgeoisie under Communist leadership—his "New Democracy" line—as an anti-Marxist betrayal of the revolution and an attempt to restore capitalism.[3] Eventually, however, the CPSU accepted the desirability of alliance with the national bourgeoisie and the two-stage revolution, and Ranadive fell from power in the CPI, to be replaced by the Andhra leadership. The Andhra leaders publicly apologized to Mao for Ranadive's attacks[4] and attempted to apply the line they had advocated. Peasant revolt, however, proved no more successful than urban insurrection, and armed struggle was finally shelved entirely, with the Andhra group in turn replaced in 1951 by a new leadership headed by Ajoy Ghosh as General Secretary.

Two lasting results flowed from these events. First, although what was then thought of in the CPI as the "Chinese path" (involving a peasant army, guerrilla warfare, the bypassing of cities and avoidance of urban insurrection, establishment of a secure base area protected from encirclement, and formation of a proletarian alliance with the peasantry and national bourgeoisie) was found to be no more applicable to India than what was then depicted as the "Soviet path" (a one-stage, proletarian, urban revolution in alliance only with peasantry),[5] a significant degree of Chinese influence was nevertheless permanently implanted and legitimized within the CPI as a source of inspiration and guidance second only to that of the CPSU.[6] Secondly, the factionalism, blatant lack of discipline, and regional disregard for central authority that had grown during the struggle against Ranadive became permanent features of CPI life, to a degree seen in few if any other Communist parties. The authority of the central CPI machinery was, henceforth, so weakened in relation to the provincial Party organizations that never again could the central Party leadership attempt in the Bolshevik manner to impose an arbitrary, rigid line upon the often defiant provinces.

Thereafter, endemic factional strife persisted in the Party, nourished by a regional particularism that caused the CPI to partake more and more of one characteristic of many bourgeois parties in federal states such as India and the United States: a tendency of national leaders to depend upon a local base rather than their national position for their standing in the Party. This tendency was further encouraged by the linguistic and caste divisions peculiar to India, which also left their imprint on the Party. Credible CPI documents published by the Democratic Research Service of India testify that it became the practice for the opposing views of leftist and rightist factions to be disseminated by their respective Politburo and Central Committee champions within the provincial committees, where each leader had his followers, while the Politburo itself at times virtually ceased to meet.[7] With the roots of their political and Party strength in the provinces or in specialized fields of activity such as the trade unions, few of the Politburo members wished to, or did, devote continuous attention to the weak Party center. This indifference—and its corollary, the continued failure of the provincial organizations to keep the center informed of what was going on throughout the Party—came to be a more or less permanent feature of CPI life and was lamented by reports delivered to Central Committee meetings and Party Congresses in 1952, 1953, 1955, 1956,[8] and again in 1961.[9]

This fragmentation of Party authority was partly responsible for the CPI's recalcitrant reaction to the gradually softening Soviet attitude toward Nehru between 1951 and 1955. By slow degrees, the Indian Party was forced to follow the evolution of Soviet policy in agreeing first that there were some positive aspects to Nehru's generally undesirable foreign policy, then that Nehru's foreign policy was generally good but that his domestic policy was bad, and finally that there were favorable features of his domestic policy as well. The CPI had to be bludgeoned and cajoled into taking each painful step along this path, usually with a considerable time lag behind the development of Soviet policy. Each gradual modification of line toward Nehru was accomplished only over the strenuous objections of a large section of the Indian Party, which did not wish to see what it regarded as opportunities to advance the cause of Communism in India by opposing Nehru all along the line to be sacrificed for the sake of Soviet foreign-policy interests. Such CPI recalcitrance was reflected in the Party program adopted in 1951,[10] and then was strongly manifested at the CPI's Third Congress, at Madurai in December, 1953.[11] While efforts to secure a rightward accommodation of the CPI line to Soviet policy were led by General Secretary Ghosh, opposition became increasingly centered in three provincial Party organizations: those of West Bengal and the Punjab—which had long traditions as centers of Indian terrorism—as well as important sections of the Andhra Communist Party. Meanwhile, the moderation of Soviet hostility to Nehru—which had been begun cautiously three years before Stalin's death[12]—accelerated greatly once Stalin disappeared from the scene. In 1954 and 1955, Nehru exchanged visits with both the Soviet and Chinese leaders, and the U.S.S.R. began a program of economic assistance to India. Internal CPI opposition increased as the Soviet tone toward Nehru grew warmer.

Thus, in September, 1954, a CPI left-faction coalition from various provinces actually succeeded in getting a Central Committee plenum to condemn the Party Politburo for having authorized publication of an article two months before praising the Nehru government with excessive warmth upon the occasion of Chou En-lai's visit to India. A later Party document commented that after the Central Committee had registered its rebuke, "even this criticism . . . was not considered enough by certain provincial committees who thought that the Politburo had not been dealt with adequately."[13]

However, when the Cominform organ published an article a month later strongly implying support for Nehru's foreign policy,[14] the CPI Politburo—"divided and demoralized" by its chastisement—was said to have been thrown into a "state of panic," and in November, 1954, it recommended to an emergency Central Committee meeting explicit rejection of the Cominform line.[15] Eventually, however, the Central Committee adopted a resolution postponing judgment on the issue, declaring that "more time and thought" were required to resolve the "important differences" within the Central Committee.[16]

Throughout 1955, the U.S.S.R. and Communist China continued to develop the soft line toward Nehru. An editorial in *Pravda* on January 26, 1955, India's Republic Day, not only praised the foreign policy of "the outstanding statesman Jawaharlal Nehru" but went on to list and praise the domestic accomplishments of the Nehru government in the fields of agriculture, consumer-goods production, education, and public health. To the discomfiture of the Andhra Communist Party, these statements were used effectively in Congress Party propaganda against the CPI in an important Andhra election campaign the following month. In April, the Bandung Conference of Asian and African leaders was held, and Chou En-lai showed the Asian bourgeoisie a disarmingly moderate image of

Chinese Communism. At about the same time, a tentative contract was signed, based on an earlier offer of Soviet aid, for construction of a large steel mill in India. In May, an editorial in the CPSU journal *Kommunist* gave the first indication of a coming change in the previously hostile Soviet appraisal of Gandhi. In June, Nehru paid an extended visit to the Soviet Union, and in November, Khrushchev and Bulganin visited India.

While these events intensified the turmoil within the Indian Party,[17] their ultimate effect was to shift the balance of forces within the CPI so as to force a relaxation of its hostile posture toward Nehru, as well as eventual public avowal of what in practice had already become primary reliance on parliamentary elections to advance the Party's fortunes. These changes in the Party's stance were formalized, after the CPSU's Twentieth Congress, in successive decisions of CPI Congresses in 1956 and 1958. However, the minority leftist faction of the Party—now again led by Ranadive—continued to oppose the soft line toward Nehru and the Indian "national bourgoisie" and to deplore the debilitating effects upon the Party's revolutionary fervor of what it regarded as excessive reliance upon "parliamentary tactics." This long-standing opposition to the CPI's adjustment to Soviet policy was later to assume major importance in connection with the events of 1959 and 1960.

EFFECTS OF THE CPSU'S TWENTIETH CONGRESS

Meanwhile, the Twentieth Congress of the CPSU, in February, 1956, and the events flowing from it, administered a series of fundamental shocks to the CPI, with results that were to affect greatly the relationship of the Indian Party to Moscow and to Peking down to the present day. The first and most important of these shocks was that of de-Stalinization, which, on the one hand, greatly intensified the spirit of cynicism, the internal disorganization, and the lack of personal discipline already widespread because of the Party's previous history, and, on the other hand, greatly accelerated the decline of the authority and prestige of the CPSU, which had already begun with the death of Stalin.[18] Moreover, de-Stalinization also eventually enhanced the appeal of the CCP to those sections of the Indian Party sympathetic to Peking's viewpoint. De-Stalinization was followed by the Soviet suppression of the Hungarian revolution and the subsequent execution of Nagy, which weakened the CPSU's position among the more moderate sections of the Indian Party, who were its natural supporters.[19] A third difficulty was, meanwhile, occasioned by the Twentieth Congress line on the possibility of a peaceful transition to socialism. A particular storm was aroused by the very extreme interpretation of that line, as applied to India, provided in the summer of 1956 by an authoritative Soviet article (by Modeste Rubinstein) in the journal *New Times*, which implied that Nehru, and not the CPI, would lead India into the socialist system.[20] This essentially revisionist viewpoint was bitterly challenged in public by General Secretary Ghosh,[21] and the CPSU soon retreated to a more orthodox position—which, however, still favored qualified CPI support for Nehru and CPI reliance primarily upon parliamentary tactics.

Although it is difficult to fix the precise point at which Chinese and Soviet policy toward the bourgeoisie of India and certain other Asian countries first began to part company, there is some evidence to suggest that it may have been as early as the fall of 1956, as a result of what the Chinese may have seen as a Soviet attempt after the Twentieth Congress to carry the agreed-upon moderate line toward the national bourgeoisie to intolerable lengths. In the above-mentioned *New Times* article, Rubinstein had declared that although India's "advance along the socialist path" under Nehru's leadership would be slower than and would differ in many respects from that of "say, China," only dogmatists would object to these peculiarities, which represented one of the "multiplicity of forms of socialist development." Shortly thereafter, on September 17, 1956, Anastas Mikoyan addressed the Eighth Congress of the CCP in Peking. He paid warm tribute to the Chinese Party and to "the distinguished Marxist-Leninist Mao Tse-tung," praising his "major contribution to Marxist-Leninist theory"; and he declared that the Chinese had found "their own distinctive new forms and methods of building socialism." The major Marxist contribution and distinctive new form that Mikoyan actually cited, however, was the Chinese alliance with the national bourgeoisie and the Chinese effort to move toward socialism through state capitalism. Later in his speech, Mikoyan dealt at length with Communist policy toward the underdeveloped countries and their national bourgeois rulers; he quoted Lenin on the "new transitional forms and ways" these countries were seeking "to avoid the torments of capitalism," and he indicated in polemical language what those forms should be. Mikoyan declared that "we must be able to see" the difference between state capitalism in India and state capitalism in the United States. He held that "Marxists cannot but regard positively" the growth of state capitalism in the newly independent countries; he suggested that this was their "new transitional form" to avoid capitalism; and he argued that this was a factor promoting growing sympathy for "socialist ideas and slogans" in such countries.[22]

In short, the evidence suggests that Mikoyan praised the Chinese use of state capitalism and their alliance with the national bourgeoisie for the building of socialism under Communist control in China as polemical justification for a sanguine Soviet attitude toward the growth of state capitalism in underdeveloped Asian countries where the national bourgeoisie and not the Communist Party was still in control. If this interpretation is correct, the Chinese may already have been objecting at this time to a distortion of their doctrine and experience to bolster policies they could not endorse.[23] To the present day, Soviet journals (unlike those in Communist China) have continued to insist upon the "progressive" role of state capitalism in underdeveloped countries such as India; and at least until the Sino-Soviet polemics of 1960 forced Moscow to harden its line somewhat, to seek to retain wide support in the world Communist movement, many Soviet statements continued to suggest ambiguously that the "socialist" inclinations of the national bourgeoisie of Asian countries—while certainly not Marxist —nevertheless should be relied upon somehow to facilitate the gradual slide of these countries into the Communist orbit.[24] By 1959 and 1960, Chinese articles, on the other hand, were denouncing people who thought that under the leadership of the bourgeoisie one could "march into the period of socialism by way of state capitalism."[25]

If Chinese doubts on this aspect of Soviet policy did begin to arise as early as the fall of 1956, they did not, however, immediately affect the Indian Communist Party. Forces within the CPI favoring parliamentary tactics and a moderate approach to Nehru received a major windfall in April, 1957, when the Communist Party was victorious in elections in Kerala and proceeded to form a government in that state—the first time in the history of the world Communist movement that a Communist Party had achieved even this limited degree of power through a parliamentary election. This event caused a wide stir in the Communist movement, as the first apparent confirmation of the CPSU's Twentieth Congress dictum on the peaceful transition to power; and it helped to keep the controlling weight of opinion within the CPI behind the moderates for the next three years. Subsequently, the CPI moved from the April, 1956, line of the Palghat (Fourth) Party Congress (where the Party cautiously acknowledged the possibility of peaceful transition to socialism through parliamentary means backed by mass movements), to the April, 1958, line of the Amritsar (Fifth) Party Congress (which exuded confidence that the parliamentary take-over in Kerala could be repeated in other Indian states and eventually even in the Centre).

Ranadive and the Party militants, however, found themselves unpleasantly restricted by the existence of the Kerala Ministry, since the CPI could not now agitate any issue that might undermine the Kerala government. The Party could not, for example, demand nationalization of industries without compensation, expropriation of foreign assets, or other steps that the Kerala regime itself was unwilling to take because of a desire to create an impression of restraint and to avoid giving New Delhi justification for pushing it out of office.

The CPI leftist faction saw its objections confirmed as the Kerala government came into increasing difficulties in the fall of 1958, partly as the result of its own imprudent actions (such as the use of its police to fire on hostile demonstrators) and partly as the result of a continuing campaign that the Congress Party and its Kerala allies were waging to unseat the Communists. This campaign appears to have occasioned a temporary shift in emphasis in the Soviet line toward Nehru. Although the central Soviet press maintained a studied silence on the Kerala events, one obscure Moscow publication broke this silence in early October to run an "Observer" editorial discussing the campaign of "provocations" against the Kerala regime; the editorial indicated a Soviet conviction that the CPI should not resign under this pressure.[26] Two months later, an article in *World Marxist Review* by Pavel Yudin, the Soviet Ambassador to the C.P.R., took Nehru to task for statements he had recently published attacking the Communists as devotees of violence. Yudin ridiculed Nehru's notion of "socialism" and made it clear that the Indian bourgeoisie would be responsible for any Communist resort to violence if it refused to allow power to pass peacefully into Communist hands. While this article may have been partly intended to put pressure on the Nehru government to prevent it from swinging further toward the West, its primary design seems to have been to attempt to induce Nehru not to dismiss the Kerala Ministry, while informing the CPI that it was permitted to build up mass agitation to bolster its bargaining position with respect to the Nehru government. At the same time, Yudin intimated that the CPI should continue to support "progressive" policies of Nehru against "imperialist" and "feudalist" forces, and thus indicated that no permanent change in line was intended.[27]

1959: TIBETAN REVOLT AND BORDER DISPUTE

That the Soviet shift in emphasis was indeed only temporary was demonstrated a month later at the CPSU's Twenty-first Congress, where Khrushchev hailed Nehru and his government in connection with the completion of the Bhilai steel plant and Mukhitdinov gave the "progressive forces of India"—the Communist Party—only secondary credit for India's economic and foreign policy achievements, giving primary credit to "the farsighted policy of the outstanding statesman of the East, Prime Minister Jawaharlal Nehru."[28] In January, 1959, the CPSU appears to have decided to bear with this leader of the Indian national bourgeoisie for a considerable distance, regardless of the outcome in Kerala; this decision was soon reflected in the Soviet attitude displayed toward New Delhi during the Tibetan revolt, and later during the Sino-Indian border controversy. It is possible that Moscow's softening of the line on Nehru was connected with the decision of the Nagpur meeting of the Indian Congress Party in January, when the left wing of the party backed by Nehru pushed through a strongly worded resolution supporting land reform. It also seems possible, however, that the decision to relax pressure on Nehru was in some way related to a broader CPSU decision taken at this time to pursue more actively the "peaceful coexistence" strategy against the Western world. The first concrete manifestation of such a broad decision was Mikoyan's self-invited exploratory trip to the United States in early January, and the second was Khrushchev's enunciation, at the end of that month, of the Twenty-first Congress thesis that wars, besides not being inevitable, could even be eliminated from the life of society while capitalism remains.

In 1959, for the first time, the CPI became gravely affected by the growing differences between the Soviet and Chinese postures toward the "imperialist" world, their attitudes toward the ruling national bourgeoisie of underdeveloped countries, and their views on the most appropriate means of Communist assumption of power. The gap between the CPSU and the CCP suddenly widened, partly as a result of events over which neither Party had control—for example, the Tibetan revolt, Nehru's decision to oust the Communist government in Kerala, Washington's decision to invite Khrushchev to the United States. It was also, however, the result of a conscious turning to the right by the CPSU and to the left by the CCP. In the fall of 1959, Khrushchev not only took a publicly neutral posture toward the Sino-Indian border dispute (to the apparent bitter resentment of Peking), but in the aftermath of his visit to the United States, adopted the softest line toward the West generally he was ever to voice publicly, while Peking grew increasingly shrill in its warnings against Western treachery and in contradiction of the Soviet line. Meanwhile, at home the CPI found itself once again subjected to sharply conflicting influences from Moscow and Peking, largely flowing from the divergent foreign policy interests of the two Communist powers. These conflicting influences were not expressed, as in 1948, in opposing "models" of armed revolution (urban insurrection versus peasant guerrilla warfare), but now rather through opposing estimates of the usefulness of Nehru's bourgeois government, opposing advice on what line to take toward that government and toward the Indian national bourgeoisie generally, and opposing attitudes on the relative importance to be assigned to parliamentary elections as instruments for Communist advance. It was against the background of these increasingly divergent Soviet and Chinese policies that the rightist and leftist factions of the CPI eventually began to identify themselves publicly with the lines associated with Moscow or Peking. Thus it was that Ranadive, the apostle of orthodoxy and militancy who had denounced Mao as heretical and revisionist, at last found himself espousing Mao's militant cause against a revisionist CPSU.

Just as the surfacing of the Sino-Indian border dispute in the fall of 1959 had its origin in events connected with the Tibetan revolt in the spring, so also the emergence of public Sino-Soviet differences in line over the border issue in the fall was preceded by more subtle differences over the Tibetan issue months before. In the beginning, this was not so: The two bloc partners made an apparently coordinated initial announcement of the Tibetan revolt on March 28, and twice in early April Moscow repeated in radio commentaries Peking's claims that Kalimpong, in northern West Bengal, had been used as a base for the Tibetan rebels, despite Nehru's public denial of this charge. Subsequently, however, the U.S.S.R. suppressed from its public coverage all such charges against India and excised hostile references to India from reports on C.P.R. articles and speeches carried in Soviet media. Moscow limited blame for the uprising to Tibetan "reactionaries," Western "imperialism," and Chiang K'ai-shek. Communist China, on the other hand, continued to repeat its statements about Kalimpong, together with public attacks against Indian "reactionaries" and "expansionists" for their sympathy with and alleged aid to the rebels. By late April, after strong criticism of the C.P.R. had been voiced by the Indian press and in the Indian Parliament, the Chinese Communists expanded their attacks into a concerted mass campaign in which the Indian Government was repeatedly implicated in the revolt and in the "abduction" of the Dalai Lama. Personal denunciations of Nehru at nationwide mass meetings in early May culminated in a May 6 *Jen-min Jih-pao* editorial article reproving Nehru's attitude toward Tibet, renewing charges of Indian interference there, and suggesting that Nehru, while often differing with the "imperialists," nevertheless was strongly influenced in his policies at times by the Indian "big bourgeoisie" tied to imperialism.

The CPI throughout this period adopted a public attitude strongly defending Communist China, but not usually going beyond the limits of the Soviet treatment of Nehru. On April 5—when the Soviet line blacking out all references to Kalimpong had not yet been clearly established—the weekly CPI organ *New Age* carried an article urging an investigation of activities in this border town, as well as a CPI Secretariat resolution suggesting the same point. After this—in line with the Soviet example—charges about Kalimpong are not known to have been made in CPI media, but Indian Party organs and spokesmen continued cautiously to defend Peking. General Secretary Ghosh, in a *New Age* article on May 10, complained that some of Nehru's statements were "heavily biased in favor of the rebels" and denied that all of India's conduct during the rebellion had been unimpeachable or that "all the blame lies with the Chinese." Along with this rather qualified justification of the C.P.R., Ghosh expressed pleasure that Nehru had "indignantly rejected" the crude attempts of the "imperialists" to change India's independent foreign policy. Ghosh showed great defensiveness over Nehru's reaction to the Chinese charge of "expansionism," professing to believe that this charge had not been intended against Nehru or the Indian Government, but only against "certain reactionary circles in India." A resolution reportedly passed by the CPI during the Sino-Soviet polemic the following year was alleged to have protested against the unwisdom of the Chinese intimations at this time that the Indian Government was "expansionist" and against the harm this brought to the Communist cause in India.[29]

The Indian Government's removal of the Communist Kerala regime came in midsummer, between the Sino-Indian controversy over the Tibetan revolt in the spring of 1959 and the outbreak of the border conflict in the fall. The CPI reacted at the time to this long-expected event with comparative restraint, attempting to capitalize on it by appealing in the role of martyr to "all democratic forces including Congressmen" to unite to defeat the threat to democracy said to have been demonstrated.[30] One result of the Kerala dismissal, however, was to strengthen the hand of the CPI leftist faction in its contention that the Amritsar line—with its implied confidence that the Party could win power through parliamentary elections—was mistaken; the resultant change in the climate of CPI opinion was demonstrated at the Sixth Party Congress, in 1961.

It is also likely that the Kerala events confirmed the Chinese Communist leadership in the estimate it had publicly expressed in May that Nehru was tending to make increasing concessions to the Indian "big bourgeoisie" and to Western "imperialism" and that this estimate in turn became one of the factors motivating the rigid C.P.R. stand as the border dispute developed. On August 28, Prime Minister Nehru publicly affirmed in the Lok Sabha charges that the C.P.R. had infringed on Indian territory in both Ladakh and the Northeast Frontier Agency, thereby inflaming Indian public opinion. Two days later, the CPI Central Secretariat issued the first in what was to be a long and varied series of statements on this matter, a vague declaration glossing over the question of border violations, holding (as the Chinese were to do) that the entire border has never been defined, making no mention of the McMahon Line, and urgently calling for negotiations. The CPI subsequently came under wide public attack as a result of its failure in this statement to take a clear-cut stand supporting the Indian Government position. Meanwhile, on September 3, a Chinese Communist note to New Delhi accused India of "aggression" along the border and demanded withdrawal of Indian troops from the disputed areas. Five days later, on September 8, Chou En-lai dispatched another letter to Nehru, professing willingness to have the border dispute subjected to negotiations, but making no specific proposal for a meeting with Nehru. Chou reiterated all Chinese claims to disputed territory and specifically rejected the validity of the McMahon Line in the east. He also charged that Indian troops were guilty of "armed attacks" on Chinese frontier outposts.

These Chinese Communist statements greatly increased the difficulties of the CPI and intensified the isolation in which it found itself. On September 8—the same day that Chou sent his letter to Nehru—*Pravda* revealed that Ajoy Ghosh was now in the Soviet Union. On the next day, the Soviet Government issued its celebrated special Tass announcement deploring the clashes on the Sino-Indian border, urging a negotiated settlement, and taking a conspicuously neutral stand on the merits of the conflicting claims.[31] It seems likely that this announcement was decided on following consultations between Ghosh and the Soviet leaders and that it was finally triggered by the unyielding stand taken by Chou in his September 8 letter.[32] The Soviet statement was obviously intended to dissociate the U.S.S.R. from the Chinese position in the minds of the Indian Government and public and simultaneously to attempt to relieve the pressure on the CPI; it was reportedly defended on these grounds in an unpublished CPI resolution the following year.[33] It is evident from subsequent CCP conduct that Communist China regarded the Soviet action as a betrayal of an obligation to support another bloc Party for the sake of further unprincipled conciliation of the Indian bourgeoisie. This event undoubtedly added to the already strong Chinese objections to the line now being taken by the CPSU toward the West in general and contributed to the eventual Chinese decision to launch an open world-wide offensive against that line in April, 1960.

In late September, the CPI Central Executive Committee met and eventually issued a lengthy resolution affirming the Party's conviction that "socialist" China could never commit aggression and stating that acceptance of neither the McMahon Line nor the line shown on Chinese maps should be made a precondition for Sino-Indian negotiations. This second CPI statement aroused a great uproar within India and was widely denounced as virtually treasonable. This reaction from all sections of the non-Communist public was to place severe pressure upon those CPI provincial organizations heavily dependent on electoral alliances with other parties; as a result of the indiscipline long prevalent in the CPI, rightist-inclined leaders of certain provincial organizations—such as those of Maharashtra and Kerala—were to succumb to this pressure and oppose the central Party line. Public statements urging support for the Indian Government position were made by such leaders as former Kerala Chief Minister E. M. S. Namboodiripad, Maharashtra Party First Secretary S. G. Sardesai, and CPI Central Secretariat member and trade-union leader S. A. Dange. Dange, Sardesai, and the Maharashtra organization were later publicly rebuked for this by the CPI National Council.[34]

Against the background of this Party discord, General Secretary Ghosh led a CPI delegation to the celebration of the C.P.R. tenth anniversary in early October, where he heard Khrushchev publicly warn the Chinese Communists against efforts to "test the stability of the capitalist system by force" and presumably attempt to dissuade the CCP both from its opposition to the peaceful coexistence line and from its rigid posture toward Nehru. Credible Indian press reports later claimed that Ghosh also remonstrated with the Chinese leaders for the attitude they had shown during the Tibetan revolt and the border dispute, to no avail.[35] The CCP reaction was apparently typified by a journal article, published in the midst of these talks, which provided the most hostile Chinese public allusion to the Indian Government since the previous spring, suggesting that "the leaders of India" had shown themselves to be "double-faced neutralists" who "maintain such intricate relations with the imperialists as to lead them to manifest an expansionist ambition."[36]

Nevertheless, following his return home, Ghosh held a press conference on October 18 in which he emphasized at great length Mao's assurances to him of the Chinese People's Republic's peaceful intentions. These remarks by Ghosh were given extensive coverage in the *New Age* of October 25; in the meantime, however, a new clash had occurred between Chinese Communist troops and Indian border guards in the Ladakh area, Indians had been killed and Indian prisoners taken by the Chinese, and Communist China had officially protested that the clash was the result of provocation by the Indian side. Ghosh was thus placed in a ridiculous position, and he reacted sharply: On October 24, the Party Central Secretariat issued a public statement calling the Ladakh clash a "tragic event" and saying that there was "no justification whatever" for the firing. At subsequent meetings at Meerut in early and mid-November of the Party's larger policy-making bodies, the Central Executive Committee and the National Council, Ghosh seems to have supported some of the demands of the rightist faction led by Dange for concessions to Indian public sentiment. After intense resistance by the Party militants,[37] the Meerut meetings eventually produced a new compromise Party resolution which, while still ambivalent, was several degrees closer to the nationalist position. The Indian Government's claims for the McMahon Line were for the first time explicitly endorsed and the Chinese claims in the eastern sector rejected; but the western border in Ladakh was declared to be undetermined, and Chou En-lai's November 7 proposal for a meeting with Nehru was welcomed without mention of the prior condition of a Chinese troop pullback, which New Delhi placed upon such a meeting.[38]

While the CPI was moving in this direction, the CPSU was passing beyond neutrality to the expression of implicit criticism of Peking's position. In his October 31 speech to the Supreme Soviet (which marked a high-water point of the peaceful coexistence line toward the West), Khrushchev expressed deep regret over the Ladakh incident of the week before, said that "nothing can compensate" the relatives of the casualties, and appealed for friendly negotiations "to the mutual satisfaction of both sides." On November 15, *New Age* published an interview by its Moscow correspondent with Khrushchev at a Kremlin reception on the evening of November 7. The *New Age* correspondent quoted Khrushchev as calling the border dispute "a sad and stupid story," as arguing that the area in dispute was uninhabited and without strategic significance, and as citing the example of the U.S.S.R.'s past cession of territory to Iran as a model of amicable settlement of such differences. Khrushchev was said to have declared, "We gave up more than we gained; what were a few kilometers for a country like the Soviet Union?" While these statements, like the one on October 31, may have been intended to impress the Indian Government, in this case their immediate effect can only have been on the CPI rank and file. Similarly, on December 22, the Soviet press departed from its previous practice of delaying reportage on Indian notes to Communist China until they could be balanced by a C.P.R. reply; now Moscow promptly reported Nehru's letter to Chou of December 21, reiterating Nehru's preconditions for a meeting. Thus for the first time the Soviet press gave currency to non-Communist criticism of a Communist power without simultaneous rebuttal.

All this helped to perpetuate and extend the division between the so-called "nationalist" and "internationalist" (or pro-Peking) wings of the CPI. In general, and with certain notable exceptions and later variations, this division corresponded fairly well to the split on domestic strategy between the rightist and leftist factions of the Party. The rightist faction was led by the Maharashtra provincial organization, with strong support from portions of the Party committees in Kerala, Andhra Pradesh, and a number of other provinces; the leftists were entrenched in the West Bengal and Punjab organizations, with considerable strength in Andhra and elsewhere. The rightists were represented on the CPI Central Secretariat by Z. A. Ahmed, by the former Party General Secretary, P. C. Joshi, and by Dange; the last-named, who became the leader of the anti-Chinese forces within the Party in the fall of 1959, had also joined the rightists in expressing support for Nehru's domestic policy following the Congress Party Nagpur meeting in January.[39] The leftists on the Central Secretariat were Ranadive, M. Basavapunniah, and Bhupesh Gupta; these three were at this time united both in their fight against any CPI expression of support for the Nehru government against the C.P.R.[40] and in their belief that irreconcilable opposition to the domestic policies of Nehru and the Congress Party as a whole was the only way in which the CPI could expand its base of popular support. Occupying a middle position on both counts in the Central Secretariat were Ghosh and Namboodiripad. As the Sino-Soviet conflict expanded in 1960, Ghosh was to edge ever closer to the rightist and nationalist line.

1960: SURFACING OF THE SINO-SOVIET DISPUTE

In 1960, the Soviet and Chinese Parties came into open conflict, and this conflict was transformed into an organizational struggle within the world Communist movement in which both sides eventually found themselves appealing to the loyalties of the key leaders of each of the principal Communist Parties of the world. The CPI eventually had to be drawn into this dispute, if only because bloc policy toward India and the strategy to be prescribed for the CPI were key matters at issue between Moscow and Peking. The extent of the dispute was first made evident to large numbers of the CPI rank and file when, in April, 1960, the CCP opened a massive public offensive against the CPSU foreign policy line through four key statements tied to the anniversary of Lenin's birth: articles in the early and mid-April *Hung Ch'i*, a *Jen-min Jih-pao* article on April 22, and a speech by propaganda department director Lu Ting-i the same day. Central to the many implicit indictments leveled at Soviet policy in these statements was the theme that the peaceful-coexistence line as enunciated by Khrushchev was dampening the militancy of revolutionary forces throughout the world. These documents were eventually published together by the Chinese Communists in a special brochure printed in many languages and distributed throughout the world; but no doubt the CPI initially became aware of them through reprints in the English-language *Peking Review*, distributed in India.

The influence of the first *Hung Ch'i* article seemed to be immediately reflected in an article Ranadive wrote in the April 24 *New Age* (weekly) on the Lenin anniversary: Ranadive put his emphasis on Lenin's call for militant and "irreconcilable" struggle and Lenin's fight against "reformist and revisionist distortion of Marxism" and failed to mention Khrushchev's name. In contrast, an article by Ghosh on the same subject in the same issue of *New Age* paid repeated tribute to Khrushchev, to Khrushchev's recent visit to India, to the spirit of Camp David and the need for negotiations. The confusion within the CPI was vividly demonstrated on May 8, when the *New Age* (weekly) carried without comment lengthy extracts from both Lu Ting-i's Lenin Day speech in the C.P.R. on April 22 and O. V. Kuusinen's address in Moscow on the same day, providing the first major Soviet public response to the CCP. Echoes of the Sino-Soviet argument were then reportedly heard at a CPI National Council meeting in May, where a leftist speaker was said to have paid tribute to the Chinese Communists for "maintaining the purity" of Marxism, while a rightist replied by insisting on the need to accept Khrushchev's "creative Marxism."[41] Ranadive in this period seemed to be trying to utilize his position as editor of the CPI monthly journal (also called *New Age*) to promote the Chinese viewpoint: He carried full-page advertisements of *Peking Review* on the back cover of both the May and June issues and reprinted the April 19 *Hung Ch'i* article "Long Live Leninism" in June. The rightist faction appears to have retaliated on July 3 by securing publication in the weekly *New Age* of excerpts from Khrushchev's June 21 speech at the Rumanian Party Congress in which he made a scarcely veiled assault on Chinese views.

Meanwhile, the second major event in the 1960 struggle between the CPSU and the CCP took place at the World Federation of Trade Unions (WFTU) meeting in Peking in the first week of June, where the Chinese Party broke Communist discipline by openly lobbying among both Party and non-Party foreign delegates in an attempt to get the WFTU to abandon the Soviet line on disarmament, war, and the nature of imperialism. Judging from the published WFTU speeches and the subsequent published accounts of Italian socialist delegates, this effort by Peking to impose its line won varying degrees of support from a considerable number of the delegates, but was eventually substantially defeated as a result of the opposition of the CPSU delegation—only, however, after a furious battle among the delegates in which all the CPSU's latent strength within WFTU was called into play.

There is reason to believe that Dange, the current leader of the right-wing faction within the CPI, played an important part in the CPSU counterattack. Dange came to China in his dual capacity as leader of a Communist-dominated Indian trade-union federation and Vice President of WFTU. The Chinese Communists published what appeared to be a highly fragmentary version of the WFTU proceedings, stressing those speeches (and portions of speeches) which had supported the Chinese line; the New China

News Agency (NCNA) accounts severely cut the speeches of delegates (such as the Italians) who are said to have backed the CPSU
—and furnished no hint of a speech by Dange at all. There are two
probable reasons for this: Dange was personally obnoxious to the
CCP; and in all likelihood there was little in his speech that could
be published in a censored version. Vitoria Foa, an Italian delegate, reported in *Avanti* on June 14 that "the Indians" were among
those delegates who had lined up solidly with the Soviets against
the Chinese, helping to "fight with great energy . . . not only in
the public debate, but also in the commissions."

At the gathering of many Communist parties at Bucharest for
the Rumanian Party Congress three weeks later—which the Albanians and the CPSU have since publicly confirmed to have
been a turning point in the relations between Khrushchev and his
bloc opponents—the CPI was represented by two of the leftists on
the Central Secretariat, Basavapunniah and Bhupesh Gupta. There
they not only heard Khrushchev publicly assail Chinese positions
without naming the C.P.R., but also, it is said, were witnesses to a
private Khrushchev address to the parties in which he supposedly
"attacked the Chinese particularly for their attitude toward India
and other Asian countries."[42] Although representatives of most of
the Communist parties that spoke at the private meetings at
Bucharest are said to have supported Khrushchev, the CPI leftist
Bhupesh Gupta is reported to have delivered an evasive speech in
which he avoided backing the CPSU against the CCP.[43]

In the wake of these events, the rightist faction of the CPI appears to have pressed an offensive against leftist-faction positions,
which they were anxious to identify clearly with CCP resistance to
CPSU authority. When a clear-cut choice was finally posed at a
Central Executive Committee meeting in early September, vacillating and opportunistic CPI leaders (the majority) swung to the
rightist side identified with the CPSU, and the Indian Party passed
and published a resolution that did not mention China but backed
Soviet positions on the averting of war, on policy toward India, on
the possibility of nonviolent transition to socialism, and on the
"creative" application of Marxist-Leninist verities. This resolution
explicitly "reaffirmed" the positive assessment of the Indian Government's foreign policy made by the Amritsar and Palghat Party
Congresses.[44]

In addition, the rightists on the Central Executive Committee are
reported to have forced through—over the strenuous objections of
Ranadive and the representatives of the West Bengal and Punjab

organizations—a secret resolution that explicitly condemned the
Chinese Communist Party. This resolution is said to have backed
the Soviet line on the significance for the bloc of the "peace zone"
and of the good will of India above all. It blamed the Indian Government for giving succor to the Dalai Lama, but attacked Peking
for having described Kalimpong as the command center of the
Tibetan revolt, for having said the Dalai Lama was brought to
India under duress, and for having used the phrase "Indian expansionism." Communist China was accused of having made a
mistaken assessment of the Indian situation "without any effort to
ascertain the views of the Communist Party of India." The
U.S.S.R., on the other hand, was said to have taken a correct stand
on the border dispute as a conflict "between two countries of the
peace camp." Allusion was apparently made to the harmful effect
the Chinese actions had had on the CPI. The CCP errors were
said to have been the result of a new and mistaken assessment of the
role of the "national bourgeoisie" in India. The CPI reaffirmed its
disagreement with this assessment and its belief in the need to
strive to make possible a peaceful accession to power. Finally, the
resolution was said to have criticized the actions taken by CCP
trade union chief Liu Ning-i at the WFTU meeting in bringing
an inter-Party dispute openly before a front organization attended
by non-Party people.[45]

The passage of this secret resolution appears to have enraged the
provincial leaders of the leftist faction, many of whom had continued to flout Indian nationalist sentiment by publicly defending
the C.P.R. throughout 1960.[46] On October 21, the West Bengal
Party reportedly adopted a resolution violently condemning the
Central Executive Committee action as "wrong and harmful," because the CEC had spoken out without having "acquainted itself
with the views of the Chinese Communist Party." The CEC was
accused of having acted solely on the basis of Soviet accusations,
plus the evidence of "one or two *Red Flag* articles and one or two
speeches," while "conveniently avoiding to take into account a
number of articles and speeches of the Soviet leaders and some
documents of the CPSU in the context of which the *Red Flag*
articles were written"—that is, the Soviet provocations that had
obliged Peking to speak out. To this clearly anti-Soviet remark, the
West Bengal Party added the comment that the CEC knew that
the Chinese delegates at Bucharest had "refuted" the CPSU criticism there "as being untrue and slanderous." The West Bengal

resolution demanded that the Indian Party take particular care in its actions

. . . because the divergencies of opinion were primarily between two great Communist parties of the world, *both of whom* have rich revolutionary experience, have successfully applied Marxism-Leninism to concrete conditions, and have led great revolutions, and both of whom exert great influence on the course of the world revolutionary movement. [Italics added.][47]

A similar resolution was reported passed by the Punjab provincial Party committee;[48] on the other hand, leftist attempts to get such resolutions adopted in Bihar and other provinces were said to have been defeated.[49] The "views of the CCP" to which the West Bengal resolution alluded had apparently been furnished the West Bengal militants as the result of the visit of a CPI delegation to the Vietnamese Party Congress in September. The CPI was represented at this Congress by the pro-Peking West Bengal peasant leader Hare Krishna Konar, and by the pro-Russian Kerala leader K. Damodaran. Konar was said to have subsequently reported to a meeting of the Calcutta District Party committee in West Bengal that Damodaran had been snubbed in Hanoi by the Chinese delegation, while he himself had had long interviews with important leaders. Konar recited a list of CCP grievances against Moscow dating back to the CPSU's Twentieth Congress and repeated the Chinese charge that Khrushchev's peaceful-coexistence line was "sowing illusions" about imperialism. He quoted the CCP as estimating that the bourgeois governments of newly independent Asian countries were bound eventually to line up with Western "imperialism" and as declaring that the Indian Government and Nehru were now demonstrating this by inclining more and more toward imperialism while showing their "true reactionary colors" in domestic policy.[50] The Chinese Communist Party thus appears to have taken direct measures in the fall of 1960 to challenge Soviet domination of the CPI and to promote its own views among sympathetic sections of the Indian Party.

The outcome of the 81-Party conference of the world Communist movement in Moscow in November, 1960, appears to have encouraged rather than chastened the CPI leftists in their defiance of the CPSU. The long struggle the Chinese Party evidently waged against the CPSU in Moscow before the eyes of the entire movement,[51] the near-standoff between Chinese and Soviet positions in the final published Statement of the Moscow conference, and the apparent failure of the CPSU to secure any meaningful guarantee against the repetition of the Chinese public attacks on Soviet policy[52] could not but encourage the militant wing of the CPI and embolden the leftists in their efforts to strengthen their position throughout the Party in preparation for the capture of Party control and of the CPI's Sixth Congress in April. Leftists made wide gains in a number of provinces in January in the choice of delegates to the Party Congress;[53] and the secretary of the West Bengal Party commitee, Promode Das Gupta, meanwhile was reported to have circulated within the Party a document entitled "Revisionist Trends in the CPI," in which he attacked Ghosh's policies as a surrender to the bourgeoisie and imperialism. Das Gupta assailed past statements by rightist CPI leaders to the effect that the Party now relied upon elections rather than civil war as the road to power and cited in contrast CCP editorials in the Sino-Soviet polemic that had insisted that the proletariat in all countries must "smash the bourgeois state apparatus." He is said to have demanded that the CPI "follow the lead" of the Chinese Party.[54]

Shortly afterward, the CPI National Council met in February, 1961, to decide on the documents to be presented to the Party Congress for approval. Central to the debate at this meeting was the concept of the "national democratic state," which had been inserted in the 1960 Moscow Statement—apparently at CPSU insistence—to connote a transitional phase between a former colony's achievement of political independence and the assumption of direct Communist control. The national democratic state was there defined as one that had won complete economic independence from the "imperialist" world and assumed close economic ties with the bloc; one that had adopted an "anti-imperialist" foreign policy; one in which the state-owned sector had become predominant in the economy; and one in which a list of "democratic reforms" and "democratic freedoms" had been achieved, two of the most important being land reform and (implicitly) freedom of activity for the Communist Party. The national democratic state would be ruled by a broad united "anti-imperialist front" embracing "all patriotic strata" of the country concerned, including national bourgeoisie, peasantry, and proletariat. Although it has been stipulated by Soviet articles that the proletariat (the Communist Party) would have some importance in this coalition, the minimum degree of Communist influence acceptable in a national democratic front and the length of time the Communist Party should be willing to wait to secure firm control have never been spelled out by Moscow. Communist China, long hostile to Soviet gradualistic and evolutionary notions on the Communist assumption of power in underdeveloped countries, has been suspicious lest the new concept be used to justify a further indefinite delay in the achievement of Communist hegemony. Unlike Moscow, Peking has, therefore, never publicly mentioned the national democratic state and, in fact, has printed a veiled attack on the concept in *Jen-min Jih-pao* of October 10, 1961, on the eve of the CPSU's Twenty-second Congress.

The alternative drafts of the CPI political resolution and of a new Party program presented at the National Council meeting by the opposing Party factions took predictably contrasting views of the new concept. For example, Ghosh's draft political resolution set forth the aim of replacing the present "vacillating" and "compromising" government with a government of a national democratic front, which in turn would facilitate the peaceful transition to socialism. It called for a broad-based campaign seeking the cooperation of "patriotic elements in every Party" to establish this front and secure gradual changes in the government's policies. In addition to endorsing the usual "united front from below" tactic of seeking to draw support from the rank and file of the Congress and of such parties as the Praja Socialists, Ghosh's resolution called for the employment of "united front from above" tactics with local Congress committees or other local organizations "to which the peasants who are not under our influence are politically attached." Ghosh identified only the extreme right of the Congress Party and of the big bourgeoisie as the enemy of the national democratic front and, consequently, declared that the "democratic forces must adopt a correct attitude toward the small and medium industrialists" who are anti-imperialist and that Communist-controlled trade unions must even abate their demands toward these industrialists in the interests of "drawing them closer to the democratic masses." While strongly criticizing the Indian Government and Nehru for their policies toward feudalism, Western loans, land reform, and the Communist Kerala regime, this draft several times praised Nehru, particularly for his foreign policy and his support for the public sector of the Indian economy.[55]

In contrast, Ranadive's draft, while also speaking of a "national democratic front," took a much harsher view of Nehru, did not support alliances with local Congress committees, was not so eager to bring wide sections of the bourgeoisie into the democratic front, and was much stronger in its exposition of the need to struggle against the policies of the Indian Government. Eventually, the rightist drafts of both the political resolution and the Party program were adopted by the National Council, but the leftists won the right to publish their alternatives and circulate them throughout the Party.[56] Also passed on to the Party Congress for a final decision was Namboodiripad's draft organizational report, which reportedly severely chastised the Party for its indiscipline and for the revisionist and "parliamentary" habits of thought he found widespread.[57] The National Council also adopted a resolution reiterating the Meerut November, 1959, formula on the border dispute, but also now upholding India's exclusive right to negotiate the boundaries of Kashmir—of which Ladakh was a part—with China (reproving reported C.P.R. feelers on this subject to Pakistan) and to carry on frontier negotiations on behalf of Bhutan and Sikkim (reproving reported Chinese efforts to bypass New Delhi in contacting those two Indian dependencies).

THE SIXTH INDIAN PARTY CONGRESS

The CPSU was represented at the CPI's Sixth Congress, in April, 1961, by a delegation headed by Presidium member Suslov, while the CCP was not represented at all.[58] The result was that the CPSU had the field to itself in providing guidance to the Indian Party at an event of central importance. In deciphering the line the Soviets wished the CPI Congress to adopt—as distinguished from the line it eventually adopted under leftist-faction pressure—a lengthy article by Ghosh published in *Pravda* on April 5 is of major importance. Ghosh's article repeated and expanded the tributes paid in his draft political resolution to Nehru's contributions to peace and disarmament and his resistance to imperialist pressures. At the same time, Ghosh added—in accordance with the trend of Soviet policy since his February draft was adopted—a lengthy, detailed criticism of the "vacillations" of the Indian Government, particularly in regard to the Congo. Ghosh's conclusion was that the CPI must organize the masses to put pressure on the Indian Government to overcome these "weaknesses" and make New Delhi's policy more "consistent."

On the internal economic situation, Ghosh's article placed only slightly more emphasis on the negative side of Nehru's policy than had his draft resolution. He declared that "it would be, of course, incorrect" to think that the Indian Government had submitted to what was described as the blackmail attempted by the "imperialists" to force a reduction of the third Five-Year Plan and a weakening of the state sector in exchange for the granting of loans to India. Nevertheless, Ghosh complained of instances of concessions made to foreign capital, of growing ties between India and foreign bourgeoisie, of the government's alleged failures to enact significant land reform, and of the dissolution of the Kerala government. He spoke of an "intensification of the contradiction between the government . . . and the people." But on the whole, in his *Pravda* appraisal of the economy, Ghosh did not lean as heavily on the negative side as he was to do in his speech to the Congress or in the final version of the political resolution, suggesting that here changes may have been forced by the need to offset leftist pressure.

On the other hand, Ghosh added an element, which he was to repeat in his Congress speech, which the leftists were to object to strongly, and which had not been found in his draft resolution: an explicit statement that the continuation of the Sino-Indian border dispute had hurt the CPI more than anything else and had been the chief factor pushing the Indian Government in the direction desired by "imperialists and reactionaries."

Finally, Ghosh's *Pravda* article called for a "broad national association of all patriotic and democratic forces"—based on the alliance between workers and peasants, the nucleus of the national democratic front—to defend the state sector, achieve land reform, control the monopolies, prevent imperialist loans, criticize harmful tendencies in government, and so generally gain influence over government policies. Ghosh called vaguely for the overcoming of differences among "democratic" forces resulting from their belonging to different political parties, but did not clearly indicate which social classes, parties, or elements of parties might belong to the national democratic front and on what basis.

To sum up: Ghosh and the CPSU had apparently agreed before the CPI Congress on a balanced line including both praise for Nehru's foreign policy and criticism of his vacillations; credit for aspects of the government's domestic policy and a certain number of detailed attacks on its faults; and emphasis on the harm being done to the Communist cause in India by the Sino-Indian dispute. They were also agreed on the need for a very broad national democratic front, but had not yet specified the make-up of that front beyond the generalized call for the inclusion of "all democratic forces."

This conclusion is supported by the nature of the speech delivered by Suslov to the Party Congress on April 8. Suslov paid emphatic tribute to the importance of India to the outcome of the

world struggle against imperialism and to the vital significance of
the Indian policy of neutrality. He pointedly warned the CPI of
the need for discipline and unity in its ranks. He spoke of the Indian Party at one point as struggling "against imperialism and feudal oppression, for national independence, and for democracy and
social progress," and at another point as working "with other national patriotic forces . . . to liquidate economic backwardness
and to establish a stable and independent economy, to strengthen
the political independence of their country, and to promote social
progress." Suslov also referred to the "specific complicated conditions" in which the CPI had to work; alluded to the CPI's task as
one of "determined struggle against imperialism and the remnants
of feudalism" (not, it will be noted, against the ruling bourgeoisie);
and called on the Indian Party "to unite into a single national democratic front all the patriotic forces interested in India's advancement along the path of economic and social progress."[59] In short,
Suslov endorsed a national democratic program for the CPI—and
a very minimal one at that—and breathed not a word about "socialism" being a goal toward which the CPI should strive. The same
was true of the CPSU message to the Congress read by Suslov; in
contrast, the CCP message read out at the same session, while generally restrained in tone, did put in a word for socialism in India.[60]
The conclusion seems inescapable that the CPSU, while not committing itself on the question of how far to carry alliances with the
Congress Party or Congress Party units, was far more in sympathy
with the general thrust of the Ghosh-Dange line than with that of
the leftists.

Nevertheless, some reports in the Indian press[61] have asserted
that it was Suslov who advised Ghosh to make some concessions to
leftist sentiments, if not to the leftist leaders themselves; such concessions were manifested in Ghosh's agreement to drop discussion
of the Party program when the Congress became deadlocked on
that issue, in Ghosh's speech to the Congress, and in the amendments to the political resolution Ghosh agreed to accept. If Suslov
did give Ghosh such advice, it would seem to have been motivated
first by the need to preserve the loyal CPSU adherent Ghosh in authority as general secretary in the face of trends that threatened
seriously to displace him; second, by the need to neutralize enough
of the following of the left-faction leaders at the Congress—while
rebuffing those leaders themselves—to head off any inclination by
the leftists to try to take the provincial organizations they con-

trolled out of the CPI;[62] and third, to prevent the leftists from seizing organizational control of CPI executive bodies.

These considerations were all reflected in the speech Ghosh delivered to the Congress on April 9,[63] and in the description of that speech published in *Pravda* three days later. Ghosh's speech was a report opening the debate on the political resolution and introducing the National Council draft. In this report, Ghosh, while praising Nehru's foreign policy in general terms, was (as in the April 5 *Pravda* article) somewhat more specific than his draft resolution had been on New Delhi's deficiencies regarding colonialism. At the same time, he placed somewhat more stress on the degree to which the Indian Government had shifted to the right and spoke more of the "anti-people measures" of the government. He devoted less attention than had his draft resolution to an explanation of how democratic tasks are in the "objective interest" of the national bourgeoisie and, in fact, spoke less of the national bourgeoisie generally, concentrating instead on the danger of the "monopolistic bourgeoisie," who were no longer portrayed as the insignificant handful the draft political resolution had described.

Ghosh now criticized the line of the 1958 Amritsar Congress and favored instead the qualified endorsement of peaceful transition made by the Palghat Congress of 1956. The Amritsar resolution was described as both reformist (because it implied a belief that the parliamentary slide into power would be both automatic and smooth) and sectarian (because it did not appeal to a broad enough united front for strictly limited, nonsocialist goals). Ghosh warned against interpreting the peaceful path to socialism as mere reliance upon Parliament alone; this he termed a reformist deception which had been exposed by the Kerala events. He predicted that the conditions of life for the masses would remain bad under the third Five-Year Plan and that class contradictions would sharpen. He cautioned that antidemocratic tendencies might increase within the ruling class, that alleged violations of parliamentary traditions by the bourgeoisie—such as the means used to expel the CPI in Kerala—might increase; even a reactionary personal dictatorship, he said, might be a possibility after Nehru's death.

All this, however, was at least offset by an emphatic restatement of many central elements of the right-wing line. Ghosh upheld his resolution's contention that conditions were, nevertheless, still favorable for the formation of a very broad national democratic front, whose chief goal would be not the replacement of the government but the enactment of a series of reforms. While making it plain that the CPI would have to fight the next election on the basis of its own program, with the government necessarily made the clear target of electoral attack—and that, therefore, any general electoral alliance with the Congress Party was impossible—Ghosh also made it plain that this did not mean abandonment of the long-term effort to draw both the following and the "progressive" section of the leadership of the Congress Party into the national democratic front.[64] As in his draft resolution, all Ghosh's allusions to Nehru except those concerning the Kerala events were favorable; blame was almost invariably placed upon "the government," not upon Nehru. Ghosh also declared that it would be a "big mistake" to equate the Congress with the rightist Indian parties. Citing the Palghat line on the need to take into account the Congress' hold on the Indian masses, Ghosh reiterated the assertions made in his draft resolution that a process of "rethinking" was going on among many Congress supporters. His draft resolution had called on the CPI to undertake joint action with local Congress Party committees in peasant areas; he now spoke similarly of the need to take into account the loyalty of Congress followers to their organizations and to Nehru, as well as the need to make direct appeals "not only to the Congress masses but also to Congress committees, taking into account the issue concerned." In short, despite his ruling out of any general alliance with the Congress Party during the election campaign, Ghosh implied that "united front from above" as well as "united front from below" tactics must be used toward the Congress in the long-term effort of building the national democratic front. This was anathema to the West Bengal left-faction leaders.

Worse still, from the point of view of the Ranadive faction, Ghosh went beyond the scope of his draft resolution to add a direct polemical attack on the "deep-rooted sectarianism" of CPI leaders who found themselves unable to mobilize the masses to combat the negative features of Indian Government foreign policy because they were not willing or "inspired" to mobilize movements in support of favorable aspects of New Delhi's policy. It is again characteristic of the CPSU's attitude that this passage was included in its entirety in *Pravda's* highly selective account of Ghosh's speech. Also included in the *Pravda* summary was a pointed attack made by Ghosh on the contention of the old 1951 CPI program that the Nehru government was pro-imperialist.

Because the CPSU was behind Ghosh and not behind Ranadive,

the amendments that the left faction finally succeeded in attaching to the political resolution were less meaningful than they would otherwise have been. As eventually published in the May 7 *New Age* (weekly), the resolution in its final form clearly showed the influence of the leftist amendments, which gave to it a more consistently militant and anti-Congress tone over-all than that of Ghosh's speech, let alone that of the original National Council draft. This was the greatest achievement the left-faction leaders were to register at the Party Congress and was a good indication of their strength among the delegates. But because the leftists were unable to follow this up by seizing organizational control of the Party, the incorporation of many militant views into the resolution did not mean enforcement of those views upon the Party as a whole, because the resolution remained sufficiently ambiguous so that the provincial Party organizations could and did find in it some language to justify the moderate or extremist course the particular faction in control of each province intended to continue to follow. And while the leftists succeeded in greatly reducing the rightist majority in the new National Council elected by the Congress, the rightists subsequently (at a National Council meeting in June) used this reduced majority to diminish greatly the previous leftist influence over the Central Executive Committee and the Central Secretariat, the two top Party organs charged with running the Party. The most important apparent effect of these changes was to ensure that until the next Party Congress the central direction of the CPI would remain in hands at least more likely than before to be loyal to the CPSU under all circumstances.

THE CPI AND KHRUSHCHEV'S NEW OFFENSIVE

When Ghosh led a CPI delegation to the CPSU's Twenty-second Congress in October, however, even moderates normally loyal to the CPSU appear to have been shaken by the violent assault made upon the Albanian leaders at the Congress in what was to prove the opening step in a campaign to force Communist China to relinquish support of Albania and thereby undermine its own challenge to CPSU authority over the international movement. Ghosh well knew the reaction this would evoke from the left-faction strongholds of the CPI, and he may have surmised that Chou En-lai's charge that the CPSU action was an un-Marxist way to try to resolve differences might receive sympathy even in sections of the Indian Party ordinarily inclined toward Moscow. In view of his subsequent public statements, Ghosh may even have felt this way himself, although he certainly held no brief for the basic views of the Albanians or the Chinese; in any case, his primary concern was to preserve his own position and, if at all possible, to prevent the public façade of CPI unity from being destroyed on the eve of a national election. In his speech to the CPSU Congress, Ghosh therefore refrained for the time being from joining in the attack on the Albanian leadership; in this evasion, he was joined at the Congress by a number of other leaders of non-bloc Communist Parties who in past statements had supported CPSU positions against the CCP.

This was not all, however: Even worse, from Ghosh's point of view, was the equally violent attack at the CPSU Congress upon Stalin. This attack placed upon the public record and even elaborated the denunciations of Stalin's crimes—and the revelations of the realities of Soviet life—that had previously been recorded only in Khrushchev's 1956 secret speech (which, while published by the West, did not have quite the same standing with non-bloc Party members as a direct, public avowal of the facts by the CPSU). Ghosh could not forget the staggering and lasting effect upon CPI morale and discipline wrought by the first great denigration of Stalin. He knew that Stalin's memory was still deeply revered by many members of all factions of the Indian Party, and he also knew that his own position was in large part dependent upon the CPI rank-and-file faith in the happiness of life in the U.S.S.R. and the eternal wisdom of the CPSU, which Khrushchev was busily demolishing. For all these reasons, it is credible that the CPI delegation protested to the CPSU, as Ghosh reported in New Age (weekly) on December 10.

The CPI had meanwhile been kept well appraised of these events through reportage in the weekly New Age, and when Ghosh and the others returned to India, they found the Party already in turmoil. Immediately after the Congress, the organ of the CPI leftists in Uttar Pradesh carried an article eulogizing the Albanians. On October 31, the Kerala Party organ, Janayangam, said it was tragic that the battle against Stalinism had degenerated into an attack on his body. The Press Trust of India (PTI) on November 12 reported that one Kerala leader had asked for the body to be sent to the Kerala Party and that Namboodiripad had publicly praised Stalin and his work. In Andhra, the leftist chieftain Sundarayya reportedly protested against the "slanders" on Stalin the New Age had been reprinting. The Yugoslav daily Borba on January 10 claimed that the West Bengal Party Secretariat had adopted another resolution opposing the CPSU: This resolution was said to have denounced the move against Stalin and to have condemned the attack on Albania as a "direct violation of the principles" of the 1960 Moscow Declaration.

Finally, Ghosh spoke out himself, in an effort to calm things down. On December 10, he published an article in *New Age* (weekly) in which he deferred to a later meeting of the National Council any evaluation of the attack on Albania "as well as the comment made by Chou En-lai on the propriety of making such open criticism." At the same time, he finally went on record with qualified support for Moscow against Albania by mildly condemning Albanian attacks on Soviet foreign policy and on the Twentieth Congress decisons as "not in conformity" with the 1960 Moscow Statement. As in 1956, he attempted to combat disillusionment with the Soviet Party with a lengthy tribute to the accomplishments of the U.S.S.R., the significance of the new CPSU program, and the role of the CPSU as the "vanguard of the world Communist movement." At the same time, he stated that a "big majority" of CPI members had been "deeply hurt" by the decision to move Stalin's body; he insisted that Stalin was a distinguished Marxist-Leninist of extreme importance; and he expressed "deep regret" that the struggle against Stalin's cult had been carried so far. Moreover, Ghosh implicitly sided with the Italian Party in declaring that the question of how the excesses occurred and how they would be prevented from recurring had not been properly answered. Ghosh added this pointed warning that Khrushchev had undermined not only Stalin's but the CPSU's authority: "The Twentieth Congress . . . not merely ended the deification of Stalin, but also demolished the belief in the infallibility *of any Party* or any leader. This was necessary, for such a belief is contrary to the very spirit of Marxism-Leninism. [Italics added.]"

Ghosh concluded by admitting that CPI members were "dumfounded and demoralized" by these events, by begging Party members to keep silent, and by declaring that it was impossible to hold a Party meeting to discuss recent developments until after the approaching elections.

By the time Ghosh wrote this article, however, another factor had arisen to exacerbate greatly relations between the CPI factions and between the Soviet Union and Communist China: a revival of the border dispute.

Throughout 1961, the Soviet and Chinese Communist policies toward the Nehru government had continued to move along widely divergent paths. The U.S.S.R. maintained a policy of economic assistance to India and continued to depict Nehru's foreign policy as generally progressive, while simultaneously sustaining discreet propaganda pressure upon the Indian Government (pressure supported by the CPI) to bend toward the Soviet view on specific topical issues. Early in the year, Soviet and CPI articles were most concerned with New Delhi's policy toward the Congo and Cuba, and later the emphasis shifted toward the Soviet resumption of nuclear testing, Nehru's stand at the neutralists' conference, and particularly the Berlin issue. After the middle of the year, the U.S.S.R. made no direct criticisms of the Indian Government. Communist China, on the other hand, throughout the year maintained a vitriolic line toward Nehru, attempting to discredit him with both the bloc and the world Communist movement and with the radical but non-Communist forces of the "national liberation movement." To maintain the single-hued portrait of Nehru as a faithful servant of American "imperialism" and enemy of both China and the U.S.S.R., C.P.R. propaganda continued to make extremely tendentious selections from Nehru's statements, going to extravagant lengths in this regard in connection with the neutralist conference and Nehru's remarks on the Berlin issue.

In the meantime, the border issue again became inflamed, with Peking and New Delhi exchanging charges of fresh border incursions in a series of notes in the summer and fall. On November 20, Nehru brought these matters to public attention before the Lok Sabha, thereby setting in motion new violent denunciations of the C.P.R. by the Indian and Western press. Already angered by this action of Nehru's, the Chinese were evidently infuriated when on November 21, the day after Nehru's statement, Ajoy Ghosh issued a public statement on his own initiative as CPI General Secretary strongly criticizing the C.P.R. Ghosh expressed "surprise and regret" at the information disclosed by the Indian Government, implicitly accepting the Indian version as beyond question. He declared that the Chinese actions could not but heighten tension and embitter relations between the two countries, and "demanded" that the C.P.R. put an end to such actions and take measures to ensure that they would not recur.[65]

After waiting two weeks, the C.P.R. in early December published the texts of the notes it had exchanged with New Delhi, followed by a ferocious *Jen-min Jih-pao* editorial denouncing the "anti-Chinese campaign launched by Nehru in India." In this editorial, the

Chinese Communists summed up all their efforts of the past year to indict Nehru as an enemy of progressive mankind and charged that he had initiated his "anti-Chinese campaign" at American instigation to hurt the bloc, as well as to bolster what Peking depicted as the sagging chances of the Congress Party in the coming Indian elections. In addition, in this editorial the CCP finally gave vent publicly to its long-held feelings about Ghosh, attacking him for having "trailed behind Nehru and hurriedly issued a statement in condemnation of China . . . without bothering to find out the truth or to look into the rights and wrongs of the case."[66]

This unprecedented CCP attack upon Ghosh was also necessarily both an indirect slap at the CPSU and, at the same time, a Chinese action in support of the leftist CPI faction and in condemnation of the rightist faction. The Peking-Nehru polemic was soon intermeshed with the broader Sino-Soviet battle going on concurrently, with Albania amplifying Chinese denunciations of the Indian Premier, and other East European states, like the U.S.S.R., refusing to do so. Even before the *Jen-min Jih-pao* editorial had been published, Moscow's alarm at the whole trend of events was made apparent when, on December 2, Tass announced that an invitation extended to Brezhnev during the summer to visit India at an opportune time was now being accepted; Brezhnev arrived on this emergency trip two weeks later.

At the same time, the Chinese actions had served to increase further the tension between the opposing groups within the CPI. The West Bengal Secretariat resolution reported by the Yugoslav press in January, 1962, is said to have formally affirmed that Ghosh's anti-Chinese statement represented "the attitude of part of the Party only."[67] The West Bengal Party organ, *Swadhinata*, published articles strongly attacking Nehru along the lines the Chinese had taken and, as had happened in the past, these articles were picked up by NCNA and *Jen-min Jih-pao*.[68] On the other hand, the CPI central newspaper *New Age*—controlled by the rightists—in November and December began to acknowledge repeatedly the existence of differences between the CPI and the Chinese Party. On December 13, the rightist CPI Central Secretariat member Z. A. Ahmed publicly declared, in response to a question about the Chinese attacks on Ghosh, that Ghosh could well look after himself "and needs no advice from outside as to what he should do in a matter with which the Indian people as a whole are vitally concerned." Ahmed dismissed as "absurd" the *Jen-min Jih-pao* con-

tention that India's foreign policy and her attitude toward the
C.P.R. were determined by the "lure of the dollar" and reasserted
CPI support for Nehru's foreign policy.[69]

By the end of 1961, then, the Indian Communist Party had
reached a point at which the right wing of the Party was openly
criticizing the CCP and was being criticized by it; was supporting
Moscow generally against Albania and China, though regretting
the means that had been used to attack Albania; was itself shocked
by and divided over the new assault on Stalin; and was publicly
regretting that Khrushchev had reopened this issue. The left wing
was publishing statements supporting the Chinese line on Nehru;
was reportedly censuring General Secretary Ghosh for his anti-
Chinese statements; had reportedly adopted at least one resolution
again opposing the CPSU; and appeared to be generally united in
opposition to the Soviet moves against Albania, the C.P.R. and
Stalin.

It was at this juncture that General Secretary Ghosh died, on
January 13, 1962, thereby multiplying the difficulties faced by the
CPSU in its efforts to hold the Indian Party together. Moscow now
had the task of finding a new leadership for the CPI, combining the
attributes of fidelity to Moscow and acceptability to the strong
CPI leftist minority hostile to the U.S.S.R. and favorable to China.
This task was not made easier by the results of the Indian national
elections in February; although the over-all position of the Com-
munist Party was not greatly changed, the CPI did much better in
provinces where its left wing was strong (West Bengal, Punjab,
Andhra, and Kerala) than in its right-wing strongholds (such as
Maharashtra, where Dange lost his parliamentary seat).

In late April, the leadership issue was at last dealt with, in an
unstable compromise typical of the CPI that settled nothing but
postponed the factional showdown. Chosen to replace Ghosh as
General Secretary was E. M. S. Namboodiripad, the former Chief
Minister of the Communist Kerala regime and a former moderate
who had made some public gestures toward the Party leftists during
1961 in response to their growing strength. At the same time, the
ill-defined post of Party Chairman was created and given to the
rightist leader Dange. As their apparent price for agreeing to
Dange's elevation, the leftist faction was given greatly augmented
representation on the Central Secretariat, which is charged with the
day-to-day running of the Party. In short, an uneasy equilibrium
was set up between the factions at the Party center, corresponding
to the general situation in the Party as a whole.

THE CHINESE MILITARY ATTACK ON INDIA

The Chinese general attack in the Northeast Frontier Agency (NEFA) and Ladakh areas on October 20, 1962, marked a watershed for the CPI, both in its attitude toward the Nehru government and in its relations with the world Communist movement. For the time being, this event left the CPI no more room for equivocation. If the Party did not issue a forthright condemnation of Peking and pledge support for the national government, it could expect most of the popular support it had painfully built up over the last decade to disappear rapidly; quite possibly, the Party itself might lose legal status. Right-wing CPI leaders such as Dange and provincial Party committees led by the rightist faction therefore responded immediately with public denunciations of the Chinese aggression. But the CPI itself did not take an official stand until the Party's National Council issued a resolution on November 1. During the twelve days between October 20 and November 1, two momentous events occurred to affect that resolution.

First, on October 22, the Cuban crisis began, and the Soviet Union apparently saw an overriding emergency touching on Soviet interests even more vital than the need to preserve the Soviet position in India. On October 25, for the first (and last) time in three years of Sino-Indian border controversy, *Pravda* published an editorial siding with Peking. This editorial implied doubt concerning the validity of the McMahon Line as the border in the Northeast Frontier Area, explicitly praised and endorsed the Chinese proposals for a cease-fire, opposed preconditions for a cease-fire (on which New Delhi was insisting), and called on Indian "progressives" (i.e., the CPI) to restrain themselves and their government. It seems likely that Moscow took this drastic step as a gesture seeking bloc solidarity at a time of military crisis. It is possible that a subsidiary motive, however, was a hope on Moscow's part that it could buy Chinese forbearance in the event that a backdown on Cuba became necessary.

If the Soviets did entertain such a hope, it quickly proved illusory, for when Khrushchev did back down over Cuba the Chinese proceeded to scourge him unmercifully in their propaganda as an appeaser; they continue to do so to the present day. In the meantime, the Chinese made it plain that the gesture of appeasement the U.S.S.R. had made toward *them* over India was entirely insufficient. On October 27, *Jen-min Jih-pao* published an editorial attack on "Nehru's philosophy" which went much further than an earlier editorial on this subject that the Chinese Party organ had published in May, 1959, shortly after the Tibetan revolt. Whereas in the earlier case Nehru had been depicted condescendingly as a confused and vacillating leader whose policy was nevertheless "generally favorable," now he was found always to have acted as a conscious agent of "reactionaries" and "imperialism" on all the really important questions of domestic and foreign policy. The Indian Communist Party was sternly admonished not to "trail behind" this reprobate by echoing his accusations against Peking, and S. A. Dange was denounced by name as a "so-called Marxist-Leninist" for having done so.[70] Finally, with regard to the Soviet Union, the editorial made it clear that nothing short of a direct condemnation of Nehru and India (which Pravda of October 25 had not contained) would satisfy Peking's conception of "proletarian internationalism";[71] it made clear, in fact, that what was being demanded of Khrushchev was the total abandonment of his India policy and of the fruits of eight years of Soviet cultivation of the Indian population and the Indian "national bourgeoisie."

Thus, by the end of October, Moscow could see that it had blundered; it had jeopardized its position in the eyes of Indian public opinion to no good purpose; Peking was not appeased over Soviet policy toward India and had not been restrained from launching violent attacks on Soviet actions over Cuba. Accordingly, in a November 5 Pravda editorial, and in subsequent Soviet comment, Moscow proceeded to edge away from the partial support it had given Peking on October 25, back toward its earlier neutral position.

The Indian Communist Party, meanwhile, fought a momentous internal battle in the last week of October, as a result of which it disregarded the public advice given it by both Moscow and Peking and adopted a position unacceptable even to the CPSU. Dange's forces in the National Council forced through a resolution that condemned Communist China unequivocally and called on Indians to unite behind Nehru "in defense of the motherland against Chinese aggression." Although Pravda of October 25 had asked the CPI not to do this, such a statement may have been regarded as inevitable by Moscow; the CPI resolution went on, however, to say that the Party was not opposed to India's "buying arms from any country on a commercial basis," and this Moscow could not stomach. By endorsing the acceptance of military aid from the "imperialist" West against Communist China, the CPI soon found itself at odds with many of Moscow's European adherents. For example, the British Party, former mentor of the CPI, in October and November took a more and more openly anti-Indian position; the Czech Party at first went so far as to repeat Peking's story that India had launched an "extensive offensive" on October 20,[72] and as late as November 8 was continuing to attack the validity of the Mc-Mahon Line;[73] and even the revisionist Italian Party complained that "we fail to understand easily the position of the Indian Communist Party."[74]

Meanwhile, however, Moscow's retreat—in the November 5 *Pravda*—back toward a posture of public neutrality helped to make the CPI's domestic position more tolerable, and the Dange leadership hastened to fortify itself at home and defend itself abroad. On the very next day, it was announced that Dange had had a talk with Nehru in which he outlined to the Prime Minister the National Council resolution and assured Nehru of the CPI's support. A few days later, the CPI weekly organ published a pugnacious defense of the Indian Party leadership against the attack made in the October 27 *Jen-min Jih-pao*; the Chinese were accused of "national chauvinism," and of having made a blatant appeal for Dange's overthrow on the eve of the National Council meeting.[75] At the same time, the CPI was reported to have written to all Communist parties of the world defending the Indian Party position and asking for pressure to be placed on Peking.[76]

By this time—early November—the central CPI leadership was at last firmly in Dange's hands, and the recalcitrant provincial Party organizations were soon to succumb as well. Although the vacillating CPI General Secretary, E. M. S. Namboodiripad, apparently refused to sign the November 1 Party resolution (as *Jen-min Jih-pao* carefully noted), he was isolated and powerless; the three leading left-faction spokesmen on the Central Secretariat had resigned following the passage of the resolution. Dange was obliged to the pressure of Indian public opinion upon the Party for pushing the leftists out of the central CPI machinery; he was obliged to the Indian Government for doing the same in the provinces. On November 7, the day after Dange spoke to Nehru, and again on November 21, the government made large-scale arrests of CPI cadres; the overwhelming majority of those arrested were leaders of the left-wing faction in New Delhi and in the provinces who had shown a lack of enthusiasm for the National Council resolution. *Jen-min Jih-pao* has furnished its own comment on what happened next:

> The Dange clique exploited the situation and sent their trusted followers, on the heels of the police, to take over the leading organs of

the Party committees in a number of states. The purpose of these actions by the Dange clique was to reconstitute the Indian Communist Party and wreck the Indian revolutionary movement so as to serve the ends of the big bourgeoisie.[77]

In November and December, the right-wing faction apparently did take advantage of the sudden departure of the leftists to seize for the first time the Party machinery in the left-wing strongholds of West Bengal and the Punjab, and to consolidate its dominant position everywhere else. This action appears to have evoked countermeasures on the part of the Party's left wing which may mark the beginning of an organizational split in the CPI. In the Punjab, the leftist provincial Party first secretary, before being arrested, is alleged to have left instructions to his followers not to cooperate with the new provincial Party leadership and to have warned "against certain weak links in the Party" who "would speak the language of the government."[78] In West Bengal, an "underground" center is said to have come into being which issued similar instructions to Party units to refuse cooperation to the "usurping" right-wing leaders of the provincial Party organization; and according to the Indian press, many local Party units in West Bengal have in fact maintained contact with this "underground" center and refused allegiance to the official Party organization.[79] The new management of the West Bengal party newspaper *Swadhinata* complained publicly that the outgoing leftist leaders had taken the organization's funds with them, mortgaged the *Swadhinata* presses, and left the newspaper in a financial and legal predicament in which it would be difficult to continue publication.[80]

Peking, of course, has sought to blame the growing organizational division in the CPI on "Dange and company," who are said to have "used the power of the Indian ruling groups to push aside the people who disagree with them . . . and to split the Party wide open."[81] At the same time, Communist China's increasingly open calls in December, January, and February for all "true Marxist-Leninists" to revolt against the policies and the "baton" of the CPSU were transparently designed to encourage factional strife in all Communist Parties, including the CPI. As justification for its own position, the CPI leadership therefore eagerly reprinted all the anti-Chinese statements made by various Communist parties as the Sino-Soviet polemic expanded, including Ulbricht's lament at the January, 1963, East German congress that the "Chinese comrades" had not adhered to peaceful coexistence "in dealing with frontier questions with India."

Moscow, however, was by no means happy at the prospect of a formal split in the CPI, and particularly unhappy at the means by which it was being brought about. While remaining careful not to jeopardize relations with New Delhi, the Soviet press repeatedly protested the jailing of CPI members (particularly that of General Secretary Namboodiripad, who was detained for a week in late November). On December 30, a *Pravda* writer deplored "attempts to interfere in the internal affairs of the Communist Party," citing a statement by an Indian Minister who was said to have declared that "the Communist Party should clear its ranks of questionable elements." Such efforts "to divide the Communists into the 'pure' and 'impure,'" *Pravda* complained, are nothing "but an attempt to kindle internal strife within the Communist Party, to split it."

In the light of this situation, Dange in December undertook a trip to consult with Communist leaders in the Soviet Union, Eastern Europe, Italy, and Britain. Peking later claimed that Nehru and Indian Home Affairs Minister Shastri had briefed Dange before his departure and that Dange had acted as an agent of New Delhi.[82] It seems likely, however, that Dange's first concern, as always, was to defend the position of S. A. Dange, and to justify in his talks with Khrushchev the actions taken by the CPI under his leadership. It has been reported in the Indian press that Dange was not altogether successful in this, and that Khrushchev remonstrated against the National Council resolution as being unnecessarily outspoken in condemning Chinese aggression and criticized the CPI for not qualifying sufficiently its support for Nehru.[83] After Dange's return, he reported first to Nehru and then to the CPI Central Executive Committee. The latter seemed to be responding to advice brought from abroad when, on January 12, it adopted a resolution which, while continuing to support the bargaining position of the Indian Government and to place the responsibility for reaching agreement upon Peking, put greatly increased emphasis on the need for a peaceful settlement and the dangerous machinations of the Western powers.[84]

This shift in the emphasis of the CPI line was reiterated in resolutions adopted by the Party's National Council in February. At the same time, the National Council finally put the CPI on public record with a formal, unequivocal denunciation of the Chinese Party's position in the Sino-Soviet conflict.[85] Finally, it was at this National Council meeting that Namboodiripad, already isolated within the leadership, resigned as CPI General Secretary and Editor of *New Age*, leaving Dange's forces in sole control.

That Moscow may have come to feel, however, that some of the CPI's right-faction leaders have carried a compliant attitude toward Nehru too far was suggested when the March, 1963, issue of the Soviet-controlled *World Marxist Review* published a review article by Namboodiripad (identified as merely a "member of the CPI Central Secretariat"). In this article Namboodiripad—speaking presumably with the endorsement of the CPSU—reiterated the basic Soviet thesis that the Indian bourgeoisie had "not exhausted its progressive role," but also emphasized the need to support the Nehru government only when it did well, criticizing it when it misbehaved. Namboodiripad chided "some comrades" for believing it possible simply to "walk in step with the government."

For Peking, of course, the matter is much more simple; and *Jenmin Jih-pao* on March 9, 1963, made its position plain with an editorial denouncing the CPI leadership in the most violent terms to date, condemning Dange as a Titoist revisionist who was now beyond the Communist pale, and as one who had betrayed and split the CPI by capitulating to Nehru and the Indian bourgeoisie.

PROSPECTS FOR THE CPI

Thus, by the spring of 1963, despite Moscow's apparent desire to restrain it, the right-wing faction was at last firmly in possession of the machinery of the Communist Party of India throughout the country, while the leftist faction—its top leaders still imprisoned—was apparently continuing to combat the authority of the Party leadership. It remained to be seen whether the leftists would eventually go on to create and announce a second Communist Party in India, as has already happened, for example, in Brazil.

There seems little doubt that a final break in relations between the Soviet and Chinese parties would in any case lead to a splitting up of the CPI. In the absence of such explicit mutual excommunication, however, there is every likelihood that the CPSU will continue to strive to maintain (or restore) a façade of unity in the Indian Party. It would do so if only because the three greatest centers of Communist popular strength in India—Kerala, Andhra, and West Bengal—are also centers of considerable left-faction strength within the Party, so that in the event of the formation of two Communist parties in India, the leftist one, oriented toward Communist China, might well take with it a fair proportion of the rank and file.

Whether, and regardless of how long, the CPSU succeeds in this effort, the fortunes of the CPI within India must in the long run be closely tied to the fortunes of the Party's factional struggle and to the choice the Party must continue to make between paths offered by Moscow and Peking. The Indian Party appears to have found itself incapable of nonalignment between the CPSU and the CCP, insofar as it involves neutrality on policy issues disputed by the two bloc leaders. In particular, the question of policy toward the Nehru government, on which many of the differences between the CPSU and the CCP have focused in recent years, cannot be evaded by the CPI, which must eventually lean to either one side or the other, since it can neither avoid having a policy toward Nehru nor reconcile the incompatible policies of the Chinese and Soviet leaderships. (This is not to say that the rightist leaders of the CPI, should they remain in control of the organization, will necessarily show complete obedience to the CPSU over the line to be followed toward Nehru; but the discrepancies between the Soviet and Indian parties on this point will continue to be secondary in comparison with the gulf between the views of each and the views of Mao Tse-tung.) Similarly, the questions of whether to continue to rely primarily upon parliamentary elections as the avenue to power, whether to seek to draw the "national bourgeoisie" into an alliance (and on what terms), and what line to take toward the left wing of the Congress Party are matters which in the past have been blurred over in compromise resolutions, but which cannot be indefinitely evaded in practice.

The cautious policies enjoined upon the CPI by Moscow over the last decade, for the sake of Soviet foreign-policy interests, have not been unprofitable for the Indian Communist Party: They have allowed it to gain a mass following and to become the second largest party in the Indian Parliament. They have not, however, brought the day of the revolutionary triumph (which in the heady days of 1948 had been thought to be just around the corner) again within sight. The harsher line apparently urged upon the CPI by Peking —similarly, dictated by Chinese national interests—has seemed to appeal to those in the Indian Party who feel (with some justice) that the Party's revolutionary élan and movement forward is slowly disappearing because of acceptance of Soviet dictates. The Party rightists, on the other hand, apparently have come to feel (even more strongly than the CPSU) that open attack upon Nehru or renouncement of the parliamentary line would cast away the gains the Party has made over the last decade. It seems likely that a clear-cut choice between the continued role of enervating "revisionism" (as the leftists see it) and a return to reckless "sectarianism" (as the rightists see it) can be made by the CPI only after the Party has permanently resolved its inner conflict over its alignment in the Sino-Soviet struggle.

NOTES

1. Until the CPI did so in August, 1962, the only Communist parties in the Far Eastern area that had followed the CPSU in criticizing Albania were those of Outer Mongolia, Ceylon, and Australia.

2. Quoted in "Struggle for People's Democracy and Socialism—Some Questions of Strategy and Tactics," *Communist* (CPI theoretical journal), II, No. 4 (June–July, 1949), 21–89.

3. *Ibid.*, pp. 77–87. See the discussions by John H. Kautsky, *Moscow and the Communist Party of India* (New York: John Wiley & Sons, 1956), pp. 73–77; and Gene D. Overstreet and Marshall Windmiller, *Communism in India* (Berkeley, Calif.: University of California Press, 1959), pp. 289–91. Although it is barely conceivable that Ranadive might have been given direct instructions by the CPSU to attack Mao, this seems unlikely, if only because by the time Ranadive wrote in July, 1949, the CPSU had already accepted the particular Maoist doctrine that was the central object of Ranadive's assault. It appears more likely that Ranadive sought justification for attack on the authority cited by his internal Party opponents in certain earlier indications of strain between Mao and Stalin at the time the CCP was coming to power in late 1948–49. Kautsky cited one such possible indication, in the Cominform journal's excision of a key point on the significance of the Chinese Communist successes when reprinting a report by the British Communist Palme Dutt on the "national liberation movement" in the fall of 1948 (*loc. cit.*, p. 55). A stronger indication may have been furnished Ranadive by the Soviet treatment afforded Anna Louise Strong and her book *Tomorrow's China* in early 1949. Based on repeated conversations with CCP leaders, this book was published by the Communist press of many countries in late 1948 and early 1949; in India, it appeared under the title *Dawn Out of China* in the fall of 1948. In this work, Miss Strong paid repeated tribute to the experience and authority of the Chinese Communist Party and Mao and the particular and unique relevance of Mao's teachings to the revolutions of Asia. She even went so far as to state explicitly that "it is to Mao Tse-tung and to Communist China much more than to present-day Moscow" that the Asian revolutions look for their "latest and most practical ideas." When she visited Moscow in early 1949, she was arrested, charged with espionage, and subsequently expelled from the country. Six years later, at a time when relations between Stalin's heirs and Mao were at their best, the Soviet press published a formal announcement acknowledging that the actions against Anna Louise Strong in 1949 had been groundless (*Pravda*, March 3, 1955). In effect, the CPSU thus admitted that the steps taken against Miss Strong had been directed against Mao, and apologized to Mao.

4. "Statement of Editorial Board of *Communist* on Anti-Leninist Criticism of Comrade Mao Tse-tung," *Communist*, III, No. 3 (July–August, 1950), 6–35.

5. One of the factors cited in CPI documents in 1951 to explain why armed peasant warfare on the Chinese model was for the time being unsuitable for India was the lack of a firm, contiguous rear such as the Chinese People's Liberation Army was said (by the Indian Communists) to have had in the Soviet Union. (See "Policy Statement," p. 21, and "Tactical Line," p. 37, in the brochure *Communist Conspiracy at Madurai*, published by the Indian organiza-

tion Democratic Research Service [Bombay: 1954].) This was to be of importance in 1959, when the Chinese Army at last made a vigorous appearance on the Tibetan borders of India, making apposite for the first time the question of whether the CPI now had its contiguous support base across the border.

6. Thus, speaking at the CPI's Fourth (Palghat) Congress in 1956, on the disturbing consequences of the CPSU's Twentieth Congress and de-Stalinization, General Secretary Ghosh singled out the CCP statement "On the Historical Experience of the Dictatorship of the Proletariat" as the most elaborate and satisfactory document on the question he had seen. Ghosh noted that Peking's statement had been reprinted in the Indian Communist press, and urged all CPI members to study it as a guide for solution of the troubles and doubts which the CPSU action had brought them. (See "Report of Ajoy Ghosh to the Fourth CPI Congress," in the Democratic Research Service brochure *Communist Double Talk at Palghat* [Bombay: 1956], pp. 117–25.) Moderates such as Ghosh did not become disenchanted with Peking until considerably later.

7. See "Report to the [Fourth] Party Congress" (p. 58) and "Organizational Methods and Practices of Party Centre" (p. 97), *Communist Double Talk at Palghat*.

8. "Review Report of the Politburo," *Communist Conspiracy of Madurai*, pp. 126–40; "Report to the Party Congress," *loc. cit.*, pp. 57–59; "Organizational Methods and Practices of Party Centre," *loc. cit.*, pp. 87, 93–103.

9. *Link* (New Delhi weekly), February 26, 1961.

10. Despite abundant indication in Soviet and Chinese publications that the appraisal of Nehru as pro-imperialist was already being revised, the 1951 CPI Program persisted in describing him as "essentially" an agent of British imperialism. (*Program of the Communist Party of India* [Bombay: Communist Party of India, 1951].) A decade later an article by Ghosh in *Pravda*, April 5, 1961, retroactively condemned this "sectarian" error.

11. See introductory remarks in *Communist Conspiracy at Madurai*, pp. 12–19.

12. This change began after the July, 1950, exchange of letters between Stalin and Nehru over a proposed settlement of the Korean problem. See the discussion by Allen S. Whiting, *China Crosses the Yalu* (New York: The Macmillan Company, 1960), pp. 60–62.

13. "Report to the Party Congress," *loc. cit.*, p. 53.

14. R. Palme Dutt, "New Features in National Liberation Struggle of Colonial and Dependent People," *For a Lasting Peace, For a People's Democracy*, October 8, 1954.

15. "Report to the Party Congress," *loc. cit.*, pp. 53–54.

16. *Ibid.*, p. 54.

17. A subsequent CPI document declared that by the summer of 1955 an "intense political struggle" had resulted within the Party which "became the main feature of inner-Party life from top to bottom," so that "even the current activity of the party came to a standstill in most provinces." ("Organizational Methods and Practices of Party Centre," *loc. cit.*, p. 94.)

18. In his speech to the CPI Palghat Congress following the CPSU's Twentieth Congress, Ghosh alluded to the consternation spreading throughout the CPI, acknowledging that "some of our comrades say that the whole moral basis on which they stood is shaken and there is nothing on which to stand." He pleaded that the Party not give way to "cynicism" regarding the U.S.S.R. and the CPSU, insisting that the Soviet Party "remains the leading Party" of the

international movement. But he clearly indicated his own dismay at the way in which de-Stalinization was being handled by Moscow; and after citing questions he said were being asked within the CPI regarding the responsibility of other CPSU leaders for Stalin's actions, he declared that he had no satisfactory answers to give and that "what replies have been given have not satisfied me." ("Report of Ajoy Ghosh to the Fourth CPI Congress," *loc. cit.*, pp. 117–25.) Subsequently, a CPI Central Committee resolution in July, 1956, warned that a wholly negative, "one-sided appraisal" of Stalin's role "causes bewilderment among the masses and can be utilized by enemies of Communism to confuse them." (*New Age* [weekly], July 15, 1956.)

19. In an open letter published in *New Age* (weekly) on November 18, 1956, Ghosh, responding to a Socialist challenge to the CPI on the Hungarian issue, defended the Soviet action apologetically, but admitted that the Party had been wrong in the past in "idealizing the U.S.S.R." and in not having paid more attention to other people's criticism of the Soviet Union.

20. Modeste Rubinstein, "A Non-Capitalist Path for Underdeveloped Countries," *New Times*, Nos. 28 and 32 (1956); reprinted in *New Age* (monthly), V, No. 10 (October, 1956), 19–28. Rubinstein cited and praised the significance of the endorsements of "socialism" for India by Nehru and the Congress Party; he hailed the growth of state capitalism in the Indian economy as a "progressive" factor (unlike state capitalism in the "imperialist" West); he cited Lenin as saying that such state capitalism is a step toward socialism; and he suggested that other necessary steps would come with the growth of the state sector under Nehru's leadership.

21. *New Age* (monthly), V, No. 10 (October, 1956), 6–18. Ghosh took umbrage at the Soviet writer's flat statement that the peaceful path to socialism "had been advocated for many years by Jawaharlal Nehru," at his whitewashing of all the "reactionary" side of the Indian Government's policies, and particularly at Rubinstein's omission of all indications that the proletariat and the Communist Party must lead the way to "socialism."

22. *Pravda*, September 18, 1956.

23. This hypothesis cannot be confirmed from Chinese publications, which are not known to have begun direct polemical attacks upon this Soviet line until three years later. Liu Shao-ch'i, in his report to the CCP's Eighth Congress, however, spoke of state capitalism as useful "under the leadership of a state where the proletariat holds power," and quoted Lenin to the effect that it was then useful in that it could be restricted. (*Jen-min Jih-pao*, September 16, 1956.) The Soviets, on the other hand, have maintained that it is also useful in countries such as India, insofar as it can be expanded.

24. See, for example, the article by G. Skorov in *Mirovaya Ekonomika i Mezhdunarodniye Otnosheniya*, April, 1958; the article by Ye. Zhukov in *World Marxist Review*, I, No. 3 (November, 1958); and Chapter 16 of the Soviet textbook *Fundamentals of Marxism-Leninism* (Moscow: 1959). As early as the summer of 1958, one Soviet book indicated disagreement with Peking on this subject by declaring that a "mechanical" imitation of the Chinese revolution in other backward countries was "impermissible"; it quoted an early Mao statement on the impossibility of the national bourgeoisie's ruling over a viable national state and directly contradicted Mao, citing India, among other countries, as evidence to the contrary. (M. S. Dzhunusov, *The Historical Experience of the Building of Socialism in Formerly Backward Countries* [Moscow: Gospolitizdat, 1958], p. 150.)

25. Shih Tsu-chih, in *Kuo-chi Wen-t'i Yen-chiu* (*Research in International Studies*), May 3, 1960. Similar statements were made by Wang Chia-hsiang in *Hung Ch'i*, No. 19, 1959, and by Hu Hsi-kuei in a broadcast over the Chinese Communist home service on January 24, 1960.

26. *Vodnyy Transport* (*Water Transportation*), October 9, 1958. The editorial ended by declaring that "in spite of all the tricks and slander, reaction in Kerala has not succeeded in causing the Communists to give up the course of selfless service to the people which they have set for themselves; the struggle in Kerala has not yet ended."

27. Yudin, "Reply to Shri Jawaharlal Nehru's 'The Basic Approach,'" *World Mcrxist Review*, I, No. 4 (December, 1958), 38–56.

28. Reported on the Soviet home service radio, January 31, 1959.

29. *Link*, September 18, 1960.

30. Ajoy Ghosh, "The Communist Party, the Vanguard for Indian Democracy," *New Age* (weekly), August 16, 1959.

31. The statement appeared in *Pravda*, September 10, 1959.

32. *Link*, February 5, 1961, claimed that Ghosh had told a recent CPI meeting that while he was in the U.S.S.R. in 1959 he had sent a message to the CCP concerning the Sino-Indian border dispute; this message supposedly was not answered.

33. *Ibid.*, September 18, 1960.

34. *New Age* (weekly), November 22, 1959.

35. *Link*, September 11, 1960.

36. *Shih-chieh Chih-shih* (*World Knowledge*) (Peking), October 5, 1959.

37. This was characterized by *New Age* (weekly), November 22, 1959, as "sharp differences in approach and emphasis and sometimes even in outlook . . . revealed in the discussion."

38. *New Age* (weekly), November 22, 1959.

39. *Bharat Jyoti* (Bombay), April 16, 1959. After publicly hailing the Nagpur decisions, Dange had reportedly told a meeting of the Communist-dominated trade-union federation that he fully endorsed the government's policy regarding the public sector of the economy and called upon the unions not to hamper its growth.

40. Basavapunniah was said to have harangued a December, 1959, meeting of the Maharashtra Party organization for three hours, insisting that India and not Communist China had committed aggression and attempting to browbeat the Maharashtrans into abstaining from future public expressions of support for New Delhi. (*Tarun Bharat* [Poona], February 6, 1960.) Basavapunniah was taking advantage of the fact that he had just temporarily assumed the post of Acting General Secretary because of the hospitalization of Ajoy Ghosh.

41. *Link*, May 22, 1960.

42. *Ibid.*, July 31, 1960. See also the New Delhi weekly *Blitz*, July 30, 1960.

43. *Link*, July 31, 1960.

44. *Hindustan Standard*, September 8, 1960. A summary of this resolution was promptly issued by Tass on September 8 and published in *Pravda* two days later.

45. *Link*, September 11 and 18, 1960.

46. For example, P. Sundarayya, leader of the leftist wing of the Andhra Pradesh Party and one of the most militant of all CPI figures, consistently espoused the Chinese Communist case against India in public meetings before and after the September Central Executive Committee resolutions were passed.

See *Indian Express*, June 22, 1960, and *Andhra Prabha*, September 18, 1960.

47. *Hindustan Times*, November 14, 1960, gives the purported text of this resolution. In a revealing passage, the West Bengal Party complains that the CEC "called its resolution an inner-Party resolution, but there can be no doubt that the CEC passed the resolution with the full knowledge that it would go to the press as usual, and the CEC passed it knowing fully the implications of its being openly published." This statement insinuates that the anti-Chinese secret resolution was leaked to the Indian press by rightist members of the Central Executive Committee, and also suggests that the West Bengal counterresolution was leaked in retaliation by the leftists—and furthermore, that such actions are now typical of life in the CPI.

48. *Navbharat Times* (Delhi), July 8, 1961.

49. *Link*, December 18, 1960.

50. *Ibid.*, October 16, 1960.

51. Among the many materials now available testifying to this Chinese struggle is the purported text of Luigi Longo's speech at the Moscow meeting, published in Italy and Poland in early 1962. (*Paese* [Rome], January 25, 1962; *Polityka* [Warsaw], February 17, 1962.) For the French Party's version of these events, see the pamphlet published by the Central Committee of the French CP, *Problèmes du movement communiste international* (Paris: January, 1963).

52. According to one report, the Chinese successfully opposed the inclusion in the 1960 Moscow Statement of a paragraph condemning factionalism in the international movement. (*Link*, July 16, 1961.)

53. *Link*, February 5, 1961.

54. *Ibid.*

55. *New Age* (weekly), March 5, 1961.

56. *Link*, February 26, 1961.

57. *Ibid.* This bow by Namboodiripad toward the leftists was testimony to their growing strength within the Party. Namboodiripad's report was, however, eventually shelved by the Congress, presumably because it was too controversial.

58. This apparently resulted from New Delhi's refusal to renew visas for a Chinese delegation to a World Peace Council meeting in India two weeks before, following a public altercation between a member of this delegation and an Indian Government official over the border dispute. (*The Washington Post*, July 15, 1961; see also Savak Katrak, "India's Communist Party Split," *The China Quarterly*, No. 7 [July–September, 1961], which contains a good account of the CPI Congress.)

59. *New Age* (weekly), April 23, 1961.

60. *Ibid.*

61. For example, the *Hindu Times*, April 11, 1961.

62. Such a leftist threat to split the Party was reported in *Link*, April 16, 1961.

63. *New Age* (monthly), X, No. 5 (May, 1961).

64. While Ghosh merely implied strongly several times that the national democratic front must include suitable elements of the national bourgeoisie, *Pravda's* April 12 report on his speech, in summarizing this portion of his remarks, took the liberty of saying so explicitly—another indication of the CPSU's position.

65. *New Age* (weekly), November 26, 1961. Ghosh's statement was printed on the first page under a screaming headline: "China Must Put an End to Such Acts."

66. *Jen-min Jih-pao*, December 7, 1961.

67. *Borba* (Belgrade), January 10, 1962.

68. One such *Swadhinata* editorial appeared on December 5, commenting on Nehru's speech in Calcutta three days before; this was reprinted in *Jen-min Jih-pao* on December 13.

69. PTI, December 13, 1961.

70. Chairman Dange thus became the second CPI leader to be so honored in a *Jen-min Jih-pao* editorial, the first having been Ghosh ten months previously.

71. This was spelled out still more forcefully by Chou En-lai in a speech on November 4, when he thanked the North Koreans for "upholding the stand of proletarian internationalism"; this he defined as "distinguishing right from wrong, upholding justice, denouncing the Indian aggression against China, supporting China's counterattacks in self-defense," and supporting China's proposals for a border settlement. (NCNA, November 4, 1962.)

72. Reported on Prague radio, October 25, 1962.

73. *Ibid.*, November 8, 1962.

74. *L'Unita* (Rome), November 11, 1962.

75. *New Age* (weekly), November 11, 1962. In another article in the same issue, Dange himself wrote that the CPI would help defend the country because Communists are committed to defend "just wars." The usual Communist criterion for a "just war," of course, would require Dange to do exactly the opposite.

76. *Statesman* (New Delhi), November 16, 1962.

77. *Jen-min Jih-pao*, March 9, 1963. The Chinese here went so far as to suggest that the Indian Government acted "on a list of names previously furnished to it" by Dange.

78. *Link*, December 16, 1962.

79. *Ibid.*, December 23, 1962.

80. *Ibid.*; *Swadhinata* (Calcutta), December 12 and 27, 1962; *Statesman*, January 9, 1963.

81. *Jen-min Jih-pao*, March 9, 1963.

82. *Ibid.*, January 15, 1963.

83. *Thought* (New Delhi weekly), December 29, 1962.

84. *New Age* (weekly), January 20, 1963. The Tass account of the resolution leaned heavily on the latter aspect of the statement.

85. *Ibid.*, February 17, 1963.

5. Indonesian Communism and the Transition to Guided Democracy

by RUTH T. McVEY

With a claimed membership of more than 2 million, Indonesia's Communist Party (PKI) is one of the largest in the world. It asserts, on the basis of its electoral gains since 1955, that it commands the largest following of any party in the country; and in this estimate it may well be correct. The Party's strength seems the more remarkable when we consider that a decade ago its membership totaled less than 8,000, and it was only beginning to recover from a disastrous rebellion against the government of the revolutionary republic, which had robbed it of a good part of its leadership and popular support.

Unlike most Communist parties, and certainly unlike most powerful ones, the PKI has managed to advance without arousing the organized opposition of the non-Communist parties. Since 1952, it has found it necessary to oppose only one of Indonesia's cabinets; and by the end of the decade, the PKI saw its opponents among the political parties reduced to ineffectiveness. The Communists have been far more effective than any other party in organizing both their own membership and their broader support in mass organization; no other political movement can claim to control labor, youth, peasant, or women's organizations of equal stature. Moreover, the Communist Party has managed to secure recognition as an integral part of Indonesian political life; and thus, without abandoning its international connections, it has gained a powerful claim to nationalist acceptance.

In the light of this achievement, it would seem natural to conclude that the PKI is well on its way to an assumption of control over Indonesian affairs. Perhaps this will eventually prove to be so; but at present the Communists' position, while powerful, is also

148

extremely delicate. The source of danger to it does not lie in the parliamentary framework but in the steady dissolution of that framework; the Party's advance has been in terms of institutions which are themselves declining. Consequently, the Communists' recent progress has rather resembled that of the squirrel on the treadmill. The course of this development, which will be described below, furnishes an interesting example of what may happen to a movement that seeks power through legitimate means in a country where the terms of legitimacy themselves are in a state of profound flux.

THE NATIONAL UNITED FRONT

The policy by which the Indonesian Communists have sought power has remained essentially the same for more than a decade, having been introduced in January, 1951, with the transfer of Party control to a younger generation of leaders headed by D. N. Aidit, M. H. Lukman, Njoto, and Sudisman. Although ideological factors were not the only ones of importance in the transfer of Party power, a major reason for this group's rejection of the older generation was its identification with policies that had been pursued by the Party in 1946–48 and which, they held, had been responsible for the PKI's eclipse at the end of that period. Since this experience and the Aidit group's analysis of it have had much to do with the strategy since followed by the PKI, they should be considered here, though it will be necessary to do so in brief and very simplified terms.

During 1946–48, while Indonesia was engaged in its revolution against the Dutch, the Communist Party remained small and did not put itself forward as a major claimant to political power. Instead of seeking influence in its own name, it entered into a broad coalition (the Left Wing, or Sajap Kiri) with other parties and mass organizations in which its interests were represented by leaders who sympathized with the PKI or were actually secret Party members.[1] The Party did not have control of the coalition, nor did it seek publicly to establish such control; its purpose was to blur the boundary between Communist and non-Communist rather than to emphasize it. In the process, the Party played the parliamentary game, acknowledged the nationalist revolutionary leadership, and pursued a relatively moderate policy regarding both domestic issues and relations with the Dutch.

This strategy afforded the Communists considerable advantage:

It allowed them to pursue, through their allied parties, a more flexible program than their own ideological commitments allowed; similarly, it enabled them to gather support from a broader segment of the populace than could be expected to adhere to a Communist Party per se. It allowed them, through their unofficial adherents, to raise mass organizations and to secure important positions within the government without obviously raising the specter of a Communist take-over. The mass strength and responsible attitude of the Left Wing recommended it for cabinet leadership, which position it enjoyed until the beginning of 1948.

The leftist alliance proved, however, to be as unreliable as it was broad. Splits occurred in its leadership when, under Cold War and domestic pressures, the Communists increasingly demanded commitment to their views. Having relied on parliamentary legality, the Communists and their allies were not in a position to offer an effective extraparliamentary challenge when the Left Wing cabinet was replaced by one that proceeded to cut down their positions in the military and the government. Not having themselves made claims to the legitimate leadership of the national revolution, the Communists found it difficult to provide reasons why, when the chips were down, popular support should be given to them rather than to the official heads of the republic. In September, 1948, when Communist relations with the government deteriorated to the point of armed conflict, the PKI found itself unable to utilize the Left's massive but amorphous strength, unable even to carry the entire Communist Party with it.

The mistakes of the Party leaders at that time, the Aidit group charged, lay in the fact that they were too accustomed to thinking in European popular-front terms, too little aware of the potentialities of the Indonesian revolution itself, and too inclined to regard the Communist Party as the representative of the proletariat alone: hence their failure to see that the PKI could and should assume the leadership of the national revolution itself, that it could and should appeal directly to the Indonesian masses instead of losing itself in a welter of allied organizations. Consequently, when they assumed control of the Party, the new leaders called for the PKI to claim in its own name hegemony over the national revolution, which was in their view still uncompleted. The Party was to establish a National United Front which would seek the loyalty of the proletariat, peasantry, and petty and national bourgeoisie through anti-imperialist and antifeudal slogans. The PKI was not to limit its membership to a small, ideologically trained elite, but was to expand to a size that would allow it broad contact with the population and thorough control over Communist-sponsored mass movements.

These criticisms of the Party's previous course and the policies proposed to mend it had a sound basis in the logic of the Indonesian political situation; but they were not founded on local considerations alone. The new PKI leadership freely acknowledged its indebtedness to the ideas propounded by Musso, an old-time Indonesian Communist who had returned from Soviet exile in 1948 to reorganize and guide the faltering Party. His proposals had reflected both Russia's conversion to the uncompromising militancy of the Zhdanov two-camp doctrine and its new-found enthusiasm for Chinese Communist revolutionary methods. In demanding a return to Musso's program, the new PKI leadership was, thus, also urging conformity with these still-valid guidelines to international Communist policy.

Having decided to assert Communist claims to national leadership, the Party leaders faced two major alternatives for implementing their decision. They could engage in a violent struggle for power with the established nationalists, or they could seek to extend their influence by more legitimate means. In principle, both would have been possible, since the Chinese example was one of armed struggle, and Soviet relations with Indonesia were very poor at that time. Musso's own intentions in 1948 seem to have been a seizure of power; it is not clear whether he envisioned a rebellion or a bloodless coup—he reportedly referred to his strategy as his "Gottwald Plan," thus intimating a Czech-type takeover[2]—but an armed clash with the authorities did ensue, resulting in total defeat for the Communists. Although the 1948 debacle augured ill for further armed adventure, insurrection was still a quite possible course of action in 1951, for the central government's authority sat lightly on the nation's shoulders, and armed opposition by diverse groups constituted a serious threat to the regime. In spite of these precedents, the Party leadership showed no apparent hesitation in choosing the peaceful road, and its subsequent successes in both the parliamentary and organizational spheres bore out the wisdom of its decision. These very triumphs carried within them the seeds of potential danger, however. The more the Party gained within the legal framework, the more dependent it became on the terms of that framework, and the more in the way of established organization and in-

fluence it had to lose by resorting to violence at any given point.
We shall presently see how, in recent years, this was to present the
Communists with a very grave problem.

Some eight months after it assumed leadership, the Aidit group
was taught a lesson that was to affect its choice of action deeply.
In order to rebuild the Party's popular strength and express its opposition to the anti-Communist Sukiman cabinet, the new PKI
command encouraged a wave of labor unrest which soon reached
such proportions that it became apparent the government must
either assert its authority or resign. In August, Sukiman gave his
answer: Accusing the Communists of having organized a plot to
overthrow the government, he ordered surprise raids on the headquarters of the PKI and its allied unions and had most of the
Communist Party and union leadership thrown into jail. It took the
PKI and its labor affiliates nearly two years to recover fully from
this blow; and from it the Party concluded that it must avoid
political isolation at all costs. As long as the Communists themselves were unable or unwilling to oppose force with violence of
their own, they must, it appeared, secure the protection of a powerful governmental ally by giving it a stake in their existence.

The PKI first sought this protection through the Nationalist Party
(PNI), to which the Communists offered their parliamentary support, modestly refraining from requiring cabinet representation in
return. The Nationalist politicians looked on the PKI's bid with
favor, for they were irritated at the cabinet demands of the Masjumi, the major Muslim party and their chief partner and rival in
government. Communist support would enable them to form a
cabinet without the Masjumi and thus give them a lever by which
to reduce the Masjumi's demands. Moreover, an expansion of the
PKI's organizational activity might help lessen the Masjumi's
much-feared grass-roots support in the coming general elections.
The PNI thus gained freedom on the parliamentary level, and the
PKI freedom to organize the masses.

The PKI was by no means unique among Communist movements in pursuing an alliance with a more powerful, non-Communist party. The strategy—a "united front from above," as it is called
in classical Communist parlance—had been frequently attempted,
most notably with the socialist parties of Europe. It had nearly
always resulted in frustration, however, for the Communists were
rarely willing to relax their own organizational and ideological activities to the extent deemed necessary by their chosen ally. In the
Indonesian case, however, this relaxation was necessary only to a

limited extent. One reason for this was that the PKI did not have to use slogans offensive to the Nationalist Party in extending its mass influence. It concentrated its domestic political attacks on the Masjumi and its smaller partner, the Indonesian Socialist Party (PSI), which the PNI was only too glad to see whittled down. It phrased its arguments against the *status quo* in nationalist terms and directed them against foreign rather than native economic interests. It pursued this line somewhat in advance of Moscow's progress in backing neutralist nationalism, but the facts that it was sailing in the direction of an increasingly prevailing ideological wind, that it was far from the Soviet center and, above all, that it was successful, seem to have protected it from international complications.

More important than the matter of agitational slogans in preserving PNI-PKI relations was the peculiar structure of Indonesian political life itself. We have noted that the PNI sought freedom in the parliamentary sphere, the PKI opportunity to expand its mass organizations. The two aims did not clash, for the two spheres of activity were to a remarkable extent distinct from each other. Despite the fact that the major parties boasted mass organizations allied to them and in theory carried their organization down to the local level, there was actually very little substance to their organizational efforts—except those of the Communists—and little cohesion between politics on the national level and on the levels below. Parliamentary politics took place more or less in a world of its own, its primary concern being the division of government power and office between national-level parties and party factions. This was most notably the case prior to the elections of 1955, when no party was really sure how much popular support it had and where that backing lay. The chief bastion of known PNI support was the government bureaucracy, but this was not a sphere that the PKI was then attempting to penetrate or combat. The interests of the PNI and PKI were thus cushioned from collision to a considerably greater extent than were those in the European-style "united front from above," in which Communist efforts to extend their own popular support inevitably clashed with socialist interests in the same sphere.[3]

The Nationalists did show alarm following the general elections of 1955 and the regional assembly elections of 1957, which revealed not only that the PKI was increasing its strength at unprecedented speed, but that its popular advances were being made at the expense of the PNI rather than the Masjumi. Moves of the PNI toward a *rapprochement* with the Masjumi floundered, however, on long-established factional quarrels and the continuing tendency of parliamentary politics to exist in its own peculiar world. The PKI, wisely refraining from forcing the issue, continued to give parliamentary support to the PNI, reserving its claims for cabinet representation as a weapon to keep the PNI from making too many concessions to its Muslim rival. Indeed, since 1952, the PKI has supported the "progressive aspects" of all the Indonesian governments except one—the Masjumi-led Harahap cabinet of 1955—although it has been directly represented in none of them.

The PKI's major concern in this period, the pursuit of mass strength, was markedly successful. The campaign to transform the Party from a small indoctrinated elite to a massive organizational force resulted in an expansion of Party membership from 7,910 in March, 1952, to 1.5 million in 1958.[4] Party units, which had existed only on Java and Sumatra in 1952, were extended throughout the Indonesian archipelago in this process.

Although the PKI's expansion of its membership was impressive in itself, the extent of the Party's influence can only be appreciated if we consider the strength of the mass organizations it controlled. Since the bases of the Communists' popular support have remained the same up to the present, it is perhaps worth while to describe them in some detail as they emerged in the period before the collapse of parliamentary democracy.

The principal source of Communist organizational strength outside the Party was the labor movement. SOBSI, the largest federation of labor unions, was in principle independent but in practice openly committed to the support of the PKI. It claimed a membership of about 2.7 million in 1957, and was estimated to control about 60 per cent of organized Indonesian labor; actually, its strength was even greater than these figures suggest, for it was by far the best organized and most active of the labor federations. Since Indonesian-owned industries were generally small, traditional, and difficult to organize, SOBSI's strength lay among the workers in large-scale foreign-run enterprises. The fact that these were foreign enterprises—and overwhelmingly Dutch, at that—gave SOBSI an excellent lever for pursuing wage and benefit demands; although the government was concerned to prevent economy-crippling strikes, it generally gave the benefit of the doubt to the unions in their disputes with management. At the same time, the fact that Indonesian-owned industries were insignificant sources of labor support made it possible for the Communists to pursue an aggressive labor policy without incurring the accusation of fomenting class warfare among Indonesians. Indeed, SOBSI publicly joined the PKI in proclaiming support of the "national entrepreneurs" as part of the four-class alliance of the National United Front.

In addition to recruiting members and engaging in political and economic agitation, SOBSI concentrated on increasing its adherents' class consciousness through indoctrination. This consciousness was admittedly at a rather low level. Not only were Indonesia's urban proletariat illiterate, inexperienced, and recently off the farm, but the bulk of SOBSI's labor strength was not located in the cities at all. Its major component unions—SARBUPRI (estate workers), SBG (sugar workers), and SARBUKSI (forestry workers)—comprised laborers in Indonesia's agricultural industries. They were a proletariat, but not an urban proletariat; and while their agrarian connections had potential advantages for organizing the peasantry, the Communists' concern that the proletarian purity of the labor movement would be diluted by the "petty bourgeois" values of the village tended to prevent their utilization of this fact.[5]

Communist strength among the peasantry was much less developed than among the proletariat. True, the Party succeeded in 1953 in amalgamating its own peasant organization, Rukun Tani Indonesia, with the larger Barisan Tani Indonesia (BTI), thus securing the most effective peasant organization in the country. The PKI also proved to be more successful than any other party in extending its organization into the villages, and elections showed its rural strength, particularly in east and central Java, to be impressive. The PKI leaders declared that the Indonesian revolution was necessarily an agrarian one and that the proletariat could not seize power without the help of the peasantry. However, like all Indonesian parties, the PKI was essentially urban-centered; and this orientation was reinforced, particularly in the early 1950's, by the fear of infecting the Party with the peasants' "petty bourgeois" spirit. Moreover, the Communists found the peasantry hard to organize and to staff with cadres—not unnaturally, for peasant society is usually a tough nut to crack politically, and PKI Party workers, like their non-Communist fellows, were not always eager to bury themselves in the countryside.[6] It was not until the end of 1960 that the PKI Central Committee found Party work among the peasantry to have reached a level that it could regard with satisfaction.[7] In considering its unhappiness with prior achievements, we should remember, however, that the PKI's performance in the agrarian sector was far superior to that of any other Indonesian

political party and very high for a Communist movement not actually engaged in promoting agrarian rebellion.

One of the most serious problems faced by the Party in its work
among the peasantry in this period was the absence of any obvious
slogan for action among that part of the population. In the rural
sector, the PKI could and did raise the antiforeign banner by supporting the claims of squatters on estate lands and the efforts of
small holders to compete with plantation producers; but this affected only certain areas and peasant groups and hence was not
sufficient as a principal vehicle of agitation. There were plenty of
poor and landless peasants, especially on Java, but no class of large
landowners to serve as an obvious target of attack; poverty arose
from an absolute shortage of land rather than the method of its
distribution. The lack of permanent and clearly defined class patterns and the small gradations in size of holdings made it difficult
to exploit distinctions without raising accusations of hairsplitting
and of setting villager against villager—most serious charges in
terms of Indonesian nationalist and traditional peasant values.
Moreover, it not infrequently happened that the Party's local activists or influential supporters were themselves better-situated villagers, and the Party hierarchy had to decide whether to forgo the
advantages of their adherence in the interests of the class struggle
or to utilize it in the name of national unity.[8]

A further problem in Indonesian Communist agrarian policy was
whether to stress individual or collective ownership of land. Usually Communist parties have played on the land hunger of the
poorer peasantry and hence have come out for individual ownership
as long as they are not in power. In Indonesia, however, historical
factors tempted the PKI to skip the individual-ownership stage of
Communist argument. In the Netherlands Indies, land was considered to belong ultimately to the Crown. Moreover, there existed
among various ethnic groups—most notably the Javanese—traditions of communal land ownership, values that had usually been
encouraged by the colonial regime and the plantations, which found
it easier to deal with villages as a unit rather than with individual owners. The share-and-share-alike communal traditions had
achieved a certain romantic aura in Dutch scholarship, and this
was picked up by many nationalist intellectuals, who saw in them
proof of a distinctive Indonesian social character nobler than that
of the competitive West. These factors would seem to have combined with the example set by the Soviet Union to cause, from 1947
to 1951, the PKI's Rukun Tani Indonesia to urge the nationaliza-

tion of land and the leftist Barisan Tani Indonesia to call for the recognition of the state's rights over all land.[9] Early in 1952, however, the PKI decided that such an emphasis followed too blindly both the colonial past and inappropriate foreign example and considered too little what the Indonesian peasant himself wanted; since then, although Party leaders have expressed admiration for China's communes,[10] they have not deviated from their stress on individual ownership of land.

The matter of the agrarian class struggle was much less quickly decided, and for most of the 1950's central Party advice on this point was highly ambivalent. Proceeding from the standpoint of the class struggle, the Party argued that rural Communists must strive to support the poor and landless peasants, neutralize the middle-level peasants, and combat even more intensely landlords and feudal remnants.[11] Proceeding from the viewpoint of the National United Front, however, the Party proclaimed that in the interests of the anti-imperialist struggle the rich peasants—the rural equivalent of the national bourgeoisie—were on the right side. A man could definitely be a progressive landlord and even, it seemed, a progressive feudal remnant if his heart was in the right place.[12]

Central to this ambivalence was the fact that little was actually known of the nature of class relationships in the rural sector. Granted that the principal problem in Java—the major area of Communist rural concern—was land shortage rather than land distribution; granted that economic distinctions were relatively minor and fluid; granted the existence of complicated village share-the-wealth mechanisms and the traditional aversion to setting neighbor against neighbor, the fact still remained that the man who cannot feed his children has powerful reason to envy the neighbor who can, even if he has only barely enough. Were there, therefore, deep resentments under the surface of village harmony, and if so was it feasible to exploit them politically?

The PKI leaders were very conscious of their ignorance of the actual nature of rural relationships, and they neither accepted the common stereotype of village harmony nor attempted to impose blindly Marxist-Leninist categories of class distinction. Instead, they called for thorough Party research into village conditions for the purpose of improving the PKI's method of approach.[13] The results of these investigations appear to have strengthened their belief that serious economic differences did exist, and, increasingly, they placed the weight of their advice to the rural cadres on the need to support the poorer against the richer peasantry. Perhaps the PKI leaders were seeing in their investigations what they wanted to see, but non-Communist studies have also shown rural indebtedness and the actual proportion of landless peasants to be far higher than the official figures indicate.[14]

A further complication in the peasant question was the fact that, while economic distinctions were difficult to define, there was a very clear contrast in outlook within the Javanese population based on socioreligious attitudes.[15] Rural Javanese society divides into *santri*—strict Muslims who tend to a relatively individualist and competitive view of life—and *abangan*, who though nominally Muslim adhere to a traditional, communalistic Javanese value system. A third group is the *prijaji*, the traditional aristocracy, which is largely urban and bureaucratic; its values are similar to those of the *abangan*. Party loyalties roughly tend to follow these socioreligious divisions, the PNI representing the *prijaji*, Nahdatul Ulama the conservative rural *santri*, Masjumi the modernist rural and commercial *santri*, and the PKI the *abangan*. The identification of the Communist-oriented Left with the *abangan* seems to have begun early in the Indonesian revolution; by 1948, it was sufficient to make the PKI's conflict with government forces a bloody battle between *santri* and *abangan* in the rural areas involved.

The PKI's identification with the *abangan* has given it the enormous advantage of a solid rural base of support in a key area of the country; and the shared social values of *prijaji* and *abangan* probably facilitated the alliance between PNI and PKI. The *abangan*, however, represent only one area of Indonesia, and the PKI has accordingly labored under the handicap of being a Javanese party. The outlook of the politically articulate group in the Outer Islands generally corresponds roughly to that of the modernist *santri*, and the Masjumi was consequently the strongest group outside Java. From the Communists' point of view this was most unfortunate, not only because the Masjumi was its principal party rival, but also because growing resentment of Java's domination helped make the PKI *persona non grata* in the Outer Islands. As centrifugal forces increased in the mid-1950's, it became clear that unless the Communists managed to overcome their identification with Java they could not extend themselves beyond that island and could not achieve a role in the central government without risking Outer Island secession.

To extend its influence beyond Java, the PKI needed two things: the firm establishment of central government authority on the Outer Islands and an entree to political affairs outside Java. The

Communists, therefore, supported the center against the provinces and pressed the government to take determined action against rebel and separationist groups. They desired no compromise solution to Islamic or regionalist dissidence, for concessions to these forces would undoubtedly strengthen the hand of the Masjumi and lessen the PKI's chances of gaining a place in the government. The Party's attitude in the struggle between regions and center thus differed from that commonly taken by Communist movements to further their fortunes in lands where they do not hold power: By and large, it has been their policy elsewhere to reduce the authority of the central government by supporting centrifugal forces.

The problem of gaining a foothold on the Outer Islands remained a knotty one for the Indonesian Communists. Although they were able to extend their organization to all major parts of the archipelago in this period, their activities in most areas were largely limited to urban and estate workers and were subject to frequent and increasing restrictions imposed by the territorial military commands, which were setting themselves up as spokesmen for regional dissidence. Nonetheless, the 1957–58 regional elections showed the Communists to have gained markedly in Outer Island strength from their 1955 general-election level, while the other major parties commonly experienced an absolute decline in votes. The PKI still lagged behind, but it seemed possible that general disillusionment with the other parties might enable it to play an increasingly significant role in politics outside Java.

The Communists further possessed a potentially dangerous veterans' association in Perbepbsi (Union of Former Armed Fighters of All Indonesia), which they tried to promote as a supplement to military efforts against Darul Islam and other rebel groups. In the military itself, the Communists lacked effective influence, however. Although Party pronouncements periodically stressed the need for securing the support of the soldiery, there is not much evidence that the Communists made a really serious effort in this direction. It is difficult to estimate the extent of sympathy for the PKI among the common soldiers; the few military units that have been rumored to be leftist have almost invariably been Javanese, and it would seem not unreasonable to suppose that their political leanings reflected their civilian attachments rather than their experience in the military.

Within the officers' corps, the influence of the PKI was even more tenuous. An occasional officer has been rumored to be pro-Communist—but in the context of Indonesian military attitudes this has meant "soft" on the PKI rather than loyal to it and, thus, is of considerably less significance than the pro-Communist label in Indonesian civilian politics. The reasons for this absence of influence lay partly in the ideological orientation of the members of the officers' corps—they have tended to be relatively favorable to the PSI and Masjumi insofar as they have borne any tolerance for civilian political groups; and they have tended to exhibit a relatively high regard for religion and low regard for anything smacking of international ties. More importantly, the Army and the PKI represent rival hierarchies competing for power by broadly comparable means. Both are elitist groups, possessing their own *esprit de corps* and their own discipline. The tendency for Army and Party loyalties to conflict has been evidenced frequently enough in Communist countries; in a non-Communist nation possessing a professional army of any standing and vested interest, it is perhaps inevitable that military officers will be little attracted to the Communists unless their triumph appears inevitable. Mavericks there have certainly been among the Indonesian officers; but they have generally been concerned with consolidating their own position, not with subordinating themselves to another hierarchy. Moreover, they have been able to operate freely only outside Java, where the authority of the central command was weak; and the political climate of the Outer Islands has hardly been conducive to a Communist-military alliance.

Through the People's Cultural Foundation, Lekra, the PKI secured the sympathy of the greater part of Indonesia's best creative artists, but otherwise the Party developed little strength among the educated classes. Its university student organizations were far weaker in their sphere than Pemuda Rakjat in the general youth field, and the PKI's influence in the white-collar class was generally restricted to the clerkship level. Whether the Communists' lack of attraction for intellectuals as intellectuals presented a real handicap is a matter for speculation: Indonesia's intelligentsia was not notably fortunate in political affairs in the 1950's; moreover, it seems to be true of Communist movements in general that the higher the proportion of intellectuals in their ranks, the more open they are to disunity and the less effective they are in organizing the masses. On the other hand, the Party's failure to attract the members of the bureaucracy, when combined with the absence of patronage powers accruing to cabinet participants, presented a serious hindrance to penetrating the state apparatus. The Communists' lack of appeal for the educated classes would appear to arise in part from the fact that the Indonesian elite tends to sympathize with the common man in a rather patrician manner, the aristocratic values of the *prijaji* having been carried over into the modern bureaucracy. To subordinate himself to the Communist leadership —which is youthful, not academically well educated, and of motley class origin—would mean losing himself in the masses to an extent generally unacceptable to the *prijaji*-oriented bureaucrat.

Here too, however, the element of individual psychological reaction is perhaps less important than the logic of the general competition for power. Only rarely have Communist movements had any real strength within the bureaucracy of a non-Communist country, and for obvious reasons. The well-situated bureaucrat has a vested interest in preserving the existing governmental system, while the less well-placed one hopes to keep and improve his position—ambitions that normally are not furthered by membership in a Communist Party. Nor could the Indonesian Communists hope for appointment of their members to significant bureaucratic positions, for the highly centralized civil service (*pamong pradja*) was virtually a closed club to outsiders who lacked patronage, educational, and class qualifications. The PKI itself did not make a concerted effort at penetrating the bureaucratic ranks. Perhaps its leaders saw such a cause as hopeless; in any event, a hands-off policy was dictated by its desire to preserve the friendship of the PNI, the party of the bureaucratic elite.

Considering the Communist position in the mid-1950's, we can observe three major points of weakness: The Party had no hold on the governmental apparatus; it was weak outside Java; and it had very little influence on the military. A way to solve the first problem—and to make a beginning with the other two—was provided in the extension of elected government to regional levels. The regional assemblies were designed to increase local democracy and autonomy; they and the executives elected by them were to share power with and eventually to replace the centrally appointed civil-service administrators on their governmental level. If the Communists were able to secure positions within this governmental structure, it would be much less easy for prompt and effective official action to be taken against them, and they would thus be less dependent on subservient alliances on the national government level as security against political isolation.

In twelve second-level (residency and city) areas of Java, the PKI acquired, through elections in 1957, an absolute majority in the legislative councils and hence absolute control of regional executives. In various other areas of Java, it shared executive responsibility with other parties either by virtue of its strength in the legislature or by virtue of the fact that regional coalition patterns deviated from those in the capital. Participation in the territorial governments gave the PKI an opportunity both to show the people what it could do if it were given a chance to hold office—and thus, by setting an example of honesty, efficiency, and achievement, to distinguish itself from the government it supported at the national level—and to demonstrate that Communist participation in or even domination over a government did not mean the eclipse of non-Communist groupings. Party comments emphasized the demonstration value of areas where the PKI had executive control; it is interesting to note that the projects they urged these governments to undertake were not principally aimed at improving the position of the proletariat or Party, but at improving general living conditions in towns and—especially—villages.[16]

With the establishment of the regional-assembly system, the PKI partly abandoned its concern for the good will of the Nationalist Party and began a campaign against the *pamong pradja*, calling it outmoded and feudalist and asking for its complete replacement by the new system. It also urged the swiftest possible extension of elected regional government to the Outer Islands—for even if the Party would be weak in assemblies there, it would have sufficient strength in many of them to form useful alliances and demonstrate its energy and concern for local problems.[17]

THE REJECTION OF PARLIAMENTARY GOVERNMENT

Under these conditions, it is little wonder that the PKI was an enthusiastic supporter of Indonesian representative democracy, and that, when Khrushchev proffered the idea of a peaceful assumption of power by Communist parties, it endorsed this as an immediate prospect for Indonesia. However, the very factors that made the parliamentary environment so advantageous to the Communists —the confusion and rivalry of the political parties, their ineffectiveness in both governmental and mass organizational fields—were to lead to the eclipse of the parliamentary system as a whole. This decline began almost as soon as the returns for the first general elections were in, for instead of providing one group with a clear mandate, they indicated that the stalemate of parliamentary forces would continue. Parliamentary decision-making reached a minimum, and this, combined with Indonesia's deepening economic crisis and the growth of regional discontent, created a stagnation in the governmental process that the country could ill afford.

On the face of it, such a paralysis of authority was anything but unfavorable to the Communists' prospects. While the PKI had prospered electorally, its parliamentary role had always been subordinate to the building of a massive disciplined organizational base. It was thus not dependent on parliamentary democracy per se, but on the dispersal of power and fragmentation of opposition that that system entailed in Indonesia. The collapse of the system should in theory have provided a golden opportunity for the Communists to press their bid for power; but, for two reasons, it did not. One was the imminent prospect of regional rebellion, and the other was the emergence of two powerful elements to fill the vacuum of authority created by the decay of parliamentary government.

We have already described the PKI's weakness in the Outer Islands and noted the Party's policy of backing the center against the regions. If the PKI had taken advantage of governmental weakness in the critical years 1956–58 to push its claim to power, it might have succeeded in establishing its authority on Java, but only at the expense of Outer Island secession. When the international context is considered, it seems unlikely that a Communist Java would have long survived; and if it had, it would have presented economic problems of near-insoluble dimensions. At the same time, as we have also noted, the PKI had been making some headway outside Java and could hope to increase its influence there, particularly if the Masjumi, which was deeply if indirectly implicated in the separationist movement, was discredited and its supporters removed from regional power. Moreover, the preponderance of Java in population and bureaucratic influence gave it a determining authority in national politics so long as a highly centralized governmental system was maintained; and the PKI thus had a vested interest in the restoration of central control. The Communists, therefore, threw their weight in the crisis, not into a move for power, but behind the emergent bastions of central control—the Army and the President.

The transfer of political power from the parliamentary parties to the military and the President took place gradually, but we may perhaps regard the events surrounding the regional rebellions of 1958 as marking a turning point. Parliament proved woefully inadequate in dealing with the rising separationist tide; when this defiance took the form of revolt, President Sukarno stepped in to declare a state of war and siege, and the central command of the Army moved to assert its authority by force. The decisiveness and effectiveness with which the military acted enhanced both its general prestige and its own unity; moreover, the imposition of nationwide martial law gave it a legitimate basis for exercising broad control over Indonesian political life.

The Communists did not at first greet this development with outward alarm; they had previously expressed considerable apprehension at the extension of military influence into Indonesian public life. A new joint leadership had arisen, they declared—that of the Army and the People; together, they would crush the rebellion and embark on the reconstruction of the nation. Since almost any political compromise with the rebels would have involved concessions injurious to Communist interests, the PKI pressed for a military solution, backing an increase in the authority of the central command in the apparent hope that it would be more amenable to central civil authority than were the regional commanders. When, in an effort at rallying popular support and strengthening its control over civilian activities, the Army undertook the creation of civilian-military Cooperation Bodies and a National Front for the Liberation of West Irian, the Party declared that they embodied the alliance of Army and People for which it had been calling and that they would provide the avenues by which the people could participate in the task of suppressing regional dissidence and rebuilding the nation.[18]

It is quite possible that the PKI's support for the Army in this period reflected Party hopes for advancement under the umbrella of the central command. The Communists may well have reckoned that the revolt would be more difficult to crush than it was and that the Army would find it necessary to rely on PKI organizations in order to secure its control.[19] Moreover, the PKI may have felt that the central army, shorn of the influence of the highly anti-Communist rebel commanders, might prove more supple in its attitude toward the Party. Whatever the PKI's hopes for profit from its cooperative attitude, however, it seems certain that the Party's principal motivation in supporting the military effort was its great fear of the effect a genuine compromise—let alone a rebel victory —would have on its political position.

With the reduction of the revolt to the proportions of a disturbance, it became clear that Indonesia had entered a new political era. Parliament and the parties had faded into the background.

Both the Army and the President had greatly enlarged their positions, and the rivalry between them for ultimate power became the leitmotiv of Indonesian politics. The Western-oriented political groups, having been implicated in the revolt, were cast beyond the pale; emotional nationalism consolidated its victory over gradualism in political and economic considerations. Dutch enterprises had been placed under Indonesian control at the end of 1957 and were subsequently nationalized; relations with Holland were broken off as part of the ever more heated campaign for the return of West Irian. The President's Political Manifesto of 1959 was declared to be the staff of Indonesian ideological life, pointing the way to the replacement of Western-derived liberal democracy by a truly national, nonparliamentary "guided democracy." Increasingly, pressure was applied to alter existing institutions, attitudes, and loyalties in conformity with official ideological requirements.

So far as the PKI has been concerned, the most salient feature of the guided democracy era has been the fact that political power, once so highly fragmented, is now concentrated in two formidable centers. The President's strength lies in his considerable stature as a popular leader, in the fact that as Indonesia's first and only president he has a title to primacy which few would question, and in his highly developed ability to play his opponents against each other. The Army, now united under the authority of the central command, possesses a virtual monopoly of force; moreover, it has embedded itself firmly in the economic and political administration of the country. It is increasingly unpopular, but it is unquestionably powerful.

In this new constellation of forces, the PKI's interest has been, first of all, to preserve what it can of the old—that is, to maintain its freedom of action and the dispersal of other sources of political power. This has involved the Party in a somewhat awkward position, for it has meant that the PKI has joined in the official denunciation of parliamentary democracy as "liberal" and "Western" and, at the same time, has appeared as one of that system's principal defenders. The Party has attempted to explain the paradox by arguing that the failings of the parliamentary system in Indonesia were not the fault of representative democracy itself, but resulted from the fact that Indonesian democracy had never been representative enough: The PKI had never been in the government in spite of its popular strength, the system of regional legislatures had not been applied broadly enough, and elections had not been promptly and frequently held. Remedy these faults, the Party argued, and the ailments of Indonesian democracy would be cured. Similarly, the Communists appeared as champions of civil liberties—particularly of freedom of speech, press, and assembly. In this they were notably unsuccessful, for military restrictions imposed in the name of security and Presidentially sponsored requirements for ideological loyalty combined to reduce civil liberties to a rapidly vanishing minimum.

Although the PKI has sought political advantage by standing four-square behind the President, its stake in the preservation of parliamentary conditions was such that its backing of his steps toward guided democracy has been simultaneously enthusiastic and reserved. Thus, the Communists' endorsement of the Presidential Concept of 1957, in which the principles of guided democracy were proclaimed, made a point of the fact that Sukarno had given assurances that the parliamentary system would not be abandoned. In 1959, its acceptance of Sukarno's Political Manifesto was openly tempered by reservations regarding the diminution of political freedoms; and it voiced sharp objections to the announcement that all senior civil-service officials were to abandon their party affiliations, even though the PKI's own membership in this category was at best minimal.[20]

In March, 1960, the PKI joined its archrival, Masjumi, in objecting to the government's cavalier attitude to parliamentary prerogatives in ramming its budget proposals through the legislature. The President's response demonstrated the fact that the party system had by now become a mere shell: "Retooling" Parliament along more cooperative lines, he appointed the new members, dividing the seats between party and functional (corporate) group representatives. Even more injurious to Communist hopes than the national Parliament's decline was the Presidential revision of the regional assemblies' functions, which resulted by 1961 in the effective restoration of the *pamong pradja* system. Although the PKI did receive some appointments to regional administrative posts, particularly in areas where the Communists were strong, the revival of the older administration robbed it of the prospects for expanded influence which the legislatures had held out [21]

Although the Communists failed to secure the advantage of a continuing representative system, they did not suffer the eclipse that system's failure brought the other parties. The PKI is now virtually the only party worth considering as a major power factor in Indonesia. The Masjumi and PSI were generally discredited as a result of the rebellion—either for their involvement or their failure to succeed—and were finally outlawed in 1960. The Nahdatul Ulama and PNI have degenerated as organizations into little more than self-perpetuating patronage machines. Only Murba, a national-Communist party, whose opinions have been widely adopted by the government ideologues, has improved its position; but it remains a splinter group at heart, a state of mind rather than a political organization. The PKI, however, is now the third political force after the President and the Army; it has attained a position of greatly enhanced prestige—but also one of great vulnerability.

COMMUNISM UNDER GUIDED DEMOCRACY

In the new power constellation, the Army has been the PKI's principal opponent. We have already described the bases for military antagonism to the Communists in the parliamentary period. These sources of friction have remained under guided democracy; indeed, they have become greatly intensified. The military's impatience with all political parties was heightened by the failure of the parliamentary system to deal with the regionalist movement. Its own effectiveness in putting down the rebellion and in assuming broad political and economic responsibilities encouraged its belief that Indonesia's salvation lay in a reordering of the state along military lines, providing it with the singleness of purpose and command that it had thus far so fatally lacked. The Communists, as a group aiming at a reordering of the state along their own lines, formed a major obstacle to these ambitions and hence appeared as a serious rival.

It might well be argued that the military, given sufficient rewards, might shift from insisting on a state run according to its own lights to one directed by or in cooperation with the Communists. The ideological orientation of the Indonesian military elite is hardly firm; its most prominent characteristic is authoritarianism, which it shares with the PKI. The Communists would be a powerful ally; they possess popular support, which the Army notably lacks. Presumably, too, they could offer an increase in the Soviet military aid which already plays a large part in bolstering the Army's power. It seems unlikely, however, that such an alliance is possible, given the intrinsic interests and present power of the military—and the open hostility between the Army and the PKI since 1959 would indicate that the military and Communist leaders share this conviction. The Army is too powerful to need to subordinate itself or to share authority with an organization that would inevitably try to absorb or unseat it. With military direction of the state such a clear possibility, why should the Army enter so potentially disadvantageous an association? The centrifugal forces within the military are the Outer Island regional commanders and the rehabilitated ex-rebel elements; they are anti-Communist, forming a continual source of pressure on the central command for firmer measures against the PKI. An alliance with the Communists would seriously alienate these forces and might reopen the Pandora's box of regionalism, on the closing of which the Army has staked so much of its prestige.

Of perhaps even greater importance are the enormous vested interests that the Army has acquired in the *status quo*. Large portions of the economic and political administration of the country are under direct or indirect Army control; from this, the military elite derives considerable power and profit. Indeed, it may be questioned whether the Army's concern for the reordering of the state is motivated as much by distress over civilian failures as it is by a desire to justify and extend the access of the military to these perquisites. At the same time, the expanded functions of the military elite frequently place it in positions automatically opposed to the Communists. The officer who is in charge of administering or advising a nationalized Dutch concern acquires management's view of labor unrest. The officer who is involved in territorial administration—either through occupying a civilian government post or a position in the military administration that parallels it—is likely to become intolerant of Communist attempts to organize popular protest. The common soldiery has also shared in the general enhancement of the military position. Unlike the Kuomintang soldier of the Chinese civil war period, the Indonesian Army man is relatively well paid and well treated, and he enjoys a position of power and privilege vis-à-vis the civilian population.

The Army's opposition to the PKI has taken two principal forms: the restriction of its activities and the establishment of competing organizations. The Communists, whose success depends so greatly on public agitation and organization, have suffered much from the restrictions placed on political party activities by the military in the name of security and patriotism—the more so since many of them have been aimed specifically at the PKI.

These measures have not been limited to the national level; regional commanders, particularly in the Outer Islands, have tended to be even stricter, probably because local sentiment is with them and Presidential influence is weaker. Thus, when in July, 1960, the central command denounced the PKI leaders for their criticism of the government, it brought the members of the Party's Politburo in for repeated interrogation; but military authorities in several Outer Island districts went a step further by placing a complete ban on PKI activities and throwing local Communist leaders in jail.

Since the Army possesses an organization that penetrates to the local levels of political activity and has the means, authority, and will to impose its decisions forcibly, its restrictive measures have been effective in reducing the PKI's public activities, disrupting its normal communications lines, and denying it easy access to the masses. In the other major sphere of military activity affecting the Communists—the establishment of competing mass organizations —the Army has been far less successful. Except for the establishment of the Veterans' Legion (Legiun Veteran), which absorbed all veterans' organizations, including the PKI's Perbepbsi, the Army did not replace existing organizations, but united them under military direction in Cooperation Bodies, which became part of the Army-sponsored National Front for the Liberation of West Irian. These bodies were composed of representatives of major organizations in their spheres of activity—labor, youth, women, religion, and so on—and existed, in theory at least, from the national down to the local or place-of-work level. As we have noted, the PKI's initial reaction to their creation in 1957 was enthusiastic, but it soon became clear that the groups presented the Communist mass organizations with an obstacle of serious proportions. Full control of the bodies lay with the military and not with the participating organizations; the groups represented in the Cooperation Bodies could effectively stalemate each others' activities, but they had little chance of furthering their own projects unless they coincided with the military's plans. By 1959, the Communists' remarks on the Army-People relationship had become almost invariably querulous, and in 1960 one Party leader, Lukman, was to declare that, however desirable a national front might be, the PKI should not again lend itself to the type of relationship represented by the Cooperation Bodies.[22]

The rise of the Army as the Communists' principal opponent gave the PKI added reason to fear isolation; and the Party, looking for support outside the failing party system, found a protector in President Sukarno. With Army-PKI rivalry replacing inter-party competition, Sukarno became more and more the arbiter between the military and the Communists, playing the one against the other and so securing his own freedom of action. Since the Army has been in a much better position to take measures reducing the Communists' strength than the PKI has been to diminish the Army's, this has generally meant that the President's role in the feud has been to protect the Communists. Thus, he intervened to secure military permission for the holding of the PKI's 1959 Congress and took away much of the humiliation involved in the Army's restrictions on the meeting by addressing it himself. He similarly lent his presence to the Seventh (1962) Congress, and under this protective shadow Aidit was emboldened to address some of his sharpest criticisms to the Party's opponents. Sukarno has rescued the PKI from some of the military's severer reprisals, such as those following the Party's July, 1960, criticisms of the government; and he has balanced Army penetration of the governmental structure to some extent by appointing PKI sympathizers to regional government posts. Under the slogan NASAKOM (unity of nationalist, socialist, and religious people), the President has urged PKI participation in the cabinet, and he has repeatedly declared his faith in the national loyalty of the Party; all of this has greatly strengthened the PKI's claims to a legitimate place in the Indonesian political sun.

To ensure itself of Sukarno's support, the PKI has had to identify itself closely with the President and his program. Given the Party's own choice of radical nationalism as its principal line of popular appeal, this has not necessitated far-reaching changes in the Communists' program; indeed, the PKI has found many of the slogans advocated by the President useful in arguing for the compatibility of Communist principles with the Indonesian way of life. This close identification, however, makes it difficult for the PKI to assert its distinctiveness from the government and its independent claims to leadership. The problem has become particularly acute with the increasingly direct participation of Sukarno in the running of the government and the steady decrease in permissible areas for criticism of the authorities.

The Communists' relationship with the President has been further complicated by Sukarno's efforts to establish a mass organization and ideological movement of his own. In the ideological sphere, these efforts reached their peak in his Political Manifesto of August, 1959; organizationally, they resulted in the proclamation in 1960 of the National Front, which was to replace the Army's languishing National Front for the Liberation of West Irian and was aimed ideally at the merger of all political elements into one monolithic national force.

The PKI's response to Sukarno's endeavors along this line has been understandably ambiguous. The Party has welcomed those aspects which were ideologically propitious—anticapitalism, anti-Westernism, the inclusion of all major (i.e., also Communist) political forces in the governing of the country. It has also found them useful in reducing its political party opponents and as a counter to the military's own ideological and organizational efforts. On the other hand, the PKI has shown deep concern at those aspects which tend to a *Gleichschaltung* of the parties and their mass organizations. In its efforts to prevent this, it has been joined by the other parties and major organizations, which, by and large, are equally unhappy at the prospect of extinction. Whether the joint foot-dragging of these groups would be enough to prevent the creation of monolithic bodies is perhaps open to question. In their resistance, they have, however, been aided by the Army-Sukarno rivalry, a reef on which all efforts toward monolithic control have so far foundered.

The attempts at establishing the National Front provide a good example of the way in which this has worked out. As noted, the Front was announced by the President as a replacement for the Army-sponsored National Front for the Liberation of West Irian. The Army was not in a good position to oppose the move, for its front had failed to attract popular support and had been seriously compromised by charges of corruption. Instead, the military began moves to transfer the Cooperation Body apparatus to the National Front system, maintaining, of course, the existing military influence in those bodies; and regional and local commanders began to work for the establishment of National Front units under their own hegemony. This, coupled with the political parties' resistance to a front comprising more than a loose coalition of existing political organizations, made the chances of its becoming an effective instrument of Presidential control rather dim; and accordingly, though reluctantly, Sukarno acceded to the watering-down of the Front to a purely formal expression of national unity.

An attempt at establishing a monolithic labor organization, OPPI, made the same year under Presidential sponsorship, met a similar fate. SOBSI adamantly refused to consider any organization in which it would not be assured complete freedom of action. Other labor groups were less opposed, however, seeing the new body as a possible instrument for reducing SOBSI's vastly superior strength to their own benefit; and the project was vigorously pushed by Labor Minister Ahem Erningpradja, who saw in it prospects for an organizational empire of his own. Whether Communist opposition would have sufficed to reverse the President's attitude is unclear; but territorial military commanders began to join non–SOBSI unions in establishing OPPI units, thus raising the specter of Army hegemony and adding considerably to the PKI's arguments for abandonment of the project.

We will notice in this connection that the PKI's attitude toward front groups has shifted markedly from that of the parliamentary era. Once eager and confident of their ability to control such alliances, the Communists are now wary. What makes the difference is the presence of the Army and/or the governmental apparatus as participants in the officially sponsored fronts; inevitably, control will rest with them. Hence, the PKI, although it continues to urge cooperation in a National United Front and to deplore the splintering of the nation's organizational life, has given no indication since its short-lived welcoming of the Cooperation Bodies that it hopes to secure control over such groups by working from within. Instead, its emphasis has been on limiting the official fronts to the loosest of coalitions by insisting on the preservation of its freedom of action within them.[23]

While the PKI has managed thus far to maintain its independence and that of the mass organizations allied to it, it has faced serious problems in mobilizing popular support. Restrictions on public demonstrations and requirements for political orthodoxy have severely limited the possibilities for gaining popularity through protest. Such demonstrations as have been organized by the Communists have generally been against officially admitted problems such as rising prices or lack of consumer goods; and they have taken the appearance more of petitions than protests. Objections on topics deemed impermissible by the authorities have generally resulted in severe punitive measures, particularly in the regions beyond Djakarta; and in cases where the Party has adopted a more extreme position than the authorities in officially approved campaigns, it has sometimes had its fingers slapped for its pains. Indeed, in a regime that bases itself so heavily on exhortation, it is difficult under the best of circumstances to compete on agitational grounds; and this, coupled with the effective imposition of restrictive measures, has turned the Party's principal emphasis to other approaches—to consolidation rather than agitation, and to constructive activities rather than critical onslaughts.

Consolidation of the Communist Party ranks actually began before the guided-democracy period, having been necessitated in the first place by the mushroom growth of the Party and its affiliates in the early and mid-1950's. The campaign began in earnest with the introduction of the first Three-Year Plan for Party organization and education in July, 1956; a second Three-Year Plan was adopted by the Party Congress of 1959. The chief emphasis of the plans was a sweeping program for the indoctrination of Party members, ranging from literacy courses at the lowest level to discussion of pure theory and international Communist relations at the Central and Major District Party schools. It was stressed that the presentation of ideology should be, at all but the highest levels, in Indonesian terms and with careful consideration of the local conditions and problems; theoretical instruction was to be extended downward gradually. The importance the Party leadership attached to the program is understandable, for restrictions on PKI agitational activity have made it imperative that the Party establish a popular hold based on something more than slogans and mass meetings. Moreover, the attempts at defining an official Indonesian national ideology cannot be overlooked as a threat to the PKI's efforts in the doctrinal field; the Party has evinced particular concern at their implications for fostering a "national nihilist" spirit among the working class.[24]

In addition to this program for ideological education, the Three-Year Plans called for a vast increase in the number of full Party members and a more rapid system of promotions to activist positions. Part of the reason for the very large percentage of candidates —70 per cent of 1954 Party membership and 50 per cent of 1959— lay in the very rapid expansion of the organization. A good part of it was also the result of the unwillingness of local unit leaders and senior members to admit the newcomers as their equals, a situation that, Party leaders stated, had created disinterest and discontent among the rank and file, robbed the Party of new blood, and discouraged potential members from joining.[25] We must remember in this connection that the PKI has very little in the way of patronage to offer its functionaries in an era when access to official perquisites has become almost necessary for survival; and so the problem of providing sufficient incentives within the Party structure to maintain the *élan* of the lower cadres has become a matter of prime importance.

The PKI has not restricted its indoctrination efforts to the Party membership, but has also made a concentrated effort to extend Marxist education to the general public. Anti-illiteracy courses have been one vehicle for this; another has been the People's University (Universitas Rakjat) system of adult education, which was begun in Djakarta under Party sponsorship in 1959 and subsequently extended to other major cities. However, much the same factors as in parliamentary days still militate against an extension of Communist influence in the bureaucracy; the *pamong pradja*, though shaken by ideological "retooling" and by the appointment of military and pro-PKI representatives to some of its posts, remains basically the closed group it was before.

It seems most unlikely that the PKI will be able to attain a foothold in the bureaucratic structure by attracting a substantial number of its members to the Party; it is equally improbable that it will again acquire an opportunity to bypass the *pamong pradja* via a revival of regional elective government. The most feasible way of penetrating the apparatus of state under the present conditions is to acquire control of a ministry, which would give the Party considerable leeway in placing its people in the bureaucratic structure belonging to it. This means participating in the government, however, and until recently the PKI showed no notable enthusiasm for sharing the odium of responsibility. As we have seen, the Party used its demands for a role in the cabinet during the parliamentary period largely as a threat to block the inclusion of the Masjumi. Otherwise, it maintained that the Communists ought to be brought into the government but not that they *had* to be, a posture which served both as a lever in securing demands on the other parties and as a demonstration of the PKI's lack of responsibility for the sad state of public affairs.

With the evolution of "guided democracy," the advantages of nonparticipation in the cabinet have become less obvious. The possibilities for opposition having grown steadily slimmer, the Party's attitude of "friendly criticism" toward the government rests perforce more on friendship than on criticism. In addition, the institutional boundaries between government and opposition have become blurred, so that it is no longer obvious who is responsible and who is not on the basis of cabinet representation. The PKI has been drawn into positions that identify it with the government; in March, 1962, it even acquired a role on the fringes of the ministerial council.[26]

The advantages of formal nonparticipation in the government have thus declined. Those of participation have increased, for control of a ministerial apparatus would provide, in addition to the usual advantages attendant on such power, an avenue of communications outside Djakarta in a situation where ordinary Party links, especially in the Outer Islands, are prey to increasing disruption. Moreover, it would give the PKI a better bargaining position vis-à-vis the other components of the bureaucracy through trading favors, for the Party's present activities among the masses depend almost completely on permission from local or regional authorities, which the Communists are at present in a poor position to extract.[27] Finally, in a post-Sukarno period, the PKI must hope for the other parties and the civilian bureaucracy to act as a buffer between it and the army. To achieve this, it must convince them that the PKI is a lesser threat to their interests than the military; a major step in this direction would be to show them that it could share the reins of government peaceably.[28]

That the PKI would appear to be seriously concerned with the need to attain a role in the cabinet was evidenced at the Party's April, 1962, Congress, when it discussed with unaccustomed concreteness the necessity of acquiring a role in the government that involved responsibility for part of the bureaucratic apparatus. At the beginning of 1963, Aidit put the Party's demands very sharply: The economic crisis, he declared, had reached such grave proportions that all the country's energies must be engaged in its solution if the nation was to avoid civil war. Hence the economic crisis must be given precedence over all other questions, even the struggle against imperialism. The energies of the Indonesian Communists, Aidit argued, must be utilized in dealing with the problem; the NASAKOM principle must be carried out, for if it was to avoid chaos the country could no longer afford to keep the PKI on the sidelines of government.[29]

Aidit was all too correct in stressing the seriousness of Indonesia's economic state, for inflation and shortages of virtually all essential goods have made life extremely hard, in rural areas as well as the towns. It therefore may be that the PKI has decided that it can no longer temporize, that the time has come to turn popular despair into anger and put itself forward aggressively as the savior of the suffering people. The argument may also, however, stem from a grave concern on the part of the PKI leaders for the vitality of their own organization under the present circumstances. The Party seems, at present, to be afflicted more by apathy than rebelliousness on the part of its following. At the time of the 1962 Party Congress, it was announced that the second Three-Year Plan had not been fulfilled. Its failure was assigned in the first place to the blows the Party had suffered since 1959, especially to the restrictions imposed by regional army commanders in the wake of the Party's July, 1960, criticisms. In some areas, the Party organization had become deeply discouraged, and in general there was a feeling among Communists that restrictions on political activity, coupled with the necessity of devoting one's personal energy to the economic struggle for survival, made it impossible to work further for the perfection of the Party.[30]

If discouragement among the Party ranks is a serious problem—and the open discussion of the issue would indicate that it is—the PKI may face the unpleasant prospect of following the other parties into relative powerlessness. The problem of attaining a government role thus becomes urgent, both as a demonstration to its following that the Party is making headway and because at a future date it may not be able to press its demands as effectively. Moreover, with the struggle for subsistence a bitter one for most Indonesians, the possession of patronage, of positions that provide access to the necessities of life, becomes essential simply to keep Party functionaries from dissipating their energies in the effort of personal survival.

In the field of labor organization, the Party has felt the limitations of the new era in Indonesian politics very strongly. Whereas a great deal of attention was once devoted to labor work in reports of PKI conclaves, unions have received much less attention in recent years. It is easy to see why: There is very little that labor organizations are now able to do. SOBSI's serious difficulties began after the seizure of Dutch-owned enterprises in December, 1957. State management and later nationalization of these firms meant that labor unrest could be construed as an act injurious to the Indonesian national interest rather than as a struggle against foreign imperialism; and so, in fact, it was. Strikes in essential (foreign-exchange–producing) enterprises had been banned even before the takeover; since then, they have become virtually impossible in all enterprises of any importance. Furthermore, the inflation-conscious government has been notably cool toward the granting of wage and salary increases. Since inflation has cut earning power severely, the unions are obviously in a difficult position. Moreover, their existence has been almost continuously threatened by official moves to consolidate labor representation for political or managerial purposes: the labor-military Cooperation Body (BUMIL), OPPI, and most recently the Army-sponsored worker-management association, PTK.[31]

Whether SOBSI has been able to keep up its members' enthusiasm under such conditions is open to some doubt. At the same time, however, we should remember that although SOBSI can protest only weakly, it still does protest, in contrast to nearly all the other labor organizations, which have tended to curry favor with the military and management in order to gain preference as bargaining agents. SOBSI's organization may be weakened by arrests and restrictions; but martyrdom has its advantages. The danger to Communist influence in the labor field is probably less that the workers will reject SOBSI's unions than that they will become apathetic in their support, unconvinced of the possibility of victory, and thus unreliable in time of crisis.

Communist work among the peasantry has not experienced the severe difficulties faced by the labor organizations. On the contrary: We have noted that it was at the end of 1960 that the PKI leadership first expressed satisfaction with work in the agrarian sector. This appears to have been partly the result of strenuous efforts undertaken during 1959 to improve the rural cadre situation and strengthen Party knowledge of agrarian affairs and partly because the PKI has succeeded in good measure in establishing its image as the one political group that is concerned with the peasants' fate. The Party evinced considerable satisfaction over its progress in rural areas at the time of its 1962 Congress. The BTI, it declared, had risen rapidly in membership to some 4.5 million, making it far and away the Party's largest mass organization. The rural cadre situation had greatly improved, though the problem of rich peasants and landlords in the Communist ranks still remained.[32]

With other parties and mass movements near extinction in the countryside, the national forces reaching down to the villages are those of the civilian government, the military, and the Communists. Army officials have tended to be arbitrary in their treatment of the peasants; moreover, it is the military that generally has the task of enforcing unpopular government measures, and it is therefore widely disliked. The villagers' attitude toward the civilian governmental apparatus has traditionally been one of both awe and opposition. Because of the highly centralized nature of the *pamong pradja*, the peasants tend to view it as the representative of the urban outside world. Their own locally financed village government (*pamong desa*) acts as a bargaining agent with this outside force; and the local prestige of the village heads depends largely on their ability to ameliorate the impact of central government demands. If the village headman is unable to prevent or evade the imposition of unpopular central policies, he runs the risk of being viewed by the villagers less as their representative against central authority than that authority's representative against them, and they will tend to look for an alternative spokesman.

Such pressures have increased in recent years, particularly for the

clearing of squatters from estate lands, the ensuring of planting
and delivery of crops desired by the government at fixed prices, and
the securing of village labor for *gotong rojong* (mutual aid) projects
not seen as immediately useful by the peasants. The Communists
have shown themselves well aware of the potentialities of the situation, for they have encouraged the absorption of the headmen into
the central government sphere by demanding the redistribution of
village land allotted for their support on the argument that the
existing system is feudal and headmen should be on centrally provided salary.

Setting the Communists up as an alternative spokesman for the
villages, the PKI's peasant organization has assumed an important
role in providing counsel to villagers in their various legal and administrative dealings with officialdom.[33] The PKI has also taken
an active part by appearing in behalf of poor peasant interests in regard to the agrarian reform laws passed in 1960, offering its services
to the committees set up at various levels to oversee their execution
and informing the peasants how they can secure the greatest benefit
from the new regulations. The Party has campaigned to raise the
pay of farm laborers, combat usurious interest rates, and reduce the
landlord's share of the harvest from the government-set 50–50 to
40–60.[34] It has also been active in organizing village-desired mutual-
aid projects, has engaged in a well-publicized campaign to improve
rice cultivation techniques, and has sponsored credit, consumer, and
producer cooperatives.

Such activities do not run counter to the government's own campaigns: At the most, they go a step further than the authorities have
in the direction of reform. The Communists are thus unlikely to
run into important official interference in carrying them out; and
at the same time, the manner in which they do so can make clear
to the peasants that they are acting as *their* spokesman and not as
an arm of central officialdom. Such a strategy is not easy to execute:
It presumes a substantial rural cadre corps, possessing considerable
skill and dedication; and there is the risk that the PKI's efforts will
not distinguish the Party's program from that of the government
sufficiently to preserve peasant loyalties should the Party and government become opponents. Again, rural discontent may reach such
proportions that Communist organizations, if they continue to act
as peasant spokesmen, are drawn into violent conflict with the
authorities—as indeed happened in Kediri in late 1961. Or the
Communists may find that too much success breeds opposition:
In West Java, for example, the military removed from office in

1961 various PKI members who had been chosen village headmen. By and large, however, the authorities are more reluctant and less able to put pressure on the peasantry than they are on labor, and the Communists' rural position is thus far more secure.

In appealing to the populace at large, the PKI has been considerably handicapped in the guided-democracy period, not only by restrictions on agitation, but also by the fact that a major line of emotional approach has been robbed of much of its force. As in the parliamentary era, the Communists have placed their principal emphasis on an appeal to radical anti-Western nationalism. This has, however, become much less useful as a weapon against the Party's political competitors, since neither Sukarno nor the Army can be as easily or as safely accused of insufficient national spirit as could the Masjumi and PSI. At the same time, the Army has been in a good position to point out the "un-national" character of the PKI, particularly in connection with the Party's defense of Indonesia's Chinese minority and its denial of religion.

Nationalism has, however, by no means lost its usefulness to the PKI. The Party has used nationalist arguments in two ways: first, to establish its claims to being a legitimate part of the national scene; and second, to demonstrate that the goals of the Indonesian nation can be achieved only through Communism. Its claims in both respects have been considerably strengthened by the fact that in recent years many of the Party's long-standing demands have become part of either governmental policy or Presidential urgings; the Party is able to point to this as proof of an *avant-garde* nationalist record. Its argument has been that the revolution begun in 1945 is as yet incomplete, that in fact it failed owing to the compromise settlement with the Dutch. Indonesia is thus still in the stage of national revolution, and the struggle can only be carried out by the expulsion of imperialist interests, the removal from power of all who would compromise on this issue, and the inclusion of the Communists in the government. The Party has differentiated itself from the government by arguing that it has not adequately pursued its own goals: It has not retooled its organs along NASAKOM lines, especially outside Djakarta; it has emphasized guidance but not democracy; it has failed to take the economic and political measures necessary to cope with inflation, shortages, and corruption; and it has pursued the anti-imperialist struggle with energy but not with consistency.

At this point, the PKI's argument branches off from the official nationalist one, though considerable effort is made to point to

elements of compatibility: National Front has gradually replaced
the term National United Front in Indonesian Communist literature, for example, blurring the distinction between the PKI's and
the President's ambitions; likewise, "guided democracy" becomes
analogous to the "national democracy" put forth by Khrushchev
as an appropriate governmental form for underdeveloped non-Communist nations. The Indonesian national revolution, the Party
claims, is at the same time a people's democratic revolution; the
truly complete achievement of independence is synonymous with
the establishment of a "people's democracy." That can only be
accomplished under the leadership of the proletariat, together with
its ally, the peasantry. It will result in a "national coalition" government, in which these classes will have a leading position, but
which will also include the petty and national bourgeoisie. Its rule
will be a dictatorship of the "people" rather than a dictatorship of
the proletariat; its purpose will be to create not socialism but people's democracy, which—bringing the argument full circle—is the
true embodiment of the republic envisioned by the 1945 revolution.[35]

Obviously, there is a rather large gap between the first and second stages of the argument: The *gotong rojong* government is not
the same as the national coalition government, the National Front
is not really the same as the National United Front, and guided
democracy is not the same as people's democracy. The difference
lies not so much in the program set by the PKI for the people's
democratic government—which is generally compatible with accepted nationalist aims—but in the fact that it presupposes Communist domination, while the other presupposes only Communist
inclusion. The gap is to be bridged, the theory runs, by the progressive strengthening of the Party's influence at the expense of a de-
caying opposition: To this end, the slogan "Develop the progressive
forces, unite with the middle-of-the-road forces, and isolate the die-
hard forces" has been offered since 1956 as a strategic guide—
although with the replacement of the Party system by more re-
doubtable contenders for power, its reiteration has acquired an
increasingly hollow ring.

THE POSSIBILITY OF RESISTANCE

Given the fact that the present constellation of forces makes an
assumption of power through parliamentary means less likely, and
given the increasing official controls over political expression, we
might expect that the Party would have second thoughts about the

policy that has brought it so near and yet so far from victory. Indeed, for some years there have been persistent rumors of a split within the Communist leadership, centering on the need for the Party to assert its own identity and to avoid the irreparable weakening of its position by submitting to the various encroachments of the President and the Army. According to these reports, the faction urging a more active policy is led by Lukman, while Aidit is the principal proponent of a more complaisant stand. However, if one can judge by published statements, the difference would appear to be one of the degree to which compromises should be made under the present policy, and not whether the policy itself should be rejected. While Lukman criticized PKI participation in the Cooperation Bodies, he has placed as much emphasis as Aidit on the need for Sukarno's protection, on the need to avoid the alienation of the non-Communist forces, and on the need to avoid being placed in an illegal opposition.[36] Since mid-1960, Party criticisms of the government have taken a more bitter (though still circumspect) tone; perhaps this portends a changing view, but there is no outward sign that such revision is the result of a decline in Aidit's influence.

The problem is where to draw the line on the question of compromise. The Party, having gained much, has much to lose; to maintain its independence effectively against both Sukarno and the Army would mean to risk uniting them against it and could lead to illegality and reduction by force. It is questionable, in the light of the Army's strength and the PKI's concentration on Java, far from outside sources of Communist aid, whether the Party's fortunes in rebellion would be much better than those of previous dissident groups. The provocation must therefore be great if the risk is to be taken; yet the very reluctance to take risks may expose the Party to the piecemeal reduction of its power.

Perhaps some evidence for the PKI's attitude on this dilemma may be found in the Party's reaction to the current Sino-Soviet ideological debate. On most points, the Indonesian Communists have placed themselves behind the Chinese position, and thus on the side of the intransigent radicals. Yet, in analyzing the significance of this for PKI policy, we are faced with a number of questions. Does the Party's stand mean that its leadership endorses for Indonesia the Chinese distrust of neutralist nationalism and aversion to halfway revolutionary measures? Or is its position in the quarrel a sop to an opposition that wishes a more aggressive course? Is the PKI's stand related to the ideological issues themselves or to the way in which these issues have been presented? Or does it relate to the presence of control by Russia or China over the Party? We cannot provide a real answer to these questions, but it may be useful to discuss some of the factors involved.

Let us first consider the problem of whether it is Soviet or Chinese power rather than the issues of the quarrel that has determined the PKI's stance. Neither the U.S.S.R. nor China is in a position to exert real pressure on Indonesia—a fact that the PKI no doubt contemplates ruefully in mulling over its current political predicament. The Party probably receives financial aid from the Soviets and/or the Chinese; how much is a matter for speculation. The U.S.S.R. has been generous with aid for the Indonesian military; whether this has given it any significant leverage in Indonesia's domestic politics is uncertain, considering the mutually exclusive interests of the Army and the PKI. It is by no means impossible that this is not even the purpose of Soviet generosity in this instance—it is hardly without precedence for the U.S.S.R. to ensure its diplomatic interests by putting its money on the horse it thinks may win. Indonesia's Chinese minority is another possible source of outside influence on the Party. The PKI has consistently defended that group's interests, at times to its bitter cost; on the other hand, the PKI has been overwhelmingly an ethnic Indonesian Party, and there seems to be little possibility of control of the PKI by the local Chinese, though they may be an important source of finances.

The whole question of financial backing becomes questionable, however, in the light of the Sino-Soviet conflict: It would seem strange that either side would allow itself to lose such an important Party simply by offering less money. Control of financial resources was doubtless a major factor in securing compliance in the days of single leadership—but not now, when there are two centers of power. The same can be said of psychological influence: Now that there are two sources of orthodoxy, the PKI leaders, who by their background were already oriented toward the Indonesian rather than the international Communist arena, have little reason to feel overwhelmed by the authority of either Moscow or Peking. If we consider the issues at stake in the quarrel, and the PKI's reasons for assuming its stand, we shall see that it is unlikely the Party considers itself a satellite of either of the major Communist powers.

In the handling of such issues as Albania, Yugoslavia, and de-Stalinization, Khrushchev has appeared as the defender of Soviet domestic and diplomatic interests, while the Chinese stand has shown more concern for the interests of Communist movements outside the bloc, especially in underdeveloped areas. Essentially, China has stressed the need to preserve the image of Communist perfection. Thus the Chinese have argued that differences of opinion should not be aired beyond the Communist ranks. Those inside the Communist family should not, like Albania, be lightly cast away. Those already beyond the pale, like Tito, should remain there; second thoughts on the subject without radical changes on the expellee's part only weaken the image of Communist infallibility. Similarly, the admission of gross misrule made in the Soviet de-Stalinization campaign shatters the image of the happy Communist state. The effects of such publicity cannot but be injurious to Communist movements in the emergent nations: With so much of their popular support—and their own internal morale—depending on their ability to offer utopia to groping men, they can ill afford public discord, inconsistency, and revelations of oppression.

It is not surprising, then, that the PKI has taken the Chinese stand. Tito remains anathema to the Party in spite of—or perhaps because of—the fact that he enjoys close relations with Sukarno. He is portrayed as the secret "running dog" of the West, an evil genius who would persuade neutralist leaders that their salvation does not lie with the Communist bloc. The PKI has criticized both dogmatism and revisionism; but as the Sino-Soviet debate over Yugoslavia waxed hotter, the Party's emphasis on the evils of revisionism seemed to take precedence. If the PKI criticisms of Yugoslav revisionism are considered to be, in fact, attacks on a moderate approach to relations with non-Communist forces—as we assume they are in the Chinese case—then this clearly involves a contradiction with the policies thus far pursued by the PKI in Indonesia. On the other hand, there are very good reasons for the PKI to feel deeply concerned about Yugoslav revisionism per se. The Indonesian political elite presently in power is strongly inclined toward collectivism and has borrowed a good many ideas from Marx, Lenin, and the latter-day examples of Communist states. At the same time, it is highly nationalistic; and this combination accounts for the popularity of the national-Communist ideas proffered by the Murba Party and its associated ideologues. The PKI, to overcome objections to its international connections, has argued that the only way Indonesia can be free of imperialist pressures and able to build the socialist state endorsed by official ideology is for it to align with the Communist camp. The argument is a weak one; yet, if the Party is ever to gain commanding influence over the present national elite, it must sell it this viewpoint. Tito, however, is the argument's living refutation, and his ties with Sukarno make him doubly dangerous in this respect. The acceptance of the Titoist position by the Communist bloc would weaken the PKI's argument fatally; and Yugoslav revisionism must therefore be opposed—not because it is moderate domestically, but because it is unaligned internationally.[37]

The motives for the PKI's stand on Albania have been clearer, since here no domestic issues have been involved. The Party indicated its position early in the quarrel—in 1959, before the public rift between Khrushchev and Hoxha. In that year, the Party journal began to exhibit a sudden interest in Albanian achievements; and the Indonesian Communist delegation to the Twenty-first Congress of the CPSU topped off its Moscow visit with a stopover in Albania, where, it was reported, "complete agreement" was reached on all issues.[38] The Party's attitude toward the Albanian question was made quite plain at the CPSU's succeeding Congress, in 1961, when Aidit refused to denounce the Albanian heresy.

In judging this aspect of the Sino-Soviet dispute, we must bear in mind that from one point of view, that of policy toward non-Communist elements, China is more intransigent, while from another, that of policy toward groups within the Communist camp, it is more moderate than the Soviet Union. Its defense of Albania is also a defense of relative autonomy within the Communist camp. The existence of considerable freedom is obviously important to China as a powerful nation with views and ambitions of its own. It is also important to the Indonesian Communists, whose advances under the Aidit leadership owed so much to the flexibility of the Party's policies and their congruence with Indonesian conditions. We might therefore expect the PKI to defend the freedom of Communist parties to determine their own internal affairs, and that, indeed, was the argument by which Aidit explained his refusal to condemn Albania on returning from the CPSU Congress in 1961. The only question that decided whether a Communist Party should be in or out of the bloc, he stated, was *whether* it was building socialism in its country; *how* it did so was its own affair. No pacts or promises were to limit participation in the bloc; it was solely an association of like-minded groups.[39]

A Communist Party's right to judge its internal affairs was therefore its own, and, as Aidit emphasized, the PKI would insist upon this prerogative: "The PKI, as I have stated many times before, and this is in accordance with the spirit of the Communist Declaration of 1960, is a Marxist-Leninist Party which stands on its own feet,

which has equal rights with the other Communist Parties and certainly does not run other parties. In accordance with Marxism-
Leninism, the PKI determines its policies by itself."[40] This stand
was endorsed by a PKI Central Committee resolution which both
asserted the equality of the Communist parties and condemned
polycentrism. The two positions were not inconsistent. The Soviet
Party, the Central Committee explained, was the acknowledged
head of the socialist group because of its role in Communist history
and because the U.S.S.R. was the country most advanced along the
path to a Communist society. This leadership, however, was merely
titular: It required respect, not obedience, from the other parties.
Only in this sense could there be a "center" of the Communist
movement. The idea of polycentrism was incorrect not because it
weakened control but because it implied any control at all. "The
question is not one of 'autonomy,' but of independence and equality for all the Communist parties. We do not live in a 'kingdom' or
'republic' composed of Communist parties, where the pressure of
the central 'government' is so strong that the question of autonomy
arises. We do not agree with the theory of polycentrism, the theory
of many centers, because . . . we do not agree with the existence
of a central system in the world Communist movement."[41]

If all Communist parties are to be granted parity, and if there is
to be no source of central command, how are the differences of
Communist opinion on international issues to be settled? That
there are such issues the PKI has hardly denied: There is the question of Stalin, for instance, whose importance for Communist history requires, in the Indonesian Party's view, that he be maintained
as a hero, if not as a god.[42] There is also the matter of the Yugoslavs,
"who by supporting the Twenty-second CPSU Congress aimed at
sowing the poison of dissension in the ranks of the socialist bloc and
the world working-class movement."[43] The PKI's only answer to the
problem is that such disagreements be settled by "consultation and
consensus"—the *musjawarah* and *mufakat* of Indonesian nationalist ideology—in accordance with the principles laid down by such
mutually determined guidelines as the 1957 and 1960 international
Communist statements.[44]

On the question of war and revolution, the PKI has taken a stand
somewhere between those of China and the Soviet Union. The
Party has claimed that there can be no compromise with the imperialist powers, that force is the only thing they understand, and
that concern for peace must not be allowed to detract from the
struggle for national liberation.[45] On the other hand, although the

Party denounced the U.S. role in the 1962 Cuban crisis in the strongest terms, it did not suggest that American force be opposed by Soviet intractability.[46] In view of the high emotional value of extreme anti-Westernism in Indonesia and the popularity of a strong stand on issues of colonialism and national interest, it is to the Party's advantage to have solid international Communist support of such matters. Not only would this help gain Indonesian sympathy for alliance with the Communist side, but also, by encouraging still more extreme nationalist endeavors, it could help isolate Indonesia further from the West. The PKI therefore has good grounds to feel that in temporizing on these issues the Soviet Union has been selling out one of Communism's best arguments in the interests of its diplomatic position.

The Party's militance on the issue of imperialism and colonialism has not been carried over to its view of relations with forces that do not fall in these categories. "To settle differences of opinion," Aidit noted in discussing the CPSU Congress, "it is necessary in my opinion to stick to 'consultation and consensus' not only among Communists, but also among parties, groups, and forces which oppose the main enemy, imperialism."[47] Theorizing on Indonesia's foreign policy, the PKI has adopted Sukarno's formulation of a world divided into two groups, the "new emerging forces" and the "old established forces." The former can develop only at the expense of the latter, and hence they are basically opposed. The "old established forces" are led by the Western imperialist powers. Both the socialist bloc and the newly independent nations are part of the emergent forces, and therefore, the PKI emphasizes, their interests vis-à-vis the imperialist-led group coincide. For Indonesia to maintain a neutral position between the Communist and Western powers is thus, in the PKI's view, inconsistent in terms of its official theory of world relations and contrary to its national interest. The national interest can only really be served by a "united front for peace and freedom" formed by the socialist bloc and the newly independent nations, whose combined strength alone can overcome the forces of imperialism and neocolonialism. As an important and dynamic power among the newly independent states, the Party has argued, Indonesia can play a glorious role in consummating this alliance.[48]

In this fashion, the "two-camp" doctrine is revived, but in a form designed to woo the nationalists rather than alienate them. Its basic assumption is Soviet rather than Chinese: The ultimate impulse of nationalism in the newly independent countries is toward the

East rather than the West. Whether the PKI is convinced in its heart of hearts that this is necessarily so is another matter. The Sino-Indian border war certainly did nothing to increase its confidence. In reporting the affair, the Party newspaper took the stand that India was to blame because it had refused to settle the dispute on the basis of consultation and consensus. China's acceptance of the Asian-African offer of mediation indicated its good will, while India's reluctance was "disappointing."[49] The imperialists were egging India on in the hope of causing a war that would push that country into the Western sphere of influence; Nehru and reactionary circles around him were held responsible for yielding to the lure of Western support, but the PKI did not stress in its newspaper reports the Chinese argument that the Indian bourgeoisie had sold out to imperialism and thus ceased to be useful in the revolutionary process.

The wider implications of the affair were by no means lost on the Party, however. It found the attitude of the Indian workers even more alarming than that of the Indian bourgeoisie; their enthusiastic support for Nehru and participation in attacks on Indian Communist headquarters demonstrated a national chauvinist tendency that "will set the Indian working class back by decades and have an injurious influence on the development of the Asian revolutionary movement."[50] With the PKI already concerned by the inroads "nationalist nihilism" might be making on the reliability of the Indonesian workers, the evidence this provided of the potential fickleness of popular support in a Communist-nationalist falling-out seems to have had a deeply unsettling effect.[51]

In theorizing on the state of Indonesia's revolutionary development, the PKI has accepted the Soviet-sponsored concept of "national democracy" as a stage between bourgeois and people's democracy, and has argued that guided democracy, when fully carried out under the NASAKOM principle, is substantially identical to this phase.[52] Although the Party has evinced concern at the growth of "bureaucratic capitalism"—both as a source of opposition to labor's demands and as a reason for the mismanagement of Indonesia's state-run enterprises—it has thus far continued to include the national bourgeoisie as a progressive force and to stress the need for good relations with it and with the non-Communist parties. Party pronouncements on the domestic situation are naturally inhibited greatly by the limitations on political expression, but the over-all tenor of the PKI's statements on the process of converting a nationalist state to a socialist one is that of emphasis on a long, hard pull toward power rather than on the expectation of inevitable and violent confrontation. This by no means implies that the Party may not change its view, even in the very near future; but if it does so, it seems most likely that this will be as a result of events in Indonesia rather than in the U.S.S.R. or China. In the last analysis, the Indonesian Communist reaction to the Sino-Soviet dispute has been determined by its stand on domestic affairs, and not the other way around. It is what happens in Indonesia that will determine whether the Party stands or falls, and the PKI has shown itself to be very much aware of this fact.

When all is said and done, the Sino-Soviet quarrel appears curiously peripheral to the Indonesian Communist situation. Neither Russia nor China in the 1960's provides much analogy to the issues faced by the PKI. It is rather China of the 1920's that appears congruent: Is Sukarno Indonesia's Sun Yat-sen, and is Army chief Nasution its Chiang K'ai-shek? The parallel is an interesting one, the more so since it has by no means been ignored by Indonesian political figures.[53] The PKI's position depends very much on the protection of one man; he may be removed by a coup, by retirement, by death. In a post-Sukarno era—and Indonesian political calculations center increasingly on such a period—would a *modus vivendi* between the Army and the PKI be possible? The military, which would undoubtedly be the major force in a post-Sukarno situation, might not wish to push the issue immediately, for a move to destroy the Party might bring civil war and would surely entail serious unrest in Java. On the other hand, there would be considerable pressure from the regional commanders for a drastic solution; and since the PKI could not hope for much more than bare tolerance, there would probably also be pressure on its leaders to make a break rather than bleed to death from the pricks of increasing minor restrictions. The specter of a second Shanghai (the Chinese Communists were crushed there by the Kuomintang in 1927) would almost surely haunt PKI thoughts of a future coexistence with the Army. At the same time, the Army must remember what happened to the Kuomintang after its initial triumph over the Communists. The unity of the military is by no means guaranteed: "Warlordism" is a distinct possibility. The economic situation is very bad and is likely to continue to be so for some time even under the best of management; a prolonged period of severe hardship for the population thus seems unavoidable, and the Army is already widely unpopular.

The parallel is, of course, by no means perfect. Java hardly provides a Yenan, remote from central government control and close to sources of outside support. It is doubtful whether the Indonesian Army would find itself fighting on two fronts in the absence of a third world war; and it could doubtless muster considerably more foreign support than could the KMT of the 1930's. Moreover, the Communists would face serious problems in extending revolutionary control successfully beyond Java, from both a logistical and a political point of view. But perhaps the greatest question mark in the whole matter of Communism's future in Indonesia is the attitude of the Indonesian people. Will their reaction to continuing hardship and frustration be one of apathy or revolt? Revolutions are not made simply by bad conditions, but because people expect more than they are getting. The Indonesian people expected much to result from their revolution against the Dutch; they did not get it, and this was one of the reasons for the instability of government in the parliamentary era. The political leadership of the guided-democracy period has based its appeal for popular support squarely on promises to relieve these frustrations. Some demands—notably, for the satisfaction of the national ego—have been met; but for the mass of the population life has become harder than before, and the chances to express and redress grievances even slimmer. The popular reaction, however, appears now to be one not of anger but of apathy, not of revolution but of resignation.

It is possible that the expectations fanned by the Japanese occupation and the revolution against the Dutch have died under long years of frustration and defeat. There is perhaps a historical parallel to this: The wave of popular expectations from political action that rose with Indonesia's first mass movement, the Sarekat Islam, was shattered by colonial government opposition and dissipated in the ill-fated rebellion led by the PKI in 1926–27. During the 1930's, when economic hardships were the greatest and the political regime the most reactionary, popular resistance was at its lowest ebb—not, we might suspect, because of contentment, but because people no longer felt anything could come of it. Possibly the same process is taking place today, in which case the PKI's position is very weak indeed. Only the future will tell, however; and in the meantime, the Party can comfort itself with the thought that, however low the fortunes of the revolutionary movement sank in the 1930's, it no more signaled the end of revolution in Indonesia than the Shanghai coup marked the end of Communism in China.

NOTES

1. The leftist leaders' claims to having been secret Communists have been disputed by non-Communist leaders who were closely associated with them. George McT. Kahin, in *Nationalism and Revolution in Indonesia* (Ithaca, N.Y.: Cornell University Press, 1952), presents evidence for both sides of the argument. The author's own research into the prewar period has tended to substantiate the evidence for Communist affiliation of those leaders who had been students in Holland, although the allegiance of Amir Sjarifuddin, the most important of the Sajap Kiri group, remains open to considerable question.

2. See Kahin, *op. cit.*, p. 275.

3. For an illuminating and thorough discussion of national-level Party relations during the 1950's, see Herbert Feith, *The Decline of Constitutional Democracy in Indonesia* (Ithaca, N.Y.: Cornell University Press, 1962); and for a treatment of the structure of government and politics below the national level, see John Legge, *Central Authority and Regional Autonomy in Indonesia* (Ithaca, N. Y.: Cornell University Press, 1961).

4. For some statistics on Party growth in this period, see *Material for the Sixth National Congress of the Communist Party of Indonesia* (Djakarta: Agitation and Propaganda Department of the C. C. of the C. P. I. [Central Committee of the Communist Party of Indonesia], n.d.), p. 63.

5. For a later PKI criticism of this tendency, see M. H. Lukman, *Tentang Front Persatuan Nasional* (*Concerning the National United Front*) (Djakarta: Pembaruan, 1960), pp. 31–32.

6. For a discussion of PKI weaknesses in peasant organization, see D. N. Aidit, "Haridepan Gerakan Tani Indonesia" ("The Future of the Indonesian Peasant Movement"), *Bintang Merah*, July, 1953, reprinted in Aidit, Asmu, Mau Tje-tung [Mao Tse-tung], *Untuk Bekerdja Lebih Baik Dikalangan Kaum Tani* (*For Better Work Among the Peasantry*) (Djakarta: Pembaruan, 1958), especially pp. 15–19; "Laporan Tambahan Mengenai Masaalah Mengembangkan Pekerdjaan Massa Kaum Tani" ("Supplementary Report Concerning the Question of Improving Mass Work in the Peasantry"), *Bintang Merah*, XIII, No. 5–7, (May–July, 1957), 200–201; and Aidit, *Untuk Demokrasi dan Kabinet Gotongrojong* (*For Democracy and a Gotong Rojong Cabinet*) (Djakarta: Pembaruan, 1959), pp. 163–64, 166.

7. See *Madju Terus Menggempur Imperialisme dan Feodalisme* (*Ever Forward to Crush Imperialism and Feudalism*) (Djakarta; Pembaruan, 1961), pp. 15–17.

8. See Aidit, *Untuk Demokrasi . . .* , p. 165; and Aidit, "Haridepan Gerakan . . . ," pp. 12–13.

9. For a later PKI analysis of this phase of policy, see Njoto, "36 Tahun Partai dan Perdjuangan Melawan Dogmatisme" ("36 Years of the Party and the Struggle Against Dogmatism"), *Bintang Merah*, XII, No. 4–5 (April–May, 1956), 119.

10. Thus Aidit, returning from the CPSU Twenty-first Congress via China, referred to the communes as the "rays of a sun which lights the broad horizons of East Asia." (*Harian Rakjat*, April 27, 1959.)

11. For examples of this analysis, see Aidit, "Haridepan Gerakan . . . ," *loc. cit.*, especially p. 12; and Asmu, "Beladjar dari Sidang Pleno DPP-BTI

ke-III" ("Learn from the Third Plenary Session of the BTI Executive"), in Aidit, Asmu, Mau Tje-tung, *op. cit.*, pp. 28–29.

12. Thus Aidit, addressing the Seventh Plenum of the Central Committee, stated that the contradiction between the peasantry and landlords who were opposed to the movements of regional dissidence did not represent a major division in Indonesian society and must be subordinated to the principal conflict against imperialism. (*Bintang Merah*, XIV, No. 11–12 [November–December, 1958], 542.) The general program drawn up in 1958 for adoption by the Sixth Party Congress referred to "advanced aristocratic elements" as being capable of supporting a people's democracy. (*Material for the Sixth National Congress . . .*, p. 92.)

13. See Asmu, *op. cit.*, for a detailed criticism of lack of knowledge of agrarian conditions on the part of the Communist rural cadres and an outline of what the Party felt should be investigated; see also "Laporan Tambahan . . . ," *loc. cit.*, p. 260; and Aidit, "Ubah Imbangan Kekuatan untuk Melaksanakan Konsepsi Presiden Soekarno 100%!" ("Change the Balance of Forces for the 100% Implementation of President Sukarno's Concept!"), *Bintang Merah*, XIII, No. 5–7 (May–July, 1957), 181. The PKI first called for intensive research into the question of rural class stratification in 1953; this demand was reiterated by the BTI executive at its Third Plenum, in 1955, and was repeated by the Party at the fifth Central Committee session, in 1957.

14. See Karl J. Pelzer, "The Agricultural Foundation," in Ruth T. McVey (ed.), *Indonesia* (New Haven, Conn.: Human Relations Area Files, 1963).

15. For a discussion of this differentiation, see Clifford Geertz, *The Religion of Java* (Glencoe, Ill.: The Free Press, 1960); and Robert Jay, "Santri and Abangan: Religious Schism in Rural Central Java" (unpublished doctoral dissertation, Harvard University, 1957).

16. For a PKI description of the Party strategy regarding the regional governments, see Aidit, "Ubah Imbangan . . . ," pp. 156–58; also the speech by Ruslan Kamaludin to the Fifth (July, 1957) Central Committee Plenum, in *Bintang Merah*, XIII, No. 8 (August, 1957), 312–14.

17. See, for example, Aidit's address in *Documents of the 6th Plenum of the Central Committee of the Communist Party of Indonesia* (Djakarta: Pembaruan, 1958); and P. Pardede, "Likwidasi Institut Pamong Pradja" ("Liquidate the Institution of the Pamong Pradja"), *Menudju Otonomi Daerah Seluas-luasnja (Toward the Broadest Possible Regional Autonomy)*, Vol. II (Djakarta: Pembaruan, 1958).

18. See Aidit, "Fase Baru dan Penjesuaian Organisasi dengan Situasi" ("The New Phase and Bringing the Organization in Line with the Situation"), *Bintang Merah*, XIV, No. 3–4 (March–April, 1958), 124; See also Bimo, "Separatisme dan Kemerdekaan" ("Separatism and Independence"), *Bintang Merah*, XIII, No. 3–4 (March–April, 1957), 80, 82; "Pernjataan Terimakasih kepada Tentara dan Rakjat" ("Declaration of Thanks to the Army and the People"), *Bintang Merah*, XIV, "Nomor Konfernas" ("National Conference Number") (June–July, 1958), 324–25; *Bintang Merah*, XIV, No. 11–12 (November–December, 1958), 558; and Aidit, *Konfrontasi Peristiwa Madiun 1948, Peristiwa Sumatera 1956 (Confrontation of the 1948 Madiun Affair and the 1956 Sumatra Affair)* (Djakarta: Pembaruan, 1958), p. 24.

19. This apparently did happen in a few places. The author was informed by Daniel Lev that in the Minangkabau area of West Sumatra, especially in the region around the separationist stronghold of Padang, non-Communist local

leaders were so involved with the rebellion that the invading central government forces named PKI members or sympathizers to many civil administrative and militia positions in spite of the intrinsic weakness of the PKI in that area. Javanese units considered to have leftist sympathies were heavily utilized by the central government in putting down the insurrection—presumably because the military command felt they would be most likely to oppose the rebels firmly. The long-run effect of this was perhaps detrimental to Communist interests, however, since a heavy toll was taken of these units' membership, resulting in their regrouping.

20. See Aidit, "Ubah Imbangan . . . ," pp. 159, 168; Persbiro Indonesia (PIA) news bulletins of August 22 and September 12, 1959; and Aidit, "The Sixth National Congress of the Communist Party of Indonesia," *Review of Indonesia*, VI, No. 11–12 (November–December, 1959), 44.

21. It might be noted that the PKI also lost a good deal of its representation in the regional legislatures, which were retooled along the same lines as Parliament. According to Aidit's report to the 1962 Party Congress, 50 per cent of the Communist representatives lost their seats (*Harian Rakjat*, May 7, 1963). Though the legislatures were no longer important as sources of power, this was certainly a blow to the Party's morale and diminished the number of positions it could provide its regional activists.

22. Lukman, *op. cit.*, pp. 54–55.

23. For an analysis of the problems of National United Front strategy under guided democracy, see Lukman, *op. cit.*, pp. 32–41.

24. See Aidit, "The Sixth National Congress . . . ," p. 46; and Aidit, *Untuk Demokrasi* . . . , pp. 48–49, 136–49. For discussions of the first two plans, see Aidit, "Ubah Imbangan . . . ," pp. 186–94; Njoto, "Masaalah Pendidikan didalam Partai" ("The Question of Education Within the Party"), *Bintang Merah*, XII, No. 7–8 (July–August, 1956), 296–307; Aidit, "The New Phase and Bringing the Organization in Line with the Situation," *Documents of the Sixth Plenum* . . . , pp. 76–80; and Aidit, *Untuk Demokrasi* . . . , pp. 133–34.

25. See Aidit, *Untuk Demokrasi* . . . , pp. 151–59; *Madju Terus* . . . , *loc. cit.*, pp. 20–25. The problem still existed in 1962: See Aidit's report to the Fourth Central Committee Plenum, in *Harian Rakjat*, April 28, 1962; and Sujana, "Soal Organisasi sesudah Congres" ("The Problem of Organization Following the Congress"), *Harian Rakjat*, May 18, 1962.

26. A Presidential reorganization of the cabinet in March brought the chairmen and vice-chairmen of Parliament and the Interim Consultative Assembly (MPRS) into that body. Aidit and Lukman, who were among the vice-chairmen of these assemblies, were thus included in the cabinet circle, though without acquiring actual ministerial power and without formally representing the PKI.

27. See *Harian Rakjat*, April 25, 1962—Aidit's statement to the April plenary session of the Central Committee—for a discussion of this point and the general problem of cabinet representation.

28. Evidence of such a bid for support may be seen in the April, 1962, Central Committee assertion that the attempts to repress the Party had thus far been foiled by the resistance of the working class and "because the other democratic parties and their followers can sense that whatever is done against the PKI is just a first step toward the smashing of all parties. In several places, there were those among the other parties which were successfully forced to join

in implementing the prohibition on the PKI, but in general the other parties of democratic traditions did not wish to be made clubs for beating the PKI." (*Harian Rakjat*, April 28, 1962.)

29. Aidit statement of January 8, 1963, as reported in the *Antara* (Djakarta) news bulletin of January 12, 1963.

30. *Harian Rakjat*, April 28, 1962 (report of the Fourth Central Committee Plenum).

31. It is interesting to note that although the PKI claimed it had succeeded in raising SOBSI membership considerably in the 1959–62 period (to about 3 million), it considered its principal achievement in the labor field to have been the prevention of the establishment of OPPI and the PTK (*Harian Rakjat*, April 28, 1962; report of the Central Committee).

32. *Harian Rakjat*, April 30, 1962.

33. I am indebted to Daniel Lev for providing me with information on BTI activities in this sphere. The importance of this function in peasant eyes can perhaps be appreciated if we note that villages were seeking this sort of representation fifty years ago. It was a major reason why they joined the Sarekat Islam, Indonesia's first mass movement and the only one in the colonial period to gain significant rural support.

34. In carrying out these campaigns, the Party has urged its cadres to take into account the economic status of those on whom the demands were made. A middle-income peasant could not be expected to concede as much as a rich one, and both of these were to be subjected to less pressure than those in the landlord category. (*Harian Rakjat*, April 30, 1962.)

35. A good statement of this analysis may be found in the preamble to the PKI constitution adopted by the Sixth Party Congress. (See *Material for the Sixth National Congress* . . . , pp. 107–8; and Lukman, "Pidato Pengantar untuk Perubahan Konstitusi Partai" ["Keynote Speech for the Changing of the Party Constitution"], in *Tentang Konstitusi PKI* [*On the Constitution of the PKI*] [Djakarta: Depagitprop CC PKI, 1959], pp. 12–30).

36. See Lukman, "Pidato Pengantar . . . ," *passim*, especially pp. 28–31; Lukman, *Tentang Front Persatuan Nasional*, especially p. 35; and Lukman, "PKI dan Pernjataan 81 Partais" ("The PKI and the Declaration of the 81 Parties"), in *41 Tahun PKI*, (*41 Years of the PKI*) (Djakarta: Pembaruan, 1961); Lukman "AD-ART PKI sesudah Kongres Nasional ke-VII" ("The Constitution and By-Laws of the PKI Following the Seventh National Congress"), *Harian Rakjat*, May 15 and 16, 1962.

37. Thus Aidit, addressing the Sixth Party Congress, emphasized Tito's bad influence on neutralist leaders, citing Nasser as an example of one who "had already sacrificed his good name as an anticolonial fighter by following in the steps of the Tito clique and carrying on the reactionary anti-Communist policy of the imperialists." (Aidit, *Untuk Demokrasi* . . . , p. 95.) And in its July, 1960, criticism of the government, the PKI sharply denounced its enthusiasm for a neutralist bloc that would include Tito. (*Harian Rakjat*, July 8, 1960.)

38. See PIA news bulletin, January 23, 1960.

39. Aidit contrasted the bloc with a treaty organization and concluded that no obligation other than that of pursuing socialism bound its members. "Participation in the socialist bloc," he continued, "is not determined by subjective judgment, but by objective evidence that a country is really constructing socialism, a society without oppression of man by man. Albania is a country

which is constructing a society of this sort, a socialist society. Comrade Khrushchev himself does not deny this." (*Harian Rakjat*, December 15, 1961.)

40. *Harian Rakjat*, December 15, 1961.

41. *Ibid.*, January 2, 1962; resolution of the Third (December, 1961) Central Committee Plenum.

42. See Aidit's report on the CPSU Congress, in *Harian Rakjat*, December
15, 1961, for a detailed exegesis on this subject. The PKI joined in the original
denunciation of the cult of individualism, but lapsed into silence on the subject of Stalin as Soviet public pronouncements on the departed leader became
more fiercely critical. In 1959, the Party expressed its disapproval of the Soviet
stand by stressing its debt to Stalin at its Sixth Congress (Lukman, "Pidato
Pengantar . . . ," p. 13) and publishing a memorial to him that emphasized
his virtues as well as noting his faults (*Stalin dan Karjanja* [*Stalin and His
Works*] [Djakarta: Pembaruan, 1959]). PKI leaders have since not neglected
opportunities to give credit to Stalin, and at the time of the Twenty-second
CPSU Congress Aidit was reported by the PKI newspaper to have visited "the
mausoleum of Lenin and Stalin" and there laid wreaths in honor of both
leaders. (*Harian Rakjat*, October 31, 1961.)

43. Politburo resolution supporting Aidit's statement on the CPSU Congress, *Harian Rakjat*, December 16, 1961.

44. *Harian Rakjat*, December 15, 1961 (Aidit's report).

45. For an example of this argument, see Aidit's reply to an invitation by the
World Peace Council to attend its July, 1962, congress on peace and disarmament. (*Harian Rakjat*, April 7, 1962.)

46. The PKI newspaper gave favorable publicity to suggestions that Cuba's
position be settled by Asian-African–sponsored mediation. Similarly it backed
Indonesia's U.N. proposal that the Far East be made a zone free of nuclear
weapons.

47. *Harian Rakjat*, December 15, 1961.

48. *Ibid.*, April 27, 1962 (report of the Fourth Central Committee Plenum).

49. The tone of PKI comments on the Sino-Indian dispute can be seen in
Harian Rakjat's editorial comment of November 17, 1962:

> We are still disappointed, however, by India's standpoint, which does not
> appreciate this demand by healthy world opinion (for a negotiated settle-
> ment) but even continues actively to import arms from America and England.
> It is easy to pick a quarrel, easy to make a commotion; but to face up to
> resistance is not a simple matter. It would do India honor to heed world
> opinion, which desires a settlement of the Sino-Indian boundary by
> negotiations.
>
> It is to be hoped that everyone will perforce realize that the progressive
> people of the world welcome every effort for the settlement of the Sino-
> Indian border by negotiations, and will oppose firmly and in anger a refusal
> to negotiate.

As a rule, the Party newspaper did not quote either Soviet or Chinese press
comments on the dispute, but drew its indicators of "healthy world opinion"
largely from Asian-African bloc statements that buttressed its stand. However,
when the U.S.S.R. decided not to send warplanes to India, Aidit cabled Khrushchev to express his appreciation of the decision, in view of Nehru's recent
desire to "seek disputes with neighboring countries." (*Harian Rakjat*, November 2, 1962.) Apparently, the PKI's attitude was still not considered hopeless

by the Indians, for the following day the Indian Ambassador made a pilgrimage to PKI headquarters to explain his country's standpoint to Aidit. It might be noted that the Indonesian Government assumed an attitude on the dispute which, while formally one of strict neutrality, tended in effect to favor the Chinese rather than the Indian position.

50. Aidit, "Revolusi Oktober, Patriotisme dan Internasionalisme" ("The October Revolution, Patriotism, and Internationalism"), *Harian Rakjat*, November 14, 1962.

51. Discussing the implications of the Sino-Indian crisis, Aidit stated:

The Communists and working class of Indonesia must draw a lesson from the experience still being undergone by the Indian working class, which is that chauvinism is a very great danger for the working-class movement and can paralyze it, and cause it to lose its prestige and orientation. We have also become more convinced that dialectics must be carried out in the united front with the bourgeoisie—that is, that there must be both unity and struggle. If there is only unity without struggle in the united front it will mean weakening one's own forces; the working-class movement will become an adjunct of the bourgeoisie, the working class a captive of the bourgeoisie, and can even be used by the bourgeoisie as bait to fish credit and arms from the imperialists and as a shield in a battle against socialism.

I have received statements from Indonesian Communists expressing concern and fear about what is now happening to the Indian working-class movement. I have already answered these statements. Concern is certainly appropriate, but fear which is carried to the point of timidity is not necessary. The Indian working class is one of experience, militance, and revolutionary tradition; it will surely be able to free itself from the grip of Mr. Nehru and his friends.

(*Harian Rakjat*, November 14, 1962.)

52. See Aidit, "Programma KPSS i bor'ba narodov za pol'noe natsional'noe osvobozhdenie" ("The Program of the CPSU and the People's Struggle for Complete National Independence"), *Kommunist*, XXXIX, No. 1 (1962), 92–95.

53. The comparison was suggested to the author by Indonesians of various political persuasions in 1959; George McT. Kahin, Herbert Feith, and Daniel Lev have told the author that, during their more recent visits to Indonesia, the parallel was not infrequently brought up.

THREE

"ROADS TO SOCIALISM": COMMUNIST REGIMES IN POWER

6. A "Straight Zigzag": The Road to Socialism in North Viet-Nam

by BERNARD B. FALL

THE ROAD TO POWER

The Democratic Republic of Viet-Nam (D.R.V.N.), better known as North Viet-Nam, shares the distinction, with Tito's Yugoslavia, of having been able to impose its Communist system largely from *within*—i.e., without the preponderant military aid and presence of a larger Communist power.[1] This fact alone would be sufficient to give the regime a special niche within the "bloc of fraternal countries," whose members depend for their existence largely on the continued presence of Russian troops (as in the cases of Hungary, Poland, and East Germany, among others) or on the proximity of Chinese Communist forces (in the case of North Korea).

In sheer military terms, North Viet-Nam can stand on its own feet as the strongest military power, bar none, in mainland Southeast Asia.[2] And the Viet-Nam People's Army (VPA) enjoys a deserved reputation of being one of the best jungle combat forces in the world; it is, furthermore, a thoroughly politicized army, of which its own commander-in-chief, Vo Nguyên Giap, has said: "Our Army was successful and mature because it is a people's army led by the Party."[3] Or, as Julien Cheverny, a French technical-assistance expert who recently spent four years in Indochina, put it in a brilliant book that is virtually unknown in the English-speaking world:

> [Viet-Nam's] Communism is not the result of an alien overlay, of a more or less well-supported invasion or importation, but has been lived with in the colonial struggle, has acquired experience during the [Indochina] war, has been broken in through the exercise of governmental powers . . .[4]

199

North Viet-Nam has another almost unique feature among Communist countries (including Yugoslavia). In its thirty-two-year-long history, the country's Communist Party has never experienced a purge of any of its major leaders. That is not to say that the Party never has had, and does not have now, "left" and "right" tendencies and wings, and even a "cult of the personality." It has all that, as will be seen later. But thus far, all such schisms have been reasonably well settled *en famille*, without any of the original leaders disappearing from either the May Day parades or the local history books. Considering the fact that at its inception in 1930 the Indochinese Communist Party (ICP) was so badly split that it looked for a while as if there were going to be, as in Burma, three different Communist parties, this is, as of mid-1963, an important achievement of the Party's leadership.

Thus, "factionalism," which was a major problem with many of the other Communist parties of the 1930's (and seems to be a problem again in the 1960's), did not affect Vietnamese Communism to the same extent. This was in part due to the fact that its leadership had to concern itself constantly with day-to-day problems of survival and did not make an attempt at contributing to the philosophies of Marxism-Leninism. In fact, as one surveys the writings of Ho Chi Minh, Vo Nguyên Giap, or the Party's avowed theoretician, Truong Chinh, one is struck by their philosophical poverty.[5]

Theirs is strictly a regime of *operators*, practitioners of the job of building the "first socialist state in Southeast Asia," content apparently to borrow the necessary ideological underpinnings from next door in Peking, or from Moscow. But the special geographical position of North Viet-Nam—separated as it was from any Soviet-bloc area by thousands of miles of hostile territory until the Chinese Reds reached the Tongking border in November, 1949—compelled the Vietnamese Communist leadership to season the over-all recipe of Communist takeovers to local tastes. As Cheverny says: "Vietnamese Communism, along with that of China, is the only one in Asia to have won its war as well as its revolution." This hard truth must constantly be kept in mind as one looks at North Viet-Nam today.

Vietnamese Communism's rise to power can be divided into three historical periods: (1) pre-independence (1920–45); (2) the war of liberation (1945–54); and (3) the post–cease-fire era (1954–63). During all three periods, several minor changes of line took

place, but the general configuration of Communist operations inside Viet-Nam followed an over-all pattern, as will be briefly shown.

THE PRE-INDEPENDENCE STRUGGLE

In the period prior to the disappearance of colonial control in
Indochina, Vietnamese Communism followed the general line of
temporary alliances with bourgeois nationalist parties that became
standard operational procedure from Cuba to China. Ho Chi
Minh's own past history[6] provides ample illustration for this. A
member of the French Socialist Party until 1920, he swung over to
the Third International when the French Communist Party was
created, went to Moscow in 1924 and worked with Borodin in
Canton during the honeymoon between the Kuomintang and the
Soviet Union, then joined the Chinese Communists for a period[7]
before starting to organize an "Indochinese" (in fact, overwhelmingly Vietnamese) Communist movement.

This was also the period when Ho and his Communists first
collaborated with anti-French Vietnamese revolutionaries living in
exile in China—some of whom were later to allege that the Vietnamese Communists were not loath to denounce to the French
police all those nationalists who, during their stay in China, refused
to collaborate with the Communist elements. The year 1930
brought about the first break of the Communist-nationalist "united
front." The nationalists—allegedly to head off a French drive
about to begin—openly rebelled at Yên-Bay in North Viet-Nam
and some other towns, only to be brutally put down by the colonial
authorities, while the Vietnamese Communists simply sat on the
sidelines.[8]

In the following period, which saw the rise of the Fascist powers
simultaneous with the proclamation of the "Dimitrov line" and the
rise to power in France of a "popular front" regime which had
liberalizing influences on political activities in the colonies, the
Indochinese Communist Party entered into a "legal struggle" phase
and took the utmost advantage of it, consolidating its hold on the
young intellectuals and organizing the plantation, factory, and
mine workers.

This brief honeymoon with the colonial power (which included
such scenes as the 1938 May Day ceremonies when the French and
the Red flags flew side by side!) ended with the new Moscow line
calling for appeasement of Hitler when he attacked Poland in September, 1939. Dutifully, like its French counterpart, the ICP came
out against the war and at the same time went underground. In a

policy statement of November 13, 1939, it sought to reconcile the irreconcilable by attacking France's war against Nazi Germany as "imperialist," while asking its adherents to struggle against Japan: "Our Party finds it to be a matter of life and death . . . to struggle against the imperialist war and policy of thievery and massacres of French imperialism . . . while at the same time struggling against the aggressive aims of Japanese Fascism . . ."[9]

It remains a matter of conjecture whether the sideswipe at Japan at a time when Moscow sought to preserve "correct" relations with the Japanese was due to a local initiative or not. It is also more than likely that several small anti-French uprisings that took place at that time—notably one in Cochinchina on November 23, 1940 —were of a nationalist nature and were only later absorbed into the local Communist mythology. The hard fact remains that at least until 1942, the ICP simply struggled to keep its apparatus—badly mauled by some large-scale arrests when the Party had gone underground in 1939—alive and in functioning order.

As World War II flared up in Asia, the ICP went along with the new "united front" line, though once more in its own good time. Ironically, it was the local Chinese generals Lung Yün[10] and Chang Fa-k'uei who, for their own shortsighted purposes, pushed the wartime alliance between Vietnamese Communists and nationalists to its ultimate conclusion: Both generals had ulterior designs upon mineral-rich and prosperous Tongking and had fully realized that the Vietnamese non-Communist parties, small and divided as they were and led by men in their seventies who had not set foot in Viet-Nam for several decades, would be incapable by themselves of "delivering" the area. They realized correctly that Ho Chi Minh and his well-disciplined Communists could.

Where the Chinese generals made their fatal mistake was in believing that they, in conjunction with their Vietnamese puppets, could maneuver and control the ICP into becoming a docile tool. But, as history shows, there were several other leaders (with greater claims to sophistication than these South China war lords) who harbored similar illusions in other parts of the world. Ho Chi Minh and his followers, cut off from the outside world, at first did not know what line to follow; it took Ho almost eighteen months of being dragged in stocks from Chinese prisons in Kweilin to other prisons in Liuchow before he saw his way clear to such a collaboration with the war lords and their Vietnamese followers. The decision (though ideologically "correct" when he finally consented) must have been prompted largely by the realization that his own chances of further surviving in jail were becoming increasingly slim. But even before he was jailed, Ho already had taken certain measures to broaden the base of the Party's struggle. In May, 1941, during the eighth session of the Central Committee of the ICP, it had been resolved to create "an enlarged national front to include not only workers and peasants . . . but also patriotic landowners"; and in the true opportunism that the circumstances demanded, "the Central Committee decided to adopt momentarily a somewhat milder slogan in the agrarian field: 'Confiscation of the land owned by traitors for distribution to the poor farmers.' "[11] That very much milder slogan was to remain the basis of the D.R.V.N.'s agrarian policy until ultimate victory was assured in 1953 and the cooperation of the landowning bourgeoisie was no longer deemed necessary.

Having decided on a "national front" policy, the ICP made approaches to various non-Communist groupings, which in May, 1941, agreed to form the Viet-Nam Doc Lap Dong Minh (Revolutionary League for the Independence of Viet-Nam), better known as the Viet-Minh. It was the Viet-Minh that in 1943 agreed to cooperate with the Chinese war lords. Too well known in Chungking and elsewhere as a Communist leader, the man previously called Nguyên Ai-Quoc now adopted the name of Ho Chi Minh ("He who enlightens"), under which he was to become famous; and on March 28, 1944, a Provisional Republican Government of Viet-Nam was proclaimed in Liuchow under the aegis of the Chinese. The Viet-Minh represented a comfortable minority in that government—surely no danger to the non-Communist majority and its Chinese backers. No one objected when the Viet-Minh elements volunteered to return to the dangers of Japanese-occupied Indochina while the pro-Kuomintang Vietnamese awaited V-J Day in China.

Thus it was the Viet-Minh that created the first anti-Japanese guerrilla forces in Viet-Nam, rescued American fliers shot down in Indochina, provided intelligence to the Allies, spread propaganda among the civilian population, and received all the credit for anti-Japanese activities during the war.

But the master stroke of the ICP was to come with V-J Day. On August 13, 1945, it held a "national conference" at the village of Tan Trao in the hill province of Tuyên-Quang, in the course of which it decided to make a bid for power before the Allies had a chance to land, thus presenting them with the *fait accompli* of Communist control. Truong Chinh, then Secretary-General of the ICP, described what went on in a short book published a year later:

In the course of this history-making Congress, the ICP proposed a clear-cut program: Guide the revolutionaries so as to disarm the Japanese *before the arrival of the Allies in Indochina*, take over the power that was in the hands of the Japanese and their puppets, and receive, *as the authority in control of the country*, the Allied forces coming to demobilize the Japanese. [Italics added].[12]

The passage is self-explanatory. It fits perfectly into the Communist pattern then being applied from Lublin to Athens to Singapore—and thanks to Allied bungling, it worked with signal success. At Tehran and Potsdam, it had been decided that Indochina would be occupied by Chinese Nationalist forces down to the 16th Parallel, while Commonwealth forces would occupy the southern half of the peninsula. Both occupations worked in favor of what the Viet-Minh and ICP now set out to do. British occupation (mainly the Twentieth Indian Division of Major General D. D. Gracey) was prompt, but was spread far too thin to have any effect on the ICP apparatus establishing control throughout the country. As for the Chinese occupation forces, they were numerous, but it took them three months to cover the 100 miles from the border to Hanoi as they slowly pilfered their way through the countryside, making themselves hated in the process and thoroughly discrediting their Vietnamese nationalist allies as well.

The "provisional government" created in 1944 in China was quietly forgotten as the Viet-Minh on August 16, 1945, proclaimed the creation of a National Liberation Committee of Viet-Nam. In striking fashion, the "Lublin process" was about to repeat itself in Southeast Asia—but without even the presence of an overwhelmingly strong Communist military force. On August 19, the Viet-Minh entered Hanoi. On August 23, Emperor Bao-Dai in Hué surrendered the grand seal of the Vietnamese Empire to representatives of the Viet-Minh and proclaimed his abdication.

On August 25, the Viet-Minh's Committee of Liberation of the Nam-Bô (South Viet-Nam) took over control of Saigon. And on August 29, a Provisional Government of the Democratic Republic of Viet-Nam was formed in Hanoi by Ho; the ICP and the Viet-Minh held all its key posts, even though it also included a few non-Communists. On September 2, 1945, the independence of Viet-Nam was solemnly proclaimed from the balcony of the Hanoi opera house, to the cheers of a crowd 500,000 strong, and Asia's second oldest (after Outer Mongolia) Communist state was born.

So far, the ICP had completely outmaneuvered its adversaries. It was to suffer a few setbacks in the South, where General Gracey dealt with the Nam-Bô committee on a "no-nonsense" basis. ("They came to see me and said 'welcome' and all that sort of thing. It was an unpleasant situation, and I promptly kicked them out.") He released the French troops who were still held in Japanese POW camps and thus started a flurry of fighting, of which the takeover of Viet-Nam had so far been largely devoid.

But in Hanoi, the Chinese Nationalists saw to it—through their greed and shortsightedness—that the Communist takeover would be as painless and thorough as possible. A "gold week" held by the Viet-Minh, in which residents of North Viet-Nam were compelled to give their gold for the "purchase" of weapons from the Chinese, was thoroughly successful and soon provided the nascent Viet-Nam People's Army (VPA) with 3,000 rifles, 50 automatic rifles, 600 submachine guns, and 100 mortars of American manufacture—plus the substantial French and Japanese stocks (31,000 rifles, 700 automatic weapons, 36 artillery pieces, and 18 tanks) that the Chinese were supposed to have secured but had not.

In the political field, the Viet-Minh movement fared equally well. Fully realizing its temporary dependency upon non-Communist good will, it took the unusual step of "dissolving" the ICP on November 11, 1945, thus becoming, no doubt, the only "people's democracy" to operate without an official Communist Party of any kind. Then, again following the Polish experience, it promised the Kuomintang generals to give the Vietnamese non-Communist parties 70 seats in the first legislature, elected in January, 1946—provided the non-Communist parties would not even try to compete in the electoral contest.[13] Knowing that they would not be able to gain even 70 seats (out of a total of about 400) in a fair fight, the nationalists agreed with alacrity, thereby sealing their doom—for the Vietnamese electorate, which, until then, had only known the Viet-Minh, was deprived of any chance of even seeing the opposition, much less voting for it.[14]

The government that resulted from the January, 1946, elections was, predictably, *not* openly Communist-dominated, in order to forestall adverse reactions from the Kuomintang generals and to continue to gain, if possible, a measure of recognition in the West. With a cold measure of realism, the ICP leadership—recognizing that the "socialist motherland" was far away and unlikely to get embroiled in Viet-Nam—made a determined drive to gain American recognition and a seat in the United Nations. Both efforts failed, of course.

Behind the façade of respectability, a relentless struggle for the consolidation of Viet-Minh power went on. Provincial mandarins (among them President Ngo Dinh Diem's brother, Ngo Dinh Khoi) were murdered; a massive drive began against the well-entrenched Trotskyites in South Viet-Nam;[15] and a clumsy attempt was made at dismantling the religious sects by killing some of their leaders (such as Huynh Phu So, young "prophet" of the Hoa-Hao).

Also, the actual levers of power were passed quietly into the hands of Viet-Minh faithfuls by the simple process of stripping the non-Communist ministerial positions of most of their responsibilities. The Ministry of Defense lost most of its control over the armed forces to a General Staff headed by Vo Nguyên Giap; and the Ministry of Interior lost its police powers to a Directorate of Security. Once more, many of the nationalists had let themselves be lured by the appearance rather than the realities of power. Others were simply frightened into total silence as the takeover spread under their very eyes. Many South Vietnamese leaders today are survivors of that category.

Thus, through the sheer energy and organizational ability of its Communist leadership, Viet-Nam had for all practical purposes become a "people's democracy," in fact as well as in name, even while its territory was still occupied by Chinese Nationalist, British, and French forces—surely a unique feat among present-day Communist governments.

THE "PERIOD OF RESISTANCE"

The outbreak of open hostilities with the French on December 19, 1946, simultaneously complicated and simplified the job of the D.R.V.N. leadership: It complicated it in the sense that the D.R.-V.N. now had to operate from a secret hiding place in the jungle; it simplified it in that the D.R.V.N. could erect its political, military, and administrative apparatus without having to worry about the niceties of democratic forms or world opinion.[16]

Normal civilian administration was abolished in favor of a system of Party-controlled Committees of Resistance and Administration, known by their Vietnamese initials as UBKC/HC. The court system was simplified to the utmost. The legislature, such as it was (the seventy appointed opposition members had shown up once, only to disappear forever in exile or death), had handed over its powers to a Permanent Committee which had powers exceeding those of the Soviet Presidium and did not meet from 1946 until 1953 (and then only for one session); the next legislative elections were held in May, 1960—fourteen years after the first.

Now that the Chinese Nationalists had disappeared as a power factor and the war was being fought along ideological lines, there was no further point in hiding the Communist character of the D.R.V.N.: During the Eleventh Party Congress, held on February 11–15, 1951, the Party was resurrected under the name of Dang Lao-Dong (Workers' Party).

At the end of January, 1953, the Party rescinded its erstwhile policy of leniency against "patriotic landlords." During the fourth meeting of the Party Central Committee, it was decided "to mobilize the farmers to struggle against the landowners." In the course of the fifth meeting of the Central Committee, in November of that year, the slogan "Land to the tillers" was adopted as official Party policy and promptly ratified by the ever-obedient National Assembly on December 1, 1953, in its first agrarian-reform law.

By the time the Indochina war ended, on July 20, 1954, the territory under effective control of the D.R.V.N. (then about 60 per cent) had become a true "people's democracy." This also seems to have been the view of the Lao-Dong Party, which held its sixth Central Committee meeting on July 15, 1954. Instead of focusing its attention upon internal problems, it now looked upon the whole situation in the light of the world-wide struggle ahead: ". . . to direct the main emphasis of the struggle against the American imperialists and the French warmongers on the basis of the victories already won; to re-establish peace in Indochina and to defeat the American plans of prolonging and generalizing the Indochina war."[17]

The occupation of all of Viet-Nam north of the 17th Parallel constituted, from the D.R.V.N.'s point of view, little else but a return to the *status quo ante bellum* of 1946, with a few differences: The French and the Chinese Nationalists had departed, never to return. The main antagonist of the D.R.V.N. was now the United States, and the D.R.V.N.'s most important ally was the People's Republic of China.

CONSTRUCTING THE SOCIALIST STATE

The 1954 Geneva cease-fire gave the D.R.V.N. something it had lacked since 1946: a well-defined territory in which it was the unchallenged authority; a chance of operating its governmental and political apparatus on a normal basis; and, above all, a fairly solid industrial base, without which it is impossible in the long run to create a state based on the "union of peasants and workers."

The post–cease-fire era in North Viet-Nam can be divided

roughly into two successive phases: the period of consolidation of power and the period of political and economic expansion. The first period began after the administrative takeover of North Viet-Nam in October, 1954, and was highlighted by a not-too-successful land reform,[18] an intermediate Three-Year Plan (1958–60), the proclamation of a new constitution in January, 1960, and new legislative elections in May of that year.

The second phase opened with the first full-fledged Five-Year Plan, adopted at the Third National Congress of the Lao-Dong Party, in September, 1960,[19] and also witnessed the beginning of determined politico-military drives to achieve limited external objectives: the destruction of a pro-American regime in South Viet-Nam in order to replace it with a neutralist regime as an intermediate step toward reunification on North Vietnamese terms; the liquidation—completed as of July, 1962—of the American hold on Laos; and the effective isolation of Cambodia. On a wider scale, the D.R.V.N. seeks to establish ties with various nonaligned countries. It has been partly successful in the countries of the "Casablanca bloc," but on a world-wide basis it trails far behind South Viet-Nam.

The territorial structure of the D.R.V.N. in 1963 is a well-integrated mixture of old and new. The basic units—village, district, and province—have remained unchanged in name and territorial extent since the French colonial period, whereas in South Viet-Nam many new provinces have been created and others have been given new and unfamiliar names. A larger wartime territorial unit, the "interzone" (lien-khu), grouping four or more provinces, was abolished in 1961. There remain three nonprovincial units of government in North Viet-Nam, two of which contain ethnic minorities and the third a key industrial area. The establishment of "autonomous areas" for the minorities was a sound administrative solution to the problem of handling people of different cultural patterns, one that no other nation of the Indochinese peninsula has thus far had the courage to envisage.[20] It provides the minority mountaineers with at least the appearance of local self-government and sometimes with somewhat more than that. Article 3 of the North Vietnamese constitution of 1960 recognizes that the D.R.V.N. is a "unified state made up of many nationalities," and the mountain area administration is to a large extent staffed with newly trained mountaineers, although certain essential positions (notably in the field of security) are in the hands of lowland Vietnamese.

There exist two autonomous zones (khu tu tri), Tay-Bac and

Viet-Bac, covering most of the northwestern and northeastern mountain areas of the D.R.V.N. Both zones have their own people's councils and administrative committees, headed by mountaineers. Tay-Bac is headed by a Thai, Lo Van Hac, while Viet-Bac is headed by a former Tay (Thô) chieftain who rose to the rank of Major General in the People's Army, Chu Van Tan. Problems concerning the minority peoples as a whole (there are, according to the 1960 census, 2.56 million of them, or 14.8 per cent of the total population) are dealt with in Hanoi by the Committee on Nationalities (Uy Ban Dan Toc), headed by Major General Lê Van Ba, himself a Tay. The third special area is Hong-Quang (a contraction for the area names of Hongay and Quang-Yen), which covers the key industrial areas north of Haiphong and exists merely for the purpose of better coordination of the industrial effort. (A third minority zone existed between 1957 and 1959; it covered the provinces of Laokay, Ha-Giang, and Yen-Bay and thus was called Lao-Ha-Yen. Its ethnic groups were, however, too diversified; problems arose, and, by "popular demand," Lao-Ha-Yen was broken up; Ha-Giang was attached to Viet-Bac, and the remaining two provinces had to submit directly to the Hanoi administration.[21]) There also exists a small "special zone" at Vinh-Linh along the 17th Parallel.

In terms of political structure, the new constitution and the ensuing legislative elections brought about great changes. The 1946 constitution—promulgated while Marshal Leclerc's tanks held Haiphong, American observers were in Hanoi, Chiang K'ai-shek's troops were barely back in Yünnan, and Mao's forces were thousands of miles away in Yenan—was a model of moderation, with its Jeffersonian echoes and invocations of the "peaceful aspirations of mankind." The 1960 constitution— framed by a legislative committee under the leadership of an old revolutionary comrade of Ho's, Tran Huy Lieu—constituted a radical and deliberate departure from the earlier model. In Tran Huy Lieu's own words: "It is necessary that it becomes clearly understood to what classes power belongs and by what classes [the state] shall be governed, so that the people may recognize without hesitation the nature of our regime. . . . It is founded on the union of workers and peasants and directed by the working class. Our [1946] Constitution does not include that essential point."[22]

As the new constitution took shape, an argument developed between the "jurists" and the "politicians," with the former advocating a brief document embodying guiding principles, while the latter "wanted above all a propaganda document that could be usefully employed in the struggle against the South Vietnamese rival regime."[23] The latter view seems to have prevailed, as the text published in 1960 shows. Its preamble is a completely doctrinaire indictment of "American imperialism," and much of the document is tailored specifically to the present transitional situation.

The major innovation in the new document is a long section (Chapter II) on the socialist transformation of the economy, while much of the remainder simply aligns the North Vietnamese constitutional structure with that of the other "people's democracies"; the new structure includes a "popular control organ," which, in later editions of the constitution, was translated by its correct Soviet term as "office of the procurator." In the field of presidential powers, the chief executive of the D.R.V.N. (there also is a prime minister) is by no means a figurehead. In fact, his extensive powers can be easily compared with those of General de Gaulle under the constitution of the Fifth French Republic, and it is not impossible that—colonial memories or not—the French example may have served as a model, just as anti-French South Vietnamese President Ngo Dinh Diem copies line for line the Economic Council of the French constitution of 1946 in his own constitution of 1956.

The May, 1960, elections proved interesting not in the final result—the Lao-Dong got the usual 99 per cent of the votes[24]—but in the reshuffling of top personalities that ensued. The newly elected National Assembly, which convened on July 7, 1960, to elect the new government, unanimously elected Ho Chi Minh to the Presidency, his old comrade Ton Duc Thang (eight years older than Ho and thus unlikely to succeed him) to the Vice Presidency, and Pham Van Dong to the Premiership. Truong Chinh, the Lao-Dong's philosopher and leader of the pro-Peking wing who had been demoted from the post of Party Secretary-General after the 1956 land-reform fiasco, was appointed to the post of President of the National Assembly, while its Vice Presidency went to Hoang Van Hoan, the D.R.V.N. longtime Ambassador to Peking. Those posts were not voted on with full unanimity. Lê-Duan, a rising Party official, was left without a government portfolio (which at the time started a flurry of speculation), but found himself amply compensated when Ho, at the Fourth Party Congress in September, 1961, divested himself of the important post of Party Secretary-General in favor of Lê-Duan. Professional "Kremlinologists" may wish to conclude from this that Lê-Duan, a true Party "machine man" with no following whatever in the country, may have received the coveted mantle of successorship to Ho ahead of Pham Van Dong or Vo Nguyên Giap. They should remember, however, that this was also said of Truong Chinh before November, 1956, when he was summarily removed from the post without much of a ripple outside the Party machinery itself. Ho, seventy-two in 1962, looks fit and energetic enough not to wish as yet to build a likely successor into his own state machinery—a view of politics he apparently shares with De Gaulle and Chiang K'ai-shek.

THE ECONOMY

In industrial development, lack of qualified cadres proved to be a major impediment. When the French evacuated North Viet-Nam, in May, 1955, there were exactly twenty-three engineers left in all of North Viet-Nam. Priority has been given to basic and heavy industry (steel mills, chemicals, refining of minerals, machine-tool construction)—a policy that, as even the D.R.V.N. now admits, "was not accepted without discussions. . . . The basic question is to know how to apply the Leninist doctrine to concrete conditions—which does not exclude much groping in the dark."[25]

That "groping in the dark" included a major error in 1955–56 in not allocating sufficient means to the minimal production of consumer goods, which led to many complaints and, at least indirectly, to the November, 1956, Nghé-An uprising. According to D.R.V.N. sources, there followed a tendency to "overcorrect" that shortcoming in 1957, and a semblance of balance was achieved in 1958 by allocating more means of production to such essentials as electric power, fertilizer plants, glass factories, and agricultural tool production.

In a personal interview with the author in 1962, members of the State Planning Board blamed many of the shortcomings on the insufficiency of industrial cadres, despite a serious effort at turning out qualified engineers as rapidly as possible. The Five-Year Plan adopted in 1960 was still being "refined" in various government departments late in 1962, and the absence of a solid statistical base[26] and the lack of proper methods of cost accounting were also cited as reasons for industrial production bottlenecks. For example, the North Vietnamese ran into a foreign-aid problem that could have been copied straight out of the notebook of Western aid planners: The donated installations were magnificent, but the share to be contributed by the D.R.V.N. in the form of labor and local materials often became in itself an insuperable burden.

But even so, the efforts made by North Viet-Nam in the indus-trial field are truly impressive. One has to have known the area prior to the French evacuation and to see it again now in order to appre-ciate in full what already has been accomplished at the price of backbreaking labor (in the literal sense, considering how much of the construction relies on human effort rather than bulldozers and other machinery) and low living standards. The steel mill of Thai Nguyên, the superphosphate plant of Phu-Tho, the Russian-built machine-tool plant in Hanoi are facts that have no counterparts as yet in South Viet-Nam. Deliveries of some consumer goods—from shoes to expensive cameras—from the Communist bloc have taken the edge off the worst hunger for such products (and their fantasti-cally high prices also serve the purpose of siphoning off excess pur-chasing power, thus stabilizing the *dong* at 3.53 to the U.S. dollar), and food, while not plentiful, has been available at supportable ra-tion levels since 1962.[27] Therefore, facile comparisons with Com-munist China's situation should, for the time being, be held in abeyance. As Tibor Mende has pointed out,[28] North Viet-Nam is sufficiently small and rich, in Communist-bloc terms, to become a sort of Communist showcase for the other countries of Southeast Asia to imitate.

The very austerity of Hanoi—there are no passenger cars except those of representatives of foreign missions or key officials, and hardly a building has been newly painted or repaired since the French left—contrasts markedly with the sizable amount of indus-trial construction going on in the countryside, which may escape the attention of the occasional Western observer if he is confined to Hanoi alone.

Some of the key industrial problems still are not resolved, in spite of the decision made by the Third Party Congress in 1960 to put the major emphasis of the 1961–65 plan on heavy industry. The shortage of electrical power—electricity is one field in which even the still nonindustrialized South beats the North and is likely to increase its lead—has not been resolved, and the problems posed by the woefully inadequate northern road net have not begun to be solved.

In July, 1962, the Lao-Dong Party's Central Committee held its seventh plenary session to re-examine once more the premises of the Five-Year Plan. The ensuing lengthy communiqué, although indi-cating, finally, a decision that "priority should be given to the ra-tional development of heavy industry," also mentioned that a similar priority was accorded to "plants producing machinery for basic production," and at the same time held out a promise that the consumer's rightful share in production would not be forgotten. In other words, nothing was really decided. While the doctrinaire adherence to the Leninist recipe of "industrialization first" may be the easiest (and safest) solution to the problem on the political level, the "concrete conditions" may dictate still another path before the whole Five-Year Plan is unveiled.

FOREIGN POLICY

In international affairs, the D.R.V.N. can point to some achievements, but it also must admit to some fairly frustrating stalemates. In Laos, its intervention has been limited—no reliable source speaks of more than 10,000 D.R.V.N. troops in Laos at any one time—but extremely efficient. The settlement that resulted in the July 23, 1962, Geneva agreement and totally neutralized Laos under a coalition government no longer under American or SEATO protection must be reckoned as an impressive achievement of Russian and North Vietnamese Cold War diplomacy. The grievous American errors committed in Laos[29] have in no small way contributed to the extent of the Viet-Minh victory.

The struggle for South Viet-Nam—in comparison to which the Laos operation is merely a sideshow—is, of course, far more complicated, and North Viet-Nam's leadership seems aware of some of the dangers involved. Hence, as far as the D.R.V.N. is concerned, the guerrilla struggle in South Viet-Nam is being carried on by a "South Viet-Nam Liberation Front" with a separate leadership, separate political groupings, and a separate flag. A special report on North Vietnamese aid to the Southern insurgents, signed by the Indian and Canadian members (with the Pole voting against it) of the three-power International Control Commission (ICC), was published on June 2, 1962, but rejected by Hanoi. The feeling of the Hanoi leadership seems to be that a protracted revolutionary struggle in South Viet-Nam would fully discredit the Ngo Dinh Diem regime by the sheer size of the U.S. commitment needed to keep it in power and would permit, in their words, "the marshaling of world public opinion against American imperialism."[30]

In Cambodia, the D.R.V.N. has conformed strictly to the theme of "peaceful coexistence" set by Prince Sihanouk, although it does not escape its share of the suspicion with which Cambodians consider all things Vietnamese, regardless of political color.[31] With

Thailand, the Hanoi regime has succeeded in establishing matter-of-fact negotiating relations whose smoothness would surprise the casual observer who simply takes at face value the loud protestations of everlasting anti-Communism coming forth from Bangkok. In August, 1959, Thailand negotiated with North Viet-Nam a repatriation accord for the 70,000-odd Vietnamese refugees living in northeastern Thailand. Without even the pretense of a consultation as to their wishes, those refugees are being shipped back to North Viet-Nam. Negotiations for a new accord were begun in the summer of 1962 between Hanoi and Bangkok on the subject of the refugees, since at that date 37,000 still had not been processed for repatriation. The whole operation is being carefully hushed up by all concerned, and particularly by the South Vietnamese.

However, Hanoi's most interesting foreign relations are those within the Communist camp, for they involve an extremely delicate balance between conflicting loyalties toward Peking and Moscow. Attempts at second-guessing on the subject have only shown, however, that, for the past eight or more years, the D.R.V.N. has at times felt more kindly toward Russia than toward Peking and at other times the reverse.[32] As one British diplomat personally acquainted with North Viet-Nam told this writer: "North Viet-Nam pursues her own policy between Peking and Moscow along a straight zigzag line."

An examination of the record will show that this paradoxical remark is about as fair a statement of the actual situation as can be expected. A visitor to Hanoi's Historical Museum will find, for example, a large room devoted to the "Heroic Struggle of the Vietnamese People Against Chinese Feudal Invaders"; and, if he is inclined to view a Hanoi-Moscow axis as more reassuring than a Hanoi-Peking axis, he may take comfort in the fact that during 1962 there was no Chinese Ambassador in Hanoi for several months or in the fact that the Laos war was almost exclusively a Russo-Vietnamese "show." On the other hand, the observer who likes to believe in Hanoi's permanent subservience to Red China can find an equally impressive array of counterarguments: Ho's own close association with the Chinese Communist Party; the economic dependence of the D.R.V.N. on Chinese aid;[33] Hanoi's qualified support of Albania; the increasing numbers of North Vietnamese technical personnel being trained (and indoctrinated) in China; the May, 1963, Ho Chi Minh–Liu Shao-ch'i joint statement; and so on.

The simple fact is that a country in North Viet-Nam's position has very little choice concerning which protector should fully preside over its destinies. It is in a position within its own bloc similar to that which a small noncommitted country such as Cambodia occupies between East and West: Its best chance of survival—and of competing for foreign aid—lies in alternately placating and playing off the two contenders against each other.

And that is exactly the "straight zigzag line" the British diplomat was talking about.

In summary, it may be said that the North Vietnamese regime has followed classical Communist policies in its rise to power and in the establishment of its state apparatus. It would be difficult to say whether the Russian or the Chinese model has been followed; in fact, for all the regime's protestations to the contrary, there is still enough of the French administrative pattern left in the machinery to make a good understanding of the former colonial administration a useful tool for the study of the D.R.V.N. Finally, it should be remembered that the rise to power of the D.R.V.N. took place under extremely adverse conditions—in fact, probably the most adverse of those of any country in the Soviet orbit—which it mastered thanks to a tactical ingenuity that can almost be considered a novel contribution to the problem of establishing a Communist regime in areas noncontiguous with the Sino-Soviet bloc. The Cuban example of Fidel Castro also comes to mind, with its initially Western-supported native guerrilla force gaining strength and slowly eliminating the non-Communist opposition until, solidly in power, it clamped its control over the whole country. While Dien Bien Phu cannot, in a military sense, be compared with the abortive Bay of Pigs landing, the net effect of military victory in both cases was that, henceforth, it will, in all probability, take a military defeat of either regime on its home grounds to change its character.

Patterns and Techniques of Social Change

Like all Communist parties recently come to power (or still aspiring to come to power), the Lao-Dong is essentially a party of petty bourgeois or even "grand bourgeois." To name a few examples, Ho Chi Minh's father was a petty mandarin; Prime Minister Pham Van Dong's father was a high court official; and Phan Ké Toai, one of the D.R.V.N.'s Vice-Premiers, was Emperor Bao-Dai's last viceroy in Tonkin.

The Lao-Dong has a total membership of fewer than 500,000, in a country of 30 million people[34]—a somewhat smaller proportion than that of other Communist parties in countries where they hold control. The bourgeois character of its leadership seems to worry the Party a great deal; so does the size of its large peasant base in comparison to its still very small number of adherents among the industrial proletariat.

In a study of the Lao-Dong leadership made in 1953 by the Party itself, it was pointed out that of 1,855 "key positions," no fewer than 1,365 were held by "intellectuals or scions of the bourgeoisie," while only 351 were held by members of the peasantry and 139 by "workers."[35] And it is an open question whether those "peasants" and "workers" were not scions of small landlords rather than of landless farmers, and supervisors rather than mine or factory hands.[36]

It was therefore unavoidable that, in the first phase of its organization, both the Party and the government had to base their operations on the voluntary cooperation of the peasantry, even the middle-level peasantry—for it is too often forgotten, even by Western scholars, that in North Viet-Nam, prior to World War II, 98.3 per cent of the tilled land was owned by small holders. In Viet-Nam, the landless-peasantry problem exists only in the deep South. In other words, to speak of "land reform" in North Viet-Nam is farcical; a Soviet agricultural expert who studied the problem just before the land reform was rammed down the throat of the D.R.V.N.'s peasantry came out with the startling but accurate figure that there were in North Viet-Nam in 1956 about 2 million hectares of agricultural land (1 hectare equals 2.4 acres) for 2.29 million landowners![37] Any redistribution of land north of the 17th Parallel merely meant to carry out a *political operation* rather than one meant to change the whole system of rural ownership, let alone to improve production.

Thus the processes of change operated mostly in the negative sense: Very little land that hitherto had not been available could be distributed,[38] but by a Population Classification Decree[39] of 1953, one class of small farmers could be pitted against a class of slightly larger landowners—thus setting into motion the process of landlord trials and executions already well known from mainland China. The arbitrariness and the social, rather than economic, character of the reform is best shown by another Soviet source, which cites the acreages of land owned by various social classes before and after the land reform:[40]

Average Acreages Before and After Land Reform
(*in hectares*)

Social Class	Before	After
Landowners	.65	.10
Rich farmers	.21	.21
Middle-level farmers	.12	.17
Poor farmers	.05	.14
Agricultural workers	.02	.15

As the above table shows, the "rich farmer" emerged comparatively even richer from the Communist land reform. In fact, he was the only one who, if he had an average family of five persons (and thus received more than one hectare), could make a decent living out of agriculture. But according to the previously cited Soviet expert Karamiychev, a total of 702,000 hectares of land were distributed to 1 million farming families, which would give each of them 0.46 hectares of rice land, or, in other words, would put them on starvation rations. But that, precisely, was the purpose of the reform: to demonstrate *ad absurdum* that the privately owned small plot was economically not viable regardless of how much the Vietnamese farmer liked it in his heart. Lenin himself had given the perfect answer to "the renegade Kautsky" when the latter accused him of betraying the small farmer's hopes of getting a small plot of his own:

> The proletarians tell the farmers: "We shall help you realize your desires in the way of an ideal capitalism—for an equalitarian redistribution of land would be nothing but an idealization of capitalism from the viewpoint of the small holder. And then we shall prove to you the impossibility of such a system and the necessity to proceed with collective cultivation of the land."

Faced with uneconomical plots, a scarcity of buffalo, and very high taxes to be paid in rice, the small peasant was the first to fall by the wayside. The rich farmer, like the kulak in Russia, was probably best equipped to withstand the pressure; he was disposed of in the usual way through land-reform tribunals. A "voluntary" movement of agricultural cooperatives was launched in the fall of 1958, and the number of kolkhozes (for that is what they were) went from 44 in 1957 to 4,722 (1958), 28,775 (1959), and finally 41,401 (1960)—constituting 85.8 per cent of all farming families in 1960.[41] By June, 1961, the figure had risen to 88 per cent.[42]

At the same time, a move was started to transform the cooperatives, in Mlle. Delattre's words, into "cooperatives of the higher

type—that is, fully socialistic ones," while similar drives were
started among nonagricultural groups, such as the fishermen and
salt producers, 77 per cent of whom were cooperativized by October, 1960.

Finally, a system of 55 state farms, copies of the Russian sov-
khozes, was set up. The People's Army itself ran 33 of them (an
indication, perhaps, of how touchy the problem was), and by mid-
1961 there were 60, with a working force of 60,000, cultivating
200,000 hectares of land.

While the countryside thus lost its small-holding aspect and
acquired a system from which only the Chinese commune is still
missing—North Viet-Nam has been exceedingly prudent in its
references to the latter—the urban areas were undergoing transformations of their own. Emphasis was placed in Lao-Dong Party
recruitment upon the nonagricultural elements. In a directive of
April, 1957 (i.e., after the November, 1956, peasant uprisings), the
Lao-Dong stressed:

> . . . that for a certain well-defined period, the Party shall above all
> grow in the cities and industrial centers with the aim of attracting
> the best sons and daughters of the working class. At the same time,
> attention will be paid to the development of the Party among the
> revolutionary intellectuals working at present in various branches of
> the public services.[43]

An extremely rapid buildup of a thoroughly politicized system of
colleges and university-type higher specialized schools further tends
to harness the youth and the urbanized working class into the new
system.

Another important element in the transformation of society was
the establishment of artisans' cooperatives in the cities. Out of a
population of 17 million in North Viet-Nam, those in nonrural
occupations, apart from the army and the administrative group,
number less than 750,000 people. Of these, 520,000 were classified
as "artisans" at the end of 1959 and, significantly, although the output of state industries rose rapidly, even by the end of the First
Three-Year Plan (1960) the output of artisans outstripped that of
all the state-owned industries.

The *social character* of the output of artisans had itself considerably
changed, however, for while in 1958 only 47,864 artisans were members of cooperatives, by 1959 more than 158,000 had joined them;
at the end of 1960, 87 per cent of all artisans had been cooperativized.[44]

Output of Production Systems in North Viet-Nam
(in percentage of total)

	1955	1957	1959	1960 (est.)
Artisan production	61.2	59.3	49.5	46.8
State industries	10.4	25.6	43.9	46.5
Private industry	28.4	15.1	6.6	6.7

This left little but the nonworking women and the aged who were as yet unorganized. That small loophole in the network of total control was successfully plugged in 1957–58 with the creation of "street and inhabitant protection committees," whose task it is to "make known and render popular the government's decisions dealing with city affairs . . . and maintain order and public safety." In Hanoi alone, the system uses 4,600 block chiefs and deputy chiefs plus 3,000 "committee members,"[45] who, in effect, see to it that everyone turns out for the spontaneous demonstrations of friendship for Albania or of "Hate America Week."

Under such a system, there is little room left for the free expression of opinion or for institutionalized change of official policies. This is left to a certain interplay of informal pressures, which will be briefly described below.

Pressure Groups in North Viet-Nam[46]

According to North Viet-Nam's second constitution, of January 1, 1960, while "all powers of the D.R.V.N. belong to the people, who exercise them through the intermediary of the National Assembly and of People's Councils [local legislatures] at every echelon, elected by it and responsible to it" (Article 4), the actual facts of government and Party operations tell a different story.

Several distinct groups hold power in the D.R.V.N. Some of them are the "traditional" Communist leaders—old Party chieftains, trade-union bosses, and a sprinkling of senior military commanders. Others spring from the ranks of the "new class"—the Party bureaucrats and the managers of the newly built (and largely still abuilding) industrial economy.

Here again, a brief comparison with the situation prevailing in other Communist-bloc countries shows that the D.R.V.N., like most Communist nations, is on the verge of switching from the "old Bolsheviks" to the "new class." The ages of the old leaders, as well as the changed situation, provide the reason for the change at this time. The old leadership (Ho Chi Minh, Ton Duc Thang) is in its seventies; Pham Van Dong, though younger, is not in good

health; and the Lao-Dong's perennial Party theoretician, Truong
Chinh, was somewhat discredited at the time of the first land-
reform fiasco in 1956 and is too closely identified with the pro-
Peking wing of Vietnamese Communism. It is, therefore, not
surprising that at the Fourth Party Congress of the Lao-Dong, in
September, 1961, the mantle of the Secretary-Generalship of the
Party fell upon Lê-Duan, a younger Party bureaucrat who had thus
far not been openly embroiled in the Moscow-Peking tug of war.

At present, then, the D.R.V.N. possesses three "power groups"
which, by virtue of their importance to the survival of the state,
may have an extra constitutional influence upon its policies: the
Communist Party and its satellite organizations, the armed forces,
and the administrators and managers.

At the same time, there exist three groups that exercise a somewhat more diffuse influence upon the affairs of the D.R.V.N. by
virtue of their sheer size or their potential influence upon the citi-
zenry at large. They could, for want of a better term, be classified as
"pressure groups." These are the intellectuals, the urban labor force,
and the peasantry.

POWER GROUPS

One of the three power groups already has been dealt with in
some detail: the ICP and Lao-Dong Party, which in 1960 num-
bered about 500,000 members.[47] Seconded by its cohort of Young
Pioneers and by a catch-all Fatherland Front, of which very little
has been heard recently as the fortunes of the Southern Liberation
Front have been rising, its influence reaches from the Presidency
of the Republic to the lowest village and army unit. As has been
shown, the Party may still suffer from "estrangement from the
broad masses," and its recent massive increase in size may perhaps
have multiplied its cadre problem more than it has strengthened
the Party's real hold on the country.

One group, on the other hand, that can lay a solid claim to being
"people-based" is the Viet-Nam People's Army. While its leader,
Giap, who holds a Ph.D. in history from the French University in
Hanoi, can certainly lay claim to the title of "intellectual," the bulk
of the division commanders and other senior officers were NCO's
in the French colonial army, or even bandits or tribal chieftains.
(Major General Chu Van Tan is a Thô tribesman.) Some (not too
many) senior commanders were trained in Communist China and
tend to be sympathetic to its views, but the overwhelming bulk of
the military leadership are personally faithful to General Giap.

The regular VPA divisions are still made up largely of villagers or even tribesmen (such as the 316th, the 324th, and the 335th divisions), and the VPA is surrounded by the aura of its unbroken victories against the French. This gives it a certain amount of assurance that the Lao-Dong does not possess. Neither the army nor the Lao-Dong has forgotten that a congress of VPA political commissars warned the civilian Party leadership in the fall of 1956 of the possibility of peasant revolt (of which the Lao-Dong was either blissfully unaware or which it did not take seriously) or that it was the VPA's 325th Division that crushed the revolt, as the civilian administration and the Party cadres fled the scene in panic. In fact, the contempt of the army for the "intellectuals" who run the country is at times so blatant that the Party newspaper, *Nhan-Dan*, openly criticized the VPA for showing "an excess of prudence when it comes to entrusting intellectuals with posts or missions in accordance with their abilities. This shows a certain narrowness of mind which operates against the intellectuals."

For the time being, the VPA is the *enfant chéri* of the regime. Giap is solidly in control of the army, and recent appointments have further strengthened the pro-Moscow trend said to be the prevailing mood in the forces. The recent influx of new Soviet weapons and the joint Soviet-D.R.V.N. operations in Laos may have further tightened such bonds, in spite of the pro-Albania mouthings of the civilian leadership and recent visits of Chinese military leaders in Hanoi, matched by rival visits of Russian senior officers.

The managerial elite, for the time being, is neither large nor proficient. It is worth mentioning only because of its *potential* influence and because it is the largest single group to receive training abroad (i.e., within the Soviet bloc). For the time being, its relatively low technical proficiency makes it a handy scapegoat for the recent production setbacks that have racked the D.R.V.N. The fact that it is at present made up largely of discharged army officers does give it, however, a certain amount of power and influence.

PRESSURE GROUPS

In any totalitarian state, pressure without power is a slender reed indeed. Of the three mentioned pressure groups, two discovered the truth of that statement the hard way—the peasantry and the intellectuals. The fate of the peasantry has already been described. That of the intellectuals was mainly a problem of love deceived. It was they who had formed the *avant-garde* of the movement throughout its formative and wartime years. To this day, South Viet-Nam cannot claim a writer comparable in stature to some of those who live in Hanoi—and in Paris (including a former South Vietnamese Ambassador who won a French literary prize). The Viet-Minh's firm anticolonialist stand, its erstwhile lack of corruption, its seeming classlessness, its Spartan way of life contained powerful appeals which Saigon could not hope to match.

On the other hand, as the regime in Hanoi settled down to the humdrum life of a backwater "people's democracy," those same intellectuals soon found themselves faced with an ideological strait-jacket whose Southern Vietnamese imitation at least has the merit of being less efficient. And, so far at least, Ngo Dinh Diem has not expressed himself on the artistic merits of arhythmic verse or abstract painting. The North, on the other hand, has set extremely strict rules on precisely those subjects.

The "Hundred Flowers" era in North Viet-Nam witnessed an explosion of anti-Party writing, poetry, and painting comparable to that in Poland of 1956–58. The repression was as brutal and narrow-minded as any to be found within the bloc. Young writers and other intellectuals by the thousands were sent to the Bac-Hung-Hai irrigation canal and other projects to work in the cold water up to their chests until "they finally understood that culture, literature, and the arts spring from the masses and are destined to serve them, for it is the masses who are most able to assimilate and to judge them."[48]

The urban labor force has, thus far, remained silent. It works hard under trying conditions, can find few satisfying consumer goods, and has in recent months been given to grumbling about its labor federation, which, instead of representing its members, seems to be on the side of the "employer," i.e., the government—a charge that, of course, is true. A social-security and old-age pension plan put into effect on January 1, 1962, might well have been designed to head off further trouble in that direction.[49]

PROBLEMS AND PROSPECTS

North Viet-Nam's major problems today are of an internal rather than an external nature. This applies even to its foreign-policy problems, the most difficult of which derives from the tension existing between the U.S.S.R. and Communist China. The D.R.V.N., historically indefensible against its northern neighbor, must walk the tightrope between ideological preferences and geopolitical and economic realities.

Nothing highlighted the regime's dilemma better than Ho Chi Minh's attitude at the memorable Twenty-second Party Congress, in October–November, 1961, in Moscow. When the Chinese leadership stomped out of the Congress, Ho could do little else but follow suit, but instead of returning home or sulking in his tent, he went on a tour of European Russia, shaking hands and making friends as if he were running for election in Minsk or Kovno. Before leaving Moscow, he wrote a brief article in which he specifically thanked the U.S.S.R. and its European satellites for their "generous and fraternal economic aid," while he just as specifically forgot to mention Communist China, which by a large margin has been the most generous donor of all.[50] Yet, upon his return home, he dutifully took up the cudgels for Albania, which Moscow was condemning and Peking was praising; Albania's seventeenth anniversary as a republic (and member of the Communist bloc) was celebrated in Hanoi with a special exhibit called "The Albanian People's Republic Victoriously Builds Socialism."

Clearly, the D.R.V.N.'s interests do not lie in becoming a totally helpless satellite of Communist China. On the other hand, it is not surrounded, like Albania, by a belt of neutral nations (neutral, that is, in the fight between Albania and Russia)—and this is, let us not forget, a situation not of its own making. In other words, there is little likelihood of North Viet-Nam becoming Khrushchev's Albania in the Far East. By its narrow-mindedness and belligerent attitude, the D.R.V.N. also has dissipated a large reservoir of genuine good will and admiration that its fight against France had created among many noncommitted nations. Thus, in 1963, it may be more isolated from the rest of Asia than when it fought for survival in the jungles of Tongking.

But isolation, perhaps, is the price the regime feels it must pay to continue its march on the road to socialism.

NOTES

1. For the military aspects of the past and present Indochina problem, see Bernard B. Fall, *Street Without Joy: Insurgency in Indochina, 1946–1963* (3d rev. ed.; Harrisburg, Pa: The Stackpole Co., 1963). Both Yugoslavia and the D.R.V.N. fought for years in isolation. (Communist China also came to power largely on its own.)

2. In a statement before the House of Commons in November, 1954, Anthony Eden, then Prime Minister, estimated the Vietnamese People's Army to have the strength of the Pakistani Army (the latter being recruited from a population of 85 million, as against North Viet-Nam's 17 million). In 1962, the North Vietnamese Army was estimated at 350,000 regular troops, plus more than 2 million trained reserves, in addition to important police and militia forces.

3. Vo Nguyên Giap, *People's War, People's Army* (Hanoi: Foreign Languages Publishing House, 1961; New York: Frederick A. Praeger, 1962 (facsimile ed.), p. 126.

4. *Eloge du Colonialisme—Essai sur les Révolutions d'Asie* (Paris: Julliard, 1961), p. 177.

5. Ho Chi Minh's magnum opus is a 1926 pamphlet against French colonialism. Truong Chinh's major writings consist of two small but interesting books written in 1946–47 (*The August Revolution* [2d ed.; Hanoi: Foreign Languages Publishing House, 1962] and *The Resistance Will Win* [Hanoi: Foreign Languages Publishing House, 1960], facsimile editions reprinted in *Primer for Revolt* [New York: Frederick A. Praeger, 1963]) and Party reports on land reform. Vo Nguyên Giap has produced a collection of speeches and essays (see above, note 3).

6. The Vietnamese Communists have thus far confused hagiography and history, although some of their writings (notably Pham Van Dong's *President Ho Chi Minh* [Hanoi, 1961]) are useful in filling in some of the gaps. Two French biographical attempts exist: Jean Lacouture, *Cinq Hommes Contre la France* (Paris: Editions du Seuil, 1961), and one chapter in Fall, *Le Viet-Minh* (Paris: Armand Colin, 1960). An M.A. thesis by Raymond L. Spencer, "The Rise of Ho Chi Minh" (George Washington University, 1957), contains some older American material on the subject. Much of what follows here has been updated with material obtained in personal interviews with Ho and some of his revolutionary associates during a stay in Hanoi in the summer of 1962. For a more detailed biography, see Fall, *The Two Viet-Nams* (New York: Frederick A. Praeger, 1963).

7. It now seems established that Ho's associations with the Chinese Communist Party have been cordial and of long duration. Having come into contact with them in Canton, Ho lost contact with them after his liberation from a British prison in Hong Kong in 1931, but was put in touch with them through French Communist leader Pierre Vaillant-Couturier in 1933. After a stay in Russia throughout the period of the Stalinist purges, Ho returned to China and the Chinese Communist Eighth Route Army in 1938. In 1940, he was the Party cell secretary for a Chinese Communist guerrilla-training mission under Yeh Chien-ying (now a Chinese Communist Field Marshal) sent to South China—which perhaps gives a clue concerning why Yeh visited Hanoi in January, 1962.

8. However, a peasant uprising took place in Nghé-An Province of Central Viet-Nam in September, 1930, in the course of which the peasants confiscated land and proclaimed local "Soviets." The ICP did not approve the rebellion, but its local federations in the area supported it.

9. Nguyên Kien Giang, *Les grandes dates du Parti de la Classe Ouvrière du Viet-Nam* (Hanoi: Editions en Langues Etrangères, 1960), p. 38.

10. Lung Yün, the war lord of Yünnan, betrayed his province to the Communists in 1949 and remained in the C.P.R. as a member of the Military Council and of the directorate of the "Revolutionary Kuomintang" faction. After a brief moment of celebrity for a strong attack on the shortcomings of Russian economic aid during the "Hundred Flowers" period, he returned to obscurity and died in Peking on June 26, 1962.

11. Nguyên Kien Giang, *op. cit.*, p. 42. (Note that the citation comes from a North Vietnamese Communist source.)

12. See *The August Revolution*, in *Primer for Revolt*, p. 14.

13. Pierre Celérier, *Menaces sur le Viet-Nam* (Saigon: IDEO, 1950), p. 48.

14. Fall, *Le Viet-Minh*, pp. 45–47 *passim*.

15. The Trotskyite leader Ta Thu Thau, a personal friend of Ho Chi Minh, was murdered by the Viet-Minh while returning from a meeting with Ho in Hanoi. Cf. Donald Lancaster, *The Emancipation of French Indo-China* (New York: Oxford University Press, 1961), p. 137.

16. Cf. the excellent article on the D.R.V.N.'s wartime grass-roots administration by George Ginsburgs, "Local Government and Administration in North Viet-Nam, 1945–1954," in P. J. Honey (ed.), *North Vietnam Today* (New York: Frederick A. Praeger, 1962), pp. 135–65.

17. Nguyên Kien Giang, *op. cit.*, p. 75.

18. For an interesting firsthand description of the "correction-of-errors" process after the land reform got out of hand, see Wilfred Burchett, *North of the 17th Parallel* (2d rev. ed; Hanoi: Red River Publishing House, 1957).

19. Jeanne Delattre, "L'Economie vietnamienne au début de son premier quinquennat," *Economie et Politique* (Paris), June, 1961, pp. 16–32.

20. For a discussion of the administration of the Indochinese ethnic minorities, see Fall, "L'Administration des minorités ethniques dans les Etats de l'ex-Indochine," *Asia/France-Asie* (Tokyo), July, 1962.

21. Based on author's interview with the Committee on Nationalities, Hanoi, July 6, 1962.

22. *Thoi-Moi* (Hanoi), December 31, 1956.

23. Much of the following information is an abridgment of Chapter VIII of Fall, *The Two Viet-Nams*.

24. Let it be noted that non-Communist rump parties continue to exist in North Viet-Nam, just as they theoretically exist in some East European "people's democracies." Both the Vietnamese Democratic and Socialist parties, representing mostly a handful of Hanoi bourgeois and intellectuals, seated candidates in the 1960 election.

25. Le Vinh, "Problèmes de l'industrialisation," in a special issue, "Viet-Nam du Colonialisme au Socialisme," of *La Nouvelle Critique* (Paris), the "highbrow" monthly of the French Communist Party, March, 1962, p. 110.

26. A statistical yearbook covering the 1958–60 Plan (*So Liêu Thong Kê* [Hanoi: Su That, 1961]) exists, but some of its figures clash with others released subsequently. As will be seen, at least three different sets of figures can be produced for almost anything.

27. An example of Communist propaganda is provided by the food statistics for North Viet-Nam put out by the French Communists. Thus, Jean Chesneaux, trying to prove the "pauperization" theory of colonial exploitation, cites that per capita rice consumption in Viet-Nam fell from 252 kilograms a year in 1900, to 226 in 1913, and to 182 in 1937 (Cf. *La Nouvelle Critique*, March, 1962, p. 23). Another French Communist, Jeanne Delattre asserts (*op. cit.*, p. 28) that the per capita rice ration was 115 kilos in 1955, 150.4 in 1957, and 172 in 1959. William Kaye, a non-Communist British economist, using North Vietnamese figures (Cf. "A Bowl of Rice Divided: The Economy of North Vietnam," in Honey, *op. cit.*, pp. 105–16) arrives at 190 (1955), 215 (1956), 190 (1957), 200 (1958), 225 (1959), and 190 (1960). *Les Nouvelles du Vietnam* (Paris), No. 1 (April, 1962), another Communist source, asserts that per capita production of rice in 1961 reached 332 kilos, while official North Vietnamese sources admit to a per capita production of only 273 kilos of non-milled rice (paddy), which loses 35 per cent of its weight during the milling

process, and thus would account for a per capita availability of about 176 kilos. (From this must be deducted the seed grain for the next year, 10–15 per cent harvesting losses, and grain used in illegal production of rice alcohol and pastry.) In mid–1962, the *actual* Hanoi rice ration was 13 kilos per month per adult and 7 kilos for children under thirteen, or a median yearly rice ration of about 150 kilos.

In South Viet-Nam in 1962, using the same calculation, there were about 275 kilos of rice available per inhabitant. To turn Professor Chesneaux' example around, the D.R.V.N. has apparently "pauperized" its people even more than the colonial regime.

28. Tibor Mende, "Les deux Viet-Nams, laboratoires de l'Asie," *Esprit*, June, 1957.

29. Cf. Fall, "The Laos Tangle," *International Journal* (Toronto), May, 1961; Fall, "Reappraisal in Laos," *Current History*, January, 1962; Fall, "Who Broke the Cease-Fire?," *The New Republic*, June 18, 1962; and Fall, "Laos—Will Neutralism Work?," *The New Republic*, July 2, 1962.

30. Interview of the author with Ho Chi Minh and Pham Van Dong, Hanoi, July 13, 1962.

31. *Réalités Cambodgiennes* (Phnom Penh), July 20, 1962, carried an article by Prince Sihanouk in which he pointed out that *both* Viet-Nams were equally unwilling to abandon territorial demands upon his country.

32. See, for example, P. J. Honey, "The Position of the D.R.V.N. Leadership and the Succession to Ho Chi Minh," in Honey, *North Vietnam Today*, pp. 47–59.

33. As Under-Secretary of State W. Averell Harriman stated the case in the course of a television interview on February 11, 1963: "Their [the D.R.V.N.'s] hearts are in Moscow, but their stomachs are in China." (Department of State, *Red China and the U.S.S.R.* [Washington, 1963], p. 28.)

34. Based on 1960 census for the North, 1961 estimates for the South. In the South, of course, the Lao-Dong is illegal, but probably has 50,000 members.

35. Fall, *Le Viet-Minh*, p. 173.

36. Hoang Quôc Viet, the leader of the North Vietnamese Trade Union Federation, for example, worked as a white-collar employee in the French coal mines for less than a year in 1925. This was the extent of his connection with industrial labor.

37. V. P. Karamiychev, in *Zemledeliye* (Moscow), October, 1957; and in *Ekonomika Sel'kogo Khozyaistva* (Moscow), V (1957). Cf. Fall, *Le Viet-Minh*, p. 284.

38. Here we rendered the Communists a great service by inciting as many persons as possible to leave North Viet-Nam. Since most of the 860,000 persons who left were farmers and about 640,000 were Catholics, we gave the D.R.V.N. at least 1 *million acres* of ownerless land to carve up among the remaining peasants and, at the same time, removed a big element of potential unrest.

39. *Decree No. 239/B.TLP*, March 2, 1953.

40. V. Zelentsov, in *Voprosy Ekonomiki* (Moscow), September, 1957, p. 62. Cf. Delattre, *op. cit.*, p. 22.

41. Delattre, *op. cit.*, p. 23.

42. Truong Van Ba, "De la réforme agraire à la coopération," *La Nouvelle Critique*, March, 1962, p. 117. The same author also notes that 9,000 cooperatives now include whole villages, but the average size of a cooperative is 70 families. By the end of the First Five-Year Plan, in 1965, the average size of

the cooperatives should reach 150 families. However, any direct question about the creation of Chinese-type communes was answered by emphatic denial. The collectives envisaged for 1965 would cover between 200 and 260 acres and include 1,400 to 1,500 persons.

43. The sudden attention paid the intellectuals arose from the fact that many of them had rapidly grown disillusioned with the postrevolutionary regimentation of the Hanoi regime. The "Hundred Flowers" period, which affected North Viet-Nam perhaps even more than Red China, became the culminating point of that tension.

44. Delattre, *op. cit.*, p. 21.

45. Radio Hanoi, July 24, 1958. Ironically, South Viet-Nam found no other solution to its own urban security problem but to create "neighborhood groups" that are line-for-line copies of their Communist counterparts—including the snooping into everyone's personal affairs.

46. A more detailed version of this section appeared in Honey, *North Vietnam Today*, pp. 60–69.

47. *Third National Congress of the Viet-Nam Workers' Party*, (Hanoi: Foreign Languages Publishing House, 1960).

48. *Hoc Tap* (Hanoi), No. 12 (December, 1958).

49. "Institution des assurances sociales au Viet-Nam Nord," *Agence France-Presse* (Hanoi), December 30, 1961.

50. Ho Chi Minh, "Certains Problèmes de l'Asie," *Temps Nouveaux* (Moscow), No. 47 (November 22, 1961).

7. North Korea and the Emulation of Russian and Chinese Behavior

by GLENN D. PAIGE

Although the Russian and Chinese Communists may make mutually exclusive claims for the relevance of their experience for the modernizing societies of the East, a review of Korean Communist experience since 1945 leads to the conclusion that there is no a priori reason for the acceptance of these claims. In fact, the Korean Communists seem to have moved from a period of heavy initial reliance upon Soviet experience, through a period of noticeable experimentation with Chinese policies, into a period of a more self-oriented search for "Korean" solutions to their developmental problems. As more extensive research on comparative Russian, Chinese, and Korean Communism is accomplished, elements of all three types of behavior probably will be distinguished in each of these periods.

While it is difficult to specify with precision the boundaries of these periods, an initial approximation might be as follows: The period of predominant Soviet emulation, 1945–58; the period of growing Chinese emulation, 1958–59; and the period of Soviet-Chinese emulation, combined with increasing emphasis upon Korean experience as a guide to future action, since 1960.

It will be noted that a concept of "emulative behavior" is being employed as a focus of analysis. By this is meant purposive organizational behavior, the object of which is to reproduce the behavior patterns (including policies) of another organization. The organizations considered here, of course, are the Korean Workers Party (KWP) and the Communist parties of the Soviet Union and China. Three factors are hypothesized to account for the emulative behavior observed in the Korean Communists: controls imposed upon them from outside Korean society; the external orientations of their own leadership; and the "objective" political, social, and economic conditions of North Korea and its international environment. This framework will underlie the descriptive analysis of Korean Communist experience since 1945.

PREDOMINANT RUSSIAN EMULATION, 1945-58

Some of the main events that took place during this first period were the organization of the North Korean Communist Party (NKCP) in October, 1945, with Kim Ilsŏng as first secretary; the organization of the New People's Party (NPP) with Kim Tubong as Chairman in March, 1946; the conduct of land reform on the basis of private peasant ownership in March–April, 1946; the nationalization of 90 per cent of major industrial enterprises in August, 1946; the merger of the NKCP and NPP into the North Korean Workers Party (NKWP) with Kim Tubong as Chairman and Kim Ilsŏng as Vice Chairman in August, 1946; the initiation of economic planning through the One-Year Plans of 1947 and 1948; the establishment of the Korean People's Democratic Republic (K.P.D.R.) in September, 1948; the execution of the Two-Year Plan of 1949–50; the merger of the NKWP and the South Korean Workers Party headed by Pak Hŏnyŏng into the Korean Workers Party, led by Kim Ilsŏng, in June, 1949; the Korean War and the start of eight years of direct Chinese involvement in Korean affairs; the beginning of agricultural collectivization in 1953–54; the conduct of the Three-Year Plan for postwar recovery in 1954–56; the Third Party Congress and the attack by the Yenan-Soviet opposition on Kim Ilsŏng, during April–September, 1956; and the beginning of the First Five-Year Plan in 1957–58.

The Korean Communists group these events into the periods of "peaceful democratic construction, 1945–50"; the "Fatherland Liberation War, 1950–53"; "postwar rehabilitation and reconstruction of the national economy, 1954–56"; and the "Five-Year Plan, 1957–61." For present purposes, however, they can be divided simply into two periods: the time when the Korean Communists explicitly were engaged in building a "socialist" society (after 1953) and the time when they were not (prior to 1950). The Korean War served as the dividing line. The bases of the evasiveness of the early period were explained, apparently candidly, by Kim Ilsŏng in 1955:

> If we had yelled about building socialism in the period of construction directly after liberation, who would have accepted it? Even the people would not have been able to come over to our side. If we ask why, it was because the Japanese imperialists had spread the evil propaganda that socialism meant sleeping under the same quilt and

eating out of the same pot. If we had not taken account of this at the time and had raised our socialist slogans we would have frightened the people, and they would not have joined us.[1]

This early equivocation was in sharp contrast to Mao Tse-tung's April, 1945, essay, "On Coalition Government," in which he declared: "We Communists never conceal our political stand. It is definite and beyond any doubt that our future or maximum program is to head China for socialism and Communism."[2]

PRIOR TO "BUILDING SOCIALISM," 1945-53

The pattern of emulation embodied in the slogan "Learn from the Soviet Union!" was established largely during the Red Army occupation of North Korea from 1945 to 1948. Human symbols of this control were Kim Ilsŏng, Korean-born but with both Manchurian and Soviet experience, who was installed as head of the NKCP with obvious Soviet support; Major General Romanenko, political officer of the occupation, who supervised the early consolidation of Communist power in North Korea; Hŏ Kai, a Soviet-Korean graduate of Moscow University, who was made chief of the organizational bureau of the NKCP and later became a member of the seven-man Military Affairs Committee charged with supreme power to prosecute the Korean War; Major General Lebedev, political adviser to Kim Ilsŏng in the initial phases of the war; some 200 Soviet-Koreans who occupied powerful positions (although nominally of secondary rank) in the Party, police, army, and administrative apparatus; and numerous Soviet advisers. In 1950, State Department analysts who studied the Soviet system of control in North Korea had concluded that Korea was "already well advanced toward becoming a Republic of the U.S.S.R."[3]

But even without the Soviet control system, it is not unlikely that the Korean Communists, had they been able to achieve power, initially would have oriented themselves primarily to the Russian rather than to the Chinese Communists for guidance and support. If it is true that the less experienced a "modernizing" elite is, the greater its reliance upon the experience of others, then the Korean Communists could have been expected to emulate at least some other Communist elite, since their own experience contained little of practical relevance for the socialist transformation of Korean society.[4] The historic Korean Communist Party—founded in Seoul in April, 1925, admitted as a section of the Comintern in March, 1926, expelled for "factionalism" in December, 1928, and unable to reorganize or to regain Comintern recognition thereafter—had bequeathed some attempts to formulate programs,[5] but little else of constructive significance. Rejected by the Russians, repressed by the Japanese, feared by their fellow countrymen, and plagued by inner dissension, the Korean Communists had demonstrated neither the organizational continuity nor the purposiveness that the Russians and Chinese had shown on the path to power. Thus it was probable that they would have been predisposed to emulate "successful" Communist experience. In 1945, this was provided by the Russians—not the Chinese.

Perhaps the most compelling support for the hypothesis that Soviet experience or lessons drawn from it would have been the primary object of emulation at this time was that the generators of the only other plausible source of guidance, the Chinese Communists, themselves apparently maintained a similar orientation toward the Soviet Union.

Certain characteristics of North Korean society at the end of the period of Japanese control in 1945 also probably were conducive to a primary Soviet orientation for a Communist-dominated Korea. Chief among these were the significant development of heavy industry in North Korea, the destruction of plant and equipment by the retreating Japanese, the dearth of skilled Korean technicians, and the consequent need for advanced technical assistance to restore North Korea's industrial operations. Before division in 1945, North Korea, with 33 per cent of a Korean population estimated at 24 million, produced 80 per cent of the peninsula's coal, 95 per cent of the iron and steel, 90 per cent of the hydroelectric power, 85 per cent of the chemicals, 35 per cent of the machinery, and 20 per cent of the consumer goods, as well as 35 per cent of Korea's food.[6] About 12 per cent of the labor force was engaged in industry of a nonagricultural nature. Thus there were reasonable grounds for the Korean Communists to seek Soviet assistance in the development of the economy—assistance that the Chinese Communists were not then in a position to give.

Some of the important measures adopted by the Korean Communists in 1945–46 bore striking resemblances to Chinese policies after 1949, but since they were pursued under Red Army control it seems reasonable to infer that the Korean similarities were more indicative of the adaptability of Soviet policy than of the emulation of Chinese experience or plans for the future. Chronologically, at least, it was quite possible for the Chinese to have learned from Korean experience (perhaps via the Russians), but further research will be needed to determine whether this, in fact, took place. In any case, the early events in North Korea showed that the Korean Communists, even under Soviet control, did not have to repeat, literally, Soviet historical experience.

The early development of North Korea's political institutions illustrates both a Korean attempt to emulate Soviet example and Soviet flexibility in adapting to local conditions. As explained by Kim Ch'angsun, one of the Republic of Korea's foremost analysts of Korean Communism, an important difference was soon observable in 1945–46 between the organizational techniques of those Communists who had been trained in the Soviet Union and those who had worked with the Chinese.[7] The former and their followers initially began to organize a Communist Party based on the workers, the poverty-stricken, the illiterate, and the outcast. They soon earned the fearful reputation of being thugs and terrorists. The alienation of the Communist Party from the populace quickly became apparent. On the other hand, the Communists from Yenan, under the banner of the New People's Party, addressed themselves mainly to the urban intelligentsia and to the rural peasantry with marked organizational success, especially in conjunction with the land reform in the spring of 1946. The Soviet response in the summer of 1946 was to abandon the attempt to form a frankly "Communist" Party and to absorb the Yenan Communists and their followers in a more amorphous North Korean Workers Party. After failing to install Kim Ilsŏng as Chairman of the amalgamated Party in August, 1946, the Soviet advisers even acquiesced in the assumption of that role by the leader of the Yenan-Koreans, Kim Tubong.

Against this background, the formal abandonment of the Korean Communist Party and the circumlocutions of Kim Ilsŏng at the time of the organization of the NKWP become interpretable as an attempted emulation and readjustment sequence. Kim explained on August 29, 1946:

A party is the *avant-garde* of a class, defending and fighting for its interests. The Communist Party . . . protects the interests of the proletariat. The New People's Party . . . protects the interests of the peasantry and the working intelligentsia. Despite the fact that the Communist and New People's parties thus represent the interests of their respective classes, they have carried out a common task from the day of their establishment—namely, the articulation of the common interests of the workers, peasants, and intelligentsia. These interests have been the basis for the struggle for democracy and also serve as the basis for the merger of the Communist and New People's parties.[8]

Later, in February, 1959, after a purge of Kim Tubong and other central Yenan-Korean figures, Kim Ilsŏng took quite a different view of the NPP. "As everyone knows," he asserted, "our Workers Party was created by merging the Communist Party and the New People's Party. The New People's Party was a petty-bourgeois party, which cannot be viewed as completely approving Communism. Therefore, all members of the Korean Workers Party cannot be regarded as Communists. This situation requires that we make every effort to educate our members and turn them into Communists."[9]

Thus, in Korea, the attempt to form a narrow proletarian-class Party was abandoned in favor of a broader type of political organization under Communist control, defined in recent Party literature as a "mass Marxist-Leninist Party of the new type which represents the interests of the Korean people and nation."[10] With over 1.3 million members (or 12 per cent of the estimated North Korean population of nearly 11 million in 1961), the KWP is proportionately one of the largest parties in the Communist bloc. Its size, defended partly by Kim Ilsŏng as required by the future task of reunification, is one of the "distinctive features" which are said to stem from "peculiarities" in its historical development. Another deviation, self-consciously explained in the orthodox interpretation of the 1956 Party regulations, is that the KWP "has the special quality of being the *avant-garde* of not only the working class but of all the laboring masses."[11] The KWP thus defines itself as a party of "all the working people," usually delineated residually as "all those who are not pro-Japanese, pro-American, dependent capitalists, landlords, or national traitors."

Two other formal North Korean political institutions developed prior to 1950 illustrate the divergences from literal Soviet experience that were possible for the Korean Communists, as for the East European Communists, even under Soviet control. The first is the tolerated existence, even nominally, of other political parties—the Democratic Party organized in November, 1945, and the Young Friends of Ch'ŏndogyo Party, formed in February, 1946. They are obviously retained for propaganda effect. But while taunting the South Koreans for the "undemocratic" suppression of KWP activities, Kim Ilsŏng has explained candidly that the North Korean parties have been permitted to exist because they have not opposed the "building of socialism."[12] The second institution that differs from Soviet experience but not from Soviet theory is the United Democratic Fatherland Front, a coalition of all "patriotic" parties, social organizations, and individuals organized in June, 1949. This

is the Korean equivalent of the Chinese People's United Democratic Front, but since similar institutions exist elsewhere—in East
Germany, for example—it is unlikely that this institution was inspired exclusively by Chinese example.

The land reform of March–April, 1946, provides a socio-economic example of North Korean and Soviet adaptability in the
attempt to induce Korean emulation of Soviet behavior. It is unlikely that there was disagreement among Korean Communists
about the ultimate objective of collectivizing agriculture as the
Russians had done. Undoubtedly, however, there were differences
of opinion as to timing and method. The decision taken was to
confiscate about 2.5 million acres and to distribute about 98 per
cent of it as nontransferable private property to more than 720,000
peasant households. Only 2 per cent was nationalized, in sharp contrast to the early Bolshevik land-nationalization program. Virtually no North Korean writer on agricultural collectivization now
fails to note that the Korean land reform differed from that of the
Russians in its private-ownership basis. The reform, essentially completed within one month, is hailed as an example of the "creative
application of Marxism-Leninism to Korean conditions." The main
"condition" seems to have been that collectivization or loss of ownership would have been abhorrent to the Korean peasants. On the
other hand, the slogan "Land to the tiller!" promised to build support for Communist control. The presence of the Red Army is customarily listed among the factors ensuring the success of the
reform.

With the completion of land reform, the question of the timing
of collectivization undoubtedly presented itself. Unlike the future
Chinese decision to continue with collectivization once land reform
had been completed in 1952, the Koreans did not immediately begin to collectivize in order to mitigate the "capitalistic evils" of
private ownership. Four years of peace and three years of war were
to elapse before the Koreans launched their program to deprive the
individual peasant of his land. The main reason for the Korean delay was probably to maximize the propaganda effect of private ownership on the farmers of South Korea and thus to increase the
probability of unification under Communist control. This decision,
like many other North Korean policies, seems to have been conditioned by the Korean Communist belief that the Party was "building socialism" before the eyes of more than half a nation of
spectators.

THE KOREAN WAR, 1950–53

The clarity of the North Korean decision to invade the Republic of Korea is matched only by the obscurity of the full extent of Russian and Chinese involvement in it. In view of the Soviet control system in North Korea, however, it is unlikely that the decision could have been made without Russian knowledge. A clearer understanding of whether the war resulted more from the emulation of Russian or Chinese behavior (or both) or from the "creative application" of Marxist-Leninist theory to Korea must await future intrabloc polemics on this subject of undoubtedly triple disgruntlement.

In any case, the war seems to have been accompanied by a slight weakening of the Soviet control system and an increase in the Chinese orientation of the North Korean leadership, but at the same time a reaffirmation of the primary Soviet orientation occurred. The probable weakening of the Soviet control system is suggested by the suicide of the Soviet-Korean Hŏ Kai after he was censured by a 1951 Central Committee plenum for defective organizational work. At first praised for his social background as the son of a truck driver and for his rare Party experience in the U.S.S.R. as an *oblast* secretary, he is posthumously derided by Kim Ilsŏng as the "Party *paksa* [Ph.D.]" and has become a symbol of "bureaucratism" in Party work. A criticism frequently made against him is that he followed a policy of "exclusivism" embodied in an attempt to limit the size of the Party and to favor the admission of workers rather than peasants.

If greater elite involvement with a plausible object of emulation is conducive to modeling behavior, then joint Sino-Korean prosecution of the war must have enhanced Korean sensitivity to the programs and policies of mainland China. One suggestion of this was the Korean emulation of the Chinese Five-Anti Campaign, which was directed against the business class. But more intimate contact apparently did not result in the displacement of Soviet-oriented leaders by Chinese-oriented leaders. In fact, General Mu Chŏng, a leading Yenan-Korean who symbolized close collaboration with the Chinese Communists, was stripped of his rank and command in December, 1950, as a hostage to the North Korean military disaster in the retreat from Pyongyang. Apparently, Kim Ilsŏng hoped to protect himself against possible displacement by a potential rival of great popularity with the Chinese forces. Later, at Chinese request, General Mu, who was performing hard labor, was transferred to China, where he subsequently died. Soviet advisers were said to have participated in planning his initial demotion.[13]

The Korean War did not change the continued primacy of leadership orientation toward the Soviet Union. This may be illustrated by a general order issued on February 8, 1953, on the occasion of the fifth anniversary of the founding of the North Korean Army.[14] "Basing itself upon advanced Soviet military science and the priceless battle experience of the Soviet Army," the document proclaimed, "the Korean People's Army has experienced great qualitative and quantitative development during the Fatherland Liberation War." The pronouncement merely credited the Chinese, who had rescued the Koreans in three years of bitter struggle, with having contributed "blood," "their finest sons and daughters," and "a fine spirit of proletarian internationalism." The same relative emphasis may be found in the orthodox interpretation of the "historical significance" of the Korean War contained in the *General History of Korea*, published by the Pyongyang Academy of Sciences in 1959.[15] References to China are not included among the five points of significance, which are asserted to be as follows: The heroism of the Korean people ensured victory; through this victory, the Korean people gained unprecedented international prestige; the war years provided invaluable experience for the people, Party, government, army, and social organizations; the Korean people and army defeated the United States; and the victory of the Korean people was also the victory of the socialist camp "headed by the Soviet Union." Later, in discussing "sources of strength," this text credits the Chinese with having demonstrated a "model of proletarian internationalism."

Wartime devastation, a reduced and psychologically exhausted population, a severe shortage of labor, little hope of unification in the immediate future, and the stimulus of China's First Five-Year-Plan apparently provided the objective conditions for the North Korean drive toward "socialism," which began immediately after the Korean armistice.

TOWARD "SOCIALISM," 1953–58

The North Korean decision to proceed with the thoroughgoing collectivization of Korean society was essentially a Korean version of Stalin's decision to build "socialism in one country"—i.e., a decision to build *socialism in one-half of a country*. Again, while the Soviet example seemed to be the end object of emulation, there appears to have been intra-Party conflict over the appropriate strategies and tactics to be pursued. In resolving these issues, the Koreans seem to have taken both Soviet and emerging parallel Chinese experience into account.

The propensity of the Korean leadership to emulate external examples during the postwar social and economic changes probably was made more certain by the elimination between 1953 and 1955 of the main domestic followers of the former underground Communist leader Pak Hŏnyŏng, who had served during the war as foreign minister and as a member of the Military Affairs Committee. The elimination of the potential domestic, or "national Communist," opposition to the Kim Ilsŏng leadership took place in two stages. First, in August, 1953, Yi Sŭngyŏp, one of the three secretaries of the Central Committee of the KWP, and nine other leaders of the former South Korean Workers Party were sentenced to death for having plotted to install Pak Hŏnyŏng as Premier through a *coup d'état*. The forces for the coup were to be guerrillas, largely of South Korean origin, who had been in wartime training under Yi's direction for operations in South Korea. The second stage in the elimination of a potential domestic leadership was reached in December, 1955, when it was announced that Pak Hŏnyŏng himself had been executed, charged mainly with being an "American spy." One informed interpretation of the two-year delay in eliminating Pak was that his prestige and influence were so great that a general uprising of his followers might have been expected if he had been killed with Yi in 1953.[16]

The general line for postwar development was articulated by Kim Ilsŏng at the sixth plenum of the KWP Central Committee in August, 1953. For industry, this was to be "the priority development of heavy industry together with the simultaneous development of light industry and agriculture."[17] For agriculture, the basic policy was to be "the gradual cooperativization of individual farming." Three periods of development were planned: a preparatory period of from six months to a year; a Three-Year Plan, 1954–56; and a Five-Year Plan, 1957–61. The main goals of this effort were to develop heavy industry, to remove "colonial economic lopsidedness" through industrial diversification, and to collectivize agriculture. The historical stage was considered to be that of "laying the bases of socialism."

The Korean formula of the "simultaneous" development of industry and agriculture apparently preceded by four years the first Chinese Communist announcement of such a policy in September,

1957.[18] The formula, paradoxically enough, seems actually to have been a defense of an orthodox Stalinist emphasis on heavy industrial development against those who wished to stress the improvement of Korean living conditions. In defending this policy, Kim Ilsŏng repeatedly argued that Korean "conditions" (including the "will" of the people, the organizational skill of the KWP, and rich natural resources) made it possible to have an industrial policy that varied from that of the U.S.S.R. Chief among these conditions, he maintained, was the fact that the Soviet Union had to carry out its economic development in isolation, whereas Korea could count upon assistance from the other countries in the Communist bloc. The implication was that while the Soviet Union was faced with the necessity of building heavy industry for survival and thus of draining finite resources away from consumption, North Korea would be able to have *both* heavy industry *and* consumer goods. In effect, Kim argued that North Korea could both emulate Soviet experience and be different from it.

The emphasis on heavy industry probably first became an intra-Party issue in 1953, when decisions were being made as to the utilization of a three-year Soviet postwar rehabilitation grant of $250 million and a four-year Chinese grant of $324 million. Only one-quarter of this aid was actually allocated for consumer goods.

In the summer of 1956, in the aftermath of the Twentieth Congress of the CPSU, the policy of the "priority development of heavy industry" became a major issue in the most serious struggle for power in North Korea since 1945. Among the other central issues in the dispute was the question of whether the KWP should emulate the Twentieth Congress decision to replace the "cult of personality" with "collective leadership." The main protagonists in the attack upon Kim Ilsŏng and the "Kapsan faction"[19] that took place at that time were the leading Yenan-Korean theoretician, Ch'oe Ch'angik, a Vice Premier, and the Soviet-Korean theoretician Pak Ch'angok, also a Vice Premier. If Kim was not faced with a combined Sino-Soviet opposition, he was at least confronted with adversaries who had strong Chinese and Russian connections.

Briefly, the sequence of events in the controversy was as follows:[20] In April, 1956, the KWP held its Third Congress. The programs for the coming Five-Year Plan were approved, and the general line of the "simultaneous" development of industry and agriculture with emphasis upon industry was reaffirmed. Although the resolutions of the Twentieth Congress were known, there was no discussion of the "Stalinist cult of the personality" and its implications for Korea.

The usual idolatry of Kim Ilsŏng was somewhat subdued, however. After the Congress, Kim journeyed for two months in the Soviet Union and East Europe, seeking support for the Five-Year Plan. In his absence, Pak Ch'angok reportedly wrote a letter to Khrushchev complaining that Kim had neglected the Twentieth Congress decisions.[21] In the meantime, he and Ch'oe opened a campaign for "collective leadership," with obvious implications, in the KWP press.

On August 30–31, at a Central Committee plenum called to hear a report on his trip, an open attack was made upon Kim Ilsŏng's "dictatorial" leadership and economic policies, with Koreans from Yenan spearheading the attack. The meeting place became a scene of tumult. Finally, Kim and his Kapsan faction held a majority and were able to expel Ch'oe, Pak, and their colleagues from the KWP as "anti-Party, factional elements." At least five of the recalcitrants fled to China for safety.

The Russian and Chinese responses to the conflict were to send First Deputy Premier Anastas Mikoyan and Marshal P'eng Tehuai to Pyongyang for an investigation. Their decision reportedly was that "since intra-Party struggles over Party problems can take place within the young and unseasoned Communist Parties of underdeveloped areas, this matter should be brought to an end in the spirit of comradely self-criticism, and the Party expulsions should be withdrawn."[22] In September, the Party memberships of Ch'oe and Pak were restored, but they did not regain their Central Committee positions; nor did their followers return to positions of power and influence. Actually, a widespread purge of those suspected of complicity in the attack upon Kim took place.

Thus, in 1956, the Koreans did not emulate the campaign against Stalin, just as, in 1957, they did not emulate the Chinese campaign to encourage open criticism of government policies, although North Korean intellectuals were fully aware that both campaigns had occurred. If anything, the Kapsan faction's control drew tighter as North and South Korean, Yenan-Korean, and Soviet-Korean rivals were progressively eliminated.

The second major set of decisions on the postwar path to "socialism" concerned the collectivization of the farming population between 1953 and 1958. Again, while there were some similarities with simultaneously unfolding Chinese experience, and certain Korean modifications, the primary object of emulation appeared to be the experience of the Soviet Union. This may be illustrated by the decisions made in North Korea about the types of collectives to be organized, the timing of entrance into them, and the handling of the *punong* (kulaks).

As in China and Vietnam, three types of agricultural collectives, always referred to as "cooperatives" in North Korean literature, were planned as the organizational alternatives to individual farming. The first was a shared "labor cooperative," the second was a pooled "land cooperative," and the third was termed a "socialist" cooperative. These paralleled the Chinese "mutual aid," "producers' cooperative," and "collective" forms. Since these three general types were also characteristic of Eastern European agricultural policy, it appears that in adopting them the Koreans and the Chinese were following Soviet policy guidance rather than emulating one another. In fact, Kim Ilsŏng has explicitly equated the Korean second and third forms with the Soviet *toz* and kolkhoz.

From the polemical tone of his early writings on collectivization and from what is known of the multifaction tensions at the time within the KWP, it can be inferred that there was a controversy over the timing and methods of collectivization that involved questions of whether to emulate the Russians, the Chinese, or neither. For example, in a November, 1954, speech,[23] Kim attacked "certain people" who believed that collectivization would be an impediment to the unification of the country. This sounded very much like an objection that Communists of South Korean Labor Party lineage might have raised. A second argument was apparently aimed at the Chinese-oriented Koreans. "Certain comrades," Kim admonished, "think that in organizing agricultural cooperatives we should proceed gradually from the first type, to the second, and then to the third. But it is wrong to think of this as progressing from the first to the third grade in school." In support of his position, Kim argued that the different forms coexisted at the outset of collectivization in the Soviet Union. Therefore, he insisted that the peasants, according to the "principle of Leninist voluntarism," should be placed in collectives "appropriate to their level of political consciousness." Thus the Koreans later claimed distinctiveness for their collectivization program in that a majority (74 per cent) of their cooperatives were of the "socialist" form from the very beginning of the program. The alternative stage-by-stage approach might well have been advocated by China-oriented Koreans because this is the general policy that was followed in China and North Viet-Nam as well. Another issue on which "certain comrades," apparently inclined toward China, were corrected was the question of the size of the collectives. Against the idea that they should be as large as 500 households, Kim insisted that they should be increased gradually from 10 or 15 to no more than 70.

A further objection to the timing of collectivization, not made in the speech cited above but later mentioned in discussions of the program, was that it should be delayed until an appropriate level of mechanization had been reached. This objection, later assigned by Kim Ilsŏng to "dogmatists," might possibly have originated with Soviet-faction members critical of the Kim leadership, although it would have been a useful argument for all who wished to use delayed collectivization as a political weapon. In any case, the precedence of social change over technological change in Korea, as in China, has become the basis for one of the principal Korean Communist claims for the distinctiveness of North Korean experience from that of the Soviet Union and the countries of Eastern Europe. It was later claimed that collectivization resulted in increased production even without mechanization.[24]

A further problem of collectivization involved the method of dealing with the rich peasants, or kulaks. Nurtured on the *History of the Communist Party of the Soviet Union (Bolsheviks)*, KWP cadres undoubtedly had come to regard it as orthodox to "rely firmly on the poor peasantry, strengthen the alliance with the middle peasantry, and wage a resolute struggle with the kulaks."[25] But Korean policy represented an obvious modification of the Soviet formula. "Firmly relying on the poor peasantry," Kim Ilsŏng explained at the KWP's Fourth Congress, in September, 1961, "[the Party] strengthened the alliance with the middle peasantry and, restricting the kulaks, gradually re-educated them."[26] Thus, while Stalin in 1929 considered the question of kulak participation in the collective farms to be "ridiculous" since they were the "sworn enemies" of the system,[27] Kim explained in 1961: "We accepted into the cooperatives all kulaks who were in agreement with the socialist transformations and who honestly tried to work, but to the handful who attempted to interfere with the cooperative movement we gave their just deserts." The objective basis of the "peaceful" disposition of the kulaks was said to be their extreme weakness, since they were reported to comprise only 0.6 per cent of the farm households.

It is not unlikely, because of the closeness of Sino-Korean relations, that the Korean policy toward the rich peasants represented, at least in part, an attempt to emulate the pacific re-education of "capitalist elements" that had become a prominent element, in theory if not always in practice, of Chinese experience. Nevertheless, at the beginning of the First Five-Year Plan, in 1957, in agricultural change, as in industrial and institutional development, the Korean Communists seem to have attempted, first of all, to follow the Soviet example. "Experience in agricultural collectivization in the U.S.S.R.," wrote Kim Ilsŏng for *Pravda* in October, 1957, "became the guiding compass of our Party's cooperativization policies."[28]

By the end of 1957, the initial year of the First Five-Year Plan, the collectivization of Korean society had been nearly completed, and a significant level of industrialization had been reached. Of total economic output, "socialist forms" were said to contribute 98.7 per cent of industrial production, 87.9 per cent of trade activity, and 98.6 per cent of agricultural production. Since the proportion of the industrial contribution to total output was said to have reached 60 per cent in 1956, North Korea was now identified as a "socialist industrial-agricultural state." Basic postwar reconstruction was declared to be over, and the "technical reconstruction" of industry was said to be a main objective. North Korea boasted that it had produced its first tractors and excavators. In August, 1958, the collectivization of Korean agriculture in 13,309 cooperatives of the *artel* type was completed. The speed of completion was hailed as a "distinctive feature" of North Korean experience; the North Korean journey to collectivization in "only four or five years" was declared to be shorter than that of the Soviet Union or of any other socialist country.

In the summer of 1958, the Korean Communists began to say that Korea was on a "high tide of socialist construction."

GROWING EMULATION OF THE CHINESE, 1958–59

In the summer and fall of 1958, when far-reaching political, social, and economic changes had already been achieved in Korean society, the Chinese began to assert independent policies alleged to be worthy of emulation by those who wished to construct a Communist society. This occurred following eight years of intimate Sino-Korean military involvement. If emulative behavior is correlated with the articulateness of the model, the plausibility of its relevance for the emulating society, and its availability to the modernizing elite, then most of these conditions prevailed in Sino-Korean relations in 1958. On October 3, a Sino-Korean Friendship Association was formed in Pyongyang for the first time.

The Korean emulation of Chinese policies that took place during 1958–59 apparently occurred in the absence of external controls by either the Soviet Union or by Communist China. If the pre-1950 Soviet control system had existed, it is improbable that it would have happened at all. On the other hand, since the Chinese Army withdrew from North Korea in October, 1958, it is not likely that the Koreans acted under Chinese military dictation. Some characteristics of the North Korean economy suggest that the Kim Ilsŏng leadership was not highly vulnerable to Russian or Chinese economic sanctions which could have induced conformity. Whereas foreign aid accounted for 33.4 per cent of state revenues in 1954, it had dropped to 4.5 per cent in 1958.[29] This, together with industrial diversification, served as the basis of the Koreans' claim that they had achieved an "independent national economy." Trade with the Soviet Union, which had accounted for 80.8 per cent of all international transactions in 1955, had declined to 57.0 per cent in 1957.[30] In the same period, China's share of Korea's foreign trade had increased from 9.0 per cent to 27.3 per cent. Assuredly, the cessation of imports of coking coal from China or of oil from the Soviet Union could have crippled North Korea's industrial and military capacities, but unless the viability of the Communist regime itself was to be risked, it was improbable that such sanctions would be applied. This is undoubtedly the key to Kim Ilsŏng's bargaining power within the bloc. As long as China and the U.S.S.R. do not act in concert, he can seek relief from one side from the pressures of the other. From both, he can demand military support.

The emulation of Chinese practices also was not accompanied by the emergence of a new China-oriented KWP leadership. On the contrary, by the end of 1958, all the Yenan-Communist leaders who were thought to have been connected with the August, 1956, incident had been arrested and purged from Party life: Kim Tubong was put under house arrest; Ch'oe Ch'angik was imprisoned; the Soviet-Korean Pak Ch'angok was also put under arrest. Nevertheless, there was no clear evidence that the adoption of Chinese policies and growing Chinese orientation meant a rejection of Soviet experience or the displacement of the Soviet Union as the primary object of emulation. Conceivably, however, if these policies had turned out to be highly successful, such a reorientation might have occurred.

In light of the above considerations, and on the basis of fragmentary evidence, the most plausible explanation of North Korea's decisions to adopt Chinese policies in 1958–59 seems now to be that the Kim Ilsŏng group became convinced that Chinese innovations actually promised solutions to Korea's own pressing economic

problems. For, whatever the reasons, the Korean Communists decided to emulate Chinese policies in at least five major respects.
They decided to imitate the frantic pace of the Great Leap Forward, to combine economic and administrative units at the lowest
rural administrative level, to reorganize the agricultural cooperatives
in the direction of the people's communes, to adopt handicraft
methods of local industrial production, and to make Party organs
directly responsible for economic and administrative decisions.

The decisions to follow Chinese practices apparently were made,
or at least confirmed, by a September, 1958, plenum of the KWP
Central Committee. Until this plenum, the slogan of the Five-Year
Plan had been "Economy and Increased Production"; afterward,
Korea was saddled with the "Flying Horse Movement," which embodied the superhuman spirit of the Great Leap Forward. The symbol of the winged horse who could travel hundreds of miles each
day was taken from a Chinese historical novel, traditionally popular
in Korea, about military exploits during the Three Kingdoms period
(221–65 A.D.). After this plenum, KWP controls were tightened,
and the North Koreans were urged to reach the portals of the "construction of Communism" in the "near future." The drive to catch
up with the Soviet Union by going beyond Soviet experience was
foretold when Kim Ilsŏng told local administrative heads in
August:

> The Soviet economy is now highly developed and the Soviet people
> are living well. But we are now living in difficult conditions. In order
> to live well quickly we must go forward faster than others. Why
> should we adhere precisely to Soviet norms of production? Is it bad
> that a Korean produces two while a Russian produces one?[31]

Thus working days were prolonged to fourteen or more hours and
all available manpower, including half of all white-collar workers,
were thrown into production. According to Lee Dong Jun, the
people were "forced to work like animals."

In October, 1958, the more than 13,000 agricultural cooperatives
were combined into 3,843 cooperatives, and their boundaries were
made coterminous with those of the lowest rural administrative
unit, the *ri*. The chairman of the people's committee at the *ri* level
thus became the chairman of the *ri* agricultural cooperative. This
change followed the similar Chinese merger of cooperatives into
communes at the *hsiang* level during the previous two months and
preceded by nearly a year a comparable reorganization in Mongolia.
The average size of the amalgamated Korean cooperatives was

approximately 300 households, or equal to that of the average Soviet kolkhoz. The vast scale of the Chinese commune was not reproduced.

The Korean Communists clearly emulated many of the principal features of the communes, although a fuller appreciation of the extent of the changes attempted awaits more intensive research. John Bradbury has documented Korean interest in them, especially that shown by Kim Ilsŏng during and after his visit to China in late November and early December, 1958.[32] Since North Korea's ratio of arable land to population was almost precisely that of China's (approximately .2 hectares per person), and since industrialization had left only 53.1 per cent of the population on the land in 1957, it was likely that the communes appeared to Kim to be a logical way to squeeze maximum production out of available land and labor force. Lee Dong Jun, until early 1959 an eyewitness to developments in North Korea, has written that a "literal" attempt was made to copy the communes: The peasants were deprived of their individual kitchen plots, tools, and domestic animals; an attempt was made to mobilize female labor for the fields by establishing nurseries and communal cooking facilities. Whether the "free supply" system was tried is not clear. Apparently, neither the establishment of communal housing nor the "arming" of the peasants was imitated, although the new cooperatives possessed certain paramilitary features such as marching to work in formations as martial music was played.

In one aspect of agricultural organization, the Koreans emulated neither the Chinese nor the Russians in the 1958–59 period. When the Chinese dissolved their version of the Soviet machine-tractor stations (MTS) and dispersed the equipment among the communes and when the Russians abolished the MTS, the Koreans did not follow these examples, but converted their former "machine-hiring stations" in name to "agricultural machinery stations," which dealt with the cooperatives on a yearly contract basis.

Another feature of the Great Leap Forward emulated by the Koreans was the attempt to use handicraft methods of industrial production, especially in the production of pig iron.[33] This was related to an attempt, not unlike Soviet experience, to decentralize certain types of modern industry in order to use local resources more efficiently and to improve administration.

In December, 1959, Kim Ilsŏng announced a major departure from the role of "checking and supervising," which had been characteristic of Korea's Marxist-Leninist Party since 1945. This decision

seemed to follow the Chinese in what H. F. Schurmann has identified as one of the most profound differences between Chinese and
Russian Communism.[34] Kim stated:

> The Standing Committee of our Party's Central Committee has
> adopted a policy to further strengthen Party leadership. People's
> committees at the provincial, city, and county level will perform their
> duties under the control of their respective Party executive commit-
> tees, and all activities within factories will be conducted under the
> leadership of factory Party committees.
>
> The highest organ within a factory is not the factory director but
> the factory Party committee. The factory director and the Party
> chairman will act under that committee. The factory Party commit-
> tee will discuss both economic and Party matters, and the factory di-
> rector and Party chairman will carry out its decisions.[35]

With this change, Korea followed China in rejecting the previous
Soviet pattern of Party avoidance of direct involvement in daily
administrative and economic operating decisions. If cross-cultural
propensity to emulate is correlated with intensity of elite involvement and the extent of past success in goal achievement through
collaboration, then it is not surprising that Kim Ilsŏng explained
that the new organizational methods had been "first tried within
the ranks of the People's Army with good results."

The role of the Korean Party in its major deviation from Soviet
experience is apparently not explainable in exactly the same terms
covering the Chinese deviation. Prior to the seizure of power, the
Korean Communists, unlike the Chinese, did not have years of
experience in which the Party was responsible for all matters of
public administration within a substantial geographical area. The
Korean equivalent of the Chinese revolutionary experience, however, may be based on the Communist leaders' assumption of responsibility for filling the vacuum left after 1945 by the withdrawal
of Japanese administrators, policemen, technicians, and businessmen. In this sense, they did not take over an operating administra-
tive-economic structure as did the Bolsheviks, but were forced to
create one. It is probably true, however, that the necessary—if not
sufficient—impetus for the drastic Korean shift to the Chinese pattern of control came from the serious economic crisis that had
developed by the end of 1959.

The goals of the First Five-Year Plan were declared achieved in
mid–1959 after only two and a half years. But in December, when
the decision to alter the role of the Party was taken, Kim Ilsŏng

complained that whereas economic progress in 1957 and 1958 had been "smooth and rapid," the year 1959 had revealed "many defects." Korea was said to be suffering from a "tension between socialist productive relations and socialist productive forces." Thus Kim complained about unplanned increases in the industrial labor force, draining of rural manpower, declining steel production, and shortages of industrial raw materials, housing, and food. Poor planning, faulty administration, and concentration on heavy industry had induced the Communist equivalent of economic depression: idle industries and shortages of raw materials and daily necessities. The Korean response to this situation was to declare 1960 as the "Year of Shock Absorption," anticipating the Chinese decision to make 1961 the "Year of Industrial Consolidation."

EMULATION OF RUSSIAN AND CHINESE BEHAVIOR AND
THE EMERGENT KOREAN SELF-IMAGE, 1960–62

In general, Chinese policies emulated by Koreans had proved no more effective in solving the economic problems of North Korea than they had been in removing the economic difficulties of mainland China. By 1960, the Koreans consequently seemed to have abandoned all their major emulation efforts except those pertaining to the meshing of economics and administration at the *ri* level and to the direct decision-making role of Party organizations. By March, 1962, the only exception seemed to be the former. If past success in goal achievement through emulation is a correlate of propensity to emulate, then it is likely that future Korean emulation of Chinese domestic policies was made less probable by the experiences of 1958–59.

While the greeting "Are you riding the Flying Horse, Comrade?" was retained, the "Year of Shock Absorption" signified a slowing down of the precipitous pace inspired by the Great Leap Forward. The main strategies of the period became the cessation of heavy industrial plant construction, the improvement of technology, and the raising of productivity in existing plant capacity. This was the year that Kim Ilsŏng told a visiting Japanese reporter that Korea had now reached the level of a "middle peasant."[36] The First Seven-Year Plan (1961–67) essentially continues the policies of 1960. Kim Ilsŏng has characterized it as "the plan for the over-all technological revolution in Korea." For the first four years, there is to be a minimum of new heavy industrial construction. Its objectives, affirmed at the Fourth Congress of the KWP, are: to "markedly raise the living standard of our people," to "strengthen the economic base," and to turn Korea into a "socialist industrial country in the ranks of the advanced industrial countries."

In agriculture, at least by 1960, North Korea had returned to the Leninist line of "electrification and mechanization," supplemented by the Asian slogan of "irrigation." Throughout the year, and until the aftermath of the Twenty-second CPSU Congress, the Koreans apparently maintained silence about the Chinese communes. By the end of 1960, the tasks of electrification and irrigation were said to have been "basically completed." While some of the features of the communes might possibly have been retained, the kitchen plots, small hand tools, chickens, pigs, rabbits, and other animals were returned to private hands. One handbook published in North Korea in 1960 exhorted the farmer to have his family increase its private production of livestock (including dogs, which are eaten in Korea) and vegetables so that they could sell them on the farmers' market and earn enough money to build a new house.[37] Another publication on industrial production explained: "The initial policy of our Party in establishing local industries . . . was to mobilize all the resources and potentialities that would promote their development, even handicraft methods. However, up to the present time, we have not been able to develop local industries using these handicraft methods. Therefore, the mechanization of all sectors of local industry must be vigorously promoted."[38]

An enlarged plenum of the Central Committee of the KWP held on March 6–18, 1962, apparently decided to revert from the Chinese to the Soviet method of Party work. "The plenum," according to *Pravda*, which could have been expected to have a keen interest in the matter, "called upon Party committees at all levels to stop substituting for administrative and economic organs, to concentrate all their efforts on Party work, and in this manner to strengthen the organizational-political work of the party."[39]

This decision, as well as the other decisions to terminate the emulation of Chinese behavior, might be interpreted as the result of Soviet pressures. Certainly, some kind of pressure must have been applied. But since most of the earlier policies were modified by the Chinese themselves and since the North Koreans have persisted in major policies sharply at variance with Soviet orthodoxy, these decisions to adopt and reject are probably more fully explainable as evidence of genuine Korean Communist attempts to find their own solutions to their developmental problems. In fact, it is the concluding thesis of this review of seventeen years of North Korean experience that, at least since 1960, the Korean Communists gradually have developed a rationale for a pattern of behavior that permits the emulation of both Chinese and Russian policies, but increasingly stresses the search for independent Korean application of "Marxist-Leninist" theory.

A speech reportedly made by Kim Ilsŏng on December 28, 1955, and (significantly) reproduced in pamphlet form for mass distribution in July, 1960, a time of noticeable strain in Sino-Soviet relations, exemplifies this dual external orientation and growing Korean self-emphasis:

> We must learn from all the socialist countries and especially from the Soviet Union.
> The important thing is to understand why we are learning. We are learning in order to be able to apply the advanced experience of the Soviet Union and the other socialist countries to the Korean revolution.
> During the war, Hŏ Kai [the Soviet-Korean], Kim Chaeuk, and Pak Iru [a leading Yenan-Korean] fought futilely over political methods to be employed within the People's Army. The people who came from the Soviet Union insisted upon the Soviet way; the people who came from China insisted upon the Chinese way. Thus they argued, saying, "The Soviet way is best" or "The Chinese way is best."
> When you eat rice it doesn't make any difference whether you use your right hand or your left or whether you use a spoon or chopsticks. Isn't it all the same as long as what you are eating gets into your mouth? What was the necessity of digging into which "way" was best in wartime. . . . This could not but weaken inner Party discipline. At that time the Central Committee decided that we should learn both from the Soviet Union and from China and creatively develop methods of political work suited to our own country.
> The important thing is to master revolutionary truth, Marxist-Leninist truth, and to apply it to the actual conditions of Korea. We cannot have an imperative principle of doing [everything] just as the Soviet Union does. Although certain people say that the Soviet way is best or that the Chinese way is best, have we not now reached the point where we can construct our own way?[40]

In April, 1955, in the same vein, Kim apparently told a KWP Central Committee plenum: "Today each person who came from the Soviet Union, China, or from South Korea must understand that he is one of the members of the Korean Workers Party."[41] According to Lee Dong Jun, the KWP leadership actually bases its policies self-consciously upon a combination of the "historical teaching of the Soviet Union," the "practical experience of the Chinese revolution," and "Marxist-Leninist theory."[42] He explains this dual Sino-Soviet orientation partly on the grounds that both China and the Soviet Union appear to be "advanced" countries in North Korean eyes.

It seems that up until early 1963, at least, the North Korean leadership has continued to maintain a primary but not exclusive orientation toward the U.S.S.R. The concept of "advancement" may help to explain why this is so. Clearly, the Soviet Union is regarded as more advanced than China. In the articulate official Korean image of the U.S.S.R., the Soviet Union is viewed as a great neighbor, the inspirer of the national independence movement, the liberator of Korea, the guarantor of the pre-1950 reforms, the supplier of great material and moral support during the Korean War, the donor of vast aid in postwar reconstruction, the most experienced country in building Communism, the strongest and technically most advanced country in the world, and the leader of (or at least the first to be mentioned among) the countries of the socialist camp. An important indication of a principal Soviet orientation has been the teaching of Russian as a second language, rather than Chinese, for three hours per week beginning in the fifth grade.[43] A similar conclusion is suggested by a Japanese report in July, 1961, that only Soviet officers were serving as advisers to the People's Army.[44] The primacy of Soviet orientation is also suggested by the order of precedence by which North Korea signed military pacts with its two neighbors in the summer of 1961—first with the U.S.S.R. and then with China. The same pattern prevailed in the conclusion of economic aid agreements in 1953. If equality of orientation had existed and it had been desired to avoid a slight to the other Party, presumably two simultaneous negotiating missions could have been dispatched. The primacy of orientation toward the U.S.S.R. and the defensiveness with which it is maintained are reflected in a statement by Kim Ilsŏng in February, 1959:

> Solidarity centered on the Soviet Union was necessary yesterday, is necessary today, and will be necessary tomorrow. This solidarity around the Soviet Union does not mean that somebody is dominating somebody else; it also does not mean that we are suffering from *sadaejuǔi* [an extremely important concept in Korean intellectual history, which refers to a kind of sycophancy before powerful nations or persons].[45]

In contrast to this basic image of the U.S.S.R., that of China is less well developed. China is viewed in KWP publications more simply as a great neighbor, a "partner in a friendship sealed in blood as eternal as the Yalu River," a donor of vast postwar aid, and an inspiring nation of growing power and prestige. In their reported diplomatic interchanges, the Koreans seem to reject—by omission —the Chinese characterization of the intimacy of Sino-Korean relations as being that of "lips and teeth" or "flesh and bones." The Koreans have preferred the less organic imagery of "members of the big family of the socialist camp," to which "headed by the Soviet Union" has been customarily appended. However, in the post-Cuban crisis in Sino-Soviet relations, there has been a noticeable increase in the warmth of Korean references to China.

If it is true that the higher the level of modernization the less extensive the emulation of external models of development, then the gradual emergence of an independent and rather well-articulated self-image in North Korea, especially after 1959, may be partly correlated with accomplished social and economic change as well as with the requirements of political strategy. The emergent Korean self-image stands in sharp contrast to the pre-1950 view of Korea as being dependent upon the "reputation of Marshal Stalin," the "heroic Red Army," and the "great Soviet Union"—Korea's "benefactors" and "liberators"—who "guaranteed freedom, independence, and democratic construction." The contemporary image contains four main components, all of which include emphasis either explicitly or implicitly upon the theme of Korea's emergence as an independent actor within the Marxist-Leninist system. They are: the distinctive path to power; the achievement of an independent national economy; the role of North Korea in the socialist camp; and North Korea's experience as an object of emulation for other underdeveloped countries.

A distinctive Korean path to power, involving the activities of an *émigré* guerrilla force with strong domestic links and the armed forces of a neighboring Communist power, is implied by the gradual elaboration of a myth about the pre-1945 Manchurian partisan activities of Kim Ilsŏng.[46] Although Soviet military action is credited with the "liberation" of Korea, a more elaborate rationale for the existence of the regime has been worked out by portraying the "true Communists led by Comrade Kim Ilsŏng" as the only legitimate heirs of the Korean revolutionary tradition and by showing that they were actively fighting for Korean independence against the Japanese in Manchuria in the 1930's. The self-definition of the Kim Ilsŏng leadership as the only "true Communists" implicitly denies the claims to leadership that might be advanced by Koreans who had been active at Yenan, in the Soviet Union, in Japan, or within Korea itself, except those of the "Kapsan Action Committee" in South Hamgyŏng Province, who are said to have worked in close collaboration with Kim Ilsŏng after 1935.

Three other aspects of the guerrilla myth are important evidence of growing self-orientation. First, the Koreans are portrayed as fighting both for the Chinese revolution and in defense of the Soviet Union; thus they claim to have made an *independent* contribution to Communist successes in China and in the U.S.S.R. Second, the myth is silent on the Party affiliation of the Manchurian Koreans. According to the Comintern policy of "one country, one party," they should have been members of the Chinese Communist Party, but this is neither claimed nor clarified. On the other hand, as the "true Korean Communists" with a domestic organizational network, they would reasonably have been expected to have received Comintern and Soviet recognition as the legitimate Korean Communist Party. This was not the case, but this is neither acknowledged nor explained. Thus the "real" Korean Communists are depicted in a nebulous organizational interstice, somewhere between the Russian and Chinese parties. Third, although Kim Ilsŏng is portrayed as having been a guerrilla in China for at least a decade, there is absolutely no acknowledgment of Mao Tse-tung as a font of revolutionary wisdom and guerrilla strategy. The failure to link Mao and Kim is probably motivated by the desire to avoid the dramatization and legitimation of the claims to leadership of those Koreans who actually were associated with the Chinese Communists at Yenan. The myth acknowledges the Soviet Union as virtually the sole source of inspiration.

The Korean Communist economic self-image emphasizes the themes of independence and industrialization. North Korea is proudly portrayed as having changed from an exploited colonial country to a "socialist industrial-agricultural state with an independent national economy." Thus the economy is described as being "self-supporting," "independent," and "balanced." The virtues of bloc economic cooperation, of course, are also praised. However, in terms of this image of independence, it is unlikely that the North Koreans are highly responsive to Soviet appeals for economic specialization and integration such as those contained in the program approved by the Council for Economic Mutual Assistance (CEMA) in Moscow in June, 1962. In Korean ears, they have a ring of Japanese colonialism. Korean failure to send an official delegation to observe this meeting can be interpreted, at least in part, on this basis. The North Koreans claimed at the Fourth Congress of the KWP, in 1961, that industrial production now contributed 70 per cent of economic output. In Korean eyes, North Korea reached a high point in economic prestige when it signed an agreement to export to China tractors, automobiles, and machine tools in 1962.[47] With rich mineral resources and growing industrial capacity, North Korea thus seeks to project upon the world and to inculcate in its youth an image of independent economic strength. That the Korean and Soviet Communists may not agree on all the implications of Korean economic development is suggested by the fact that although Kim Ilsŏng reported to the Fourth Congress that the "sprouts of Communism" were appearing in Korea, a contemporary Soviet article centered upon the problems of building the "bases of socialism" there.[48]

The symbol that suggests most clearly the emergence of a more self-conscious attempt to build an image of a Korean path to socialism is the "Ch'ŏngsanni spirit and method." In February, 1960, Kim Ilsŏng spent two weeks at the Ch'ŏngsanni agricultural cooperative, where he engaged in direct discussions with members of the collective about its problems and attempted to develop solutions for them. Later, Kim did the same thing at the Taean Electrical Factory and at other industrial and agricultural installations. The "Ch'ŏngsanni spirit" thus has come to signify stress on the primacy of political enthusiasm in overcoming economic difficulties, reminiscent of Maoist thought but always coupled with a strong concern for mechanization. The "Ch'ŏngsanni method" briefly has been generalized into a technique by which cadres and administrators at upper levels descend to lower levels for the purpose of helping to innovate solutions to practical problems there. It may be that partial analogues for such behavior may be found in both Russian and Chinese experience, but for North Koreans the "Ch'ŏngsanni spirit and method" has repeatedly been described as "an epoch-making development in our country's history," with strong nationalist overtones.

The developing image of North Korea's role in the socialist camp, in addition to emphasizing the "obligations of proletarian internationalism," advances significant claims to independent recognition. For example, the Korean Communists view themselves as the "eastern sentinel of the socialist camp," making an independent contribution to the military defense of both China and the Soviet Union. As the "shock troops of the world revolutionary and workers' movements" during the Korean War, they claim to have achieved universal prestige. Since the outbreak of the war is depicted as part of a long-range American plan to establish a continental base from which to attack China and the Soviet Union, the Koreans view themselves as having made great sacrifices in Chinese and Russian interests. The legends of heroic deeds during the war reflect an apparent Korean need to build a self-image in which they are not merely the passive recipients of Chinese salvation. For each tale of Chinese heroism on behalf of Koreans, there is a story of courageous Korean assistance to the Chinese. Chinese General Yang Yung effectively appealed to this Korean self-image when he said at the 1961 anniversary celebration of the Chinese entrance into the war: "We are very grateful to the Korean people because they have defended with their own blood the security of China and of the whole socialist camp."[49]

There is little doubt that the Korean Communists view their own accomplishments as suitable for emulation by other emerging nations of Asia and Africa. They offer, after all, the only case in the bloc except North Viet-Nam of building socialism in a former colonial country. After official visitors to Pyongyang are escorted to the Museum of the Korean Revolution, the Fatherland Liberation War Memorial Hall, and the Industrial and Agricultural Exhibition Hall, they customarily avow their interest in Korean experience. "All that we saw," reported Thakin San Wie of Burma in October, 1961," has convinced us that it is unnecessary any longer for the Burmese people to rely upon the West, as in the past when it was a colony, and that the Asian people, like the Korean people, will be able to turn the underdeveloped area into a rich land by the energy of their own workers and technicians." A month earlier, Madeira Keita of Mali said, "We think that experiences of Korea are of international significance and give practical possibility to the African people, particularly to the newly liberated peoples like the Malian people, and we sincerely believe that the Malian people should assimilate the experience of Korea as much as possible."[50] In reply to such remarks, Korean spokesmen fail to specify that their own policies were based upon the emulation of Russian and Chinese experience; thus they accept the proffered role as an independent model of development.

Both the Chinese and Russians acknowledge and thereby reinforce the Korean image of "sucessful" accomplishment. The most effective appeals are made by the Chinese when they say they have "learned from" Korean experience. This was declared by Teng Hsiao-p'ing at the Fourth Congress of the KWP.[51] A recent Soviet article, polemical in tone and possibly intended in this case to blunt

Chinese claims for leadership in the underdevolped areas, declared: "He who wants to understand what socialism does in former colonial and semicolonial countries can familiarize himself with the development, of course, of the Korean Democratic People's Republic."[52]

The North Korean emulation of Soviet and Chinese policies since 1945, the consequent changes that have taken place, the external orientations of the Communist leadership, and the gradual articulation of an image of independence within a Marxist-Leninist framework suggest the hypothesis that there is a level of modernization at which a modernizing elite begins to emphasize its own past experience as a principal guide to future action. In this sense, the Korean Communists undoubtedly conceive of the planned future Communist transformation of South Korea as involving the application neither of a Russian nor of a Chinese model of development, but rather a Korean one which incorporates primarily Russian and secondarily Chinese experience. The proportions in which these elements might be combined is suggested by the list of references cited in the bibliography of *Political Economy*, a standard KWP text published in 1960:[53]

Author	Number of Citations
Kim Ilsŏng	84
Lenin	33
KWP	16
Marx and Engels	15
Khrushchev	5
Stalin	4

Significantly, no works of Mao Tse-tung were listed. Yet, as earlier and later events have shown, this is apparently not to be interpreted as evidence either of North Korean failure to learn from Chinese experience or of unwillingness to emulate Chinese policies. This may be seen in Korean behavior in the aftermath of the Twenty-second Congress of the CPSU.

THE SITUATION AFTER THE TWENTY-SECOND PARTY CONGRESS

Between the CPSU Twenty-second Congress and early 1963, the North Koreans deviated in several major respects from Soviet policy. They refused to sever relations with Albania and, in fact, entered into new economic agreements with Tirana. They continued bitter attacks on Yugoslavia, against which the North Koreans hold a special grudge because of Yugoslav abstention from the Security

Council vote of June 25, 1950. They persisted in a sharp polemic against "revisionism" that was far more intense than their strictures against "dogmatism." They refused to open intra-Party discussion of "Stalinism" and its implications. They supported China in the Sino-Indian border war. And they sought unsuccessfully to speak in defense of China at the East German Party Congress. These were not the first Korean deviations from Soviet policy (they had attempted to emulate the Chinese communes in 1958 and had supported Chinese border claims against India despite Soviet neutrality in 1959), but apparently, the wider the Sino-Soviet rift has become, the more the Korean Communists have been seen to adopt "Chinese" positions.

This deviant behavior may be analyzed in terms of the three factors hypothesized to account for Korean emulation that were suggested at the beginning of this chapter: external control, external orientation, and "objective" conditions. First of all, they support the conclusion that it is no longer tenable to regard North Korea as being under direct Soviet control. On the other hand, they do not conclusively demonstrate that the KWP now acts under the dictation of the CCP.

In the second place, it is not certain that this behavior indicates a reorientation from a primary "Soviet model" of development to a primary "Chinese model." Here it may be useful to distinguish between general and specific propensities to emulate (i.e., between whole models and parts of models) and between objects of emulation (e.g., between domestic and foreign policies). Viewed in this manner, it seems likely that the "more advanced Soviet Union," by and large, still serves as the principal object of goal orientation for the Korean Communists. Yet, while they appear to be Soviet-oriented in this sense, and in terms of the primacy of Russian technologies within their society, they also obviously find themselves at variance with several current Soviet policies. An oversimplified but perhaps not too misleading interpretation is that they are pro-Soviet but anti-Khrushchev.

There are at least two major policies identified with Soviet Premier Khrushchev that the Kim Ilsŏng leadership must find particularly distasteful. In a land where the cult of the leader is promoted with such intensity as in North Korea, Khrushchev's espousal of a somewhat more relaxed collegial rule is not likely to find warm receptivity. The Korean Communists have two terms for the word "comrade"—an honorific one (t'ongji) and an ordinary one (tongmu). At least one high official is known to have been dismissed at least partly for failure to apply the honorific form to Kim Ilsŏng.[54] "Leader Study Rooms" in which the exploits of partisan hero Kim are studied without "disrespectful" coughing or conversation also dot the nation. Kim undoubtedly believes that emulation of the Khrushchevian style of leadership, even verbally, in the context of the harsh discipline to which the North Korean people have been subjected, and against a background of repressed factional grievances, would lead to his own downfall. Thus, in his report on the Twenty-second Congress, Kim declared that the "Stalinist cult of the personality" would not become a subject of discussion within the KWP because it was purely an "internal problem of the CPSU."[55] KWP cordiality toward Albania can be understood in part as a vicarious defense of the Kapsan faction's rule—i.e., a defense of a Stalinist leadership's ability to maintain itself in power with Chinese support against Soviet and domestic attack.

The Kapsan faction also probably finds itself in agreement with Chinese dissatisfaction with the Khrushchevian policy of "peaceful coexistence." In Korean Communist eyes, this policy must have appeared to have suffered a disastrous defeat with the successful *coup d'état* in the Republic of Korea in May, 1961.[56] North Korean fear and apprehension may be inferred from the haste with which the North Korean regime concluded military agreements with both the U.S.S.R. and Communist China in the summer of 1961. Kim Ilsŏng reportedly told the Supreme People's Assembly in 1958 that "coexistence" would be impossible as long as the "hated Americans" maintained forces in the South.[57] Kim is also on record as being of the opinion that whereas North Korea alone could not defeat American military power in South Korea under normal circumstances, it could easily do so if the United States was engaged in a plethora of military actions around the globe.[58] Thus the Korean Communists have a direct and selfish interest in favoring Chinese encouragement of widespread revolutionary wars in underdeveloped areas: the unification of Korea under Communist domination. It is ominous indeed, then, that since the December, 1962, plenum of the KWP Central Committee the slogans "A weapon in one hand—a hammer and sickle in the other!" and "Arm all the people!" have been raised in North Korea.[59] These slogans were emphasized in the celebrations in Peking on February 8, 1963, which marked the fifteenth anniversary of the Korean People's Army, where there were frequent omissions of the word "peaceful" in referring to Korean unification. The present trend seems to be toward increased North Korean bellicosity.

Finally, a dual pattern of emulation with a Soviet emphasis seems plausible for the Pyongyang leadership domestically because North Korea has the characteristics of both a modern industrial state based on Soviet technology and an Asian agricultural state, similar in many respects to China. In this sense, both Russian and Chinese experience and future innovations would appear to be of interest to the Korean Communist leaders. Therefore, both the Soviet and Chinese "models" and their future ramifications may be viewed as of some "relevance" for Communist North Korea, although the extent to which Russian and Chinese policies are followed and to which Korean policies are improvised will depend upon the orientations of the incumbent Pyongyang leadership. In these orientations, feelings of Sino-Korean cultural affinity, reinforced by wartime collaboration, can be expected to play a part.

Unless Soviet or Chinese leaders can establish mutually exclusive control over the Korean Communists, the near future will undoubtedly witness more North Korean emulation of both Russian and Chinese behavior as in the slogan "peace and revolution" advanced by the North Korean Ambassador to Moscow on July 5, 1962.[60] In the near future, as now, the visitor to North Korea may expect to see Koreans in their Lenin caps and Mao uniforms, as well as Western and Korean clothes, hustling amidst the massive, Moscow-like buildings of the new Pyongyang—on Kim Ilsŏng Square, on Stalin Avenue, and in Mao Tse-tung Plaza—their speech peppered with Russian and Chinese terms such as *kampaniya* (campaign) and *chakp'ung* (the Chinese *tso-feng*—style of work). If he listens carefully, he should also be able to hear behind the city noises the age-old Korean cry of lament: "*Aigo.*"

NOTES

1. Kim Ilsŏng, "Sahoejuŭi hyŏngmyŏngŭi hyŏn kyedane issŏsŏ tang mit' kukka saopŭi myŏt kaji munjedŭre taehayŏ" ("On Various Problems of Party and Government Work in the Present Stage of the Socialist Revolution"), in *Kim Ilsŏng sŏnjip* (*Selected Works of Kim Ilsŏng*) (Pyongyang: KWP Press, 1960), IV, 258.

2. Mao Tse-tung, *Selected Works* (New York: International Publishers, 1956), IV, 274.

3. *North Korea: A Case Study in the Techniques of Takeover* (U.S. Department of State [Washington, 1961]), p. 120.

4. On the pre-1945 history of Korean Communism, see Robert A. Scalapino and Chong-sik Lee, "The Origins of the Korean Communist Movement," *Journal of Asian Studies*, XX, No. 1 (November, 1960), 9–31, and XX, No. 2 (February, 1961), 149–67; Glenn D. Paige, "Korea and the Comintern, 1919–35," *Bulletin of the Korean Research Center*, No. 13 (December, 1960), pp. 1–25;

and Chong-sik Lee, "Korean Communists and Yenan," *The China Quarterly*, No. 9 (January–March, 1962), pp. 182–92.

5. E.g., "Platform of Action of the C.P. of Korea," *Inprecorr*, No. 11 (February 23, 1934), pp. 303–5, and No. 14 (March 2, 1934), pp. 355–58.

6. Edwin W. Pauley, *Report on Japanese Assets in Soviet-Occupied Korea to the President of the United States* (Washington: U.S. Government Printing Office, 1946), p. 3.

7. Kim Ch'angsun, *Pukhan sibonyŏn sa* (*Fifteen-Year History of North Korea*) (Seoul: Chimungak, 1961), pp. 97 ff. This is the most important work in print on North Korean politics since 1945. The present study is heavily indebted to it, but differs mainly in its explicit conclusion that the Kim Ilsŏng leadership has achieved a measure of independence from both Soviet and Chinese control.

8. Kim Ilsŏng, "Nodongdangŭi ch'angnipkwa tangmyŏnhan che kwaŏpe taehayŏ" ("The Founding of the Workers Party and Various Present Tasks"), *Selected Works*, I (1955), 230.

9. Kim Ilsŏng, "Chosŏn nodongdang chungang wiwŏnhoe 1959 nyŏn 2-wŏl chŏnwŏn hoeŭieso han kyŏllon" ("Concluding Remarks at the February, 1959, Plenum of the CC of the KWP"), *Selected Works*, VI (1960), 266.

10. *Taejung chŏngch'i yongŏ sajŏn* (*Everybody's Dictionary of Political Terms*) (Pyongyang: KWP Press, 1959), p. 240.

11. *Chosŏn nodongdang kyuyak haesŏl* (*Interpretation of the Korean Workers Party Regulations*) (Tokyo: Hagu sŏbang, 1960), p. 31.

12. Kim Ilsŏng, "Uri tang sabŏp chŏngch'aegŭi kwanch'ŏrŭl wihayŏ" ("For the Accomplishment of Our Party's Judicial Policies"), *Selected Works*, V (1960), 443.

13. Kim Ch'angsun, *op. cit.*, p. 124.

14. *Wei cheng-ch'ü tzŭ-yu tu-li ti Ch'ao-hsien jen-min cheng-i ti tsu-kuo chieh-fang chan-cheng* (*The Korean People's Righteous Fatherland Liberation War for Freedom and Independence*) (Pyongyang: KWP Press, 1955), p. 300.

15. *Chosŏn t'ongsa* (Tokyo: Hagu sŏbang, 1959), III, 264–71.

16. Kim Ch'angsun, *op. cit.*, p. 149.

17. Kim Ilsŏng, "Modun kŏsŭl chŏnhu inmin kyŏngje pokku palchŏnŭl wihayŏ" ("All for the Postwar Reconstruction and Development of the People's Economy"), *Selected Works*, IV (1960), 9.

18. Donald S. Zagoria, *The Sino-Soviet Conflict* (Princeton, N.J.: Princeton University Press, 1962), p. 87.

19. This is a generic term used in North Korea to refer to the immediate supporters of Kim Ilsŏng. The "Kapsan" faction has come to be distinguished from the "Soviet," "Yenan," and "domestic" factions.

20. Account based mainly upon Kim Ch'angsun, *op. cit.*, pp. 150 ff.

21. Lee Dong Jun, *Hwansanggwa hyŏnsil: naŭi kongsanjuŭi kwan* (*Fantasy and Fact: My Observations of Communism*) (Seoul: Tongbang t'ongsin sa, 1961), p. 187. Until his escape in early 1959, the author of this important work was a writer for *Pravda* in Pyongyang.

22. Kim Ch'angsun, *op. cit.*, p. 157.

23. Kim Ilsŏng, "Nongch'ŏn kyŏngniŭi kŭmhu palchŏnŭl wihan uri tangŭi chŏngch'aege kwanhayŏ" ("Our Party's Policies for the Further Development of the Agricultural Economy"), *Selected Works*, IV (1960), 180 ff.

24. For a theory that would not support this claim, see Hoang Van Chi, "Collectivization and Rice Production," *The China Quarterly*, No. 9 (January–

260   GLENN D. PAIGE

March, 1962), pp. 94–104. It should be borne in mind, however, that only about one-quarter of North Korea's arable land consists of paddy fields.

25. History of the Communist Party of the Soviet Union (Bolsheviks) (Moscow: Foreign Languages Publishing House, 1952), p. 448.

26. Kim Ilsŏng, "Otchetnyi doklad Tsentral'nogo Komiteta Trudovoi Partii Korei IV syezdu partii," Kommunist, No. 14 (September, 1961), p. 96.

27. J. V. Stalin, Works (Moscow: Foreign Languages Publishing House, 1955), XII, 177.

28. Kim Ilsŏng, "Widaehan 10-wŏrŭi sasangŭn sŭngnihago itta" ("The Ideas of Great October Are Winning"), Selected Works, V (1960), 209.

29. Yoon T. Kuark, "A Comparative Study of Economic Development Between South and North Korea During the Post-War Period" (unpublished paper, University of Minnesota, 1961), p. 27. See also Kim Samgyu, Chōsen no shinjitsu (The Truth About Korea) (Tokyo: Shiseidō, 1960), p. 74.

30. Real volume grew from 164 million to 250 million rubles, however. (Kuark, op. cit., p. 58.)

31. Kim Ilsŏng, "Si, kun inmin wiwŏnhoeŭi tangmyŏnhan myŏt' kaji kwaŏpe taehayŏ" ("On Various Tasks Confronting City and County People's Committees"), Selected Works, VI (1960), 9.

32. John Bradbury, "Sino-Soviet Competition in North Korea," The China Quarterly, No. 6 (April–June, 1961), pp. 15–28. See also Philip Rudolph, "North Korea and the Path to Socialism," Pacific Affairs, XXXII, No. 2 (June, 1959), 131–43.

33. Philip Rudolph, North Korea's Political and Economic Structure (New York: Institute of Pacific Relations, 1959), p. 45.

34. H. F. Schurmann, "Organizational Contrasts Between Communist China and the Soviet Union," in Kurt London (ed.), Unity and Contradiction (New York: Frederick A. Praeger, 1962), pp. 65–99.

35. Kim Ilsŏng, "Sahoejuŭi kyŏngje kŏnsŏresŏ chegidoenun tangmyŏnhan myŏt' kaji kwaŏptŭre taehayŏ" ("On Various Present Tasks Raised by Socialist Economic Construction"), Selected Works, VI (1960), 528.

36. Torimoto Kenrō, "Seiji no hanashi" ("The Political Story"), in Muraoka Hirohito et al., Kita Chōsen no kiroku (Report on North Korea) (Tokyo: Shindoku shosha, 1960), p. 190.

37. Nongŏp hyŏptong chohabŭi chŏngch'i kyŏngjejŏk konggohwarŭl wihan myŏt' kaji munje (Various Problems in the Political and Economic Strengthening of the Agricultural Cooperatives) (Pyongyang: KWP Press, 1960), p. 190.

38. Kyŏngje sangsik (Economic Fundamentals) (Pyongyang: KWP Press, 1960), p. 90.

39. Pravda, March 12, 1962, p. 5.

40. Kim Ilsŏng, Sasang saŏpesŏ kyojojuŭi wa hyŏngsikjuŭirŭl t'oejihago chuch'erŭl hwangniphal te taehayŏ (On Exterminating Dogmatism and Formalism and Establishing Independence in Ideological Work) (Pyongyang: KWP Press, 1960), pp. 11–12.

41. Kim Ilsŏng, "On Various Problems of Party and Government Work . . . ," p. 269.

42. Lee Dong Jun, op. cit., p. 275.

43. Song Chihak, Chōsen kyōiku shi (History of Korean Education) (Tokyo: Kuroshiyo shuppan, 1960), p. 230.

44. Asahi (Tokyo), July 14, 1961, p. 3.

45. Kim Ilsŏng, "Concluding Remarks at the February, 1959, Plenum . . . ," pp. 249–50.

46. A standard version is Yi Nayŏng, *Chosŏn minjok haebang t'ujaeng sa* (*History of the Korean People's Liberation Struggle*) (Tokyo: Hagu sŏbang, 1960).

47. *Peking Review*, January 19, 1962, p. 22.

48. S. V. Kim. "Voprosy stroitel'stva osnov sotsializma v koreiskoi narodno-demokraticheskoi respublike," *Narody Azii i Afriki* (*Peoples of Asia and Africa*), No. 2 (1962), pp. 18–29.

49. North Korean radio broadcast, October 25, 1961.

50. *Ibid.*, September 29 and October 23, 1961.

51. *Jen-min Jih-pao* (Peking), September 13, 1961, p. 4.

52. E. Kuskov, "Mezhdunarodnoe znachenie stroitel'stva kommunizma v SSSR," *Politicheskoe samoobrazovanie*, No. 6 (June, 1962), p. 14.

53. *Chŏngch'i kyŏngje hak* (*Political Economy*) (Pyongyang: KWP Press, 1960).

54. Lee Dong Jun, *op. cit.*, p. 193.

55. *Kuan-yü ts'an-chia su-lien kung-ch'an-tang ti 22-tz'ŭ tai-piao ta-hui ti Ch'ao-hsien lao-tung-tang tai-piao-t'uan ti kung-tso* (*On the Work of the KWP Delegation at the 22nd CPSU Congress*), supplement to *Hsin Ch'ao-hsien* (*New Korea*), No. 21 (1961), p. 4.

56. There is evidence to suggest, however, that the Pyongyang leadership first suspected that the coup had been carried out by pro-Communist elements. Since May, 1961, it has made repeated conciliatory gestures toward the Seoul junta. See Paige, "Korea," in Cyril E. Black and Thomas Perry Thornton (eds.), *Communism and Political Revolution* (Princeton, N. J.: Princeton University Press, 1963).

57. Lee Dong Jun, *op. cit.*, p. 280.

58. Kim Ilsŏng, *On Exterminating Dogmatism* . . . , p. 21. See also *Selected Works*, IV (1960), 343.

59. *Jen-min Jih-pao*, January 15, 1953, p. 3.

60. *Pravda*, July 6, 1962, p. 4.

8. The Mongolian People's Republic and Sino-Soviet Competition

by ROBERT A. RUPEN

The Mongolian People's Republic (M.P.R.) has a small and scattered population, with fewer than 1 million inhabitants in an area of 600,000 square miles. Geographically, it is remote, largely semi-desert, and landlocked between the giants of China and the U.S.S.R. And it possesses a very primitive economy. These facts have led it to depend heavily on foreign models for development and change.

Before 1911, Manchu China exercised control over, and greatly influenced, Mongolian society and government. Since 1921, however, the principal model for Mongolian development has been the Soviet Union; even by 1911, in fact, Russians had already begun to play that role. Thus Chinese-Russian rivalry for predominance in Mongolia bears a historical, "nationalistic," and non-Communist element of real importance.

From 1921 until the Chinese Communists established their regime in Peking in October, 1949, Russia alone exerted Communist influence in Outer Mongolia; the "new China" did not move seriously to reassert its influence in the area until 1952. The Russian Communists had operated in and influenced Mongolian society and government for thirty years, therefore, when the Chinese Communists began to re-enter the scene, and the U.S.S.R. had impressed on the M.P.R. its pattern of education, government, and organization and, to some degree, even its dress, diet, and language. In the past decade of Sino-Soviet "socialist competition" in the M.P.R., Chinese influence has once again become a factor in the situation, but, to date, it has not displaced or even seriously challenged the predominance of Russian influence.

The nature of the indigenous Mongolian society and economy, based on livestock-herding and nomadic organization, and its racial and religious characteristics, distinctively Mongolian and Buddhist, also affect the M.P.R.'s susceptibility to influence by outside models. There exist for Mongolia not only the over-all Communist models of Russia and China, but also the racial and social models provided by Buryat-Mongolia in the U.S.S.R. and Inner Mongolia in China, the traditional religious model of Tibet, and the nomadic model of Kazakhstan and Soviet Central Asia. Buryat-Mongolia has often influenced the M.P.R. in more important ways than has the U.S.S.R. Inner Mongolia has sometimes exerted a more immediate influence than China. And Soviet experience in handling the nomads of Central Asia has also affected the M.P.R. There exists, in short, a Mongolian and nomadic world within the Communist one.

Nevertheless, typically Soviet phenomena appear in all aspects of Mongolian organization and society, and the M.P.R. has experienced, on a small scale, many of the same phases of development and changes as the U.S.S.R. Many of these changes have closely followed those in the Soviet model: Widespread purges, ruthless collectivization, Stalinism and the "cult of personality," the post-Stalin "thaw," and educational reform have all occurred in the M.P.R. at approximately the same time, and in much the same way, as in the U.S.S.R. The Soviet model has inspired the Mongolian Party, its governmental organization, its constitution, its Five-Year Plans for economic development, its Academy of Sciences, its army, its secret police, its architecture, and much of its literature. Ulan Bator, the capital, mirrors Moscow: It has its Sukhe Bator Square, its mausoleum for revolutionary leaders, its rising apartment buildings, and its May Day parades. Russians have trained the M.P.R.'s teachers, often in Soviet schools. Mongolian pupils and students learn from textbooks translated from Russian ones. Mongolian leaders and officials usually speak fluent Russian. And perhaps it is relevant to note that the head of the Party and the Government in the M.P.R. has a Russian wife. On June 7, 1962, the M.P.R. joined the Council for Economic Mutual Assistance (CEMA) as a full member. (It is the only Asian Communist state to do so.)

REASSERTION OF CHINESE INFLUENCE

China thus faces a serious problem in reasserting its influence in the M.P.R. Insofar as contemporary China is Communist, much of what it represents has already been impressed upon Mongolia by the U.S.S.R. Insofar as contemporary China is Chinese, it represents imperialistic territorial ambitions, which in many respects frighten the Mongols. Insofar as Communist China is Stalinist and opposed to liberalizing tendencies, it challenges trends favored by the Mongols. Moreover, since Mongolia has already for many years accepted and to a considerable extent been made over in the Soviet image, what alternative can China offer? China's industrial and agricultural weakness means that the U.S.S.R. can easily trump every Chinese economic card. In Mongol eyes, also, the U.S.S.R. poses no immediate or direct threat to Mongolian territory; too few Russians live too far away. The Chinese, however, could easily swamp the Mongols. Hence, the M.P.R. deals cautiously and warily with China, and it would not lightly act to cut its ties with its Soviet protector, even if it could.

But China's re-entry on the Mongolian scene has already affected the M.P.R. in many ways, and it has led the Russians to take conscious counteraction. As a result, Sino-Soviet "socialist competition" may well lead to an acceleration of Mongolian economic development. In the past, the Mongols themselves, generally easygoing, have, for the most part, left it to the Russians to determine the pace of their development, and the Russians for a long time contented themselves with controlling Mongolian foreign affairs and showed relatively little interest in rapid Mongolian development. Now, however, Chinese influence poses a challenge to which there has already been a clear Soviet response.

After Stalin's death, on March 5, 1953, and before Khrushchev established himself as effective successor, China apparently moved to exploit the Russian interregnum and attempted to displace the U.S.S.R. as protector of the M.P.R. This conclusion, while admittedly speculative, is supported by the following facts, which suggest a steady growth of Chinese influence immediately after 1953.

Sometime in 1954, Jargalsaikhan, who served as the first Mongolian Ambassador to Peking, from 1950 to 1953, replaced Lkhamsurun as M.P.R. Minister of Foreign Affairs. This change may well have increased Chinese influence in the M.P.R.

On September 24, 1954, Ho Ying replaced Chi Ya-t'ai as Chinese Ambassador to Ulan Bator. Ho had been Deputy Director of the Asian Affairs Department in Peking's Foreign Ministry, and his appointment to Ulan Bator signified higher-level Chinese representation there.

C. L. Sulzberger, in a dispatch sent from New Delhi on February 13, 1955, reported, apparently on the basis of information from Indian officials, that when Bulganin and Khrushchev visited Peking in October, 1954, "They are said to have recognized that the Outer M.P.R., while retaining independence, should eventually come within China's sphere of influence."[1] There has been no substantiation of any such agreement, but it at least suggests that some Asian observers had concluded that Peking was rapidly increasing its influence in the M.P.R.

In November, 1954, Ulanfu—a member of the Chinese Communist Party Central Committee—headed a large Chinese delegation to the M.P.R.'s Twelfth Party Congress in Ulan Bator, and his speech strongly stressed closer Mongolian-Chinese relations. By contrast, a comparatively small and low-level Soviet delegation appeared at the Congress, headed by P. T. Komarov, Deputy Chairman of the CPSU's Commission on Party Control.

The role of China in the M.P.R., vis-à-vis the U.S.S.R., probably attained its peak in August, 1956, when there were more than 10,000 Chinese laborers working in the country and Peking made a grant of 160 million rubles to the M.P.R. At the same time, Soviet influence appeared to be declining. The last Russian soldiers withdrew from the M.P.R. in 1956, and the number of Russian civilians there was greatly reduced. Continuation of this trend might, before many years, have changed the M.P.R.'s basic orientation from Moscow to Peking.[2]

But the U.S.S.R. then acted to oppose Chinese "displacement," and on May 15, 1957, Bulganin and Tsedenbal issued a joint statement that reasserted Moscow's role—a document of great significance in Sino-Soviet relations as well as in M.P.R. affairs.[3]

Now Soviet aid to the M.P.R. far exceeds China's. Moreover, the Soviet Union still overwhelmingly dominates the Mongolian export and import trade. And Russian cultural influence continues to affect Mongolia far more than does that of the Chinese. Many Mongols study in the U.S.S.R. (2,000 in 1960–61), while only a handful (fewer than 150 a year) study in China. Many Mongols speak and read the Russian language fluently; few know Chinese.

Nevertheless, there has been significant evidence of renewed Chinese influence in the M.P.R. There were recently some 20,000 unskilled and semiskilled Chinese laborers there. The M.P.R.'s pattern of equating administrative-territorial units (the *somon*) with livestock collectives directly parallels Chinese organizational forms in the Inner Mongolian Autonomous Region and differs from earlier Mongolian practice. There is some reason to believe that the Chinese Communists' new steel complex at Paotow, in Inner Mongolia, has stirred the M.P.R. to begin to establish its own steel industry. The Chinese Communists have made a loan of 200 million "old" rubles to support the M.P.R.'s Five-Year Plan (1961–65).

New transportation ties have increased Sino-Mongolian contacts, and since 1956 there has been a direct rail connection from Peking to Ulan Bator. And, of course, in addition to the exchange of official representatives, new links have been created through friendship societies, cultural visits, joint statements, conferences, and the like. Each of these developments deserves attention.

The scant and scattered population in the M.P.R. makes labor a scarce commodity and creates problems for the country's economic development. In addition, apathy and even resistance to disciplined work obstruct the formation of a trained and reliable indigenous Mongolian labor force. The Mongols have not adapted well to factory work, and they practically refuse to do construction work. They seem to believe that the Chinese are much better suited to labor of this sort, and they would rather import Chinese to dig ditches and put up buildings and bridges than do it themselves. Even before the days of predominant Soviet influence, Chinese provided "coolie" labor to Outer Mongolia, and for the past seven years the Chinese Communists have been sending construction workers, ditch-diggers, and the like. On the basis of a prior Sino-Mongolian agreement, the first Chinese laborers arrived in the M.P.R. in May, 1955. By August, 1956, some 10,000 Chinese worked in the country, building bridges and apartments, warehouses and factories. In 1958, 2,400 additional Chinese workers arrived. Then, in September, 1960, a new Sino-Mongolian agreement provided for a continuing supply of Chinese labor. On May 5, 1961, 754 more Chinese arrived in Ulan Bator for this purpose, and on July 29, 1961, still more. The wages of these laborers and the costs of materials they employ constitute the major use of Chinese loans and grants to the M.P.R. There is no comparable Russian program.

But, throughout 1962, only withdrawals of Chinese labor from Mongolia were reported, and few Chinese workers remained there in 1963.

While collectivization of livestock and the organization of co-operatives in the M.P.R. have generally followed the Russian pattern, the recent merging of basic territorial units (*somons*) with cooperatives appears to follow the Chinese model rather than any Russian example. It is relevant to note that only Chinese sources, and not Russian ones, have described this development in the M.P.R. An article published in China in July, 1959, described amalgamation of M.P.R. cooperatives and *somons* as follows:

To strengthen and develop the production and organization of the cooperatives, the Central Committee of the Party has decided to abolish the *bag* [the smallest administrative unit, encompassing about 50 families] and to combine the *somon* [about 150 families] . . . with the corresponding cooperative. This forms the so-called "*somon* cooperative." Implementation of this decision was begun . . . in the first part of 1959. . . . More than 1,700 *bag* governments have been abolished, and the 370 *somons* have been reorganized and transformed into 426 *somon* cooperatives.[4]

Significantly, a Secretary of the Chinese Communist Party reported similar developments in Inner Mongolia. In an article published in June, 1961, he indicated that in 1959 the former 2,200 livestock cooperatives in that area were transformed into 150 livestock communes (in 1959, 694 cooperatives were consolidated into 389 in the M.P.R.), and he concluded: "Normally, a commune is equivalent to the original *somon* in size. When the *somon* is small, there is one commune in one *somon*, and when the *somon* is big, there are several communes in one *somon*."[5]

No matter how radical the Communist leadership in Outer Mongolia (or in the U.S.S.R.) has been on occasion, it has never tried to shift the country's economic base away from livestock-raising. The regime has always based Mongolian economic development plans on its livestock industry. It has always aimed to increase the quantity and improve the quality of the animals raised, and it has based the limited industrial development of the country—meat-packing, leather-working, wool-processing—for the most part on livestock products. Other industries have had supporting roles. Coal mining has provided power for such industries. Agriculture has supplied fodder. Biological laboratories and factories have produced serums to control and eliminate animal diseases.

It now seems possible, however, that the M.P.R. may embark on new experiments, partly as a result of the influence of the Chinese model. China has established in Inner Mongolia, at Paotow, a major industrial complex, which turned out 70,000 tons of steel in 1959, is scheduled to attain 500,000 tons annual production, and will ultimately be one of China's largest producers. This observer would suggest that steel production will begin in the M.P.R. more because Inner Mongolia now produces steel at Paotow than because conditions favorable for it exist in Outer Mongolia. The first recorded mention of steel production in the M.P.R. occurred in Chou En-lai's conversations with Tsedenbal, which took place in Ulan Bator during May 27–June 1, 1961. There soon followed an announcement of plans for the construction at Darkhan of Outer Mongolia's first steel plant, with an annual capacity of 300,000 tons.

The Russians may actually build the plant to maintain their predominant position, but the impetus appears to have been Chinese.

LOANS AND GRANTS

Both the Soviet Union and Communist China have made significant loans and grants to the M.P.R., which may be summarized as follows:

	U.S.S.R.	Communist China
1947–57	900-million rubles, loans and grants	
1956–59		160-million-ruble grant
1958–60	200-million-ruble loan; 100-million-ruble grant	
1959–61		100-million-ruble loan
1961–65	615-million-ruble loan; deferment of payment of 245 million rubles owed U.S.S.R.	200-million-ruble loan

The timing of the announcement of these loans and grants suggests a pattern of Soviet reaction to Chinese moves. In August, 1956, China extended to the M.P.R. a grant of 160 million rubles. As if to answer the Chinese challenge and to emphasize its own longer record of aiding the M.P.R., the Soviet Union, in the Bulganin-Tsedenbal joint statement of May 15, 1957, publicized, for the first time, the amount of its past and promised loans and gifts, and it detailed the uses to which the money was being put. It was only after the Chinese had announced, in May, 1960, a 200-million-ruble loan to the Mongols for the 1961–65 period that the Russians, on September 9, announced their own 615-million-ruble loan for the same period.[6]

Another important development in Sino-Mongolian relations in recent years has been the construction of a major rail line linking the two countries. A trans-Mongolian railroad had long been planned and discussed by Russians, Chinese, and Mongols,[7] and in 1949 the Russians actually completed the first section of such a line, stretching from the Soviet border to Ulan Bator. Then, on September 15, 1952, the U.S.S.R., the M.P.R., and China signed an agreement to extend this railroad from Ulan Bator to the Chinese town of Chining. The Chinese began building the section within their own territory (the Chining-Erhlien line) in May, 1953, and 25,000 construction workers completed the job by December 11, 1954; this 337-kilometer (210 miles) stretch comprises the only wide-gauge (Russian) track in China. Finally, the Trans-Mongolian railroad began operations on January 1, 1956. To date, however, it appears to have been more important in Sino-Soviet than in Sino-Mongolian trade. But conceivably it may become increasingly significant in the latter; when Sino-Russian trade reportedly declined, the Chinese announced that the first through passenger train ran from Peking to Ulan Bator on January 16, 1962, stating that such trains would operate regularly, once a week.

In official representation, as in other fields, Chinese activities have increased in recent years, but quite clearly the U.S.S.R. still holds a superior position. The U.S.S.R. maintains not only an Ambassador in the M.P.R. (currently K. V. Rusakov), but also a full-time "adviser to the Soviet Ambassador" (V. I. Ivanenko) and a trade representative to Ulan Bator (N. A. Simagin), as well as a consul in the city of Choibalsan in eastern Mongolia. Other evidence of the predominance of Soviet influence can also be cited. Within Mongolia, former diplomatic representatives to the U.S.S.R. generally now occupy more important positions than those who have represented the M.P.R. in Peking. The head of the Mongolian-Soviet Friendship Society (Tsende) clearly outranks the head of the Mongolian-Chinese Friendship Society (Maidar). And the U.S.S.R.'s delegation to the Mongolian Fourteenth Party Congress and celebration of the fortieth anniversary of the Mongolian Revolution in July, 1961, headed by Suslov, significantly outnumbered and outranked the Chinese group headed by Ulanfu.

While any examination of the biographies and careers of Mongolian leaders and officials clearly indicates a far closer Mongol attachment to the U.S.S.R. than to China, the careers of important Mongols who have spent time in China are of considerable interest. The first M.P.R. Ambassador to Peking, Jargalsaikhan, who served there from July, 1950, to June, 1953, returned home to become Mongolian Minister of Foreign Affairs during 1954 and 1955. Later, he became head of the Party's Foreign Relations Section, and he was then Chairman of the Great Khural from March, 1959, to July, 1960. Currently, Jargalsaikhan heads the M.P.R.'s United Nations delegation in New York, which, of course, removed him from Mongolia and contacts with China. Ochirbat replaced Jargalsaikhan in Peking and served there from July, 1953, to May, 1957. After the Bulganin-Tsedenbal joint statement reasserting Soviet supremacy in Mongol affairs, Ochirbat was recalled and sent as Ambassador first to East Germany and then to Mali. His replacement in Peking, S. Luvsan, served there from May, 1957, to June, 1959. Thereafter,

Luvsan became a Deputy Prime Minister for a brief period and
then was appointed Ambassador to Moscow in March, 1960. His
successor in Peking, D. Sharav, served from July, 1959, to June,
1962; his present position is not known. The present Ambassador,
D. Tsevegmid, who succeeded Sharav, is definitely a Soviet-oriented
Mongol.

Four major top-level purges have occurred in the past five years,
but no clear linkage to Sino-Soviet relations emerges. Nationalistic
strivings and competition for power may have been of greater importance. But the purges make quite clear that internal political
stability did *not* follow the Soviet reassertion of primary influence
in 1957, except that Tsedenbal "won" in every case, and the Russians back Tsedenbal.

A two-stage purge that took place in November, 1958, and
March, 1959, saw the replacement of Damba by Tsedenbal as First
Secretary of the Party, and Sürenjav by Tsende as Second Secretary.
There were other important changes as well: Both Damdin and
Lamchin were replaced, by Tömör-Ochir and Baljinyam, as regular
members of the Politburo, while Molomjamts and Jagvaral replaced
Balgan and Samdan as candidate members; and Dügerjav, Chairman of the Committee on Party Control, was replaced by Genden.
Although in Damba's case it had first been reported that the Politburo met on November 20–22, 1958, to relieve him "at his own request," in March, 1959, a Party plenum announced Damba had
been dismissed for "lack of principle and dishonesty before the
Party, stupid idealist-political backwardness, conservatism and in-
ertia, egotism and faulty self-criticism, opportunistic conciliation
with distortions, and defects in work."[8] It is conceivable that this
purge may have been related to the Sino-Soviet competition for influence: Damba's term as First Secretary (April, 1954, to November, 1958) corresponded roughly with the period of special Chinese
activity in the M.P.R., so that labeling him "pro-Chinese" would
appear reasonable. However, the evidence is by no means wholly
clear, and it is difficult to arrive at firm conclusions about the significance or meaning of the purge.

On July 4, 1960, the Politburo member and Party Secretary,
Tömör-Ochir (who had joined the Politburo at the time of Damba
purge in November, 1958) was removed. Others replaced at the
same time were two Politburo candidates; the Chairman and the
Secretary of the Presidium of the Great Khural; the Chairmen of
the Mongolian-Soviet Friendship Society, of the Committee of
Peace and Friendship Organizations, of the Geological Research

Bureau, and of the Committee of Sciences; and the Ministers of Transport and Communications and of Trade Resources.

On January 29, 1962, at the same Central Committee meeting that announced "de-Choibalsanization" and an attack on the "cult of personality" in the M.P.R., Tömör-Ochir rejoined the Politburo, replacing the man who had replaced him in July, 1960 (Baljinyam).[9] The same January, 1962, meeting replaced the Chairman of the Party's Central Revision Commission, the Chairman of the Administration of State Farm Affairs, and the Head of the Foreign Affairs Committee of the Great Khural.

Direct Soviet interference in Mongolian internal affairs was evidenced more openly than usual in May, 1962. The Mongols celebrated the eight-hundredth anniversary of the birth of Genghis Khan on May 31, 1962, and on that date dedicated a 36-foot monument at his reputed Mongolian birthplace, issued memorial stamps, and held ceremonies in the capital and at the site.[10] But the Russians attacked this manifestation of nationalism through an article in *Voprosy Istorii* (*Questions of History*) by the old Soviet diplomat, I. Maiskii, and another in *Istoriya S.S.S.R.* (*History of the U.S.S.R.*).[11] Both these articles appeared in the U.S.S.R. in May, and both strongly attacked Genghis Khan as a feudal lord who delayed historical progress and development. The effect of the Russian attacks became evident on September 10, 1962, when a special Mongolian Party Central Committee meeting replaced Tömör-Ochir as Politburo Member and Party Secretary, specifically making him the scapegoat for the Genghis Khan anniversary celebration.[12]

L. F. Il'ichev, the Secretary of the Central Committee of the Communist Party of the Soviet Union, led the Soviet delegation to Ulan Bator for a Mongolian Party meeting dealing with questions of ideological work, January 8–10, 1963, where Tömör-Ochir's replacement on the Politburo, Lkhamsüren, labeled Genghis Khan a reactionary.[13]

INNER MONGOLIA AND THE M.P.R.

While the Inner Mongolian example affects the M.P.R. in some fields (the *somon* cooperatives and steel production have already been cited as examples), influence also flows the other way. The Inner Mongols established "their own" university at Küke Khoto in October, 1957, and this may have been at least partly because the M.P.R. operated one in Ulan Bator. However, a potentially far more important influence from the M.P.R. on the Inner Mongolian

Autonomous Region (I.M.A.R), the idea of adopting the Cyrillic script for the Mongolian language in Inner Mongolia, was discussed but ultimately rejected.

A meeting held in Küke Khoto in Inner Mongolia from May 22 to 29, 1956, reported the official replacement of the traditional Mongolian alphabet (vertical script) by Cyrillic. However, the Mongols in China never did actually start using the Cyrillic script, which has been employed in the M.P.R. since 1945, and the Chinese subsequently announced, in early 1958: "Whenever a nationality [in China] constructs or reforms its script, it should always take the Latin script as its basis."[14]

This language issue has important political implications. A Russian, speaking on the subject in Peking just three weeks before the initial Küke Khoto announcement of the adoption of Cyrillic, stated: "Scientific and cultural cooperation between the Chinese People's Republic and the M.P.R. must clearly be strengthened . . . [and it is desirable to] have a common literary language, cementing the popular masses into a unified national monolith."[15] If the Mongols in China had actually adopted the Cyrillic alphabet, M.P.R. textbooks and other publications would then, of course, have been easily employed in the I.M.A.R.

But it did not work out that way. Clearly, considerations larger than Mongolia alone affected this matter. Sino-Soviet relations may also have been involved. In May, 1956, for example, Serdyuchenko, a member of the Academy of Pedagogical Sciences of the R.S.F.S.R. and author of a book entitled *The Chinese Language and Reform*, observed in Peking: "The Russian language has become the language of socialist culture. . . . The Russian language has become the international language for all that is changing and progressive in the world. . . . [Use of the Russian alphabet] makes learning of the Russian language quicker and easier."[16] He seemed, in short, to imply that China should adopt the Cyrillic script for transliteration of Chinese as well as Mongol. However, the Chinese chose to adopt the Latin alphabet instead.

Top Chinese Communist Mongols have played an important role in Peking's relations with Ulan Bator. For example, Ulanfu (Yün Tse), an alternate member of the Chinese Communist Party's Politburo and long-time I.M.A.R. leader, headed the Chinese delegation in Ulan Bator at the Twelfth Mongolian Party Congress, in November, 1954; at the Thirteenth, in March, 1958; and at the Fourteenth, in July, 1961. He also represented China at the ceremonies on the Mongolian border marking the opening of the Trans-Mongolian railroad, on January 1, 1956. Another "Chinese" Mongol, Chi Ya-t'ai, also now a top I.M.A.R. official, served as first Chinese Ambassador to Ulan Bator, from July, 1950, to September, 1954, and is a Deputy Chairman of the Sino-Mongolian Friendship Society. Of five official delegates from the Chinese People's Republic to the First International Congress of Mongolists, which met in Ulan Bator in September, 1959, two were Mongols from Küke Khoto.

Both Ulanfu and Chi Ya-t'ai attended the Mongol-Tibetan School in Peking in the early 1920's, when that institution trained personnel for duty in minority areas. The trainees were largely Chinese, but included a few "natives" trusted for their loyalty to China, as evidenced by facility in the Chinese language and other marks of Sinification. Then, about 1924, both Ulanfu and Chi Ya-t'ai joined the Chinese Communist Party, and they subsequently supported Chinese Communists against Mongolian "bourgeois nationalists."[17] They are now among the few high-ranking, influential Mongols in the Chinese Communist regime.

PAN-MONGOLISM

Extensive and intensive Sinification has to a considerable extent "denationalized" the Inner Mongols in China. Chinese have been moving into Inner Mongolia in substantial numbers for more than a century, and now they outnumber the Mongols in the I.M.A.R. about eight to one. Partly in response to a sense of threat from the Chinese, Inner Mongolian nationalism has historically been primarily anti-Chinese. The Japanese attempted to exploit this fact and tried to use "Pan-Mongolism" to win the support of the Khalkhas of Outer Mongolia during the Sino-Japanese War.

Actually, there have been five periods in this century when the merging of Inner and Outer Mongolia, either as a self-governing unit or under unified foreign control, has appeared to be at least a theoretical possibility, although the possibility may, in fact, have always been more theoretical than real.

During 1911–15, several Inner Mongolian princes fled to Urga (the present Ulan Bator) and pressed a very willing Autonomous Government of Outer Mongolia to "liberate" Inner Mongolia from China. However, Czarist Russia forced the Autonomous Government to forgo such action, and the Inner Mongols lost their dominant influence in Urga.[18]

In 1919–20, Semenov's anti-Bolshevik movement, supported by Japan after February, 1918, adopted a specific Pan-Mongolian aim

after the so-called Dauria Conference of February, 1919. The Inner
Mongolian Lama, Neisse Gegen, functioned as nominal leader.
This attempt ended ignominiously in January, 1920, however, when
a Chinese garrison on the Russo-Mongolian border captured the
movement's leaders and shot Neisse Gegen.[19]

In 1925–26, during the struggle between two Chinese warlords,
Feng Yü-hsiang and Chang Tso-lin, Feng obtained Russian mili-
tary aid and political support, and the Soviet-Feng plan for a time
apparently included the aim of uniting Inner and Outer Mongolia.
But Chang Tso-lin defeated Feng, who was forced to flee from
North China to Urga and Moscow.[20]

During the 1930's, a strong Inner Mongolian nationalist move-
ment led by Teh Wang was exploited by the Japanese as an anti-
Communist group that would "liberate" Outer Mongolia and join
it to Inner Mongolia in a greater Mongolian state. It, too, failed.
The U.S.S.R. dealt a final blow to all such Japanese and Inner
Mongolian pretensions at Nomonkhan in 1939.

During 1945–47, the U.S.S.R., in conjunction with the M.P.R.,
apparently aimed to add Inner Mongolia to the territory subject to
Soviet influence. However, the Chinese Communists, led by Ulanfu
in Inner Mongolia, frustrated this attempt, and, on May 1, 1947,
established an Inner Mongolian regime loyal to the Chinese Communist movement of Mao Tse-tung.

In the complex relations between various Mongol groups and
areas, Inner Mongolia has generally represented conservative and
traditional social values, including maintenance of the power of the
princes and the importance of the Buddhist Church. Buryat-Mongolia, by contrast, has represented liberal and modernizing trends.
Outer Mongolia has usually stood between them. To the Mongols,
therefore, "the south"—China, Japan, and Inner Mongolia—has
symbolized limited or no social change, whereas "the north"—Russia and Buryat-Mongolia—has represented substantial change. The
south has appealed to the old and conservative Khalkhas, the north
to the young and radical ones. Japan, until its defeat in 1945, not
only championed Mongolian conservatism, but also greatly complicated indigenous nationalism by drawing all Mongolia directly into
the Japanese-Russian struggle and world politics.

DE-STALINIZATION

In recent years, one of the clues to relative Chinese and Russian
influence in many Communist countries has been the manner in

which local Communists have handled the questions of de-Staliniization, the "cult of personality," and Albania.

Choibalsan, the Mongolian revolutionary hero and Prime Minister from 1939 until his death in Moscow in 1952, was in many respects the M.P.R.'s "little Stalin." He followed Stalin's orders and suggestions slavishly, and within the M.P.R. he was deified in much the same way as Stalin was in the U.S.S.R. Selections from a poem published in celebration of Choibalsan's fiftieth birthday, in 1945, suggest how closely the Mongolian "cult of personality" paralleled the Soviet one:

> Raising a powerful song,
> Honor to the leader, Choibalsan!
>> You were born, to the Mongols' happiness,
>> Exactly a half-century ago!
> You gave us luck,
> You guarded freedom,
>> Firm fighter for the right,
>> Stalin's pupil!
> Your heroic honor
> Will inspire legends throughout the centuries.
>> Live and work for us in good fortune,
>> Live tens of centuries!
> We remember your teachings,
> To raise our cultural level.
>> Together with our beloved leader,
>> To create a beautiful life.[21]

It is not surprising, therefore, that steps toward "de-Choibalsanization" in the M.P.R. followed de-Stalinization in the U.S.S.R. By 1958, in fact, it appeared that Choibalsan's reputation was being deliberately relegated to the shadows, and when this writer visited the M.P.R., Mongols attempted to discourage the purchase of Choibalsan's collected works, saying, "There is little worth while to be found in them." However, subsequent developments have not been entirely consistent. Whereas, in July, 1961 (when the celebration of the fortieth anniversary of the Mongolian revolution took place), Choibalsan's collected speeches were published in a Russian edition and were reviewed entirely favorably by a Russian in a learned Russian journal, six months later, on January 29, 1962, the Central Committee of the Mongolian People's Revolutionary Party (MPRP), following the line of the Twenty-second Congress of the CPSU, demanded "decisive measures to ensure complete liquidation of the harmful consequences of Choibalsan's cult of personality in all spheres of life."[22]

Tsedenbal has not replaced Choibalsan as a political deity in the M.P.R., and he is more nearly a "little Khrushchev'" than a "little Stalin." Under his leadership, the "thaw" has definitely reached Mongolia; one significant sign of this is the fact that Western non-Communist travelers can now visit the country.

On the Albania issue, the stand of the M.P.R. is strongly pro-Soviet. At the Twenty-second CPSU Congress, the M.P.R. followed the Soviet example and openly denounced "the anti-Leninist splitting activities of the Albanian Party leaders."[23] Earlier, the Mongols had also supported the Soviet Union at the meeting of eighty-one Communist parties in Moscow in November, 1960. Actually, the Mongols have supported the U.S.S.R. on all crucial issues in Communist bloc affairs in recent years with such consistency that the predominance of Soviet influence on the M.P.R.'s foreign policy is indisputable.

PRINCIPAL DOMESTIC PROBLEMS OF THE M.P.R.

Examination of the principal domestic problems of the M.P.R. also throws some light on the relative contribution and influence of the U.S.S.R. and China and their "agents"—Buryat-Mongolia and Inner Mongolia. These problems may be divided into those already basically solved and those still unsolved. Among the problems already solved, from the M.P.R.'s point of view, are: the status of the Buddhist Church, the place of the secular aristocracy, the nation's general illiteracy and lack of technical training, control of the national economy, the need for language reform and development, poor administration, untrained and incompetent officials, ineffective central government, and the need to form an army.

While the regime's accomplishments in the above fields are noteworthy, the M.P.R. has yet to solve some very basic problems, including its general dependence on foreigners, its shortage of labor, the continued existence of "bourgeois nationalism," the continuing problem of settling the nomads, and the fundamental need to increase the number of livestock in the M.P.R.

Lamaist Buddhism, the religion that traditionally dominated all aspects of Mongolian life, has been essentially eliminated in the M.P.R. Only a small and "tame" Buddhist Church remains. It plays no role in the government or the economy, both of which it formerly dominated. The Mongolian Church suffered a most brutal and thorough attack in the 1930's, and nothing of importance survived. Only an empty shell remains.

Until recently, Inner Mongolia represented an area where the Buddhist Church could continue to survive, but the Chinese Communists' current policies hardly encourage religiously inclined Khalkhas to look southward for support. For example, in an address to the lamas of the Silingol League, in Inner Mongolia, Ulanfu declared on July 10, 1958:

> Now the social order is changed. Feudal and capitalist society are overthrown, but the lamas are still here. What must be done? They must just change, too, serve the new society, and walk the socialist road. . . . The Red Star Cooperative . . . has decided that each lama shall put in 260 days of labor a year . . . . Only by labor can one have food . . . . If a lama joins a cooperative . . . can he recite sutras? After joining and completing the fixed number of labor days, he can dispose of the remainder of his time, and may recite sutras.[24]

Furthermore, Peking's handling of the Tibetan revolt and its denunciations of the Dalai Lama must provide convincing evidence that Communism and Buddhism cannot coexist peacefully for long, even in China.

It is true, of course, that the Chinese Communists established a Chinese Buddhist Association in 1953 and published a beautifully illustrated book, *Buddhism in New China*, in 1956. They also support a journal entitled *Modern Buddhism* (*Hsien-tai Fo-hsüeh*) and utilize, or exploit, the Panchen Lama. The Russians, too, refurbish monasteries and permit circumscribed Buddhist activity. Not surprisingly, the M.P.R. does the same. However, none of the Communist regimes offers to the Buddhists more than superficial basis for hope in the future.

During World War II, the M.P.R. did permit the existence of a strictly controlled "official church," and a limited state-restricted Buddhist organization operates today. In addition, there are still some older Mongols who profess Buddhism and pray in the privacy of their yurts, without official interference. But as a vital institution, Lamaist Buddhism has been destroyed in the M.P.R.

Formerly, the old aristocracy, the princes, dominated both the central and local governments in Outer Mongolia and controlled much property and many people. However, soon after 1921, they lost their political functions, and by the early 1930's they had lost all their property as well. For a brief period in the 1930's, Inner Mongolia (Teh Wang and the Japanese) offered some hope and support to the Khalkha princes, but the defeat of Japan in 1945 completely destroyed the possibility of help from that quarter. Meanwhile, in Inner Mongolia, the Chinese Communists quickly eliminated the surviving local aristocrats. The traditional Mongol aristocracy has thus met a fate similar to that of the traditional church.

Development of education probably represents Communism's most positive accomplishment in Outer Mongolia. Construction of schools has accompanied the destruction of churches. All Mongols now go to school. For most Mongols, four years of schooling assure at least general literacy and some systematic training. And there do exist many seven-year and ten-year schools, mainly in the cities and towns, and some higher education as well. The University of Ulan Bator serves some 2,500 students, and various technical institutes provide other advanced schooling. Besides the educational system proper, the Mongolian Academy of Sciences unites leading scholars in all fields. The truly remarkable performance in education has changed the whole country. Some Mongols oppose Communism, but none denies the evident results in education.

The first teachers in the M.P.R.'s schools were Russians and Buryat-Mongols. Now Mongols learn to teach in Mongolian pedagogical institutions, and Mongols staff the schools at all levels. In the past, it was necessary for foreigners, mainly Russians, to come to Mongolia to operate the machinery and equipment supplied to the M.P.R. Then Mongols went to the U.S.S.R. for training (a few also went to Germany in the 1920's). Now the domestic educational system trains most of the required engineers and machine operators.

The Soviet educational system provides a model that the M.P.R. has closely imitated. For example, in August, 1961, following the Soviet lead, the M.P.R. announced that its seven- and ten-year schools would be transformed into eight-year and eleven-year general schools and polytechnical schools.

In Inner Mongolia, the Chinese Communists have also placed great stress on education. They recently announced with pride that 180,000 Mongolian children in the I.M.A.R. now attend primary and secondary schools, using Mongolian-language textbooks, that half the adult Mongolian population under forty is now literate, that the teachers' college in Küke Khoto has trained more than 900 teachers of Mongolian nationality, and that a university (started in 1957, and now having 3,000 students) and a veterinary college are operating, also at Küke Khoto.[25]

But the M.P.R. can more than match these Inner Mongolian accomplishments. With fewer than 1 million people (compared with China's 1.5 million Mongols), the M.P.R., as of September 1, 1961, had 111,500 pupils enrolled in 327 primary and middle schools, staffed by 3,734 Mongolian teachers. The M.P.R. University in Ulan Bator opened in 1942, and it is claimed that there are now 5,600 college-level students and 8,900 students in special and secondary technical schools in the M.P.R. The M.P.R Veterinary Institute was established in 1958, and at least three teachers' colleges are in operation. And in 1961, the M.P.R. literacy rate was officially claimed to be 72.2 per cent.[26]

The Chinese Communist regime can bring about, and probably has actually already brought about, an educational revolution in Inner Mongolia, but its model offers no particular attraction to the M.P.R., which did the same thing earlier, on the Russian pattern.

The apparatus of economic as well as political control imposed by the M.P.R. on the Mongols has been enormously strengthened during the past decade. With the effective collectivization of practically all the nomads and most of their livestock during 1957–59, nationalization of the economy in the M.P.R. was completed, since all other economic enterprises had long been incorporated into the "socialist sector."

The major instruments of economic control, operating under the over-all control of the Mongolian People's Revolutionary Party, included in 1961: 337 cooperatives (since 1959, combined with *somons* into *somon* cooperatives), enrolling more than 99 per cent of total *arat* households and owning about 80 per cent of total livestock (approximately 17 million head); 36 Machine Livestock Stations (M.Zh.S.); and 28 state farms (goskhozes). Except for the *somon* cooperative organization, which is apparently based on Chinese practice, all of the M.P.R.'s political and economic instruments copy Soviet prototypes.

The M.P.R. has also become a country of Five-Year Plans: the First Five-Year Plan (1948–52)—the abortive First Five-Year Plan of 1931–35 is never mentioned; the Second Five-Year Plan (1953–57); the Three-Year Plan (1958–60); and the Third Five-Year Plan (1961–65). The U.S.S.R. will supply approximately 15 per cent of total M.P.R. investment in the Third Five-Year Plan, while China will supply about 5 per cent. The Russians also appear to be far more actively involved in the M.P.R. planning than the Chinese. For example, it was to Moscow, not Peking, that a member of the Mongolian Politburo, Molomjamts, went in 1960 for consulta-

tion about the scope and direction of the Third Five-Year Plan.
Further evidence of Soviet involvement in Mongolian planning was
provided when Sambu, also a member of the Mongolian Politburo,
emphasized in a speech in Moscow in April, 1960: ". . . an event
in the spring of 1959 of historical significance for the development
of new Mongolia: stressing agriculture on the initiative of Khrushchev."[27] M.P.R. economic policies often echo the current Soviet
line.

The M.P.R.'s lack of machinery and equipment has been met,
and continues to be met, by imports from abroad, mainly from the
U.S.S.R., but to a much lesser extent from East European countries
and China as well in recent years. In the Three-Year Plan period
(1958–60), for example, the Soviet Union supplied the M.P.R.
with 2,500 tractors and 3,000 trucks.

The nationalization of land in the M.P.R., which took place as
early as 1924, did not profoundly affect the Mongolian economy or
society because land had never been considered "private property"
in the Western sense. However, the attack on the Buddhist Church
had very great economic effects. The Church and its leaders had, in
fact, fulfilled the functions of economic entrepreneurs as well as
theocrats, and the regime's anti-Church policies included confiscation of its property and economic resources. By 1938, the Church
owned *no* livestock, whereas it had previously owned millions of
head. The regime also drove out the other "businessmen" of Mongolia, the Chinese; confiscatory government measures, plus conditions of civil war in North China which severed normal trade,
brought about their exodus by 1929.

Forcible collectivization of the nomads was then attempted in
1929–31, but it was quickly abandoned when the nomads slaugh-
tered over one-third of their animals.[28] When collectivization was
finally carried out successfully in 1957–59, the government did not
employ force in the same direct way; instead, it achieved its goals
by exerting more subtle economic pressures, through taxation and
control of markets. Today the country is almost completely collec-
tivized, but some private ownership of livestock continues in the
collectives.

It is legitimate to ask why, after so many years of inaction after
1931, the regime moved so vigorously and rapidly in collectivizing
during 1957–59. Was this a "great leap forward" on the Chinese
pattern? Perhaps it represented a Soviet-inspired reaction to Chinese policies. Collectivization had always remained a Communist
goal for Mongolia;[29] and perhaps the Russians stepped in vigorously

in 1957, following the rapid collectivization program that took place in China during 1955–56, to prod their Mongolian satellite into action. Chinese influence may, therefore, have indirectly affected the timing and speed of the operation. No major production-increase campaign followed collectivization in the M.P.R., however, as it did in China during the Great Leap Forward of 1958; the Mongols are not really the "great leap forward" type.

In their efforts to modernize, the Mongols were hampered by significant language problems which restricted communication both at home and abroad. The old written language did not correspond to the spoken language, and local dialects added to the problem. Moreover, the traditional language included practically no technical or scientific vocabulary. The limited knowledge of foreign languages in old Mongolia did not provide much help. The Church's "intellectuals" knew Tibetan, and some princes knew classical Chinese, but knowledge of the modern world required Western languages.

Eventually, Russian became the principal medium for introduction of Western influence into Mongolia, mainly via the Buryat-Mongols, who had long been Russian subjects and thus acted as a cultural bridge. As early as 1914, a few Outer Mongols studied in Russia, and many went there after 1921. Thereafter, the Russian language was taught in Mongolian schools, and as Mongolian education became universal, knowledge of Russian spread fairly widely. Today, Russian is the principal second language in Outer Mongolia, and it is an important link between the M.P.R. and the U.S.S.R.

Reform of the Mongolian language has affected most of the population of the M.P.R. even more directly. Since 1946, the language has been taught in Cyrillic script, on the basis of a single dialect of the spoken language enriched by Russian technical and scientific vocabulary; as a result, practically all Mongols now speak and write a common unified language.[30] A population now generally literate in a common language has provided the basis for greatly improved internal communication through the press and radio, which have been widely developed in recent years.

But the language-script question remains alive despite the official use of the Cyrillic script for more than fifteen years in the M.P.R. At an ideological conference in Ulan Bator in January, 1963, Lkhamsüren complained, "Some persons are obstructively minimizing the progressive significance of the new written language and advocating return to the old written language."[31]

Poor administration, untrained and incompetent officials, and ineffective government have long plagued Outer Mongolia. However, mainly through Russian and Buryat-Mongolian example and training, Khalkha Mongols have come gradually to appreciate the importance of these matters. The centralized Party training plays a large role in the effort to solve these problems, and much "Party schooling" deals more with the mundane, practical details of operating the government than with broad theoretical "Communist" postulates. Now competent Mongolian officials, trained in Mongolia, run the country with reasonable efficiency. The threat of separatist movements and disregard of orders from the capital, common in the old days, pose no serious problems today.

One special related problem was the prevalence of fiscal irresponsibility and outright dishonesty and graft. Perhaps the most notorious example of fiscal irresponsibility under the old regime was committed in 1913 by the ruling theocrat, the Jebtsun Damba Khutukhtu. When he received a Russian loan to bolster his deficit-plagued government, his first expenditure was the purchase of an elephant for his private zoo! The "Communist" governments of the 1920's were not much better, and officials deflected considerable sums of public funds into their own pockets or channeled such funds into useless projects. Until recently, the Mongols neither understood nor showed any real interest in elemental economics.

Now, however, some of the highest officials of the Mongolian government, including the two top leaders, Tsedenbal and Tsende, are trained economists, and a successful political career depends to a considerable extent upon ability to deal with economic problems. Arithmetic and accounting have become top-priority subjects in all the schools. Reforms in currency, banking, and taxes have eliminated the former chaos, and a fairly unified and rational system has been evolved. Planning operates with at least a degree of realism, and the regime husbands resources with some care. Statistics has become a recognized field of study. The first Mongolian census (1918) and the first Mongolian statistical handbooks (1960 and 1961) represent landmarks in this area.[32]

All these developments have been directed by the Mongolian People's Revolutionary Party. The MPRP functions now as a typical Communist Party, an elite minority organized on the basis of "democratic centralism." A small Politburo directs the Party, and the Party runs the country. Top government jobholders, ministers and the like, commonly occupy Party positions as well; and at the local level, experienced Party men fill practically all chairmanships

or directorships of the *aimaks* (administrative regions) and col-
lective farms. Their usual education at the Higher Party School in
Ulan Bator trains them in administration as well as in Communist
theory. Because of the long history of close ties with the Soviet
Party, their external orientation is more toward Moscow than
Peking.

The development of a modern army has been a significant element in the development of the M.P.R., and it doubtless provides
a further tie with the U.S.S.R. At first, the Mongols strenuously resisted all attempts by Russians and others to help form an effective
army in Mongolia. The Buddhist Church was particularly opposed.
However, the destruction of the Church in the 1930's permitted
formation of the Mongolian Army at that time, and eventually,
during World War II, it operated as an adjunct of the Soviet Far
Eastern Red Army. The army is not of great military importance
today, but it could be expanded with relative ease. Any expansion
would depend on Russian equipment, but competent Mongolian
officers have been trained in modern weaponry and warfare, and
there are now Mongolian pilots, tank drivers, and the like who
can use whatever equipment is available.

The army does not at present impose a heavy burden on the economy. Military expenditures accounted for only 4.6 per cent of the
1961 M.P.R. budget, compared to 46.6 per cent of the 1940 budget.
But the fact that the M.P.R. built an army of considerable size
twenty years ago definitely affects the character of Mongolian society today. The development of an effective military establishment
dealt a blow to traditional passivity and lack of "national" commitment, and the army constituted an important instrument of education and social change, as well as a fighting force. As one Russian
historian put it:

> The *arats* with past service in the MPRA [Mongolian People's
> Revolutionary Army] and transferred from it to the reserve were the
> first representatives of the people's intelligentsia . . . . The MPRA
> instructed the *arat* youth to handle bayonet and knife, machine gun
> and cannon, airplane and tank; it taught it the national language and
> converted the soldier into a cultured, politically aware soldier-citizen,
> a guide in the progressive ideas of the people's democracy and a
> leader of the masses in the task of social-economic reconstruction of
> society.[33]

Despite the many accomplishments mentioned above, the
M.P.R. still faces some serious and basic problems; for only one of

them—the shortage of labor—can the Chinese offer a solution more readily than the Russians. For the others, the Russians can offer at least as satisfactory solutions as the Chinese.

Most change in Mongolia is easily traced to foreign initiative—mainly Russian, but also Chinese, and even Japanese as well. The considerable physical development of the capital city of Ulan Bator offers one illustration. The Russians built, and initially operated, the first sizable factory in the city. Japanese prisoners of war built the university and many of the government buildings. And Chinese have put up most of the apartment buildings, new bridges, and the sports stadium. Almost nowhere in the city can one find a project of any type conceived, constructed, and operated by Mongols. Mongols now do run most organizations and enterprises, however. Since the Buryats lost their dominant position in the ruling elite (in the early 1930's), and since numerous Russian "advisers" left the country (particularly since 1956), the Mongols have replaced them in practically all important managerial positions; the Chinese who have come to Mongolia in recent years have served only at the lowest unskilled and semiskilled levels.

The M.P.R. is still very much dependent on foreign economic assistance. Economic self-sufficiency could probably never be attained except at a very low level of subsistence by a country like Mongolia, which depends heavily on imports for a great range of significant items, including tea, textiles, and machinery. The problem lies in the question of repayment, for Mongolia's trade imbalance continues and even grows. Essentially, Mongolia's only important exports consist of livestock and livestock products, and the livestock sector of the M.P.R. economy continues to stagnate. The Mongolian economy has not "taken off" and seems to get no closer to doing so. And the cutoff of Soviet largesse would doom hopes for Mongolian economic development.

The M.P.R. constitutes in large part an empty land—a land of vast area, sparsely populated. Moreover, the common Mongolian resistance to any form of systematic work performed at regular hours at a fixed place aggravates the general shortage of manpower. The Mongol wants to be independent, but not at the price of hard work, and forty years of Communist exhortation and pressure have had only limited effect. It is difficult to conceive, therefore, of substantial economic development without more people.

The Chinese can help, and to some extent already have helped, to solve this Mongolian problem, but since Chinese assistance of this sort could easily deluge and submerge the country, the Mongols are cautious and wary about it. So long as the Mongols can control Chinese immigration, and they have thus far done so, they can benefit from Chinese labor. But uncontrolled Chinese immigration could be a disaster, and the Mongols know it.

The Mongol conceives of himself as independent, whatever the outside opinion of him may be. He attempts doggedly and persistently to dodge and avoid complete foreign subjugation and control. Yet the M.P.R. is clearly dependent on outside aid and support. This creates a basic unsolved problem, both for the Communist regime in Mongolia and for the U.S.S.R. It is an interesting paradox that Mongolian nationalism is probably stronger now than it was before 1921, for at that time the illiterate Mongol was bounded by limited local horizons and was little affected by the ineffective central government. In recent decades, the Mongols have been "nationalized," and Mongolian nationalism has developed, too. It is difficult to know what the long-run consequences of this may be.

SETTLEMENT OF THE NOMADS

Communists do not like nomads, which means, in effect, they do not like typical Mongols. One of the M.P.R.'s basic aims, therefore, is to settle the wanderer—to fix his residence and control his actions. Consequently, the regime attempts to eliminate the yurt, the wood-framed, felt-covered tent in which most Mongols still live; tearing down yurts and putting up buildings constitute one aspect of the official campaign against nomadism. But despite the government's policy, permanent buildings still appear rarely in Mongolia, except in the capital city of Ulan Bator. Yurts are cheap, whereas building materials are scarce and expensive, and modern construction requires skills that few Mongols possess or care about.

Some restriction of mobility has already resulted, however, from the cumulative effects of changes in the yurts themselves; wooden floors, iron stoves, more furniture, and sometimes electricity have been added, and all these things make moving a greater chore. And urbanization has slowly developed; the population of Ulan Bator alone now exceeds 160,000 (of the total Mongolian population of fewer than 1 million). Settlement remains a fundamental goal of the regime.

The Bulganin-Tsedenbal joint statement of May 15, 1957, restated as a task for 1958–60 what had been repeatedly stated as an official goal at least since the 1930's: the "gradual transference of the *arat* population to a settled form of life."[34] Collectivization is intended to end nomadism. The equation is specific and conscious,

as a Mongolian author indicated in 1959: "transition to a settled
way of life through the S.Kh.O. [agricultural cooperative]." The
aim is the "transfer of all agricultural cooperatives to a settled
existence." This aim was reiterated on April 7, 1960, when Ulan
Bator announced: "A socialist emulation drive for making fixed
abodes for the herdsmen is being launched." Half the nomads of
Bulgan Aimak were to be "fixed" in wooden houses by July, 1961;
all the herdsmen of Bayan Ülegei (Kazakh) Aimak, entirely nomadic in 1958, were to be settled by the end of 1960. The implications of this policy are stated openly: "[Settlement] organically
includes an alteration of the entire tenor of life for the Mongolian
population, [involving] change in manners and customs observed
for thousands of years."[35] Despite all this, however, large-scale
settlement still lies in the future; to date, it remains an unsolved
problem.

The Chinese Communists are pursuing a similar policy. As early
as November 14, 1955, *Jen-min Jih-pao* set the task: "We must . . .
systematically and gradually assist and guide the herdsmen to grow
fodder crops and . . . to settle down and build permanent homes."
And in February, 1962, it stated: "68 per cent of the nomads in
pastoral Inner Mongolia—71,000 families—have settled down in
new homes during the past year."[36] Thus Mongols in the M.P.R.
who resist settlement and attempt to continue their traditional nomadic existence cannot look to China or the I.M.A.R. for any sympathetic consideration. Once again, China offers the M.P.R. no
viable alternative to measures already officially adopted on the basis
of the Soviet example.

Even the M.P.R.'s failures reflect the Soviet example. Despite
continuing emphasis since 1921 on the need to develop the livestock
economy, the results to date in the M.P.R. have been far from satisfactory. Actually, the total number of animals in the country in
1940 (27.4 million) exceeded the number *planned* for 1962 (20.95
million). Furthermore, although the planners have always attempted to increase the number of cattle and decrease the number
of horses, the relative number of horses steadily increases. Obviously, the nomads resist the bureaucrats. The planned figures for
livestock over the past decade show clearly the failure of official
policy: 31 million for 1952, 27.5 million for 1957, 25 million for
1960, 23.5 million for 1961, and 21 million for 1962.

Livestock and livestock products, including wool, comprise the
basis of the Mongolian economy and the country's only substantial
available exports. The U.S.S.R., as the greatest importer, is most

affected when the livestock sector of the Mongolian economy stagnates. This gives the Soviet Union a direct interest, therefore, in improving the situation, but it may well be reluctant to exert too much pressure on the Mongols lest they turn to China. In recent years, the Mongols have consistently received more goods from the U.S.S.R. than they have sent in return, and the 1960 Soviet loan included a "moratorium" on 245 million "old" rubles owed by the M.P.R. Increased Mongolian production, based on an improved livestock situation, would go largely to the U.S.S.R. for repayment, and the Soviets' past willingness to trade without full repayment may account for Mongolian lassitude.

Since early 1959, the M.P.R. has also attempted to develop agriculture on a substantial scale for the primary purpose of supporting the livestock economy, which depends on reliable fodder and food supply. (The Chinese have followed a similar policy in the I.M.A.R.) One significant fact about this agricultural program in the M.P.R. is that it now depends on Russian machinery and Mongolian labor. In the "old days," what little farming was done in Outer Mongolia was done by Chinese. None of the Chinese who came to the M.P.R. recently for labor engaged in agriculture.

The goal for grain has been to supply all domestic needs without recourse to imports (from the U.S.S.R.). But production fell off badly in 1961—120,000 tons, compared to 260,000 tons in 1960—and the U.S.S.R. continues to send grain and flour to the M.P.R.

BALANCE SHEET

In summary, the M.P.R. has solved many of its basic problems mainly by following the Russian model; however, the Chinese have also followed the Soviet model, and in dealing with most of the same problems in the I.M.A.R., China's policy has differed only in details. Similarly, for the unsolved problems, the Chinese and Russian examples appear much the same to the M.P.R., but it has been the U.S.S.R. that has been active on the scene in the M.P.R. for at least twenty-five years while China was absent, at least until recently. Perhaps now the Chinese do, in effect, cause the Russians to act more vigorously and rapidly in relations with the M.P.R., but the Chinese would face great difficulties in any attempt to replace Russian influence. Manpower constitutes the most effective tool the Chinese possess, but any attempt to make massive use of it would frighten the Mongols into even closer dependence on the Russians.

On the basis of developments since May, 1957, at least, it appears that the Soviet Union will respond to Chinese policies with moves of its own to "protect" the M.P.R. from Chinese designs and to maintain its own superior position. It is possible, of course, that at any time the U.S.S.R. and China might make an over-all accommodation regarding Mongolia that would result in a fundamental change in Mongolia's position, in which case the Mongols could do little to protect themselves. The Mongols can never be entirely relaxed or secure between 220 million Russians and 700 million Chinese, but the present balance of forces is about as favorable for them as they can hope for. Any shift toward greater Chinese influence might remove the spur to increased Russian aid and assistance.

The training and education of Mongols, under the inspiration of a "big brother" model, have wrought many significant changes in the M.P.R. However, the basic pattern and scale of the economy have remained surprisingly stable. No economic miracle has occurred in Mongolia. Nonetheless, any observer at all familiar with "old Mongolia" finds the changes astounding. The Buddhist Church, whose arm reached everywhere and whose hand was inserted into every Mongolian pocket and purse, is gone. The Communist Party has, in a sense, replaced it, but with a radically different doctrine and a far more efficient organization. Forty thousand Party members run the country more completely and thoroughly than did 80,000 lamas. The comparison is intriguing, but not very useful. Old Mongolia is gone forever, and even where appearances have changed little, the underlying spirit has changed much. No objective observer can argue that there has been no "progress." Mongolia is a healthier land today than it ever was, and not only in the strictly physical sense.

NOTES

1. *The New York Times*, February 14, 1955.

2. In 1950, the Chinese disclaimed any desire to reassert Chinese control over the M.P.R.:

> During the time the new Sino-Soviet Treaty and Agreements were signed, the Foreign Ministers of China and the Soviet Union exchanged notes to the effect that both governments affirmed that the independent status of the M.P.R. was fully guaranteed as the result of its plebiscite of 1945 and the establishment with it of diplomatic relations by the People's Republic of China.
>
> To each and every truly patriotic Chinese, our recognition of Mongolia as an independent state was a right and proper act, but to the reactionary bloc of the Kuomintang, which was somewhat compelled to accord recognition to Mongolia, it has always been a bitter memory. It was they who, after giving

due recognition, fabricated rumors bringing insults to the Mongolian people and to the Soviet Union. "The independence of Mongolia is the loss of Chinese territory," they said. Among our people, there are some who are not familiar with the actual conditions and who have been contaminated with the sentiments of "suzerainty," and they think the map of China appears out of shape and unreal without Mongolia. These are the people who have been intoxicated by the poison of "Hanism" propagated by the Kuomintang reactionary bloc. . . . While the various ethnical groups within China were still under the oppression of both imperialism and feudalism and while their liberation was still very far off, Mongolia found rightful assistance from a socialist country—the Soviet Union—and by its own hard struggle achieved liberation and independence. Such liberation and independence we Chinese should hail, and we should express our respect to the Mongolian people. We should learn from them, we should not oppose their independence, we should not drag them to share our suffering. They attained liberation twenty-eight years ago and now march forward to socialism; as for us, we have just liberated ourselves. . . . Therefore, our attitude should be one recognizing its independence and not one pulling them back to our fold and making them follow us again.

In regard to Inner Mongolia, Tibet, and other ethnical groups, the present question is not how to divide ourselves and each try to become independent, but to unite our efforts to build a strong, new, democratic China since we all have been liberated more or less during the same period.
(*New China Daily* [Nanking], March 5, 1950).

3. Text in *Izvestia*, May 17, 1957; excerpts in *Current Digest of the Soviet Press*, IX, No. 20 (June 26, 1957), 27–28.

4. Pao Yen, in *Shih-chieh Chih-shih* (*World Knowledge*) (Peking), July 20, 1959, pp. 11–12; translated in *Weekly Information Report on Communist China*, No. 280 (October 13, 1959), Sum. 2371, p. 56.

5. Wang To, in *Min-tsu T'uan-chieh* (*Unity of Nationalities*), No. 6 (June 6, 1961); translated in *Selections from China Mainland Magazines* (hereafter cited as SCMM), No. 274 (August 14, 1961), pp. 21–35.

6. Cf. Rupen, "Outer Mongolia, 1957–1960," *Pacific Affairs*, XXXIII, No. 2 (June, 1960), 126–43; and Rupen, "Sino-Soviet Rivalry in Outer Mongolia," *Current Scene* (Hong Kong), I, No. 11 (August 31, 1961).

7. The first detailed reference appears to have been in A. I. Verblyuner, "Proekt postroiki zheleznoi dorogi ot Myslovska do Troitsko-Savska i Kyakhty v svyazi' s ee prodolzheniem po Mongolii cherez Urgu do Kalgana" ("Project for Construction of a Railroad from Mysovsk to Troitskosavsk and Kyakhat in Connection with Its Extension Across Mongolia Through Urga to Kalgan"), *Trudy Troitsko-Savsko-Kyakhtinskago otd. Priamurskago otd. Russkago Geograficheskago Obshchestva* (*Works of the Troiskosavsk-Kyakhta Branch of the Pri-Amur Section of the Russian Geographical Society*), XII, Nos. 1–2 (1909), 11–40. See also I. J. Korostovetz, *Von Cinggis Khan zur Sowjetrepublik* (Berlin and Leipzig: Walter de Gruyter and Co., 1926), p. 177; and Gerard Friters, *Outer Mongolia and Its International Position* (Baltimore, Md.: The Johns Hopkins Press, 1949), p. 89.

8. *Izvestia*, November 23, 1958; *Pravda*, April 1, 1959; *The New York Times*, April 1, 1959.

9. XIV *s'ezd M.N.R.P.* (*Fourteenth Congress of the Mongolian People's Revolutionary Party*) (Moscow: Gosudarstvennoe izdatel'stvo politicheskoi literatury, 1962), p. 199. Baljinyam joined the Politburo with Tömör-Ochir in

November, 1958, but replaced Tömör-Ochir as a Party Secretary in July, 1960. Then, in January, 1962, Tömör-Ochir replaced Baljinyam both as Politburo member and Party Secretary. On March 3, 1962, Baljinyam was appointed M.P.R. Ambassador to Poland.

10. "Genghis Khan—Founder of Mongolian National State," *Mongolia Today* (New Delhi), No. 28 (July–August, 1962), pp. 14–19.

11. I. Maiskii, "Genghis Khan," *Voprosy Istorii (Questions of History)*, No. 5 (1962), pp. 74–83; N. Merpert, B. Pashuto, and L. Cherepnin, "Genghis Khan i ego nasledie" ("Genghis Khan and His Heritage"), *Istoriya S.S.S.R. (History of the U.S.S.R.)*, No. 5 (1962), pp. 92–119.

12. *Pravda*, November 1, 1962; reprinted from *Unen* (Ülan Bator), September 11, 1962.

13. *Pravda*, January 9, 1963.

14. *Min-tsu T'uan-chieh (Unity of Nationalities)*, No. 2 (1958), pp. 6–7.

15. G. Serdyuchenko, "O novom mongol'skom pis'me" ("Concerning the New Mongolian Script") (Peking: May 7–11, 1956).

16. *Ibid.*

17. See Chi Ya-t'ai in *Min-tsu T'uan-chieh (Unity of Nationalities)*, No. 7 (July 6, 1961), translated in SCMM, No. 281 (October 2, 1961), pp. 21–24; Shih Yun, in *Li-shih Yen-chiu (Historical Research)*, No. 6 (December 15, 1961), translated in SCMM, No. 299 (February 7, 1962), pp. 1–17.

18. See Owen Lattimore, *The Mongols of Manchuria* (New York: The John Day Co., 1934), p. 127; Anna Louise Strong, *China's Millions*, Vol. II (New York: Coward-McCann, Inc., 1928); H. G. C. Perry-Ayscough and R. B. Otter-Barry, *With the Russians in Mongolia* (London: John Lane, 1914), p. 117.

19. Cf. James Morley, *The Japanese Thrust into Siberia, 1918* (New York: Columbia University Press, 1957); "K sobytiyam v Mongolii" ("About Events in Mongolia"), *Russkoe Obozrenie (Russian Survey)* (Peking), I, No. 2. Semenov himself escaped; ultimately, he fell into the hands of Soviet troops in Manchuria in 1945, underwent trial in Moscow during August 28–30, 1946, and was executed. (M. I. Gubel'man, *Bor'ba za Sovetskii Dal'nii Vostok, 1918–1922 [Struggle for the Soviet Far East, 1918–1922]* [Moscow: Voennoe izdatel'stvo ministerstva oborony S.S.S.R., 1958], p. 75. See also Grigorii Semenov's autobiography, *O sebe [About Myself]* [Harbin: Izdatel'stvo "Zarya," 1938].)

20. See Korostovetz, *op. cit.*, p. 343; K. Fuse, *Soviet Policy in the Orient* (East Peking: Enjinsha, 1927), p. 193; David J. Dallin, *The Rise of Russia in Asia* (New Haven, Conn.: Yale University Press, 1949), pp. 225–26. The matter is complicated, however, since the First Inner Mongolian Party Congress, in October, 1925, in Kalgan, "consciously did not fan Pan-Mongolist tendencies, clearly understanding that the immediate task was not the union of all ethnographic Mongolia into a single unified state." (I. Genkin, "Dva s'ezda mongol'skoi narodnoi partii" ["Two Congresses of the Mongolian People's Party"], *Novyi Vostok [New Orient]*, XII [1926], 195. See also C. M. Wilbur and J. How, *Documents on Communism, Nationalism and Soviet Advisers in China, 1919–1927* [New York: Columbia University Press, 1956], pp. 330–31; and Strong, *op. cit.*)

21. In *Pod sol'ntsem svobodnoi Mongolii (Under the Sun of Free Mongolia)* (Moscow: Izdatel'stvo inostrannoi literatury, 1951), p. 122.

22. *The New York Times*, February 1, 1962. The favorable review of Choibalsan's collected speeches was that of A. T. Yakimov, in *Narody Azii i Afriki (Peoples of Asia and Africa)*, No. 6 (1961), pp. 168–70.

23. *Mongolia Today* (New Delhi), No. 11 (December, 1961), p. 25.
24. *Survey of the China Mainland Press* (hereafter cited as SCMP), No. 1837 (July 24, 1958).
25. *Ibid.*, No. 2681 (February 19, 1962).
26. *BBC Weekly News Summary of World Broadcasts—Far East* (hereafter cited as BBC-FE), No. 127 (September 20, 1961); *Mongolia Today*, No. 21 (July, 1961), p. 21; *Narodnoe khozyaistvo M.N.R. za 40 let (People's Economy of the M.P.R. for 40 Years)* (Ulan Bator: Gosudarstvennoe tsentral'noe statisticheskoe upravlenie soveta ministrov M.N.R., 1961); BBC-FE, No. 113 (November 1, 1961) and No. 136 (November 22, 1961).
27. *Izvestia*, April 13, 1960.
28. Gendun, "Iz doklada premerministra M.N.R." ("From the Report of the Prime Minister of the M.P.R."), *Tikhii Okean (Pacific Ocean)*, No. 3 (January–March, 1935).
29. Some years after the collapse of the collectivization campaign of 1929–31, Choibalsan spoke on this subject, in January, 1938: "The peasants of the U.S.S.R. have attempted to find a happier, more prosperous life through kolkhozes. We believe that there will come a time when our *arats* will themselves wish to form kolkhozes. We oppose the repetition of leftist errors, we will resolutely fight against any attempt at forced collectivization of kolkhozes." ("Vystuplenie chlena prezidiuma Ts.K. M.N.R.P. marshala M.N.R. Choibalsana na Ulan Batorskom gorodskom aktive M.N.R.P. [sobranie aktiva M.N.R.P. g. Ulan-Batora proiskhodilo 19–21 yanvarya 1938 g.]" ["Address of the member of the presidium of the Central Committee of the M.P.R.P., Marshal Choibalsan, to the Ulan Bator City group of the M.P.R.P. (meeting of January 19–21, 1938)"], *Sovremennaya Mongoliya [Contemporary Mongolia]* [Ulan Bator], No. 27 [1938], pp. 3–13.)
30. For text of official resolutions (see *Konstitutsiya i osnovnye zakonodatel'-nye akty M.N.R. (Constitution and Basic Laws of the M.P.R.)* (Moscow: Izdatel'stvo inostrannoi literatury, 1952). For a discussion of implementation, see A. R. Rinchine, *Uchebnik mongol'skogo yazyka (Textbook of the Mongolian Language)* (Moscow: Izdatel'stvo literatury na inostrannykh yazykakh, 1952), p. 5. G. I. Mikhailov refers to numerous Mongolian articles on the subject in "Yazykovedenie v M.N.R." ("Language Study in the M.P.R."), *Voprosy yazykoznaniya (Questions of Language Study)*, No. 1 (1953), pp. 104–8.
31. *Pravda*, January 9, 1963.
32. Details of 1918 census in I. Maiskii, *Sovremennaya Mongoliya (Contemporary Mongolia)* (Irkutsk: 1921). The statistical handbooks are: *BNMAU-un 1921–1958 onuudun ardun aj akhui soëlun khögjilt (Statistikiin emkheltgei) (Development of the People's Economy of the M.P.R., 1921–1958 [Statistical Handbook])* (Ulan Bator: 1960), translated in *Joint Publications Research Service* (hereafter cited as JPRS), No. 9987 (September 14, 1961); and *Narodnoe khozyaistvo M.N.R. za 40 let.*
33. I. J. Slatkin (Zlatkin), *Die Mongolische Volksrepublik* (Berlin: Dietz Verlag, 1954), pp. 228–29.
34. *Izvestia*, May 17, 1957. Choibalsan stated in a speech in 1940:

Beginning in 1941, it is necessary to embark on the task of gradual transfer from yurts to houses, especially in the cities. Houses are stronger, longer-lasting, better protected from the rain, a house is warmer and more comfortable than a yurt. Life in a house induces culture. All central organs, beginning with the Central Committee and the government, must decrease construction of new yurts and think about construction of houses. This must be carried out in all the *aimak* administrations and *aimaks* of the Khangai zone [northern Mongolia], where rich forests are to be found.

It will be more difficult to carry out this measure in the Gobi, but in time yurts here, too, will be replaced by houses.

This in general does not mean that I wish to destroy existing yurts. I have in mind to decrease expenditure on new yurts and assign the funds for that purpose to construction of houses. It is impossible to think that we shall always lead a nomadic existence—we must leave the old, backward life and build a new one.

(*Sovremennaya Mongoliya* [*Contemporary Mongolia*] [Ulan Bator], No. 42–43 [1940], p. 48.)

A rare note of tolerance was struck in *Pravda* on June 12, 1961, however: "As long as livestock is kept on remote pastures and the honorable profession of the shepherd exists, the yurt will exist as well." The article then described an experimental synthetic yurt, with walls of foam plastic and transparent plastic windows, resistant to rot and fire, and much lighter in weight than the traditional wood-framed felt yurt. (Translated in *Current Digest of the Soviet Press*, XIII, No. 24 [July 12, 1961], pp. 29–30.)

35. JPRS, No. 3180 (April 18, 1960), p. 18 (see also p. 9); G. S. Matveeva, *Sotsialisticheskie preobrazovaniya v sel'skom khozyaistve M.N.R.* (*Socialist Reforms in Agriculture of the M.P.R.*) (Moscow: Izdatel'stvo vostochnoi literatury, 1960), p. 111; SCMP, No. 2239 (April 18, 1960), p. 53.

36. BBC-FE, No. 147 (February 7, 1962).

NOTES ON THE CONTRIBUTORS

Bernard B. Fall, Professor of International Relations at Howard University, is the author of *Street Without Joy* and *The Two Viet-Nams*.

Harry Gelman, a specialist in Indian and Sino-Soviet affairs, studied at the School of Slavonic and East European Studies of London University. He is currently a Senior Fellow at the Research Institute on Communist Affairs, Columbia University.

Paul F. Langer is on the staff of The RAND Corporation, where he specializes in Far Eastern affairs. He has authored and co-authored several books, among them *Red Flag in Japan* and *Japan Between East and West*, and has contributed articles on problems of Asia and Asian–Communist bloc relations to major periodicals in this country and abroad.

Ruth T. McVey, a Research Associate of the Center for International Studies at the Massachusetts Institute of Technology, has also worked as Research Associate in Southeast Asia Studies at Yale University and on Cornell University's Modern Indonesia Project.

Robert C. North is Professor of Political Science and Director of the Studies in International Conflict and Integration at Stanford University. His books include *Kuomintang and Chinese Communist Elites* and *M. N. Roy's Mission to China* (co-author).

Glenn D. Paige, who served as Research Adviser at the Graduate School of Public Administration, Seoul National University, is currently Assistant Professor of Politics at Princeton University.

Robert A. Rupen has published numerous articles in scholarly journals on various aspects of modern Mongolia. An Associate Professor of Political Science at the University of North Carolina, he has also taught at Bryn Mawr College and Columbia University.

Donald S. Zagoria is an Assistant Professor of Government at Columbia University and a Senior Fellow of its Institute on Communist Affairs. He is the author of *The Sino-Soviet Conflict, 1956–1961*, and his articles have appeared in *Foreign Affairs*, *The China Quarterly*, *Problems of Communism*, *Survey*, and *The New Leader*.